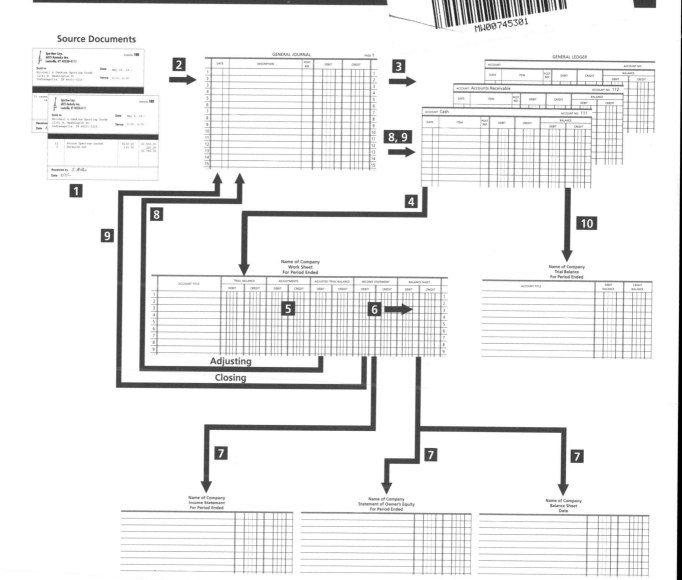

Steps in the Accounting Cycle

During Accounting Period:
1. Analyze source documents.
2. Journalize the transactions.
3. Post to the ledger accounts.

End of Accounting Period:
4. Prepare a trial balance.
5. Determine and prepare the needed adjustments on the work sheet.
6. Complete an end-of-period work sheet.
7. Prepare an income statement, statement of owner's equity, and balance sheet.
8. Journalize and post the adjusting entries.
9. Journalize and post the closing entries.
10. Prepare a post-closing trial balance.

Publishing Team Director:	Diane Longworth Myers
Senior Acquisitions Editor:	Gary L. Bauer
Developmental Editors:	Tom Bormann, Minta Berry
Production Editor:	Shelley Brewer
Production House:	Berry Publication Services
Cover Design:	Fusion Design
Cover Photograph:	Guildhaus Photography
Internal Design:	Lesiak/Crampton Design
Opener Illustrations:	Cary Rillo
Manufacturing Coordinator:	Sue Disselkamp
Marketing Manager:	Dreis Van Landuyt

Library of Congress Cataloging-in-Publication Data:
Heintz, James A.
    College accounting / James A. Heintz, Robert W. Parry, Jr. -- 15th
  ed.
        p.   cm.
    Includes index.
    ISBN 0-538-85202-X
    1. Accounting.   I. Parry, Robert W. . II. Title.
  HF5635.H444 1995
  657'.044--dc20   95-9583
                                                            CIP

Annotated Instructor's Edition, Chapters 1–28   ISBN: 0-538-85245-3
Annotated Instructor's Edition, Chapters 1–15   ISBN: 0-538-85543-6
Student Edition, Chapters 1–28   ISBN: 0-538-85202-X
Student Edition, Chapters 1–20   ISBN: 0-538-85205-4
Student Edition, Chapters 1–15   ISBN: 0-538-85204-6
Student Edition, Chapters 1–10   ISBN: 0-538-85203-8

2 3 4 5 6 7 8 9 Ki 3 2 1 0 9 8 7 6
Printed in the United States of America

I ⓉP
International Thomson Publishing
South-Western College Publishing is an ITP Company.
The ITP trademark is used under license.

Dedication

We are grateful to our wives,

Celia Heintz and Jane Parry

and our children,

Andrea Heintz, John Heintz, Jessica Jane Parry, and Mitch Parry

for their love, support, and assistance during the creation of this fifteenth edition. We especially appreciate Jessie Parry's willingness to let us use her name throughout the first six chapters.

PREFACE

Anyone who desires a successful career in business and not-for-profit organizations must understand accounting. This textbook is designed for students of accounting, business administration, office technology, computer science, and other disciplines. As students begin their study of accounting, this book will thoroughly and efficiently introduce fundamental accounting concepts and principles. This new edition maintains the strong tradition of emphasizing student understanding.

IMPORTANT FEATURES OF THE FIFTEENTH EDITION

The basic foundation that has made this text a market leader for many years has been retained in the fifteenth edition. In response to user feedback, focus group interviews, surveys, and independent reviews by accounting educators, numerous improvements have been made. The text presentation has been refined throughout, new materials have been added, and both print and computerized supplements have been revised and added. The text and all accompanying supplements have been crafted to guide students to success.

Learning Objectives

Each chapter begins with learning objectives. The learning objectives are restated at the beginning of the appropriate text section for ease of reference. The learning objectives are also keyed to the Key Points summaries, end of chapter exercises and problems, testbank, and study guide.

The following illustration shows Learning Objective 5 from Chapter 3 as it appears in the text, in the Key Points summary, and in an exercise.

THE TRIAL BALANCE

LO5 Prepare a trial balance.

5 A trial balance shows that the debit and credit totals are equal. A trial balance can also be used in preparing the financial statements.

5 **EXERCISE 3A9 TRIAL BALANCE** The following accounts have normal balances. Prepare a trial balance for Juanita's Delivery Service as of September 30, 19--.

Chapter Opening Vignettes

Along with the learning objectives, each chapter begins with a brief narrative that sets the stage for the chapter material. These vignettes include realistic business decisions and pose real-world questions. They are designed to help students understand the purpose of the chapter and why the chapter topics are important.

Learning Keys

Throughout the text, learning keys emphasize important new points. These keys direct student attention to such things as the application of new accounting concepts, how to journalize and post a transaction, relationships among accounts, and how to make an important calculation. A learning key from page 45 is shown below.

 Debits are always on the left and credits are always on the right for all accounts.

Key Steps

Key steps are incorporated frequently to show students how to accomplish specific objectives. The steps are used for many purposes, including how to prepare a bank reconciliation or a work sheet, how to post subsidiary and general ledger accounts, and how to find the cause of errors in a bank reconciliation or trial balance.

Illustrations

Accounting documents and records, diagrams, and flow charts are used throughout the text to help students visualize important concepts. Illustrations are used particularly when any new accounting principles or procedures are introduced. Important examples are as follows:

- **Use of the accounting equation.** In analyzing business transactions, students must understand the impact of an event on specific accounts in the accounting equation. Throughout Chapters 2 and 3, we repeat the accounting equation as a header for each entry made for specific transactions. This enables the student to see where each account fits in the equation, how the account is increased or decreased, and the effect each entry has on the balance of the equation.
- **Owner's equity umbrella.** In Chapter 3, the owner's equity umbrella illustrates how revenue, expense, and drawing affect owner's equity.
- **Accounting equation and financial statements.** In Chapter 2, we illustrate the direct linkages between the balances in the accounting equation and the financial statements.
- **Trial balance and financial statements.** In Chapter 3, we show how a trial balance is used to develop a set of financial statements.

- **Work sheet and financial statements.**   In Chapter 6, we show the linkages (a) between the Income Statement columns of the work sheet and the income statement, and (b) between the Balance Sheet columns of the work sheet and the statement of owner's equity and balance sheet.
- **Work sheet and cost of goods sold.**   In Chapter 14, we illustrate the linkages between the information extended to the Income Statement columns of the work sheet and the cost of goods sold section of the income statement.
- **Work sheet and closing entries.**   In Chapter 15, we illustrate the linkages between the Income Statement and Balance Sheet columns of the work sheet and the closing entries.

Key Points

Each chapter ends with a summary of key points. This provides an efficient way for students to review important chapter material.

Key Terms

At the end of each chapter, a list is provided of all important new terms introduced in the chapter. Each term is followed by the page number on which the term is first used in the chapter and a definition.

Review Questions

Review questions are provided at the end of each chapter. The questions provide students with an opportunity to immediately test their recall of important chapter concepts.

Managing Your Writing

A new and innovative section on Managing Your Writing has been added to Chapter 1. This section presents a twelve-step process that will help students become more efficient and effective writers. As part of this emphasis on writing, we have added a Managing Your Writing assignment at the end of each chapter. Each assignment provides an opportunity to apply critical thinking and writing skills to issues directly related to material in the chapter.

Demonstration Problem and Solution

Complete demonstration problems and solutions are provided for each chapter. The problems are a comprehensive application of key concepts and principles introduced in the chapter. They are useful in a variety of classroom settings. Students may work through the problems and solutions independently to gain confidence before working the Series A and B problems. Demonstration problems also can be used effectively as in-class examples.

Exercises and Problems

Three complete sets of exercises and problems have been prepared to facilitate instructor usage and student learning. At the end of each chapter, there are two sets (Series A and B) of exercises and problems. A third set, with and without solutions, is available when the study guide is adopted. Each exercise reinforces one concept developed in the chapter. Each problem links related concepts. All exercises and problems are keyed to the chapter learning objectives.

Mastery Problems

A comprehensive mastery problem follows the exercises and problems at the end of each chapter. This problem is usually similar to the demonstration problem in content and purpose. Mastery problems help develop critical thinking skills and can be used either to test or to further strengthen the students' overall grasp of the chapter materials.

Comprehensive Problems

A comprehensive problem is provided at the end of Chapter 6 and Chapter 15. Each problem permits the student to review the entire accounting cycle. Comprehensive Problem 1 deals with a service business; a merchandising business is the focus of Comprehensive Problem 2.

EMPHASIS ON SOUND PEDAGOGY

Our concern throughout the text is to facilitate student learning. Several dimensions of this sound pedagogy are worth emphasizing.

- **Work sheet acetates.**   This multi-layer presentation (Chapter 5) of the work sheet provides the most effective demonstration of work sheet preparation found anywhere. Students easily see how the work sheet is built.

- **Accounts receivable—Notes receivable.**   Notes receivable generally appear before accounts receivable on the balance sheet. In terms of student understanding, however, these two accounts come in the opposite order. Therefore, we cover the simpler, easier to understand subject of accounts receivable first (Chapter 16). Students are then better able to follow the notes receivable presentation (Chapter 17).

- **Payroll.**   This sometimes difficult subject is taught in two chapters, taking advantage of the natural break between employee and employer taxes and related issues. All coverage is current as of the date of publication, including the separation of the FICA tax into its Social Security and Medicare components.

- **Voucher system.**   This important topic is integrated into the sequence on accounting for a merchandising business (Chapters

11–15). By presenting this subject immediately following purchases and cash payments (Chapter 12), the student is shown the voucher system as a natural expansion of accounting for purchases.

- **Sales and cash receipts—Purchases and cash payments.** For sound learning and efficiency of presentation, each of these pairs of topics belongs together. The natural sequence of sales and cash receipts is reflected in Chapter 11. Similarly, Chapter 12 addresses the related activities of purchases and cash payments.

- **Depreciation methods.** Complete coverage of various depreciation methods is provided in Chapter 19. In addition, to accommodate students who may not enroll in a course that covers Chapter 19, Chapter 5 and its Appendix introduce the straight-line, sum-of-the-years'-digits, double-declining-balance, and modified accelerated cost recovery system depreciation methods.

- **Statement of cash flows.** We provide the most thorough coverage of the statement of cash flows of any text in our market. Because of the importance of the statement of cash flows today, we provide an introduction to this financial statement early in the text in an Appendix to Chapter 6. This Appendix explains the purpose of the statement of cash flows; illustrates the statement format using the direct method; and introduces operating, investing, and financing activities that are key sections of the statement. This early presentation allows students to develop a sense of the importance of managing cash flows without introducing the complexities of preparing the formal financial statement.

  Chapter 24 contains a complete discussion and illustration of the direct method of reporting cash flows from operating activities, which is preferred by the FASB. The Appendix to Chapter 24 illustrates the indirect method, which currently is used by most companies.

- **Accounting forms.** All journals, ledgers, and statements are presented on rulings. This emphasizes structure and helps students learn more quickly how to prepare these documents.

- **Color.** All journals are on blue rulings to differentiate these chronological records from ledgers and other processing documents, which are shown in yellow. Financial statements are white. Source documents vary in color, in the same manner as real-life documents.

- **Accounting relationships.** Color is used to show accounting relationships. This helps the student see the important relationships more easily. Pages 28 and 66 are two examples of this frequently used pedagogical aid.

- **Arrow pointers and text pointers.** Arrow pointers and text pointers emphasize the sources and calculations of numbers. For example, Figure 6-3 shows number pointers that point from the source number to the resulting number, and text pointers contain additional information.

FOR THE INSTRUCTOR

All complete learning packages include strong supplements. The supplements that have been designed for use by instructors are described below.

Annotated Instructor's Edition

New for this edition of the text is a complete Annotated Instructor's Edition. This special volume contains many valuable features. The first 32 pages are designed as a "walk through" the *College Accounting* learning package. In addition to introducing the package, the authors have included material on classroom preparation techniques and cooperative learning ideas. The remainder of the Annotated Instructor's Edition contains teaching tips, active learning ideas, check figures, and references to the teaching transparencies. All these components appear in the margins next to the appropriate material in the student text.

Solutions Manual

Two volumes (Chapters 1–15 and Chapters 16–28) contain complete solutions to Review Questions, Managing Your Writing activities, Series A and Series B Exercises and Problems, Mastery Problems, and Comprehensive Problems. The solutions appear on accounting rulings.

Solutions Transparencies

Series A and Series B Exercises and Problems, Mastery Problems, and Comprehensive Problems are supplied on acetates for use in classroom presentations. All solutions appear on accounting rulings.

Instructor's Resource Guide

This helpful resource supplements the Annotated Instructor's Edition. It provides complete teaching outlines with examples and activities for each chapter. In addition, brief class quizzes are included.

Testbank, Microexam, and Teletests

Over 2,000 true/false, multiple choice, and problem items are included in the testbank. Completely revised to match the changes made in this edition of the text, the testbank is a useful resource for developing testing materials. In addition to the printed supplement, Microexam provides access to the testbank in a computerized format. This easy-to-use software creates customized tests. Teletests are also available with this edition of the text.

Achievement Tests

Two sets of preprinted achievement tests are available. The tests have been completely restructured, with two tests now available for each chapter.

Teaching Transparencies

New, full-color transparencies of many illustrations in the text are available for classroom use. These transparencies are referenced in the Annotated Instructor's Edition for ease of use.

PowerPoint® Presentations

Complete classroom presentations for each chapter have been designed using Microsoft's popular presentation software. The presentations may be used with any computer that has PowerPoint installed.

Videos

Videos are available for Chapters 1–15 of the text. The videos highlight the key points of each chapter and present a problem and solution that correlates with the topics addressed in the chapter.

FOR THE STUDENT

Working Papers

Accounting rulings are available for all Series A and Series B Exercises and Problems, Mastery Problems, and Comprehensive Problems. Separate books are available for Chapters 1–10, Chapters 1–15, Chapters 11–20, and Chapters 16–28.

Study Guide

A solid tool for reinforcement, the study guide contains a discussion of learning objectives, questions, exercises, problems, and practice test questions. The study guide is available both with and without solutions, so that instructors can decide how the study guides will be used. Separate books are available for Chapters 1–10, Chapters 1–15, Chapters 11–20, and Chapters 16–28.

Solutions Software

General ledger software designed by Klooster and Allen is available for use with selected problems and practice sets. Opening balances, charts of accounts, and problem setup are provided for these problems. As students complete the problems, they gain valuable experience with full-functioning general ledger software.

Spreadsheet Software

Selected problems from the text can be completed using commercial spreadsheet software. Templates contain the basic problem setup; students learn to use the spreadsheet to solve the problems.

Tutorial Software

This computerized study guide is ideal to reinforce the concepts introduced in class, to allow students to review material missed, and to help students prepare for tests.

Practice Sets

Numerous practice sets (manual and computerized) are available for use with *College Accounting*. Each practice set is self contained; most include realistic source documents.

Check Figures

Check figures for the Series A and Series B Exercises and Problems and Mastery Problems are available on separate printed sheets.

RELATED MATERIALS

As world leader in accounting publishing, South-Western College Publishing has a wealth of resources available to complement its texts. Several have been designed to specifically accompany *College Accounting*. These include *Accounting for a Legal Office* and *Accounting for a Medical Office* and *Integrated Accounting*. The first two can be used in any classroom setting where additional coverage of specialized accounting procedures is desired. They are especially helpful to students preparing for a career in the legal or medical fields.

Integrated Accounting is available for IBM (DOS and Windows™) and Macintosh computers. Accounting applications for proprietorships, partnerships, and corporations; service and merchandising businesses; departmentalized and nondepartmentalized businesses; and voucher systems are included.

ACKNOWLEDGMENTS

We gratefully acknowledge the helpful input received from instructors and students. Your suggestions in reviews, surveys, feedback, and focus groups were instrumental in the preparation of the 15th edition. Several individuals deserve special recognition for their in-depth reviews, verification of solutions, and help with the text and supplements: Doug Cloud, Pepperdine University; Lynne Fowler, Heald Business College; Beth King, Heald Business College; Michael D. Lawrence, Portland Community College; Greg Lowry; Thomas E. Lynch, Hocking College; Leland Mansuetti, Sierra College; Fred McCracken, Indiana Business College; Betsy Ray, Indiana Business College; Marsha Schomburg; and Keith Weidkamp, Sierra College.

Further we would like to thank the Community and Career College Team members at South-Western College Publishing who worked with us on this edition: Diane Longworth Myers, Publishing Team Director; Gary Bauer, Senior Acquisitions Editor; Tom Bormann, Developmental Editor; Shelley Brewer, Production Editor; Sue Disselkamp, Manufacturing Coordinator; Dreis Van Landuyt, Marketing Manager; and Holly Knoechel and Meghan Kenney, Team Assistants. In addition, we thank Berry Publication Services for coordinating the development and production of the text. The following individuals deserve special recognition for their work with Berry Publication Services: Sara Myers, Joe Myers, Scott Ellis, and especially Minta Berry who played a key role in every phase of this revision of **_College Accounting_**.

Jim Heintz
Rob Parry

CONTENTS IN BRIEF

CONTENTS

Part 1 Accounting for a Service Business   1

Part 2 Specialized Accounting Procedures for Service Businesses and Proprietorships 203

PART

1

Accounting for a Service Business

1

Introduction to Accounting

*Careful study of this chapter
should enable you to:*

LO1 Describe the purpose of accounting.

LO2 Describe the accounting process.

LO3 Define three types of business ownership structures.

LO4 Classify different types of businesses by activities.

LO5 Identify career opportunities in accounting.

So, you have decided to study accounting. Good decision. A solid foundation in accounting concepts and techniques will be helpful. This is true whether you take a professional position in accounting or business, or simply want to better understand your personal finances and dealings with businesses. Knowledge of how accounting works will help you evaluate the financial health of businesses and other organizations. It will also give you a solid approach to dealing with financial and business transactions in your personal life.

Accounting is the language of business. You must learn this language to understand the impact of economic events on a specific company. Common, everyday terms have very precise meanings when used in accounting. For example, you have probably heard terms like asset, liability, revenue, expense, and income. Take a moment to jot down a brief definition for each of these terms. After reading and studying Chapter 2, compare your definitions with those developed in this text. This comparison will show whether you can trust your current understanding of accounting terms. Whether you intend to pursue a career in accounting or simply wish to understand the impact of business transactions, you need a clear understanding of this language.

THE PURPOSE OF ACCOUNTING

LO1 Describe the purpose of accounting.

The purpose of accounting is to provide financial information about the current operations and financial condition of a business to individuals, agencies, and organizations. As shown in Figure 1-1, owners, managers, creditors, and government agencies all need accounting information. Other users of accounting information include customers, clients, labor unions, stock exchanges, and financial analysts.

FIGURE 1-1 Users of Accounting Information

USER	INFORMATION NEEDED
Owners— Present and future	Firm's profitability and current financial condition
Managers— May or may not own business	Detailed measures of business performance
Creditors— Present and future	Whether the firm can pay bills on time so they can decide whether to extend credit
Government Agencies— National, state, and local	To determine taxes which must be paid and for purposes of regulation

THE ACCOUNTING PROCESS

LO2 Describe the accounting process.

Accounting is the art of gathering financial information about a business and reporting this information to users. The six major steps of the accounting process are analyzing, recording, classifying, summarizing, reporting, and interpreting (Figure 1-2). Computers are often used in the recording, classifying, summarizing, and reporting steps.

- **Analyzing** is looking at events that have taken place and thinking about how they affect the business.
- **Recording** is entering financial information about events into the accounting system. Although this can be done with paper and pencil, most businesses use computers to perform routine record keeping operations.
- **Classifying** is sorting and grouping similar items together rather than merely keeping a simple, diary-like record of numerous events.
- **Summarizing** is bringing the various items of information together to determine a result.
- **Reporting** is telling the results. In accounting, it is common to use tables of numbers to report results.
- **Interpreting** is deciding the importance of the information in various reports. This may include percentage analyses and the use of ratios to help explain how pieces of information relate to one another.

FIGURE 1-2 The Accounting Process

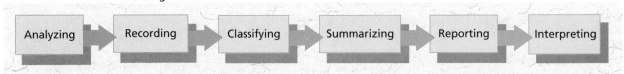

Generally accepted accounting principles (GAAP) are followed during the accounting process. The Financial Accounting Standards Board develops these accounting rules, called GAAP, to provide procedures and guidelines to be followed in the accounting and reporting process.

THREE TYPES OF OWNERSHIP STRUCTURES

LO3 Define three types of business ownership structures.

One or more persons may own a business. Businesses are classified according to who owns them and the specific way they are organized. Three types of ownership structures are (1) sole proprietorship, (2) partnership, and (3) corporation (Figure 1-3). Accountants provide information to owners of all three types of ownership structures.

Sole Proprietorship

A **sole proprietorship** is owned by one person. The owner is often called a proprietor. The proprietor often manages the business. The owner assumes all risks for the business, and personal assets can be taken to pay creditors. The advantage of a sole proprietorship is that the owner can make all decisions.

FIGURE 1-3   Types of Ownership Structures—Advantages and Disadvantages

TYPES OF OWNERSHIP STRUCTURES		
Proprietorship	**Partnership**	**Corporation**
■ One owner	■ Two or more partners	■ Stockholders
■ Owner assumes all risk	■ Partners share risks	■ Stockholders have limited risk
■ Owner makes all decisions	■ Partners may disagree on how to run business	■ Stockholders may have little influence on business decisions

Partnership

A **partnership** is owned by more than one person. One or more partners may manage the business. Like proprietors, partners assume the risks for the business, and their assets may be taken to pay creditors. An advantage of a partnership is that owners share risks and decision making. A disadvantage is that partners may disagree about the best way to run the business.

Corporation

A **corporation** is owned by stockholders (or shareholders). Corporations may have many owners, and they usually employ professional managers. The owners' risk is usually limited to their initial investment, and they usually have very little influence on the business decisions.

TYPES OF BUSINESSES

LO4 Classify different types of businesses by activities.

Businesses are classified according to the type of service or product provided. Some businesses provide a service. Others sell a product. A business that provides a service is called a **service business**. A business that buys a product from another business to sell to customers is called a **merchandising business**. A business that makes a product to sell is called a **manufacturing business**. You will learn about all three types of businesses in this book. Figure 1-4 lists examples of types of businesses organized by activity.

CAREER OPPORTUNITIES IN ACCOUNTING

LO5 Identify career opportunities in accounting.

Accounting offers many career opportunities. The positions described below require varying amounts of education, experience, and technological skill.

FIGURE 1-4 Types and Examples of Businesses Organized by Activities

SERVICES	MERCHANDISING	MANUFACTURING
Travel Agency	Department Store	Automobile Manufacturer
Computer Consultant	Pharmacy	Furniture Maker
Physician	Jewelry Store	Toy Factory

Accounting Clerks

Businesses with large quantities of accounting tasks to perform daily often employ **accounting clerks** to record, sort, and file accounting information. Often accounting clerks will specialize in cash, payroll, accounts receivable, accounts payable, inventory, or purchases. As a result, they are involved with only a small portion of the total accounting responsibilities for the firm. Accounting clerks usually have at least one year of accounting education.

Bookkeepers and Para-Accountants

Bookkeepers generally supervise the work of accounting clerks, help with daily accounting work, and summarize accounting information. In small-to-medium-sized businesses, the bookkeeper may also help managers and owners interpret the accounting information. Bookkeepers usually have one to two years of accounting education and experience as an accounting clerk.

Para-accountants provide many accounting, auditing, or tax services under the direct supervision of an accountant. A typical para-accountant has a two-year degree or significant accounting and bookkeeping experience.

Accountants

The difference between accountants and bookkeepers is not always clear, particularly in smaller firms where bookkeepers also help analyze the accounting information. In large firms, the distinction is clearer. Bookkeepers focus on the processing of accounting data. **Accountants** design the accounting information system and focus on analyzing and interpreting information. They also look for important trends in the data and study the impact of alternative decisions.

Most accountants enter the field with a college degree in accounting. Accountants are employed in public accounting, private (managerial) accounting, and in governmental and not-for-profit accounting (Figure 1-5).

Public Accounting.   Public accountants offer services in much the same way as doctors and lawyers. The public accountant can achieve professional recognition as a **Certified Public Accountant** (CPA). This is done by meeting certain education and experience requirements as determined by each state, and passing a uniform examination prepared by the American Institute of Certified Public Accountants.

Many CPAs work alone, while others work for major accounting firms that vary in scope and size. Services offered by public accountants are listed on the next page.

ACCOUNTING CLERK

Travel agency is looking for an accounting clerk to handle bookkeeping tasks. 1–3 years experience with an automated accounting system required.

BOOKKEEPING/ACCOUNTING

Service company has an opening for a full charge bookkeeper/accountant. Previous accounting experience with an associates degree preferred. Salary commensurate with experience. Excellent knowledge of LOTUS 1-2-3 required.

ACCOUNTANT

Responsibilities include accounts receivable, accounts payable, and general ledger. Familiarity with computerized systems a must. Supervisory experience a plus.

FIGURE 1-5 Accounting Careers

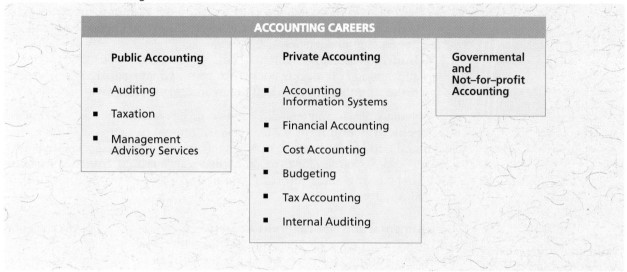

- **Auditing.**   Auditing involves the application of standard review and testing procedures to be certain that proper accounting policies and practices have been followed. The purpose of the audit is to provide an independent opinion that the financial information about a business is fairly presented.
- **Taxation.**   Tax specialists advise on tax planning, prepare tax returns, and represent clients before governmental agencies such as the Internal Revenue Service.
- **Management Advisory Services.**   Given the financial training and business experience of public accountants, many businesses seek their advice on a wide variety of managerial issues. Often accounting firms are involved in designing computerized accounting systems.

Private Accounting (Managerial Accounting).   Many accountants are employees of private business firms. The **controller** oversees the entire accounting process and is the principal accounting officer of the company. Private or managerial accountants perform a wide variety of services for the business. These services are listed below.

- **Accounting Information Systems.**   Accountants in this area design and implement manual and computerized accounting systems.
- **Financial Accounting.**   Based on the accounting data prepared by the bookkeepers and accounting clerks, the accountant prepares various reports and financial statements.
- **Cost Accounting.**   The cost of producing specific products or providing services must be measured. Further analysis is also done to determine whether the products and services are produced in the most cost-effective manner.
- **Budgeting.**   In the budgeting process, accountants help managers develop a financial plan.

- **Tax Accounting.**   Instead of hiring a public accountant, a firm may have its own accountants. They focus on tax planning, preparation of tax returns, and dealing with the Internal Revenue Service and other governmental agencies.
- **Internal Auditing.**   Internal auditors review the operating and accounting control procedures adopted by management. They also make sure that accurate and timely information is provided.

A managerial accountant can achieve professional status as a **Certified Management Accountant** (CMA). This is done by passing a uniform examination offered by the Institute of Management Accounting. An internal auditor can achieve professional recognition as a **Certified Internal Auditor** (CIA) by passing the uniform examination offered by the Institute of Internal Auditors.

ACCOUNTANT

Assist fiscal officer in not-for-profit accounting. Experience in payroll, payroll taxes, and LOTUS 1-2-3 helpful. Qualifications: accounting degree or equivalent. $22–$25K.

Governmental and Not-for-Profit Accounting.   Thousands of governmental and not-for-profit organizations (states, cities, schools, churches, and hospitals) gather and report financial information. These organizations employ a large number of accountants. While the rules are somewhat different for governmental and not-for-profit organizations, many accounting procedures are similar to those found in profit-seeking enterprises.

Job Opportunities

Job growth in some areas will be much greater than in others. Notice in newspaper advertisements that accountants and accounting clerks are expected to have computer skills. Computer skills definitely increase the opportunities available to you in your career. Almost every business needs accountants, accounting clerks, and bookkeepers. Figure 1-6 shows the expected growth for different types of businesses. Notice that growth will be greatest in the service businesses. Chapters 2 through 10 introduce accounting skills that you will need to work in a service business. Chapter 11 begins the discussion of merchandising businesses. Accounting for manufacturing businesses is addressed in the last chapters of the book. Figure 1-7 shows the expected demand for accounting skills.

Regardless of the type of career you desire, writing skills are important in business and your personal life. Becoming a good writer requires practice and a strategy for the process used to prepare memos, letters, and other documents. On pages 10 and 11, Ken Davis offers an excellent approach to managing your writing. Take a moment to read Ken's tips. Then, practice his approach by completing the writing assignments as you finish each chapter.

KEY POINTS

1   The purpose of accounting is to provide financial information about a business to individuals and organizations.

2   The six major steps of the accounting process are analyzing, recording, classifying, summarizing, reporting, and interpreting.

FIGURE 1-6   Expected Growth

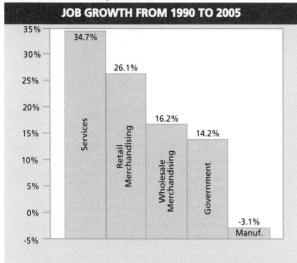

The growth in the number of new jobs from 1990 to 2005 will vary according to industry. The major area of growth is in service businesses. Service businesses that provide services to health care and business will provide the most opportunities. For example, many job opportunities will be available with temporary help agencies and computer and data processing services. Opportunities within manufacturing businesses will decrease. Part of the decrease will result from continued automation. Employment for technical workers within manufacturing will probably even increase.

Source: Bureau of Labor Statistics (1992)

FIGURE 1-7   Expected Demand

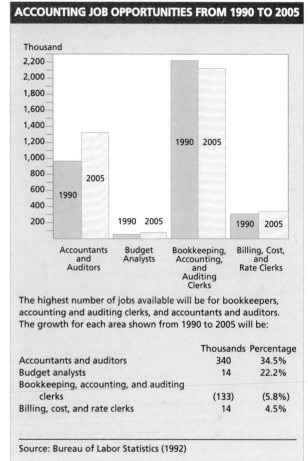

The highest number of jobs available will be for bookkeepers, accounting and auditing clerks, and accountants and auditors. The growth for each area shown from 1990 to 2005 will be:

	Thousands	Percentage
Accountants and auditors	340	34.5%
Budget analysts	14	22.2%
Bookkeeping, accounting, and auditing clerks	(133)	(5.8%)
Billing, cost, and rate clerks	14	4.5%

Source: Bureau of Labor Statistics (1992)

3 Three types of business ownership structures are sole proprietorship, partnership, and corporation.

4 Different types of businesses classified by activities are a service business, a merchandising business, and a manufacturing business.

5 Career opportunities in accounting include work in public accounting, private accounting, and governmental and not-for-profit accounting.

KEY TERMS

accountant 6   Designs the accounting information system and focuses on analyzing and interpreting information.

accounting 3   The art of gathering financial information about a business and reporting this information to users.

accounting clerk 6   Records, sorts, and files accounting information.

Managing Your Writing

KEN DAVIS

Here's a secret: the business writing that you and I do—the writing that gets the world's work done—requires no special gift. It can be *managed,* like any other business process.

Managing writing is largely a matter of managing time. Writing is a process, and like any process it can be done efficiently or inefficiently. Unfortunately, most of us are pretty inefficient writers. That's because we try to get each word, each sentence, right the first time. Given a letter to write, we begin with the first sentence. We think about that sentence, write it, revise it, even check its spelling, before going on to the second sentence. In an hour of writing, we might spend 45 or 50 minutes doing this kind of detailed drafting. We spend only a few minutes on overall planning at the beginning and only a few minutes on overall revising at the end.

That approach to writing is like building a house by starting with the front door: planning, building, finishing—even washing the windows—before doing anything with the rest of the house. No wonder most of us have so much trouble writing.

Efficient, effective writers take better charge of their writing time. They *manage* their writing. Like building contractors, they spend time planning before they start construction. Once construction has started, they don't try to do all of the finishing touches as they go.

As the illustration on the next page shows, many good writers break their writing process into three main stages: planning, drafting, and revising. They spend more time at the first and third stages than at the second. They also build in some "management" time at the beginning and the end, and some break time in the middle. To manage *your* writing time, try the following steps.

At the *MANAGING* stage (perhaps two or three minutes for a one-hour writing job), remind yourself that writing *can* be managed and that it's largely a matter of managing time. Plan your next hour.

At the *PLANNING* stage (perhaps 20 minutes out of the hour):

1. *Find the "we."* Define the community to which you and your reader belong. Then ask, "How are my reader and I alike and different?"—in knowledge, attitudes, and circumstances.

2. *Define your purpose.* Remember the advice a consultant once gave Stanley Tool executives: "You're not in the business of making drills; you're in the business of making holes." Too many of us lose sight of the difference between making drills and making holes when we write letters and memos. We focus on the piece of writing—the tool itself—not its purpose. The result: our writing often misses the chance to be as effective as it could be. When you're still at the planning stage, focus on the outcome you want, not on the means you will use to achieve it.

3. *Get your stuff together.* Learn from those times when you've turned a one-hour home-improvement project into a three- or four-hour job by having to make repeated trips to the hardware store for tools or parts. Before you start the drafting stage of writing, collect the information you need.

4. *Get your ducks in a row.* Decide on the main points you want to make. Then, make a list or rough outline placing your points in the most logical order.

At the *DRAFTING* stage (perhaps 5 minutes out of the hour):

5. *Do it wrong the first time.* Do a "quick and dirty" draft, without editing. Think of your draft as a "prototype," written not for the end user but for your own testing and improvement. Stopping to edit while you draft breaks your train of thought and keeps you from being a good writer. (Hint: if you are writing at a computer, try turning off the monitor during the drafting stage.)

At the *BREAK* stage (perhaps 5 minutes):

6. *Take a break and change hats.* Get away from your draft, even if for only a few minutes. Come back with a fresh perspective—the reader's perspective.

At the *REVISING* stage (perhaps 25 minutes):

7. *Signal your turns.* Just as if you were driving a car, you're leading your reader through new territory. Use "turn signals"—*and, in addition, but, however, or, therefore, because, for example*—to guide your reader from sentence to sentence.

8. *Say what you mean.* Put the point of your sentences in the subjects and verbs. For example, revise "There are drawbacks to using this accounting method" to "This accounting method has some drawbacks." You'll be saying what you mean, and you'll be a more effective communicator.

9. *Pay by the word.* Reading your memo requires work. If your sentences are wordy and you are slow to get to the point, the reader may decide that it is not worth the effort. Pretend you are paying the reader by the word to read your memo. Then, revise your memo to make it as short and to the point as possible.

10. *Translate into English.* Keep your words simple. (Lee Iacocca put both these tips in one "commandment of good management": "Say it in English and keep it short.") Remember that you write to express, not impress.

11. Finish the job. Check your spelling, punctuation, and mechanics.

Finally, at the *MANAGING* stage again (2 to 3 minutes):

12. Evaluate your writing process. Figure out how to improve it next time.

By following these 12 steps, you can take charge of your writing time. Begin today to *manage your writing*. As a United Technologies Corporation advertisement in *The Wall Street Journal* admonished, "If you want to manage somebody, manage yourself. Do that well and you'll be ready to stop managing and start leading."

Dr. Ken Davis is Professor of English and coordinator of the Applied Writing Group at Indiana University-Purdue University at Indianapolis. He is president of Komei, Inc., a global communication consulting company.

accounting information systems 7   Accountants in this area design and implement manual and computerized accounting systems.

analyzing 4   Looking at events that have taken place and thinking about how they affect the business.

auditing 7   Reviewing and testing to be certain that proper accounting policies and practices have been followed.

bookkeeper 6   Generally supervise the work of accounting clerks, help with daily accounting work, and summarize accounting information.

budgeting 7   The process in which accountants help managers develop a financial plan.

Certified Internal Auditor 8   An internal auditor who has achieved professional recognition by passing the uniform examination offered by the Institute of Internal Auditors.

Certified Management Accountant 8   An accountant who has passed an examination prepared by the Institute of Management Accounting.

Certified Public Accountant 6   A public accountant who has met certain education and experience requirements and has passed an examination prepared by the American Institute of Certified Public Accountants.

classifying 4   Sorting and grouping similar items together rather than merely keeping a simple, diary-like record of numerous events.

controller 7   The accountant who oversees the entire accounting process in a private business firm.

corporation 5   A type of ownership structure in which stockholders own the business. The owners' risk is usually limited to their initial investment, and they usually have very little influence on the business decisions.

cost accounting 7   Determining the cost of producing specific products or providing services and analyzing for cost effectiveness.

financial accounting 7   Preparing various reports and financial statements based on the accounting data prepared by the bookkeepers and accounting clerks.

generally accepted accounting principles 4   Procedures and guidelines developed by the Financial Accounting Standards Board to be followed in the accounting process.

internal auditing 8   Reviewing the operating and accounting control procedures adopted by management and seeing that accurate and timely information is provided.

interpreting 4   Deciding the importance of the information on various reports.

management advisory services 7   Providing advice to businesses on a wide variety of managerial issues.

manufacturing business 5   A business that makes a product to sell.

merchandising business 5   A business that buys products to sell.

para-accountant 6   A paraprofessional that provides many accounting, auditing, or tax services under the direct supervision of an accountant.

partnership 5   A type of ownership structure in which more than one person owns the business.

recording 4   Entering financial information into the accounting system.

reporting 4   Telling the results of the financial information.

service business 5   A business that provides a service.

sole proprietorship 4   A type of ownership structure in which one person owns the business.

summarizing 4   Bringing the various items of information together to explain a result.

tax accounting 8   Accountants in this area focus on planning, preparing tax returns, and dealing with the Internal Revenue Service and other governmental agencies.

REVIEW QUESTIONS

1. What is the purpose of accounting?
2. Identify four user groups normally interested in financial information about a business.
3. Identify the six major steps of the accounting process and explain each step.
4. Identify the three types of ownership structures and discuss the advantages and disadvantages of each.
5. Identify three types of businesses according to activities.
6. What are the main functions of an accounting clerk?
7. Name and describe three areas of specialization for a public accountant.
8. Name and describe six areas of specialization for a managerial accountant.

MANAGING YOUR WRITING

1. Prepare a one-page memo to your instructor that explains what you hope to learn in this course and how this knowledge will be useful to you.
2. If you started a business, what would it be? Prepare a one-page memo that describes the type of business you would enjoy the most. Would it be a service, merchandising, or manufacturing business? Explain what form of ownership you would prefer and why.

SERIES A   EXERCISES

1   **EXERCISE 1A1 PURPOSE OF ACCOUNTING**   Match the following users with the information needed.

1. Owners
2. Managers
3. Creditors
4. Government agencies

a. Whether the firm can pay its bills on time
b. Detailed, up-to-date information to measure business performance (and plan for future operations)
c. To determine taxes to be paid and whether other regulations are met
d. The firm's current financial condition

2   **EXERCISE 1A2 ACCOUNTING PROCESS**   List the six major steps of the accounting process in order (1–6) and define each.

_____ Recording
_____ Summarizing
_____ Reporting
_____ Analyzing
_____ Interpreting
_____ Classifying

SERIES B   EXERCISES

1   **EXERCISE 1B1 PURPOSE OF ACCOUNTING** Describe the kind of information needed by the users listed.

Owners (present and future)
Managers
Creditors (present and future)
Government agencies

2   **EXERCISE 1B2 ACCOUNTING PROCESS**   Match the following steps of the accounting process with their definitions.

Analyzing	**a.** Telling the results
Recording	**b.** Looking at events that have taken place and thinking about how they affect the business
Classifying	
Summarizing	**c.** Deciding the importance of the various reports
Reporting	**d.** Bringing together information to explain a result
Interpreting	**e.** Sorting and grouping like items together
	f. Entering financial information into the accounting system

2

Analyzing Transactions: The Accounting Equation

Have you ever heard the expression "garbage in, garbage out"? Computer users commonly use it to mean that if input to the computer system is not correctly entered, the output from the system will be worthless. The same expression applies in accounting. If the economic events and their impact on the accounting equation are not properly understood, the events will not be correctly entered into the accounting system. This will make the outputs from the system (the financial statements) worthless.

The entire accounting process is based on one simple equation, called the accounting equation. In this chapter, you will learn how to use this equation to analyze business transactions. You also will learn how to prepare financial statements that report the effect of these transactions on the financial condition of a business.

THE ACCOUNTING ELEMENTS

LO1 Define the accounting elements.

Before the accounting process can begin, the entity to be accounted for must be defined. A **business entity** is an individual, association, or organization that engages in economic activities and controls specific economic resources. This definition allows the personal and business finances of an owner to be accounted for separately.

Three basic accounting elements exist for every business entity: assets, liabilities, and owner's equity. These elements are defined below.

Pay close attention to the definitions for the basic accounting elements. A clear understanding of these definitions will help you analyze even the most complex business transactions.

Assets

Assets are items owned by a business that will provide future benefits. Examples include money, merchandise, furniture, fixtures, machinery, buildings, and land.

Liabilities

Liabilities represent something owed to another business entity. The amount owed represents a probable future outflow of assets as a result of a past event or transaction. Liabilities are debts or obligations of the business that can be paid with cash, goods, or services.

The most common liabilities are accounts payable and notes payable. An **account payable** is an unwritten promise to pay a supplier for assets purchased or services received. Formal written promises to pay suppliers or lenders specified sums of money at definite future times are known as **notes payable**.

Owner's Equity

Owner's equity is the amount by which the business assets exceed the business liabilities. Other terms used for owner's equity include **net worth** and **capital**. If there are no business liabilities, the owner's equity is equal to the total assets.

The owner of a business may have business assets and liabilities as well as nonbusiness assets and liabilities. For example, the business owner probably owns a home, clothing, and a car, and perhaps owes the dentist for dental service. These are personal, nonbusiness assets and liabilities. According to the **business entity concept**, nonbusiness assets and liabilities are not included in the business entity's accounting records.

 The business entity's accounting records are separate from the owner's nonbusiness assets and liabilities.

If the owner invests money or other assets in the business, the item invested is reclassified from a nonbusiness asset to a business asset. If the owner withdraws money or other assets from the business for personal use, the item withdrawn is reclassified from a business asset to a nonbusiness asset. These distinctions are important and allow the owner to make decisions based on the financial condition and results of the business apart from nonbusiness affairs.

THE ACCOUNTING EQUATION

LO2 Construct the accounting equation.

The relationship between the three basic accounting elements—assets, liabilities, and owner's equity—can be expressed in the form of a simple equation known as the **accounting equation**.

$$\text{Assets} = \text{Liabilities} + \text{Owner's Equity}$$

 If you know two accounting elements, you can calculate the third element.

Total assets	$60,400
Total liabilities	−5,400
Owner's equity	$55,000

This equation reflects the fact that both outsiders and insiders have an interest in all of the assets of a business. *Liabilities represent the outside interests of creditors. Owner's equity represents the inside interests of owners. When two elements are known, the third can always be calculated.* For example, assume that assets on December 31 total $60,400. On that same day, the business liabilities consist of $5,400 owed for equipment. Owner's equity is calculated by subtracting total liabilities from total assets, $60,400 − $5,400 = $55,000.

$$\text{Assets} = \text{Liabilities} + \text{Owner's Equity}$$

$$\$60,400 = \underbrace{\$5,400 + \$55,000}_{\$60,400}$$

ANALYZING BUSINESS TRANSACTIONS

LO3 Analyze business transactions.

A **business transaction** is an economic event that has a direct impact on the business. A business transaction almost always requires an exchange between the business and another outside entity. We must be able to measure this exchange in dollars. Examples of business transactions include buying goods and services, selling goods and services, buying and selling assets, making loans, and borrowing money.

All business transactions affect the accounting equation through specific accounts. An **account** is a separate record used to summarize changes in each asset, liability, and owner's equity of a business. **Account titles** provide a description of the particular type of asset, liability, or owner's equity affected by a transaction.

Three basic questions must be answered when analyzing the effects of a business transaction on the accounting equation.

1. **What happened?**
   - Make certain you understand the event that has taken place.
2. **Which accounts are affected?**
   - Identify the accounts that are affected.
   - Classify these accounts as assets, liabilities, or owner's equity.
3. **How is the accounting equation affected?**
   - Determine which accounts have increased or decreased.
   - Make certain that the accounting equation remains in balance after the transaction has been entered.

EFFECT OF TRANSACTIONS ON THE ACCOUNTING EQUATION

LO4 Show the effects of business transactions on the accounting equation.

Each transaction affects one or more of the three basic accounting elements. A transaction increases or decreases a specific asset, liability, or owner's equity account. Assume that the following transactions occurred during June 19--, the first month of operations for Jessie Jane's Campus Delivery.

TRANSACTION (a):   Investment by owner

An Increase in an Asset Offset by an Increase in Owner's Equity. Jessica Jane opened a bank account with a deposit of $2,000 for her business. The new business now has $2,000 of the asset Cash. Since Jane contributed the asset, the owner's equity element, Jessica Jane, Capital, increases by the same amount.

Assets	=	Liabilities	+	Owner's Equity
Items Owned		Amounts Owed		Owner's Investment
				Jessica Jane,
Cash	=			Capital
(a) $2,000				$2,000

TRANSACTION (b):   Purchase of an asset for cash

An Increase in an Asset Offset by a Decrease in Another Asset. Jane decided that the fastest and easiest way to get around campus and find parking is on a motor scooter. Thus, she bought a motor scooter (delivery equipment) for

$1,200, cash. Jane exchanged one asset, cash, for another, delivery equipment. This transaction reduces Cash and creates a new asset, Delivery Equipment.

	Assets		=	Liabilities	+	Owner's Equity
	Items Owned			Amounts Owed		Owner's Investment
	Cash +	Delivery Equipment =				Jessica Jane, Capital
	$2,000					$2,000
(b)	−1,200	+$1,200				
	$ 800	$1,200				$2,000
	└── $2,000 ──┘				└── $2,000 ──┘	

TRANSACTION (c):   Purchase of an asset on account

An Increase in an Asset Offset by an Increase in a Liability.   Jane hired a friend to work for her, which meant that a second scooter would be needed. Given Jane's limited cash, she bought the dealer's demonstration model for $900. The seller agreed to allow Jane to spread the payments over the next three months. This transaction increased an asset, Delivery Equipment, by $900 and increased the liability, Accounts Payable, by an equal amount.

	Assets		=	Liabilities	+	Owner's Equity
	Items Owned			Amounts Owed		Owner's Investment
	Cash +	Delivery Equipment =		Accounts Payable	+	Jessica Jane, Capital
	$ 800	$1,200				$2,000
(c)		+ 900		+900		
	$ 800	$2,100		$900		$2,000
	└── $2,900 ──┘			└── $2,900 ──┘		

TRANSACTION (d):   Payment on a loan

A Decrease in an Asset Offset by a Decrease in a Liability.   Jane paid the first installment on the scooter of $300. (See transaction (c).) This payment decreased the asset, Cash, and the liability, Accounts Payable, by $300.

	Assets		=	Liabilities	+	Owner's Equity
	Items Owned			Amounts Owed		Owner's Investment
	Cash +	Delivery Equipment =		Accounts Payable	+	Jessica Jane, Capital
	$ 800	$2,100		$900		$2,000
(d)	−300			−300		
	$ 500	$2,100		$600		$2,000
	└── $2,600 ──┘			└── $2,600 ──┘		

Expanding the Accounting Equation: Revenues, Expenses, and Withdrawals

In the preceding sections, three key accounting elements of every business entity were defined and explained: assets, liabilities, and owner's equity. To complete the explanation of the accounting process, three additional elements must be added to the discussion: revenues, expenses, and withdrawals.

Revenues.   **Revenues** represent the amount a business charges customers for products sold or services performed. Customers generally pay with cash or a credit card, or they promise to pay at a later date. Most businesses recognize revenues when earned, even if cash has not yet been received. *Revenues increase both assets and owner's equity.*

Expenses.   **Expenses** represent the decrease in assets (or increase in liabilities) as a result of efforts made to produce revenues. Common examples of expenses are rent, salaries, supplies consumed, and taxes. As expenses are incurred, either assets are consumed (supplies), cash is paid (wages), or a promise is made to pay cash at a future date. The promise to pay in the future represents a liability. Most businesses recognize expenses when incurred, even if cash has not yet been paid. *Expenses either decrease assets or increase liabilities. Expenses always reduce owner's equity.*

 LEARNING KEY It is important to remember that expenses do not always reduce cash.

If total revenues exceed total expenses of the period, the excess is the **net income** or net profit for the period.

Revenues Greater than Expenses = Net Income

On the other hand, if expenses exceed revenues of the period, the excess is a **net loss** for the period.

Expenses Greater than Revenues = Net Loss

The owner can determine the time period used in the measurement of net income or net loss. It may be a month, a quarter (three months), a year, or some other time period. The concept that income determination can be made on a periodic basis is known as the **accounting period concept**. Any accounting period of twelve months is called a **fiscal year**. The fiscal year frequently coincides with the calendar year.

Withdrawals

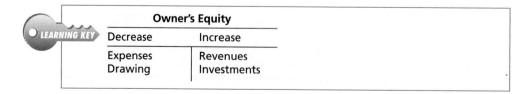

	Owner's Equity	
Decrease		Increase
Expenses		Revenues
Drawing		Investments

Withdrawals, or **drawing**, reduce owner's equity as a result of the owner taking cash or other assets out of the business for personal use. Since earnings are expected to offset withdrawals, this reduction is viewed as temporary.

The accounting equation is expanded to include revenues, expenses, and withdrawals. Note that revenues increase owner's equity, while expenses and drawing reduce owner's equity.

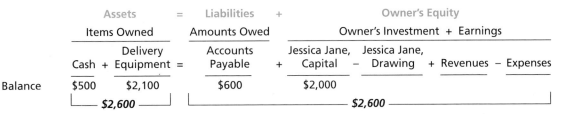

	Assets	=	Liabilities	+		Owner's Equity			
	Items Owned		Amounts Owed			Owner's Investment + Earnings			
	Cash + Delivery Equipment =		Accounts Payable	+	Jessica Jane, Capital	– Jessica Jane, Drawing	+ Revenues	– Expenses	
Balance	$500 $2,100		$600		$2,000				
	⌐——— $2,600 ———⌐		⌐———————————————— $2,600 ————————————————⌐						

Effect of Revenue, Expense, and Withdrawal Transactions on the Accounting Equation

To show the effects of revenue, expense, and withdrawal transactions, the example of Jessie Jane's Campus Delivery will be continued. Assume that the following transactions took place in Jane's business during June 19--.

TRANSACTION (e):   Delivery revenues earned in cash

An Increase in an Asset Offset by an Increase in Owner's Equity Resulting from Revenue. Jane received $500 cash from clients for delivery services. This transaction increased the asset, Cash, and increased owner's equity by $500. The increase in owner's equity is shown by increasing the revenue, Delivery Fees, by $500.

	Assets	=	Liabilities	+		Owner's Equity			Description
	Items Owned		Amounts Owed			Owner's Investment + Earnings			
	Cash + Delivery Equipment =		Accounts Payable	+	Jessica Jane, Capital	– Jessica Jane, Drawing	+ Revenues	– Expenses	
	$ 500 $2,100		$600		$2,000				
(e)	+500						+$500		Delivery fees
	$1,000 $2,100		$600		$2,000		$500		
	⌐——— $3,100 ———⌐		⌐———————————————— $3,100 ————————————————⌐						

TRANSACTION (f):   Paid rent for month

A Decrease in an Asset Offset by a Decrease in Owner's Equity Resulting from an Expense. Jane rents a small office on campus. She paid $200 for office rent for June. This transaction decreased both Cash and owner's equity by $200. The decrease in owner's equity is shown by increasing an expense called Rent Expense by $200. An increase in an expense decreases owner's equity.

	Assets	=	Liabilities	+		Owner's Equity				
	Items Owned		Amounts Owed			Owner's Investment + Earnings				
	Cash +	Delivery Equipment =	Accounts Payable	+	Jessica Jane, Capital	−	Jessica Jane, Drawing	+ Revenues	− Expenses	Description
	$1,000	$2,100	$600		$2,000			$500		
(f)	−200								+$200	Rent Expense
	$ 800	$2,100	$600		$2,000			$500	$200	
	$2,900				$2,900					

TRANSACTION (g):   Paid telephone bill

A Decrease in an Asset Offset by a Decrease in Owner's Equity Resulting from an Expense. Jane paid $50 in cash for telephone service. This transaction, like the previous one, decreased both Cash and owner's equity. This decrease in owner's equity is shown by increasing an expense called Telephone Expense by $50.

	Assets	=	Liabilities	+		Owner's Equity				
	Items Owned		Amounts Owed			Owner's Investment + Earnings				
	Cash +	Delivery Equipment =	Accounts Payable	+	Jessica Jane, Capital	−	Jessica Jane, Drawing	+ Revenues	− Expenses	Description
	$800	$2,100	$600		$2,000			$500	$200	
(g)	− 50								+ 50	Telephone Exp.
	$750	$2,100	$600		$2,000			$500	$250	
	$2,850				$2,850					

> **LEARNING KEY** Revenue is recognized even though cash is not received.

TRANSACTION (h):   Delivery revenues earned on account

An Increase in an Asset Offset by an Increase in Owner's Equity Resulting from Revenue. Jane extends credit to regular customers. Often delivery services are performed for which payment will be received later. This is known as offering services "on account." Since revenues are recognized when earned, an increase in owner's equity must be reported by increasing the revenue account. Since no cash is received at this time, Cash cannot be increased. Instead, an increase is reported for another asset, Accounts Receivable. *The total of Accounts Receivable at any point in time reflects the amount owed to Jane by her customers.* Deliveries made on account amounted to $600. Accounts Receivable and Delivery Fees are increased.

	Assets		=	Liabilities	+		Owner's Equity				
	Items Owned			Amounts Owed			Owner's Investment + Earnings				
	Cash +	Accounts Receivable +	Delivery Equipment =	Accounts Payable	+	Jessica Jane, Capital	−	Jessica Jane, Drawing	+ Revenues	− Expenses	Description
	$750		$2,100	$600		$2,000			$ 500	$250	
(h)		+$600							+600		Delivery Fees
	$750	$600	$2,100	$600		$2,000			$1,100	$250	
	$3,450					$3,450					

TRANSACTION (i):   Purchase of supplies

An Increase in an Asset Offset by a Decrease in an Asset.   Jane bought pens, paper, delivery envelopes, and other supplies for $80 cash. These supplies should last for several months. Since they will generate future benefits, the supplies should be recorded as an asset. The accounting equation will show an increase in an asset, Supplies, and a decrease in Cash.

	Assets			=	Liabilities	+	Owner's Equity				
	Items Owned				**Amounts Owed**		**Owner's Investment + Earnings**				
Cash +	Accounts Receivable +	Supplies +	Delivery Equipment =		Accounts Payable	+	Jessica Jane, Capital −	Jessica Jane, Drawing +	Revenues −	Expenses	Description
$750	$600		$2,100		$600		$2,000		$1,100	$250	
(i) −80		+$80									
$670	$600	$80	$2,100		$600		$2,000		$1,100	$250	
└─── $3,450 ───┘					└─────── $3,450 ───────┘						

TRANSACTION (j):   Payment of insurance premium

> **LEARNING KEY**   Both supplies and insurance are recorded as assets because they will last for several months.

An Increase in an Asset Offset by a Decrease in an Asset.   Since Jane plans to graduate next January, she paid $200 for an eight-month liability insurance policy. Insurance is paid in advance and will provide future benefits. Thus, it is treated as an asset. We must expand the equation to include another asset, Prepaid Insurance, and show that Cash has been reduced.

	Assets				=	Liabilities	+	Owner's Equity				
	Items Owned					**Amounts Owed**		**Owner's Investment + Earnings**				
Cash +	Accounts Receivable +	Supplies +	Prepaid Insurance +	Delivery Equipment =		Accounts Payable	+	Jessica Jane, Capital −	Jessica Jane, Drawing +	Revenues −	Expenses	Description
$670	$600	$80		$2,100		$600		$2,000		$1,100	$250	
(j) −200			+$200									
$470	$600	$80	$200	$2,100		$600		$2,000		$1,100	$250	
└─── $3,450 ───┘						└─────── $3,450 ───────┘						

TRANSACTION (k):   Cash receipts from prior sales on account

An Increase in an Asset Offset by a Decrease in an Asset.   Jane received $570 in cash for delivery services performed for customers earlier in the month (see transaction (h)). Receipt of this cash increases the cash account and reduces the amount due from customers reported in the accounts receivable account. *Notice that owner's equity is not affected in this transaction. Owner's equity increased in transaction (h) when revenue was recognized as it was earned, rather than now when cash is received.*

	Cash +	Accounts Receivable +	Supplies +	Prepaid Insurance +	Delivery Equipment =	Accounts Payable +	Jessica Jane, Capital −	Jessica Jane, Drawing +	Revenues −	Expenses	Description
	$ 470	$600	$80	$200	$2,100	$600	$2,000		$1,100	$250	
(k)	+570	−570									
	$1,040	$ 30	$80	$200	$2,100	$600	$2,000		$1,100	$250	

Assets $3,450 = Liabilities + Owner's Equity $3,450

TRANSACTION (l):   Purchase of an asset on credit making a partial payment

An Increase in an Asset Offset by a Decrease in an Asset and an Increase in a Liability. With business increasing, Jane hired a second employee and bought a third motor scooter. The scooter cost $1,500. Jane paid $300 in cash and will spread the remaining payments over the next four months. The asset Delivery Equipment increases by $1,500, Cash decreases by $300, and the liability, Accounts Payable, increases by $1,200. *Note that this transaction changes three accounts. Even so, the accounting equation remains in balance.*

	Cash +	Accounts Receivable +	Supplies +	Prepaid Insurance +	Delivery Equipment =	Accounts Payable +	Jessica Jane, Capital −	Jessica Jane, Drawing +	Revenues −	Expenses	Description
	$1,040	$30	$80	$200	$2,100	$ 600	$2,000		$1,100	$250	
(l)	−300				+1,500	+1,200					
	$ 740	$30	$80	$200	$3,600	$1,800	$2,000		$1,100	$250	

Assets $4,650 = Liabilities + Owner's Equity $4,650

TRANSACTION (m):   Payment of wages

A Decrease in an Asset Offset by a Decrease in Owner's Equity Resulting from an Expense. Jane paid her part-time employees $650 in wages. This represents an additional business expense. As with other expenses, Cash is reduced and owner's equity is reduced by increasing an expense.

	Cash +	Accounts Receivable +	Supplies +	Prepaid Insurance +	Delivery Equipment =	Accounts Payable +	Jessica Jane, Capital −	Jessica Jane, Drawing +	Revenues −	Expenses	Description
	$740	$30	$80	$200	$3,600	$1,800	$2,000		$1,100	$250	
(m)	−650									+650	Wages Expense
	$ 90	$30	$80	$200	$3,600	$1,800	$2,000		$1,100	$900	

Assets $4,000 = Liabilities + Owner's Equity $4,000

TRANSACTION (n):   Deliveries made for cash and credit

An Increase in Two Assets Offset by an Increase in Owner's Equity. Total delivery fees for the remainder of the month amounted to $900: $430 in cash and $470 on account. Since all of these delivery fees have been earned, the revenue account increases by $900. Also, Cash increases by $430 and Accounts Receivable increases by $470. Thus, revenues increase assets and owner's equity. Note, once again, that one event impacts three accounts while the equation remains in balance.

	Assets				=	Liabilities	+	Owner's Equity					
	Items Owned					Amounts Owed		Owner's Investment + Earnings					
Cash +	Accounts Receivable +	Supplies +	Prepaid Insurance +	Delivery Equipment =		Accounts Payable	+	Jessica Jane, Capital	–	Jessica Jane, Drawing	+ Revenues	– Expenses	Description
$ 90	$ 30	$80	$200	$3,600		$1,800		$2,000			$1,100	$900	
(n) +430	+470										+900		Delivery Fees
$520	$500	$80	$200	$3,600		$1,800		$2,000			$2,000	$900	
└─────── $4,900 ───────┘						└─────── $4,900 ───────┘							

TRANSACTION (o):   Withdrawal of cash from business

LEARNING KEY Withdrawals by the owner are reported in the drawing account. Withdrawals are the opposite of investments by the owner. Recall the business entity concept. The owner of the business and the business are separate economic entities. Thus, personal transactions must not be included with those of the business. If this is allowed, it will be very difficult to evaluate the performance of the business.

A Decrease in an Asset Offset by a Decrease in Owner's Equity Resulting from a Withdrawal by the Owner. At the end of the month, Jane took $150 in cash from the business to purchase books for her classes. Since the books are not business related, this is a withdrawal. Withdrawals can be viewed as the opposite of investments by the owner. Both owner's equity and Cash decrease.

	Assets				=	Liabilities	+	Owner's Equity					
	Items Owned					Amounts Owed		Owner's Investment + Earnings					
Cash +	Accounts Receivable +	Supplies +	Prepaid Insurance +	Delivery Equipment =		Accounts Payable	+	Jessica Jane, Capital	–	Jessica Jane, Drawing	+ Revenues	– Expenses	Description
$520	$500	$80	$200	$3,600		$1,800		$2,000			$2,000	$900	
(o) –150										+$150			
$370	$500	$80	$200	$3,600		$1,800		$2,000		$150	$2,000	$900	
└─────── $4,750 ───────┘						└─────── $4,750 ───────┘							

Figure 2-1 shows a summary of the transactions. Use this summary to test your understanding of transaction analysis by describing the economic event represented by each transaction. At the bottom of Figure 2-1, the asset accounts and their totals are compared with the liability and owner's equity accounts and their totals.

FIGURE 2-1 Summary of Transactions Illustrated

					SUMMARY						
	Assets					= **Liabilities** +		**Owner's Equity**			
	Items Owned					Amounts Owed		Owner's Investment + Earnings			
Transaction	Cash +	Accounts Receivable +	Supplies +	Prepaid Insurance +	Delivery Equipment =	Accounts Payable	+ Jessica Jane, Capital	− Jessica Jane, Drawing	+ Revenues	− Expenses	Description
Balance											
(a)	2,000						2,000				
Balance	2,000						2,000				
(b)	(1,200)				1,200						
Balance	800				1,200		2,000				
(c)					900	900					
Balance	800				2,100	900	2,000				
(d)	(300)					(300)					
Balance	500				2,100	600	2,000				
(e)	500								500		Delivery Fees
Balance	1,000				2,100	600	2,000		500		
(f)	(200)									200	Rent Exp.
Balance	800				2,100	600	2,000		500	200	
(g)	(50)									50	Tele. Exp.
Balance	750				2,100	600	2,000		500	250	
(h)		600							600		Delivery Fees
Balance	750	600			2,100	600	2,000		1,100	250	
(i)	(80)		80								
Balance	670	600	80		2,100	600	2,000		1,100	250	
(j)	(200)			200							
Balance	470	600	80	200	2,100	600	2,000		1,100	250	
(k)	570	(570)									
Balance	1,040	30	80	200	2,100	600	2,000		1,100	250	
(l)	(300)				1,500	1,200					
Balance	740	30	80	200	3,600	1,800	2,000		1,100	250	
(m)	(650)									650	Wages Exp.
Balance	90	30	80	200	3,600	1,800	2,000		1,100	900	
(n)	430	470							900		Delivery Fees
Balance	520	500	80	200	3,600	1,800	2,000		2,000	900	
(o)	(150)							150			
Balance	370	500	80	200	3,600	1,800	2,000	150	2,000	900	

Cash	$ 370	Accounts Payable	$1,800	
Accounts Receivable	500	Jessica Jane, Capital	2,000	
Supplies	80	Jessica Jane, Drawing	(150)	Amounts in ( ) are subtracted
Prepaid Insurance	200	Delivery Fees	2,000	
Delivery Equipment	3,600	Rent Expense	(200)	
		Telephone Expense	(50)	
Total assets	$4,750	Wages Expense	(650)	
		Total liabilities and owner's equity	$4,750	

As with the running totals in the table, the listing immediately following provides proof that the accounting equation is in balance.

FINANCIAL STATEMENTS

LO5 Prepare a simple income statement, statement of owner's equity, and balance sheet.

Three financial statements commonly prepared by a business entity are the income statement, statement of owner's equity, and balance sheet. The transaction information gathered and summarized in the accounting equation may be used to prepare these financial statements. Figure 2-2 shows the following:

1. A summary of the specific revenue and expense transactions and the ending totals for the asset, liability, capital, and drawing accounts from the accounting equation.
2. The financial statements and their linkages with the accounting equation and each other.

Note that each of the financial statements in Figure 2-2 has a heading consisting of:

HEADING FOR FINANCIAL STATEMENTS	1. The name of the firm	Jessie Jane's Campus Delivery
	2. The title of the statement	Income Statement, Statement of Owner's Equity, or Balance Sheet
	3. The time period covered or the date of the statement.	For Month Ended June 30, 19—, or June 30, 19—

The income statement and statement of owner's equity provide information concerning events covering a period of time, in this case, *the month ended* June 30, 19--. The balance sheet, on the other hand, offers a picture of the business *on a specific date*, June 30, 19--.

The Income Statement

Income Statement			Income Statement		
Revenues	$500		Revenues	$500	
Expenses	400		Expenses	700	
Net income	$100		Net loss	$200	

The **income statement**, sometimes called the **profit and loss statement** or **operating statement**, reports the profitability of business operations for a specific period of time. Jane's income statement shows the revenues earned

FIGURE 2-2 Summary and Financial Statements

	Assets					=	Liabilities	+	Owner's Equity				
	Items Owned						Amounts Owed		Owner's Investment + Earnings				
Transaction	Cash +	Accounts Receivable +	Supplies +	Prepaid Insurance +	Delivery Equipment =		Accounts Payable	+	Jessica Jane, Capital	− Jessica Jane, Drawing	+ Revenues	− Expenses	Description
(e)											500		Delivery Fees
(f)												200	Rent Exp.
(g)												50	Tele. Exp.
(h)											600		Delivery Fees
(m)												650	Wages Exp.
(n)											900		Delivery Fees
Balance	370	500	80	200	3,600		1,800		2,000	150	2,000	900	

Jessie Jane's Campus Delivery
Income Statement
For Month Ended June 30, 19--

Revenues				
Delivery fees				$2 0 0 0 00
Expenses				
Wages expense		$ 6 5 0 00		
Rent expense		2 0 0 00		
Telephone expense		5 0 00		
Total expenses			9 0 0 00	
Net income			$1 1 0 0 00	

$ at top of column

Subtotal underline

Jessie Jane's Campus Delivery
Statement of Owner's Equity
For Month Ended June 30, 19--

Jessica Jane, capital, June 1, 19--				$2 0 0 0 00
Net income for June		$1 1 0 0 00		
Less withdrawals for June		1 5 0 00		
Increase in capital			9 5 0 00	
Jessica Jane, capital, June 30, 19--			$2 9 5 0 00	

$ on total

Jessie Jane's Campus Delivery
Balance Sheet
June 30, 19--

Assets				Liabilities		
Cash	$	3 7 0 00		Accounts payable	$1 8 0 0 00	
Accounts receivable		5 0 0 00				
Supplies		8 0 00		Owner's Equity		
Prepaid insurance		2 0 0 00		Jessica Jane, capital	2 9 5 0 00	
Delivery equipment	3 6 0 0 00					
				Total liabilities and		
Total assets	$4 7 5 0 00			owner's equity	$4 7 5 0 00	

Double underline

for the month of June. Next, the expenses incurred as a result of the efforts made to earn these revenues are deducted. If the revenues are greater than the expenses, net income is reported. If not, a net loss is reported.

By carefully studying the income statement, it is clear that Jane earns revenues in only one way: by making deliveries. If other types of services were offered, these revenues would also be identified on the statement. Further, the reader can see the kinds of expenses that were incurred. The reader can make a judgment as to whether these seem reasonable given the amount of revenue earned. Finally, the most important number on the statement is the net income reported. This is known as the "bottom line."

The Statement of Owner's Equity

Owner's equity is affected by two basic types of transactions:

INFORMATION ON STATEMENT OF OWNER'S EQUITY	1. Investments and withdrawals by the owner, and
	2. Profits and losses generated through operating activities.

The **statement of owner's equity** illustrated in Figure 2-2 reports on these activities for the month of June. Jane started her business with an investment of $2,000. During the month of June she earned $1,100 in net income and withdrew $150 for personal expenses. This resulted in a net increase in Jane's capital of $950. Jane's $2,000 original investment, plus the net increase of $950, results in her ending capital of $2,950.

Note that Jane's original investment and later withdrawal are taken from the accounting equation. *The net income figure could have been computed from information in the accounting equation. However, it is easier to simply transfer net income as reported on the income statement to the statement of owner's equity.* This is an important linkage between the income statement and statement of owner's equity.

If Jane had a net loss of $500 for the month, the statement of owner's equity would be prepared as shown in Figure 2-3.

FIGURE 2-3 Statement of Owner's Equity with Net Loss

Jessie Jane's Campus Delivery
Statement of Owner's Equity
For Month Ended June 30, 19--

Jessica Jane, capital, June 1, 19--		$2 0 0 0 00
Less: Net loss for June	$ 5 0 0 00	
Withdrawals for June	1 5 0 00	
Decrease in capital		6 5 0 00
Jessica Jane, capital, June 30, 19--		$1 3 5 0 00

The Balance Sheet

The **balance sheet** reports a firm's assets, liabilities, and owner's equity on a specific date. It is called a balance sheet because it confirms that the accounting equation has remained in balance. It is also referred to as a **statement of financial position** or **statement of financial condition**.

```
                    Balance Sheet
                  ─────────────────
         Assets        Liabilities +
                       Owner's Equity
         ──────        ──────
          xxx           xxx
```

As illustrated in Figure 2-2, the asset and liability accounts are taken from the accounting equation and reported on the balance sheet. *The total of Jane's capital account on June 30 could have been computed from the owner's equity accounts in the accounting equation ($2,000 – $150 + $2,000 – $900). However, it is simpler to take the June 30, 19--, capital as computed on the statement of owner's equity and transfer it to the balance sheet.* This is an important linkage between these two statements.

GUIDELINES FOR PREPARING FINANCIAL STATEMENTS
1. Financial statements are prepared primarily for users not associated with the firm. Therefore, to make a good impression and enhance understanding, they must follow a standard form with careful attention to placement, spacing, and indentations.
2. All statements have a heading with the name of the company, name of the statement, and accounting period or date.
3. Single rules (lines) indicate that the numbers above the line have been added or subtracted. Double rules (double underlines) indicate a total.
4. Dollar signs are used at the top of columns and for the first amount entered in a column beneath a ruling.
5. On the income statement, a common practice is to list expenses from highest to lowest dollar amount, with miscellaneous expense listed last.
6. On the balance sheet, assets are listed from most liquid to least liquid. **Liquidity** measures the ease with which the asset will be converted to cash. Liabilities are listed from most current to least current.

OVERVIEW OF THE ACCOUNTING PROCESS

LO6 Define the three basic phases of the accounting process.

Figure 2-4 shows the three basic phases of the accounting process in terms of input, processing, and output.

- **Input.** Business transactions provide the necessary **input**.
- **Processing.** Recognizing the effect of these transactions on the assets, liabilities, owner's equity, revenues, and expenses of a business is the **processing** function.
- **Output.** The financial statements are the **output**.

FIGURE 2-4   Input, Processing, and Output

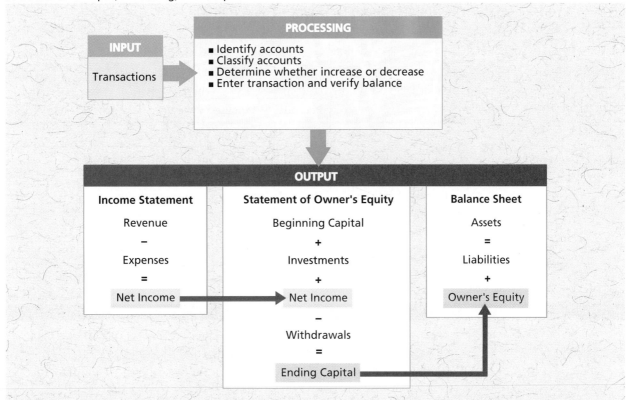

KEY POINTS

1   The three key accounting elements are assets, liabilities, and owner's equity. Owner's equity is expanded to include revenues, expenses, and drawing.

2   The accounting equation is:

Assets = Liabilities + Owner's Equity

3   Three questions must be answered in analyzing business transactions.

1. What happened?
2. Which accounts are affected?
3. How is the accounting equation affected?

4   Each transaction affects one or more of the three basic accounting elements. The transactions described in this chapter can be classified into five groups:

1. Increase in an asset offset by an increase in owner's equity.
2. Increase in an asset offset by a decrease in another asset.
3. Increase in an asset offset by an increase in a liability.
4. Decrease in an asset offset by a decrease in a liability.
5. Decrease in an asset offset by a decrease in owner's equity.

5 The purposes of the income statement, statement of owner's equity, and balance sheet can be summarized as follows.

STATEMENT	PURPOSE
Income statement	Reports net income or loss
	Revenues − Expenses = Net Income or Loss
Statement of owner's equity	Shows changes in the owner's capital account
	Beginning Capital + Investments + Net Income − Withdrawals = Ending Capital
Balance sheet	Verifies balance of accounting equation
	Assets = Liabilities + Owner's Equity

KEY TERMS

account 18 An account is a separate record used to summarize changes in each asset, liability, and owner's equity of a business.

account title 18 An account title provides a description of the particular type of asset, liability, owner's equity, revenue, or expense.

account payable 16 An unwritten promise to pay a supplier for assets purchased or services rendered.

accounting equation 17 The accounting equation consists of the three basic accounting elements: assets = liabilities + owner's equity.

accounting period concept 20 The concept that income determination can be made on a periodic basis.

assets 16 Items a business owns that will provide future benefits.

balance sheet 30 Reports assets, liabilities, and owner's equity on a specific date. It is called a balance sheet because it confirms that the accounting equation is in balance.

business entity 16 An individual, association, or organization that engages in economic activities and controls specific economic resources.

business entity concept 17 The concept that nonbusiness assets and liabilities are not included in the business entity's accounting records.

business transaction 17 An economic event that has a direct impact on the business.

capital 16 Another term for owner's equity, the amount by which the business assets exceed the business liabilities.

drawing 21 Withdrawals that reduce owner's equity as a result of the owner taking cash or other assets out of the business for personal use.

expenses 20 The decrease in assets (or increase in liabilities) as a result of efforts to produce revenues.

fiscal year 20 Any accounting period of twelve months' duration.

income statement 27   Reports the profitability of business operations for a specific period of time. (Also called the profit and loss statement or operating statement.)

input 30   Business transactions provide the necessary input for the accounting information system.

liability 16   Something owed to another business entity.

net income 20   The excess of total revenues over total expenses for the period.

net loss 20   The excess of total expenses over total revenues for the period.

net worth 16   Another term for owner's equity, the amount by which the business assets exceed the business liabilities.

note payable 16   A formal written promise to pay a supplier or lender a specified sum of money at a definite future time.

operating statement 27   Another name for the income statement, which reports the profitability of business operations for a specific period of time.

output 30   The financial statements are the output of the accounting information system.

owner's equity 16   The amount by which the business assets exceed the business liabilities.

processing 30   Recognizing the effect of transactions on the assets, liabilities, owner's equity, revenues, and expenses of a business.

profit and loss statement 27   Another name for the income statement, which reports the profitability of business operations for a specific period of time.

revenues 20   The amount a business charges customers for products sold or services performed.

statement of financial condition 30   Another name for the balance sheet, which reports assets, liabilities, and owner's equity on a specific date.

statement of financial position 30   Another name for the balance sheet, which reports assets, liabilities, and owner's equity on a specific date.

statement of owner's equity 29   Reports beginning capital plus net income less withdrawals to compute ending capital.

withdrawals 21   Reduce owner's equity as a result of the owner taking cash or other assets out of the business for personal use.

REVIEW QUESTIONS

1. Why is it necessary to distinguish between business assets and liabilities and nonbusiness assets and liabilities of a single proprietor?
2. List the three basic questions that must be answered when analyzing the effects of a business transaction on the accounting equation.
3. Name and define the six major elements of the accounting equation.
4. What is the function of an income statement?
5. What is the function of a statement of owner's equity?
6. What is the function of a balance sheet?
7. What are the three basic phases of the accounting process?

Write a brief memo that explains the differences and similarities between expenses and withdrawals.

DEMONSTRATION PROBLEM

Damon Young has started his own business, Home and Away Inspections. He inspects property for buyers and sellers of real estate. Young rents office space and has a part-time assistant to answer the phone and help with inspections. The transactions for the month of September are as follows:

(a) On the first day of the month, Young invested cash by making a deposit in a bank account for the business, $15,000.
(b) Paid rent for September, $300.
(c) Bought a used truck for cash, $8,000.
(d) Purchased tools on account from Crafty Tools, $3,000.
(e) Paid electricity bill, $50.
(f) Paid two-year premium for liability insurance on truck, $600.
(g) Received cash from clients for service performed, $2,000.
(h) Paid part-time assistant (wages) for first half of month, $200.
(i) Performed inspection services for clients on account, $1,000.
(j) Paid telephone bill, $35.
(k) Bought office supplies costing $300. Paid $100 cash and will pay the balance next month, $200.
(l) Received cash from clients for inspections performed on account in (i), $300.
(m) Paid part-time assistant (wages) for last half of month, $250.
(n) Made partial payment on tools bought in (d), $1,000.
(o) Earned additional revenues amounting to $2,000: $1,400 in cash and $600 on account.
(p) Young Withdrew cash at the end of the month for personal expenses, $500.

REQUIRED

1. Enter the transactions in an accounting equation similar to the one illustrated below. After each transaction, show the new amount for each account.

Assets						=	Liabilities	+	Owner's Equity				
Items Owned							Amounts Owed		Owner's Investment + Earnings				
Cash +	Accounts Receivable +	Supplies +	Prepaid Insurance +	Tools +	Truck =		Accounts Payable	+	Damon Young, Capital –	Damon Young, Drawing +	Revenues –	Expenses	Description

2. Compute the ending balances for all accounts.
3. Prepare an income statement for Home and Away Inspections for the month of September 19--.

4. Prepare a statement of owner's equity for Home and Away Inspections for the month of September 19--.

5. Prepare a balance sheet for Home and Away Inspections as of September 30, 19--.

SOLUTION

1, 2.

	Assets						=	Liabilities	+	Owner's Equity					
	Items Owned							Amounts Owed		Owner's Investment + Earnings					
	Cash +	Accounts Receivable +	Supplies +	Prepaid Insurance +	Tools +	Truck =		Accounts Payable	+	Damon Young, Capital −	Damon Young, Drawing	+ Revenues	− Expenses	Description
Bal. (a)	15,000									15,000				
Bal. (b)	15,000 (300)									15,000			300	Rent Exp.
Bal. (c)	14,700 (8,000)					8,000				15,000			300	
Bal. (d)	6,700				3,000	8,000		3,000		15,000			300	
Bal. (e)	6,700 (50)				3,000	8,000		3,000		15,000			300 50	Utilities Exp.
Bal. (f)	6,650 (600)			600	3,000	8,000		3,000		15,000			350	
Bal. (g)	6,050 2,000			600	3,000	8,000		3,000		15,000		2,000	350	Inspect. Fees
Bal. (h)	8,050 (200)			600	3,000	8,000		3,000		15,000		2,000	350 200	Wages Exp.
Bal. (i)	7,850	1,000		600	3,000	8,000		3,000		15,000		2,000 1,000	550	Inspect. Fees
Bal. (j)	7,850 (35)	1,000		600	3,000	8,000		3,000		15,000		3,000	550 35	Teleph. Exp.
Bal. (k)	7,815 (100)	1,000	300	600	3,000	8,000		3,000 200		15,000		3,000	585	
Bal. (l)	7,715 300	1,000 (300)	300	600	3,000	8,000		3,200		15,000		3,000	585	
Bal. (m)	8,015 (250)	700	300	600	3,000	8,000		3,200		15,000		3,000	585 250	Wages Exp.
Bal. (n)	7,765 (1,000)	700	300	600	3,000	8,000		3,200 (1,000)		15,000		3,000	835	
Bal. (o)	6,765 1,400	700 600	300	600	3,000	8,000		2,200		15,000		3,000 2,000	835	Inspect. Fees
Bal. (p)	8,165 (500)	1,300	300	600	3,000	8,000		2,200		15,000	500	5,000	835	
Bal.	7,665	1,300	300	600	3,000	8,000		2,200		15,000	500	5,000	835	

Cash	$ 7,665	Accounts Payable	$ 2,200
Accounts Receivable	1,300	Damon Young, Capital	15,000
Supplies	300	Damon Young, Drawing	(500)
Prepaid Insurance	600	Inspection Fees	5,000
Tools	3,000	Rent Expense	(300)
Truck	8,000	Utilities Expense	(50)
		Wages Expense	(450)
Total assets	$20,865	Telephone Expense	(35)
		Total liabilities and owner's equity	$20,865

3.

Home and Away Inspections
Income Statement
For Month Ended September 30, 19--

Revenues			
Inspection fees			$5 0 0 0 00
Expenses			
Wages expense	$ 4 5 0 00		
Rent expense	3 0 0 00		
Utilities expense	5 0 00		
Telephone expense	3 5 00		
Total expenses			8 3 5 00
Net income			$4 1 6 5 00

4.

Home and Away Inspections
Statement of Owner's Equity
For Month Ended September 30, 19--

Damon Young, capital, September 1, 19--		$15 0 0 0 00
Net income for September	$4 1 6 5 00	
Less withdrawals for September	5 0 0 00	
Increase in capital		3 6 6 5 00
Damon Young, capital, September 30, 19--		$18 6 6 5 00

5.

Home and Away Inspections
Balance Sheet
September 30, 19--

Assets		Liabilities	
Cash	$7 6 6 5 00	Accounts payable	$2 2 0 0 00
Accounts receivable	1 3 0 0 00		
Supplies	3 0 0 00	Owner's Equity	
Prepaid insurance	6 0 0 00	Damon Young, capital	18 6 6 5 00
Tools	3 0 0 0 00		
Truck	8 0 0 0 00	Total liabilities and	
Total assets	$20 8 6 5 00	owner's equity	$20 8 6 5 00

1   **EXERCISE 2A1 ACCOUNTING ELEMENTS**   Label each of the following accounts as an asset (A), a liability (L), or owner's equity (OE), using a format as follows.

Item	Account	Classification
Money in bank	Cash	
Office supplies	Supplies	
Money owed	Accounts Payable	
Office chairs	Office Furniture	
Net worth of owner	John Smith, Capital	
Money taken by owner	John Smith, Drawing	
Money owed by customers	Accounts Receivable	

2   **EXERCISE 2A2 THE ACCOUNTING EQUATION**   Using the accounting equation, compute the missing elements.

Assets	=	Liabilities	+	Owner's Equity
_____	=	$24,000	+	$10,000
$25,000	=	$18,000	+	_____
$40,000	=	_____	+	$15,000

3   **EXERCISE 2A3 EFFECTS OF TRANSACTIONS (BALANCE SHEET ACCOUNTS)**   Alice Stern started a business. During the first month (February 19--), the following transactions occurred. Show the effect of each transaction on the accounting equation: *Assets = Liabilities + Owner's Equity*. After each transaction, show the new account totals.

(a) Invested cash in the business, $20,000.
(b) Bought office equipment on account, $3,500.
(c) Bought office equipment for cash, $1,200.
(d) Paid cash on account to supplier in (b), $1,500.

4   **EXERCISE 2A4 EFFECTS OF TRANSACTIONS (REVENUE, EXPENSE, WITHDRAWALS)**   Assume Alice Stern completed the following additional transactions during February. Show the effect of each transaction on the basic elements of the expanded accounting equation: *Assets = Liabilities + Owner's Equity [Capital − Drawing + Revenues − Expenses]*. After each transaction show the new account totals.

(e) Received cash from a client for professional services, $2,500. REV.
(f) Paid office rent for February, $900. CASH ASS REDUCED
(g) Paid February telephone bill, $73.
(h) Withdrew cash for personal use, $500.
(i) Performed services for clients on account, $1,000.
(j) Paid wages to part-time employee, $600.
(k) Received cash for services performed on account in (i), $600.

1/5 **EXERCISE 2A5 FINANCIAL STATEMENT ACCOUNTS**   Label each of the following accounts as an asset (A), liability (L), owner's equity (OE), revenue (R), or expense (E). Indicate the financial statement on which the account belongs: income statement (IS), statement of owner's equity (SOE), or balance sheet (B), in a format similar to the following.

Account	Classification	Financial Statement
Cash		
Rent Expense		
Accounts Payable		
Service Fees		
Supplies		
Wages Expense		
Ramon Martinez, Drawing		
Ramon Martinez, Capital		
Prepaid Insurance		
Accounts Receivable		

5 **EXERCISE 2A6 STATEMENT OF OWNER'S EQUITY REPORTING NET INCOME**   Betsy Ray started an accounting service on June 1, 19--, by investing $20,000. Her net income for the month was $10,000 and she withdrew $8,000. Prepare a statement of owner's equity for the month of June.

5 **EXERCISE 2A7 STATEMENT OF OWNER'S EQUITY REPORTING NET LOSS**   Based on the information provided in Exercise 2A6, prepare a statement of owner's equity assuming Ray had a net loss of $3,000.

SERIES A   PROBLEMS

1 **PROBLEM 2A1 THE ACCOUNTING EQUATION**   Dr. John Schleper is a chiropractor. As of December 31, he owned the following property that related to his professional practice:

Cash	$ 4,750
Office Equipment	$ 6,200
X-ray Equipment	$11,680
Laboratory Equipment	$ 7,920

He also owes the following business suppliers:

Chateau Gas Company	$2,420
Aloe Medical Supply Company	$3,740

REQUIRED

1. From the preceding information, compute the accounting elements and enter them in the accounting equation shown as follows.

Assets	**=**	**Liabilities**	**+**	**Owner's Equity**
_____	+	_____	+	_____

2. During January, the assets increase by $7,290, and the liabilities increase by $4,210. Compute the resulting accounting equation.
3. During February, the assets decrease by $2,920, and the liabilities increase by $2,200. Compute the resulting accounting equation.

2 **PROBLEM 2A2 EFFECT OF TRANSACTIONS ON ACCOUNTING EQUATION**   Jay Pembroke started a business. During the first month (April 19--), the following transactions occurred.

(a)   Invested cash in business, $18,000.
(b)   Bought office supplies for $4,600: $2,000 in cash and $2,600 on account.
(c)   Paid one-year insurance premium, $1,200.
(d)   Earned revenues totaling $3,300: $1,300 in cash and $2,000 on account.
(e)   Paid cash on account to the company that supplied the office supplies in (b), $2,300.
(f)   Paid office rent for the month, $750.
(g)   Withdrew cash for personal use, $100.

REQUIRED
Show the effect of each transaction on the basic elements of the accounting equation: *Assets = Liabilities + Owner's Equity [Capital – Drawing + Revenues – Expenses]*. After each transaction, show the new account totals.

5 **PROBLEM 2A3 INCOME STATEMENT**   Based on Problem 2A2, prepare an income statement for Jay Pembroke for the month of April 19--.

5 **PROBLEM 2A4 STATEMENT OF OWNER'S EQUITY**   Based on Problem 2A2, prepare a statement of owner's equity for Jay Pembroke for the month of April 19--.

5 **PROBLEM 2A5 BALANCE SHEET**   Based on Problem 2A2, prepare a balance sheet for Jay Pembroke as of April 30, 19--.

SERIES B   EXERCISES

1 **EXERCISE 2B1 ACCOUNTING ELEMENTS**   Label each of the following accounts as an asset (A), liability (L), or owner's equity (OE) using the following format.

Account	**Classification**
Cash	
Accounts Payable	
Supplies	
Bill Jones, Drawing	
Prepaid Insurance	

continued

Account	Classification
Accounts Receivable	
Bill Jones, Capital	

2 **EXERCISE 2B2 THE ACCOUNTING EQUATION**   Using the accounting equation, compute the missing elements.

Assets	=	Liabilities	+	Owner's Equity
_____	=	$20,000	+	$5,000
$30,000	=	$15,000	+	_____
$20,000	=	_____	+	$10,000

3 **EXERCISE 2B3 EFFECTS OF TRANSACTIONS (BALANCE SHEET ACCOUNTS)**   Jon Wallace started a business. During the first month (March 19--), the following transactions occurred. Show the effect of each transaction on the accounting equation: *Assets = Liabilities + Owner's Equity*. After each transaction, show the new account totals.

(a)   Invested cash in the business $30,000.
(b)   Bought office equipment on account, $4,500.
(c)   Bought office equipment for cash, $1,600.
(d)   Paid cash on account to supplier in (b), $2,000.

4 **EXERCISE 2B4 EFFECTS OF TRANSACTIONS (REVENUE, EXPENSE, WITHDRAWALS)**   Assume Jon Wallace completed the following additional transactions during March. Show the effect of each transaction on the basic elements of the expanded accounting equation: *Assets = Liabilities + Owner's Equity [Capital – Drawing + Revenues – Expenses]*. After each transaction show the new account totals.

(e)   Performed services and received cash, $3,000.
(f)   Paid rent for March, $1,000.
(g)   Paid March telephone bill, $68.
(h)   Jon Wallace withdrew cash for personal use, $800.
(i)   Performed services for clients on account, $900.
(j)   Paid wages to part-time employee, $500.
(k)   Received cash for services performed on account in (i), $500.

1 **EXERCISE 2B5 FINANCIAL STATEMENT ACCOUNTS**   Label each of the following accounts as an asset (A), liability (L), owner's equity (OE), revenue (R), or expense (E). Indicate the financial statement on which the account belongs: income statement (IS), statement of owner's equity (SOE), or balance sheet (B), in a format similar to the following.

Account	Classification	Financial Statement
Cash		
Rent Expense		
Accounts Payable		
Service Fees		

continued

Account	Classification	Financial Statement
Supplies		
Wages Expense		
Amanda Wong, Drawing		
Amanda Wong, Capital		
Prepaid Insurance		
Accounts Receivable		

5 EXERCISE 2B6 STATEMENT OF OWNER'S EQUITY REPORTING NET INCOME   Efran Lopez started a financial consulting service on June 1, 19--, by investing $15,000. His net income for the month was $6,000 and he withdrew $7,000 for personal use. Prepare a statement of owner's equity for the month of June.

5 EXERCISE 2B7 STATEMENT OF OWNER'S EQUITY REPORTING NET LOSS   Based on the information provided in Exercise 2B6, prepare a statement of owner's equity assuming Lopez had a net loss of $2,000.

SERIES B   PROBLEMS

1 PROBLEM 2B1 THE ACCOUNTING EQUATION   Dr. Patricia Parsons is a dentist. As of January 31, Parsons owned the following property that related to her professional practice:

Cash	$3,560
Office Equipment	$4,600
X-ray Equipment	$8,760
Laboratory Equipment	$5,940

She also owes the following business suppliers:

Cupples Gas Company	$1,815
Swan Dental Lab	$2,790

REQUIRED

1. From the preceding information, compute the accounting elements and enter them in the accounting equation as show below.

Assets	=	Liabilities	+	Owner's Equity
___	=	___	+	___

2. During February, the assets increase by $4,565, and the liabilities increase by $3,910. Compute the resulting accounting equation.
3. During March, the assets decrease by $2,190, and the liabilities increase by $1,650. Compute the resulting accounting equation.

2 PROBLEM 2B2 EFFECT OF TRANSACTIONS ON ACCOUNTING EQUATION   David Segal started a business. During the first month (October 19--), the following transactions occurred.

(a) Invested cash in the business, $15,000.
(b) Bought office supplies for $3,800: $1,800 in cash and $2,000 on account.
(c) Paid one-year insurance premium, $1,000.
(d) Earned revenues amounting to $2,700: $1,700 in cash and $1,000 on account.
(e) Paid cash on account to the company that supplied the office supplies in (b), $1,800.
(f) Paid office rent for the month, $650.
(g) Withdrew cash for personal use, $150.

REQUIRED
Show the effect of each transaction on the basic elements of the accounting equation: *Assets = Liabilities + Owner's Equity [Capital – Drawing + Revenues – Expenses]*. After each transaction, show the new account totals.

5 **PROBLEM 2B3 INCOME STATEMENT**   Based on Problem 2B2, prepare an income statement for David Segal for the month of October 19--.

5 **PROBLEM 2B4 STATEMENT OF OWNER'S EQUITY**   Based on Problem 2B2, prepare a statement of owner's equity for David Segal for the month of October 19--.

5 **PROBLEM 2B5 BALANCE SHEET**   Based on Problem 2B2, prepare a balance sheet for David Segal as of October 31, 19--.

MASTERY PROBLEM

Lisa Vozniak started her own business, We Do Windows. She offers interior and exterior window cleaning for local area residents. Lisa rents a garage to store her tools and cleaning supplies and has a part-time assistant to answer the phone and handle third-story work. (Lisa is afraid of heights.) The transactions for the month of July are as follows:

(a) On the first day of the month, Vozniak invested cash by making a deposit in a bank account for the business, $8,000.
(b) Paid rent for July, $150.
(c) Purchased a used van for cash, $5,000.
(d) Purchased tools on account from Clean Tools, $600.
(e) Purchased cleaning supplies that cost $300. Paid $200 cash and will pay the balance next month, $100.
(f) Paid part-time assistant (wages) for first half of month, $100.
(g) Paid for advertising, $75.
(h) Paid two-year premium for liability insurance on van, $480.
(i) Received cash from clients for services performed, $800.
(j) Performed cleaning services for clients on account, $500.
(k) Paid telephone bill, $40.
(l) Received cash from clients for window cleaning performed on account in (j), $200.

(m) Paid part-time assistant (wages) for last half of month, $150.
(n) Made partial payment on tools purchased in (d), $200.
(o) Earned additional revenues amounting to $800: $600 in cash and $200 on account.
(p) Vozniak withdrew cash at the end of the month for personal expenses, $100.

REQUIRED
1. Enter the above transactions in an accounting equation similar to the one illustrated below. After each transaction, show the new amount for each account.

Assets						=	Liabilities	+	Owner's Equity				
Items Owned							Amounts Owed		Owner's Investment + Earnings				
	Accounts		Prepaid				Accounts		Lisa Vozniak,	Lisa Vozniak,			
Cash +	Receivable +	Supplies +	Insurance +	Tools +	Van =		Payable	+	Capital	– Drawing	+ Revenues	– Expenses	Description

2. Compute the ending balances for all accounts.
3. Prepare an income statement for We Do Windows for the month of July 19--.
4. Prepare a statement of owner's equity for We Do Windows for the month of July 19--.
5. Prepare a balance sheet for We Do Windows as of July 31, 19--.

3

The Double-Entry Framework

Careful study of this chapter should enable you to:

LO1 Define the parts of a T account.

LO2 Foot and balance a T account.

LO3 Describe the effects of debits and credits on specific types of accounts.

LO4 Use T accounts to analyze transactions.

LO5 Prepare a trial balance.

How do you keep track of your personal finances? Perhaps you make a list of your earnings and other cash inflows. Then you prepare a list of how the money was spent. Businesses need to do this, too. However, since businesses earn and spend money in many different ways, and enter thousands of transactions, a systematic approach must be followed. This is called the double-entry framework.

The terms asset, liability, owner's equity, revenue, and expense were explained in Chapter 2. Examples showed how individual business transactions change one or more of these basic accounting elements. Each transaction had a dual effect. An increase or decrease in any asset, liability, owner's equity, revenue, or expense was *always* accompanied by an offsetting change within the basic accounting elements. The fact that each transaction has a dual effect upon the accounting elements provides the basis for what is called **double-entry accounting**. To understand double-entry accounting, it is important to learn how T accounts work and the role of debits and credits in accounting.

THE T ACCOUNT

LO1   Define the parts of a T account.

The assets of a business may consist of a number of items, such as cash, accounts receivable, equipment, buildings, and land. The liabilities may consist of one or more items, such as accounts payable and notes payable. Similarly, owner's equity may consist of the owner's investments and various revenue and expense items. A separate account is used to record the increases and decreases in each type of asset, liability, owner's equity, revenue, and expense.

The T account gets its name from the fact that it resembles the letter T. As shown below, there are three major parts of an account:

1. the title,
2. the debit, or left side, and
3. the credit, or right side.

Title	
Debit = Left	Credit = Right

 LEARNING KEY | Debits are always on the left and credits are always on the right for all accounts.

The debit side is always on the left and the credit side is always on the right. This is true for all types of asset, liability, owner's equity, revenue, and expense accounts.

BALANCING A T ACCOUNT

LO2   Foot and balance a T account.

To determine the balance of a T account at any time, simply total the dollar amounts on the debit and credit sides. These totals are known as **footings**. The difference between the footings is called the **balance** of the account. This amount is then written on the side with the larger footing.

In Chapter 2, the accounting equation was used to analyze business transactions. This required columns in which to record the increases and decreases in various accounts. Let's compare this approach with the use of a

T account for the transactions affecting cash. When a T account is used, increases in cash are recorded on the debit side and decreases are recorded on the credit side. Transactions for Jessie Jane's Campus Delivery are shown below.

COLUMNAR SUMMARY (From Chapter 2, page 26)			T ACCOUNT FORM				
Transaction	Cash				Cash		
			(a)	2,000	(b)	1,200	
(a)	2,000		(e)	500	(d)	300	
(b)	(1,200)		(k)	570	(f)	200	
(d)	(300)		(n)	430	(g)	50	
(e)	500				(i)	80	
(f)	(200)		footing→	3,500	(j)	200	
(g)	(50)				(l)	300	
(i)	(80)				(m)	650	
(j)	(200)				(o)	150	
(k)	570					3,130←footing	
(l)	(300)						
(m)	(650)		Balance	370			
(n)	430						
(o)	(150)						
Balance	370						

DEBITS AND CREDITS

LO3   Describe the effects of debits and credits on specific types of accounts.

To **debit** an account means to enter an amount on the left or debit side of the account. To **credit** an account means to enter an amount on the right or credit side of the account. *Debits may increase **or** decrease the balances of specific accounts. This is also true for credits. To learn how to use debits and credits, it is best to reflect on the accounting equation.*

Assets		=	Liabilities		+	Owner's Equity	
Debit	Credit		Debit	Credit		Debit	Credit
+	–		–	+		–	+

LEARNING KEY   Debits increase assets and decrease liabilities and owner's equity. Credits decrease assets and increase liabilities and owner's equity.

Assets

Assets are on the left side of the accounting equation. Therefore, increases are entered on the left (debit) side of an asset account and decreases are entered on the right (credit) side.

Liabilities and Owner's Equity

Liabilities and owner's equity are on the right side of the equation. Therefore, increases are entered on the right (credit) side and decreases are entered on the left (debit) side.

Normal Balances

A **normal balance** is the side of an account that is increased. Since assets are debited for increases, these accounts normally have **debit balances**. Since liability and owner's equity accounts are credited for increases, these accounts normally have **credit balances**. Figure 3-1 shows the relationship between normal balances and debits and credits.

FIGURE 3-1   Normal Balances

ACCOUNT	ACCOUNTING EQUATION	INCREASE	DECREASE	NORMAL BALANCE
Assets	Left	Debit	Credit	Debit
Liabilities	Right	Credit	Debit	Credit
Owner's Equity	Right	Credit	Debit	Credit

Expanding the accounting equation helps illustrate the use of debits and credits for revenue, expense, and drawing. Since these accounts affect owner's equity, they are shown under the "umbrella" of owner's equity in the accounting equation in Figure 3-2.

FIGURE 3-2   The Accounting Equation and the Owner's Equity Umbrella

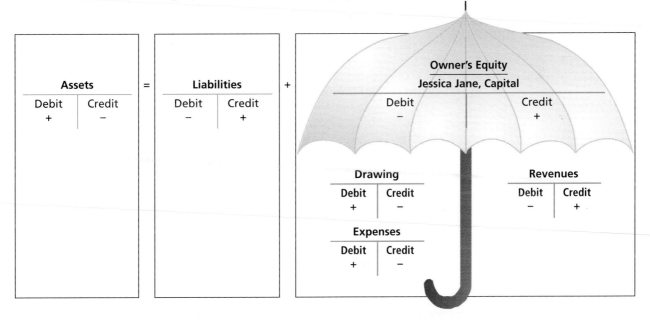

Revenues

Revenues increase owner's equity. Revenues could be recorded directly on the credit side of the owner's capital account. However, readers of financial statements are interested in the specific types of revenues earned.

Therefore, specific revenue accounts, like delivery fees, sales, and service fees, are used. These specific accounts are credited when revenue is earned.

Expenses

As expenses increase, owner's equity decreases. Expenses could be recorded on the debit side of the owner's capital account. However, readers of financial statements want to see the types of expenses incurred during the accounting period. Thus, specific expense accounts are maintained for items like rent, wages, advertising, and utilities. These specific accounts are debited as expenses are incurred.

 LEARNING KEY   You could credit the owner's capital account for revenues and debit the capital account for expenses and withdrawals. However, using specific accounts provides additional information. Remember: an increase in an expense decreases owner's equity.

Drawing

Withdrawals of cash and other assets by the owner for personal reasons decrease owner's equity. Withdrawals could be debited directly to the owner's capital account. However, readers of financial statements want to know the amount of withdrawals for the accounting period. Thus, it is easier to maintain this information in a separate account.

Normal Balances for the Owner's Equity Umbrella

Since expense and drawing accounts are debited for increases, these accounts normally have **debit balances**. Since revenue accounts are credited for increases, these accounts normally have **credit balances**. Figure 3-3 shows the normal balances for the owner's equity accounts.

FIGURE 3-3   Normal Balances for the Owner's Equity Umbrella

ACCOUNT	OWNER'S EQUITY UMBRELLA	INCREASE	DECREASE	NORMAL
Revenues	Right	Credit	Debit	Credit
Expenses	Left	Debit	Credit	Debit
Drawing	Left	Debit	Credit	Debit

TRANSACTION ANALYSIS

LO4   Use T accounts to analyze transactions.

In Chapter 2, you learned how to analyze transactions by using the accounting equation. Here, we continue to use the accounting equation, but add debits and credits by using T accounts. As shown in Figure 3-4, the three basic questions that must be answered when analyzing a transaction are essentially the same, but expanded slightly to address the use of T accounts. You must determine the location of the account within the accounting equation. You must also determine whether the accounts should be debited or credited.

FIGURE 3-4   Steps in Transaction Analysis

1. What happened? Make certain you understand the event that has taken place.
2. Which accounts are affected? Once you have determined what happened, you must: ■ Identify the accounts that are affected. ■ Classify these accounts as assets, liabilities, owner's equity, revenues, or expenses. ■ Identify the location of the accounts in the accounting equation and/or the owner's equity umbrella—left or right.
3. How is the accounting equation affected? ■ Determine whether the accounts have increased or decreased. ■ Determine whether the accounts should be debited or credited. ■ Make certain that the accounting equation remains in balance after the transaction has been entered. (1) Assets = Liabilities + Owner's Equity. (2) Debits = Credits for every transaction.

LEARNING KEY   Proper use of debits and credits helps to keep the accounting equation in balance.

Debits and Credits: Asset, Liability, and Owner's Equity Accounts

Transactions (a) through (d) from Jessie Jane's Campus Delivery (Chapter 2) demonstrate the double-entry process for transactions affecting asset, liability, and owner's equity accounts.

As you study each transaction, answer the three questions: (1) What happened? (2) Which accounts are affected? and (3) How is the accounting equation affected? The transaction statement tells you what happened. The analysis following the illustration of each transaction tells which accounts are affected. The illustration shows you how the accounting equation is affected.

TRANSACTION (a):   **Investment by owner**

Jessica Jane opened a bank account with a deposit of $2,000 for her business (Figure 3-5).

Analysis: As a result of this transaction, the business acquired an asset, Cash. In exchange for the asset, the business gave Jessica Jane owner's equity. The owner's equity account is called Jessica Jane, Capital. The transaction is entered as an increase in an asset and an increase in owner's equity. Debit Cash and credit Jessica Jane, Capital for $2,000.

FIGURE 3-5 Transaction (a): Investment by Owner

Assets	=	Liabilities	+	Owner's Equity
Debit / Credit + / –		Debit / Credit – / +		Debit / Credit – / +
Cash				**Jessica Jane, Capital**
(a) 2,000				(a) 2,000
└── $2,000 ──┘		└────── $2,000 ──────┘		

ACCOUNT AFFECTED	CLASSIFICATION	LOCATION IN EQUATION	INCREASE OR DECREASE	DEBIT OR CREDIT
Cash	Asset	Left	Increase	Debit
Capital	Owner's Equity	Right	Increase	Credit

TRANSACTION (b):   Purchase of an asset for cash

Jane bought a motor scooter (delivery equipment) for $1,200 cash (Figure 3-6).

FIGURE 3-6 Transaction (b): Purchase of an Asset for Cash

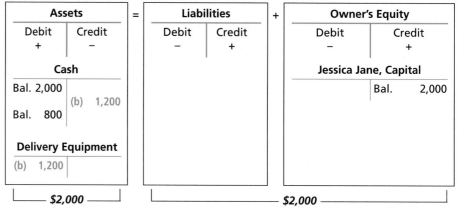

Assets	=	Liabilities	+	Owner's Equity
Debit / Credit + / –		Debit / Credit – / +		Debit / Credit – / +
Cash				**Jessica Jane, Capital**
Bal. 2,000				Bal. 2,000
(b) 1,200				
Bal. 800				
Delivery Equipment				
(b) 1,200				
└── $2,000 ──┘		└────── $2,000 ──────┘		

Analysis: Jane exchanged one asset, Cash, for another, Delivery Equipment. Debit Delivery Equipment and credit Cash for $1,200. Notice that the total assets are still $2,000 as they were following transaction (a). Transaction (b) shifted assets from cash to delivery equipment, but total assets remained the same.

ACCOUNT AFFECTED	CLASSIFICATION	LOCATION IN EQUATION	INCREASE OR DECREASE	DEBIT OR CREDIT
Delivery Equipment	Asset	Left	Increase	Debit
Cash	Asset	Left	Decrease	Credit

TRANSACTION (c):   Purchase of an asset on account

Jane bought a second motor scooter on account for $900 (Figure 3-7).

FIGURE 3-7   Transaction (c): Purchase of an Asset on Account

Assets		=	Liabilities		+	Owner's Equity	
Debit	Credit		Debit	Credit		Debit	Credit
+	−		−	+		−	+
Cash			**Accounts Payable**			**Jessica Jane, Capital**	
Bal. 800				(c) 900			Bal. 2,000
Delivery Equipment							
Bal. 1,200							
(c) 900							
Bal. 2,100							
└─── *$2,900* ───┘			└─────── *$2,900* ───────				

Analysis: The asset, Delivery Equipment, increases by $900 and the liability, Accounts Payable, increases by the same amount. Thus, debit Delivery Equipment and credit Accounts Payable for $900.

ACCOUNT AFFECTED	CLASSIFICATION	LOCATION IN EQUATION	INCREASE OR DECREASE	DEBIT OR CREDIT
Delivery Equipment	Asset	Left	Increase	Debit
Accounts Payable	Liability	Right	Increase	Credit

TRANSACTION (d):   Payment on a loan

Jane made the first $300 payment on the scooter purchased in transaction (c) (Figure 3-8).

FIGURE 3-8   Transaction (d): Payment on a Loan

Assets		=	Liabilities		+	Owner's Equity	
Debit	Credit		Debit	Credit		Debit	Credit
+	−		−	+		−	+
Cash			**Accounts Payable**			**Jessica Jane, Capital**	
Bal. 800				Bal. 900			Bal. 2,000
	(d) 300		(d) 300				
Bal. 500				Bal. 600			
Delivery Equipment							
Bal. 2,100							
└─── *$2,600* ───┘			└─────── *$2,600* ───────				

Analysis: This payment decreases the asset, Cash, and decreases the liability, Accounts Payable. Debit Accounts Payable and credit Cash for $300.

ACCOUNT AFFECTED	CLASSIFICATION	LOCATION IN EQUATION	INCREASE OR DECREASE	DEBIT OR CREDIT
Accounts Payable	Liability	Right	Decrease	Debit
Cash	Asset	Left	Decrease	Credit

Notice that for transactions (a) through (d), the debits equal credits and the accounting equation is in balance. Review transactions (a) through (d). Again, identify the accounts that were affected and how they were classified (assets, liabilities, or owner's equity). Finally, note each account's location within the accounting equation.

Debits and Credits: Including Revenues, Expenses, and Drawing

> Revenues increase owner's equity and are on the credit side of the capital account. Expenses and drawing reduce owner's equity and are on the debit side of the capital account.

Transactions (a) through (d) involved only assets, liabilities, and the owner's capital account. To complete the illustration of Jessie Jane's Campus Delivery, the equation is expanded to include revenues, expenses, and drawing. Remember, revenues increase owner's equity and are shown under the credit side of the capital account. Expenses and drawing decrease owner's equity and are shown under the debit side of the capital account. The expanded equation is shown in Figure 3-9.

FIGURE 3-9 The Expanded Accounting Equation

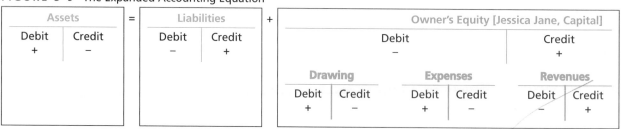

TRANSACTION (e): Delivery revenues earned in cash

Jane made deliveries and received $500 cash from clients (Figure 3-10).

FIGURE 3-10 Transaction (e): Delivery Revenues Earned in Cash

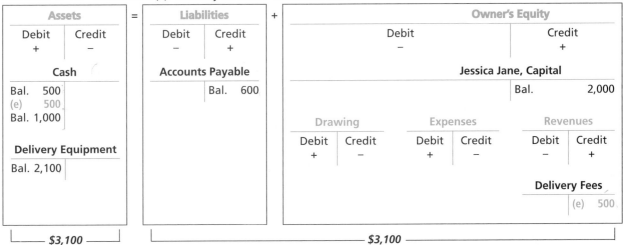

Analysis: The asset, Cash, and the revenue, Delivery Fees, increase. Debit Cash and credit Delivery Fees for $500.

ACCOUNT AFFECTED	CLASSIFICATION	LOCATION IN EQUATION	INCREASE OR DECREASE	DEBIT OR CREDIT
Cash	Asset	Left	Increase	Debit
Delivery Fees	Revenue	Right O.E.—Right Side	Increase	Credit

TRANSACTION (f): Paid rent for month

Jane paid $200 for office rent for June (Figure 3-11).

FIGURE 3-11 Transaction (f): Paid Rent for Month

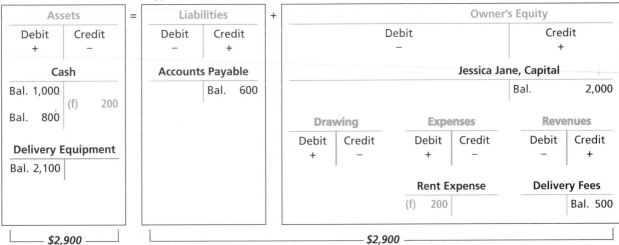

Analysis: Rent Expense increases and Cash decreases. Debit Rent Expense and credit Cash for $200.

A debit to an expense account increases that expense and decreases owner's equity. Notice that the placement of the plus and minus signs for expenses are opposite the placement of the signs for owner's equity. Note also that expenses are located on the left (debit) side of the owner's equity umbrella.

ACCOUNT AFFECTED	CLASSIFICATION	LOCATION IN EQUATION	INCREASE OR DECREASE	DEBIT OR CREDIT
Rent Expense	Expense	Right O.E.—Left Side	Exp.— Increases; O.E.— Decreases	Debit
Cash	Asset	Left	Decrease	Credit

TRANSACTION (g):   Paid telephone bill

Jane paid for telephone service, $50 (Figure 3-12).

FIGURE 3-12 Transaction (g): Paid Telephone Bill

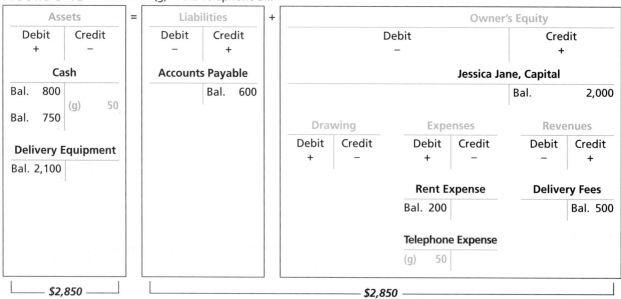

Analysis: This transaction, like the previous one, increases an expense and decreases an asset. Debit Telephone Expense and credit Cash for $50.

ACCOUNT AFFECTED	CLASSIFICATION	LOCATION IN EQUATION	INCREASE OR DECREASE	DEBIT OR CREDIT
Telephone Expense	Expense	Right O.E.—Left Side	Exp.—Increases; O.E.—Decreases	Debit
Cash	Asset	Left	Decrease	Credit

TRANSACTION (h):   Delivery revenues earned on account

Jane made deliveries on account for $600 (Figure 3-13).

FIGURE 3-13 Transaction (h): Delivery Revenues Earned on Account

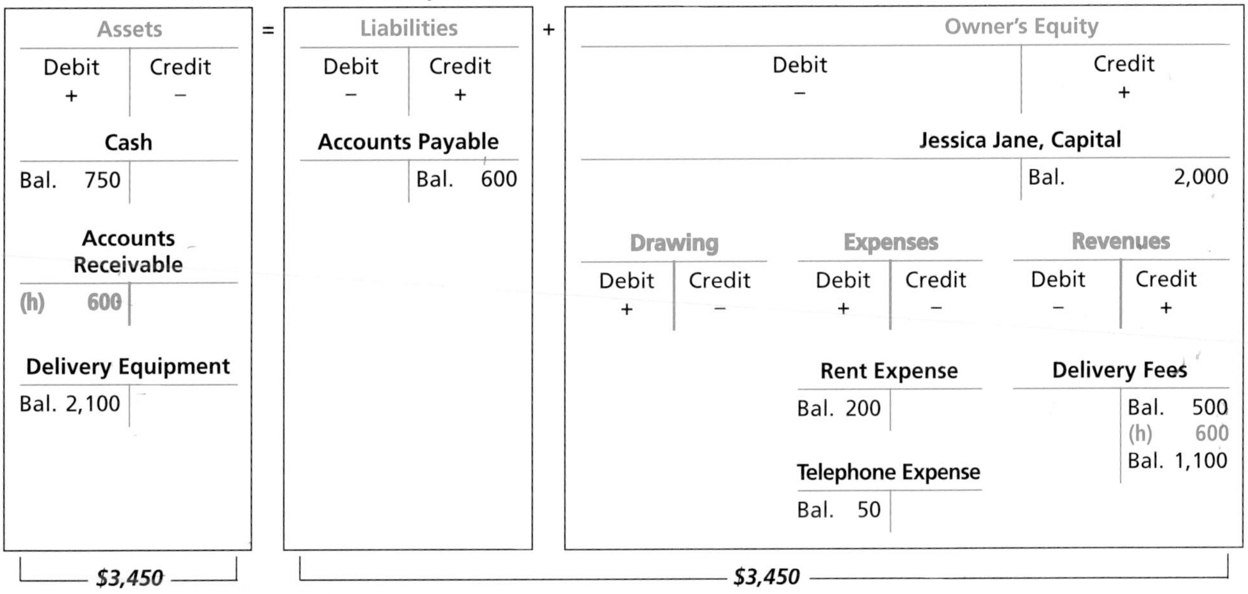

Analysis: As discussed in Chapter 2, delivery services are performed for which payment will be received later. This is called offering services "on account" or "on credit." Instead of receiving cash, Jane receives a promise that her customers will pay cash in the future. Therefore, the asset, Accounts Receivable, increases. Since revenues are recognized when earned, the revenue account, Delivery Fees, also increases. Debit Accounts Receivable and credit Delivery Fees for $600.

ACCOUNT AFFECTED	CLASSIFICATION	LOCATION IN EQUATION	INCREASE OR DECREASE	DEBIT OR CREDIT
Accounts Receivable	Asset	Left	Increase	Debit
Delivery Fees	Revenue	Right O.E.—Left Side	Increase	Credit

Review transactions (e) through (h). Two of these transactions are expenses and two are revenue transactions. Each of these transactions affected the owner's equity umbrella. Three transactions affected Cash and one transaction affected Accounts Receivable. Keep in mind that expense and revenue transactions do not always affect cash.

Notice that the debits equal credits and the accounting equation is in balance after each transaction. As you review transactions (e) through (h), identify the accounts that were affected and classify each account (assets, liabilities, owner's equity, revenue, or expense). Notice each account's location within the accounting equation and the owner's equity umbrella.

TRANSACTION (i):   Purchase of supplies

Jane bought pens, paper, delivery envelopes, and other supplies for $80 cash (Figure 3-14).

FIGURE 3-14 Transaction (i): Purchase of Supplies

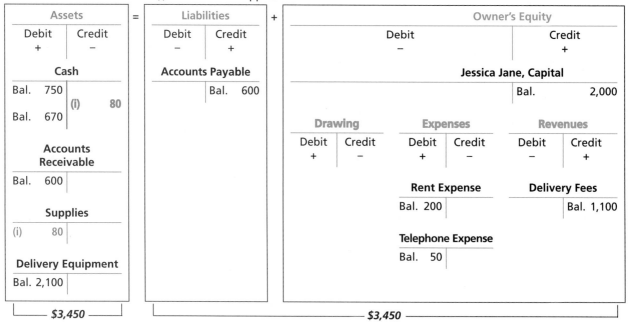

Analysis: These supplies will last for several months. Since they will generate future benefits, the supplies should be recorded as an asset. An asset, Supplies, increases, and an asset, Cash, decreases. Debit Supplies and credit Cash for $80.

ACCOUNT AFFECTED	CLASSIFICATION	LOCATION IN EQUATION	INCREASE OR DECREASE	DEBIT OR CREDIT
Supplies	Asset	Left	Increase	Debit
Cash	Asset	Left	Decrease	Credit

TRANSACTION (j):   **Payment of insurance premium**

Jane paid $200 for an eight-month liability insurance policy (Figure 3-15).

FIGURE 3-15 Transaction (j): Payment of Insurance Premium

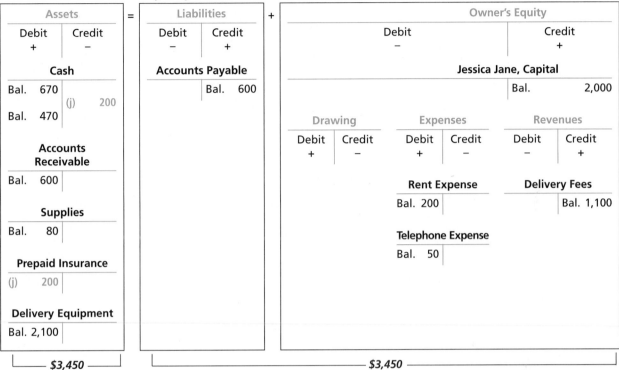

Analysis: Since insurance is paid in advance and will provide future benefits, it is treated as an asset. Therefore, one asset, Prepaid Insurance, increases and another, Cash, decreases. Debit Prepaid Insurance and credit Cash for $200.

ACCOUNT AFFECTED	CLASSIFICATION	LOCATION IN EQUATION	INCREASE OR DECREASE	DEBIT OR CREDIT
Prepaid Insurance	Asset	Left	Increase	Debit
Cash	Asset	Left	Decrease	Credit

Transactions (i) and (j) both involve an exchange of cash for another asset. As you analyze these two transactions and answer the three questions about these transactions, you may wonder why prepaid insurance and supplies are assets while the rent and telephone bill in transactions (f) and (g) are expenses. Prepaid insurance and supplies are assets because they will last for more than one month. Jessica Jane pays her rent and her telephone bill each month so they are classified as expenses. If Jessica Jane paid her rent only once every three months, she would need to set up an asset account called Prepaid Rent. She would debit this account when she paid the rent.

TRANSACTION (k):   Received cash from prior sales on account

Jane received $570 in cash for delivery services performed for customers earlier in the month (see transaction (h)) (Figure 3-16).

FIGURE 3-16   Transaction (k): Received Cash from Prior Sales on Account

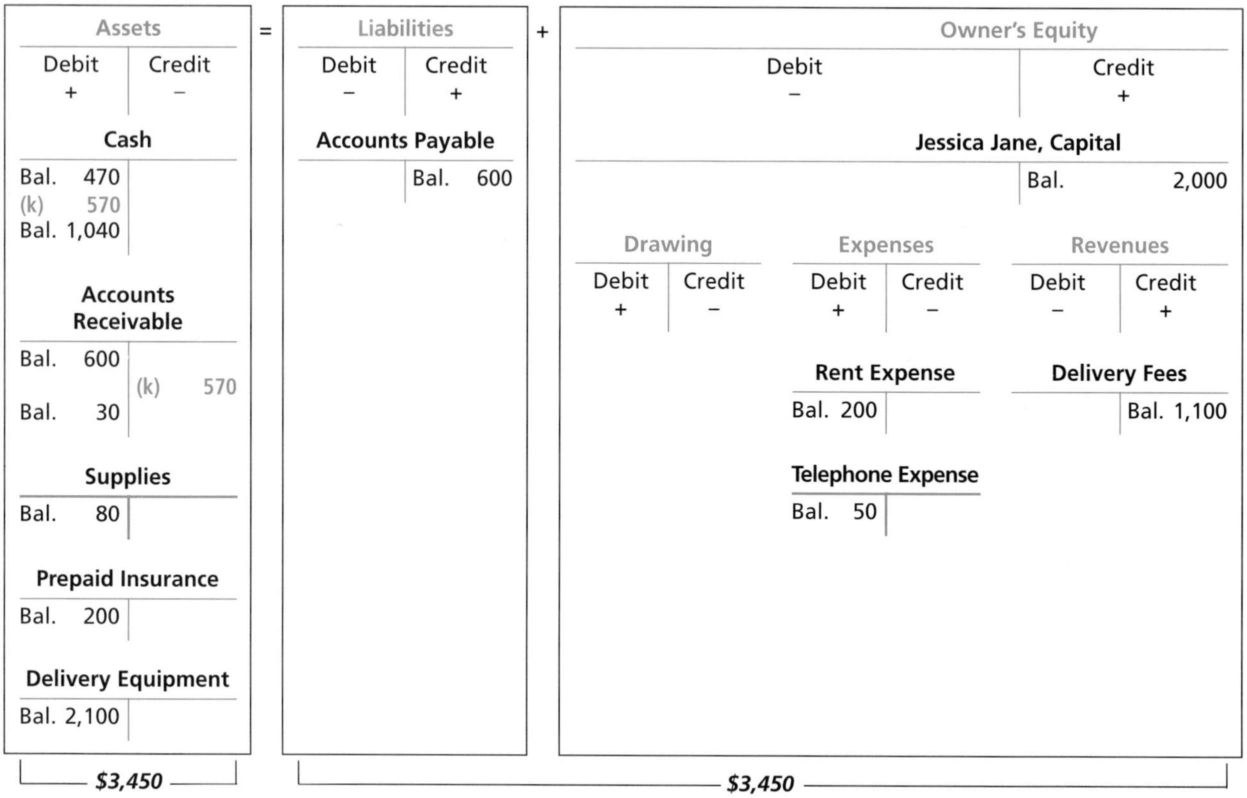

Analysis: This transaction increases Cash and reduces the amount due from customers reported in Accounts Receivable. Debit Cash and credit Accounts Receivable $570.

As you analyze transaction (k), notice which accounts are affected and the location of these accounts in the accounting equation. Jessica Jane received cash, but this transaction did not affect revenue. The revenue was recorded in transaction (h). Transaction (k) is an exchange of one asset (Accounts Receivable) for another asset (Cash).

ACCOUNT AFFECTED	CLASSIFICATION	LOCATION IN EQUATION	INCREASE OR DECREASE	DEBIT OR CREDIT
Cash	Asset	Left	Increase	Debit
Accounts Receivable	Asset	Left	Decrease	Credit

TRANSACTION (I): Purchase of an asset on credit making a partial payment

Jane bought a third motor scooter for $1,500. Jane made a down payment of $300 and spread the remaining payments over the next four months (Figure 3-17).

FIGURE 3-17 Transaction (l): Purchase of an Asset on Credit Making a Partial Payment

Assets	=	Liabilities	+	Owner's Equity

Assets

Debit +	Credit −

Cash

Bal. 1,040	
	(l) 300
Bal. 740	

Accounts Receivable

Bal. 30	

Supplies

Bal. 80	

Prepaid Insurance

Bal. 200	

Delivery Equipment

Bal. 2,100	
(l) 1,500	
Bal. 3,600	

$4,650

Liabilities

Debit −	Credit +

Accounts Payable

	Bal. 600
	(l) 1,200
	Bal. 1,800

Owner's Equity

Debit −	Credit +

Jessica Jane, Capital

	Bal. 2,000

Drawing

Debit +	Credit −

Expenses

Debit +	Credit −

Rent Expense

Bal. 200	

Telephone Expense

Bal. 50	

Revenues

Debit −	Credit +

Delivery Fees

	Bal. 1,100

$4,650

Analysis: The asset, Delivery Equipment, increases by $1,500, Cash decreases by $300, and the liability, Accounts Payable, increases by $1,200. Thus, debit Delivery Equipment for $1,500, credit Cash for $300, and credit Accounts Payable for $1,200. This transaction requires one debit and two credits. Even so, total debits ($1,500) equal the total credits ($1,200 + $300) and the accounting equation remains in balance.

ACCOUNT AFFECTED	CLASSIFICATION	LOCATION IN EQUATION	INCREASE OR DECREASE	DEBIT OR CREDIT
Delivery Equipment	Asset	Left	Increase	Debit
Cash	Asset	Left	Decrease	Credit
Accounts Payable	Liability	Right	Increase	Credit

TRANSACTION (m):   Payment of wages

Jane paid her part-time employees $650 in wages (Figure 3-18).

FIGURE 3-18 Transaction (m): Payment of Wages

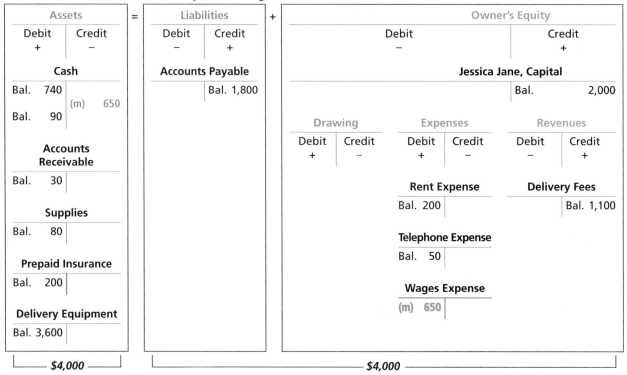

Analysis: This is an additional business expense. Expenses increase and Cash decreases. Debit Wages Expense and credit Cash for $650.

ACCOUNT AFFECTED	CLASSIFICATION	LOCATION IN EQUATION	INCREASE OR DECREASE	DEBIT OR CREDIT
Wage Expense	Expense	Right O.E.—Left Side	Exp.— Increases; O.E.— Decreases	Debit
Cash	Asset	Left	Decrease	Credit

TRANSACTION (n):   Deliveries made for cash and credit

Total delivery fees for the remainder of the month amounted to $900: $430 in Cash and $470 on account (Figure 3-19).

FIGURE 3-19   Transaction (n): Deliveries Made for Cash and Credit

Assets			=	Liabilities			+	Owner's Equity			

Assets = $4,900

Liabilities + Owner's Equity = $4,900

Cash:
- Debit +, Credit −
- Bal. 90
- (n) 430
- Bal. 520

Accounts Receivable:
- Bal. 30
- (n) 470
- Bal. 500

Supplies:
- Bal. 80

Prepaid Insurance:
- Bal. 200

Delivery Equipment:
- Bal. 3,600

Accounts Payable:
- Debit −, Credit +
- Bal. 1,800

Jessica Jane, Capital:
- Debit −, Credit +
- Bal. 2,000

Drawing: Debit +, Credit −

Expenses: Debit +, Credit −
- Rent Expense: Bal. 200
- Telephone Expense: Bal. 50
- Wages Expense: Bal. 650

Revenues: Debit −, Credit +
- Delivery Fees: Bal. 1,100 / (n) 900 / Bal. 2,000

Analysis: Since the delivery fees have been earned, the revenue account increases by $900. Also, Cash increases by $430 and Accounts Receivable increases by $470. Note once again that one event impacts three accounts. This time we have debits of $430 to Cash and $470 to Accounts Receivable, and a credit of $900 to Delivery Fees. As before, the total debits ($430 + $470) equal the total credits ($900) and the accounting equation remains in balance.

ACCOUNT AFFECTED	CLASSIFICATION	LOCATION IN EQUATION	INCREASE OR DECREASE	DEBIT OR CREDIT
Cash	Asset	Left	Increase	Debit
Accounts Receivable	Asset	Left	Increase	Debit
Delivery Fees	Revenue	Right O.E.—Right Side	Increase	Credit

TRANSACTION (o):   Withdrawal of cash from business

At the end of the month, Jane withdrew $150 in cash from the business to purchase books for her classes (Figure 3-20).

FIGURE 3-20 Transaction (o): Withdrawal of Cash from Business

Assets		=	Liabilities		+	Owner's Equity	

Assets	
Debit +	Credit −
Cash	
Bal. 520	
	(o) 150
Bal. 370	
Accounts Receivable	
Bal. 500	
Supplies	
Bal. 80	
Prepaid Insurance	
Bal. 200	
Delivery Equipment	
Bal. 3,600	

$4,750

Liabilities	
Debit −	Credit +
Accounts Payable	
	Bal. 1,800

Owner's Equity	
Debit −	Credit +
Jessica Jane, Capital	
	Bal. 2,000

Drawing	
Debit +	Credit −
Jessica Jane, Drawing	
(o) 150	

Expenses	
Debit +	Credit −
Rent Expense	
Bal. 200	
Telephone Expense	
Bal. 50	
Wages Expense	
Bal. 650	

Revenues	
Debit −	Credit +
Delivery Fees	
	Bal. 2,000

$4,750

Analysis: Cash withdrawals decrease owner's equity and decrease cash. Debit Jessica Jane, Drawing and credit Cash for $150.

Withdrawals are reported in the drawing account. Withdrawals by an owner are the opposite of an investment. You could debit the owner's capital account for withdrawals. However, using a specific account tells the user of the accounting information how much was withdrawn for the period.

ACCOUNT AFFECTED	CLASSIFICATION	LOCATION IN EQUATION	INCREASE OR DECREASE	DEBIT OR CREDIT
Drawing	Drawing	Right O.E.—Left Side	Drawing Increases; O.E. Decreases	Debit
Cash	Asset	Left	Decrease	Credit

As you analyze transactions (l) through (o), make certain that you understand what has happened in each transaction. Identify the accounts that are affected and the locations of these accounts within the accounting equation. Notice that the accounting equation remains in balance after every transaction and debits equal credits for each transaction.

Summary of Transactions

In illustrating transactions (a) through (o), each T account for Jessie Jane's Campus Delivery shows a balance before and after each transaction. To focus your attention on the transaction being explained, only a single entry was shown. In practice, this is not done. Instead, each account gathers all transactions for a period. Jessica Jane's accounts, with all transactions listed, are shown in Figure 3-21. Note the following:

1. The footings are directly under the debit (left) and credit (right) sides of the T account for those accounts with more than one debit or credit.
2. The balance is shown on the side with the larger footing.
3. The footing serves as the balance for accounts with entries on only one side of the account.
4. If an account has only a single entry, it is not necessary to enter a footing or balance.

FIGURE 3-21   Summary of Transactions (a) Through (o)

Assets		=	Liabilities		+	Owner's Equity	
Debit +	Credit −		Debit −	Credit +		Debit −	Credit +

Cash

(a)	2,000	(b)	1,200
(e)	500	(d)	300
(k)	570	(f)	200
(n)	430	(g)	50
	3,500	(i)	80
		(j)	200
		(l)	300
		(m)	650
		(o)	150
			3,130
Bal.	**370**		

Accounts Receivable

(h)	600	(k)	570
(n)	470		
	1,070		
Bal.	**500**		

Supplies

(i)	80	

Prepaid Insurance

(j)	200	

Delivery Equipment

(b)	1,200	
(c)	900	
(l)	1,500	
Bal.	**3,600**	

Accounts Payable

(d)	300	(c)	900
		(l)	1,200
			2,100
		Bal.	**1,800**

Jessica Jane, Capital

	(a)	2,000

Drawing

Debit +	Credit −

Jessica Jane, Drawing

(o)	150	

Expenses

Debit +	Credit −

Rent Expense

(f)	200	

Telephone Expense

(g)	50	

Wages Expense

(m)	650	

Revenues

Debit −	Credit +

Delivery Fees

	(e)	500
	(h)	600
	(n)	900
	Bal.	**2,000**

$4,750   *$4,750*

THE TRIAL BALANCE

LO5   Prepare a trial balance.

A trial balance provides proof that total debits equal total credits and shows that the accounting equation is in balance.

Recall the two very important rules in double-entry accounting.

1. The sum of the debits must equal the sum of the credits. This means that at least two accounts are affected by each transaction.
2. The accounting equation must remain in balance.

In illustrating the transactions for Jessie Jane's Campus Delivery, the equality of the accounting equation was verified after each transaction. Because of the large number of transactions entered each day, this is not done in practice. Instead, a trial balance is prepared periodically to determine the equality of the debits and credits. A **trial balance** is a list of all accounts showing the title and balance of each account.

A trial balance of Jessica Jane's accounts, taken on June 30, 19--, is shown in Figure 3-22. This date is shown on the third line of the heading. The trial balance shows that the debit and credit totals are equal in amount. This is proof that (1) in entering transactions (a) through (o), the total of the debits was equal to the total of the credits, and (2) the accounting equation has remained in balance.

A trial balance is not a formal statement or report. Normally, it is only seen by the accountant. As shown in the summary illustration on page 66, a trial balance can be used as an aid in preparing the financial statements.

FIGURE 3-22   Trial Balance

Jessie Jane's Campus Delivery
Trial Balance
June 30, 19--

ACCOUNT TITLE	ACCOUNT NO.	DEBIT BALANCE	CREDIT BALANCE
Cash		3 7 0 00	
Accounts Receivable		5 0 0 00	
Supplies		8 0 00	
Prepaid Insurance		2 0 0 00	
Delivery Equipment		3 6 0 0 00	
Accounts Payable			1 8 0 0 00
Jessica Jane, Capital			2 0 0 0 00
Jessica Jane, Drawing		1 5 0 00	
Delivery Fees			2 0 0 0 00
Rent Expense		2 0 0 00	
Telephone Expense		5 0 00	
Wages Expense		6 5 0 00	
		5 8 0 0 00	5 8 0 0 00

KEY POINTS

1 The parts of a T account are:

1. the title,
2. the debit or left side, and
3. the credit or right side.

Title	
Debit = Left	Credit = Right

2 Rules for footing and balancing T accounts are:

1. The footings are directly under the debit (left) and credit (right) sides of the T account for those accounts with more than one debit or credit.
2. The balance is shown on the side with the larger footing.
3. The footing serves as the balance for accounts with entries on only one side of the account.
4. If an account has only a single entry, it is not necessary to enter a footing or balance.

3 Rules for debits and credits. (See illustration on page 67.)

1. Assets are on the left side of the accounting equation. Therefore, increases are entered on the left (debit) side of an asset account and decreases are entered on the right (credit) side.
2. Liabilities and owner's equity are on the right side of the accounting equation. Therefore, increases are entered on the right (credit) side and decreases are entered on the left (debit) side.
3. Revenues are on the right side of the owner's equity umbrella. Therefore, increases are entered on the right (credit) side and decreases are entered on the left (debit) side.
4. Expenses and drawing are on the left side of the owner's equity umbrella. Therefore, increases are entered on the left (debit) side and decreases are entered on the right (credit) side.

4 Picture the accounting equation in your mind as you analyze transactions. When entering transactions in T accounts:

1. The sum of the debits must equal the sum of the credits.
2. At least two accounts are affected by each transaction.
3. When finished, the accounting equation must remain in balance.

5 A trial balance shows that the debit and credit totals are equal. A trial balance can also be used in preparing the financial statements.

SUMMARY

Jessie Jane's Campus Delivery
Trial Balance
June 30, 19--

ACCOUNT TITLE	ACCOUNT NO.	DEBIT BALANCE	CREDIT BALANCE
Cash		3 7 0 00	
Accounts Receivable		5 0 0 00	
Supplies		8 0 00	
Prepaid Insurance		2 0 0 00	
Delivery Equipment		3 6 0 0 00	
Accounts Payable			1 8 0 0 00
Jessica Jane, Capital			2 0 0 0 00
Jessica Jane, Drawing		1 5 0 00	
Delivery Fees			2 0 0 0 00
Rent Expense		2 0 0 00	
Telephone Expense		5 0 00	
Wages Expense		6 5 0 00	
		5 8 0 0 00	5 8 0 0 00

Jessie Jane's Campus Delivery
Income Statement
For Month Ended June 30, 19--

Revenue:			
Delivery fees			$2 0 0 0 00
Expenses:			
Wages expense		$ 6 5 0 00	
Rent expense		2 0 0 00	
Telephone expense		5 0 00	
Total expenses			9 0 0 00
Net income			$1 1 0 0 00

Jessie Jane's Campus Delivery
Statement of Owner's Equity
For Month Ended June 30, 19--

Jessica Jane, capital, June 1, 19--			$2 0 0 0 00
Net income for June		$1 1 0 0 00	
Less withdrawals for June		1 5 0 00	
Increase in capital			9 5 0 00
Jessica Jane, capital, June 30, 19--			$2 9 5 0 00

Jessie Jane's Campus Delivery
Balance Sheet
June 30, 19--

Assets			Liabilities		
Cash	$ 3 7 0 00		Accounts payable	$1 8 0 0 00	
Accounts receivable	5 0 0 00				
Supplies	8 0 00		Owner's Equity		
Prepaid insurance	2 0 0 00		Jessica Jane, capital	2 9 5 0 00	
Delivery equipment	3 6 0 0 00				
			Total liabilities and		
Total assets	$4 7 5 0 00		owner's equity	$4 7 5 0 00	

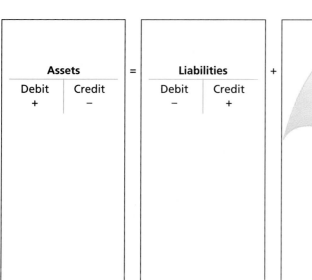
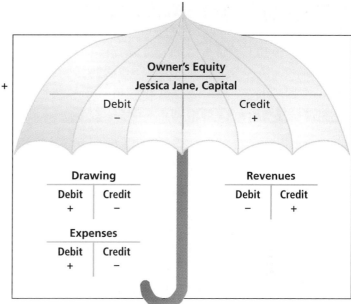

balance 45   The difference between the footings of an account.

credit 46   To enter an amount on the right side of an account.

credit balance 47   The normal balance of liability, owner's equity, and revenue accounts.

debit 46   To enter an amount on the left side of an account.

debit balance 47   The normal balance of asset, expense, and drawing accounts.

double-entry accounting 45   A system in which each transaction has a dual effect on the accounting elements.

footings 45   The total dollar amounts on the debit and credit sides of an account.

normal balance 47   The side of an account that is increased.

trial balance 64   A list of accounts showing the title and balance of each account.

REVIEW QUESTIONS

1. What are the three major parts of a T account?
2. What is the left side of the T account called? the right side?
3. What is a footing?
4. What is the relationship between the revenue and expense accounts and the owner's equity account?
5. What is the function of the trial balance?

MANAGING YOUR WRITING

Write a one-page memo to your instructor explaining how you could use the double-entry system to maintain records of your personal finances. What types of accounts would you use for the accounting elements?

DEMONSTRATION PROBLEM

Celia Pints opened We-Buy, You-Pay Shopping Services. For a fee that is based on the amount of research and shopping time required, Pints and her associates will shop for almost anything from groceries to home furnishings. Business is particularly heavy around Christmas and in early summer. The business operates from a rented store front. The associates receive a commission based on the revenues they produce and a mileage reimbursement for the use of their personal automobiles for shopping trips. Pints decided to use the following accounts to record transactions:

Assets	Owner's Equity
Cash	Celia Pints, Capital
Accounts Receivable	Celia Pints, Drawing
Office Equipment	Revenue
Computer Equipment	Shopping Fees
Liabilities	Expenses
Accounts Payable	Rent Expense
Notes Payable	Telephone Expense
	Commissions Expense
	Utilities Expense
	Travel Expense

The following transactions are for the month of December 19--.

(a) Pints invested cash in the business, $30,000.
(b) Bought office equipment for $10,000. Paid $2,000 in cash and promised to pay the balance over the next four months.
(c) Paid rent for December, $500.
(d) Provided shopping services for customers on account, $5,200.
(e) Paid telephone bill, $90.
(f) Borrowed cash from the bank by signing a note payable, $5,000.
(g) Bought a computer and printer, $4,800.
(h) Collected cash from customers for services performed on account, $4,000.
(i) Paid commissions to associates for revenues generated during the first half of the month, $3,500.
(j) Paid utility bill, $600.
(k) Paid cash on account for the office equipment purchased in transaction (b), $2,000.
(l) Earned shopping fees of $13,200: $6,000 in cash and $7,200 on account.
(m) Paid commissions to associates for last half of month, $7,000.

(n) Paid mileage reimbursements for the month, $1,500.
(o) Paid cash on note payable to bank, $1,000.
(p) Pints withdrew cash for personal use, $2,000.

REQUIRED

1. Enter the transactions for December in T accounts. Use the accounting equation as a guide for setting up the T accounts.
2. Foot the T accounts and determine their balances as necessary.
3. Prepare a trial balance of the accounts as of December 31 of the current year.
4. Prepare an income statement for the month ended December 31 of the current year.
5. Prepare a statement of owner's equity for the month ended December 31 of the current year.
6. Prepare a balance sheet as of December 31 of the current year.

SOLUTION

1, 2.

Assets		=	Liabilities		+	Owner's Equity	
Debit +	Credit −		Debit −	Credit +		Debit −	Credit +

Cash

(a) 30,000	(b) 2,000
(f) 5,000	(c) 500
(h) 4,000	(e) 90
(l) 6,000	(g) 4,800
45,000	(i) 3,500
	(j) 600
	(k) 2,000
	(m) 7,000
	(n) 1,500
	(o) 1,000
	(p) 2,000
	24,990
Bal. 20,010	

Accounts Receivable

(d) 5,200	(h) 4,000
(l) 7,200	
12,400	
Bal. 8,400	

Office Equipment

(b) 10,000	

Computer Equipment

(g) 4,800	

Accounts Payable

(k) 2,000	(b) 8,000
	Bal. 6,000

Notes Payable

(o) 1,000	(f) 5,000
	Bal. 4,000

Celia Pints, Capital

	(a) 30,000

Drawing		Expenses		Revenues	
Debit +	Credit −	Debit +	Credit −	Debit −	Credit +

Celia Pints, Drawing

(p) 2,000	

Rent Expense

(c) 500	

Telephone Expense

(e) 90	

Commissions Expense

(i) 3,500	
(m) 7,000	
Bal. 10,500	

Utilities Expense

(j) 600	

Travel Expense

(n) 1,500	

Shopping Fees

	(d) 5,200
	(l) 13,200
	Bal. 18,400

———— $43,210 ————   ———————————— $43,210 ————————————

3.

We-Buy, You-Pay Shopping Services
Trial Balance
December 31, 19--

ACCOUNT TITLE	DEBIT BALANCE	CREDIT BALANCE
Cash	20 0 1 0 00	
Accounts Receivable	8 4 0 0 00	
Office Equipment	10 0 0 0 00	
Computer Equipment	4 8 0 0 00	
Accounts Payable		6 0 0 0 00
Notes Payable		4 0 0 0 00
Celia Pints, Capital		30 0 0 0 00
Celia Pints, Drawing	2 0 0 0 00	
Shopping Fees		18 4 0 0 00
Rent Expense	5 0 0 00	
Telephone Expense	9 0 00	
Commissions Expense	10 5 0 0 00	
Utilities Expense	6 0 0 00	
Travel Expense	1 5 0 0 00	
	58 4 0 0 00	58 4 0 0 00

4.

We Buy, You-Pay Shopping Services
Income Statement
For Month Ended December 31, 19--

Revenue:			
Shopping fees			$18 4 0 0 00
Expenses:			
Commissions expense	$10 5 0 0 00		
Travel expense	1 5 0 0 00		
Utilities expense	6 0 0 00		
Rent expense	5 0 0 00		
Telephone expense	9 0 00		
Total expenses			13 1 9 0 00
Net income			$ 5 2 1 0 00

5.

We-Buy, You-Pay Shopping Services Statement of Owner's Equity For Month Ended December 31, 19--								
Celia Pints, capital, December 1, 19--						$30 0 0 0 00	
Net income for December	$5 2 1 0 00					
Less withdrawals for December	2 0 0 0 00					
Increase in capital					3 2 1 0 00	
Celia Pints, capital, December 31, 19--					$33 2 1 0 00	

6.

We-Buy, You-Pay Shopping Services Balance Sheet December 31, 19--					
Assets		**Liabilities**	
Cash	$20 0 1 0 00	Accounts payable	$ 6 0 0 0 00
Accounts receivable	8 4 0 0 00	Notes payable	4 0 0 0 00
Office equipment	10 0 0 0 00	Total liabilities	$10 0 0 0 00
Computer equipment	4 8 0 0 00		
		Owner's Equity	
		Celia Pints, capital	33 2 1 0 00
		Total liabilities and	
Total assets	$43 2 1 0 00	owner's equity	$43 2 1 0 00

SERIES A   EXERCISES

2 **EXERCISE 3A1 FOOT AND BALANCE A T ACCOUNT**   Foot and balance the cash T account shown.

Cash

500	100
400	200
600	

3 **EXERCISE 3A2 DEBIT AND CREDIT ANALYSIS**   Complete the following questions using either "debit" or "credit."

(a) The cash account is increased with a _____.
(b) The owner's capital account is increased with a _____.
(c) The delivery equipment account is increased with a _____.
(d) The cash account is decreased with a _____.
(e) The liability account Accounts Payable is increased with a _____.
(f) The revenue account Delivery Fees is increased with a _____.

continued

(g) The asset account Accounts Receivable is increased with a _____.

(h) The rent expense account is increased with a _____.

(i) The owner's drawing account is increased with a _____.

2/3/4   **EXERCISE 3A3 ANALYSIS OF T ACCOUNTS**   Jim Arnold began a business called Arnold's Shoe Repair.

1. Create T accounts for Cash; Supplies; Jim Arnold, Capital; and Utilities Expense. Identify the following transactions by letter and place on the proper side of the T accounts.
   (a) Arnold invested cash in the business, $5,000.
   (b) Purchased supplies for cash, $800. *Iv. Asset*
   (c) Paid utility bill, $1,500. *Deb. Exp.*
2. Foot the T account for Cash and enter the ending balance.

3   **EXERCISE 3A4 NORMAL BALANCE OF ACCOUNT**   Indicate the normal balance (debit or credit) for each of the following accounts.

1. Cash
2. Wages Expense
3. Accounts Payable
4. Owner's Drawing
5. Supplies
6. Owner's Capital
7. Equipment

4   **EXERCISE 3A5 TRANSACTION ANALYSIS**   Sheryl Hansen started a new business on May 1, 19--. Analyze the following transactions for the first month of business using T accounts. Label each T account with the title of the account affected and then place the dollar amount on the debit or credit side.

(a) Hansen invested cash in the business, $4,000.

(b) Bought equipment for cash, $500.

(c) Bought equipment on account, $800.

(d) Paid cash on account for equipment purchased in transaction (c), $300.

(e) Owner withdrew cash for personal use, $700.

2   **EXERCISE 3A6 ANALYSIS OF T ACCOUNT**   From the transactions in exercise 3A5, analyze the transactions affecting Cash, foot the T account, and indicate the ending balance.

2/4   **EXERCISE 3A7 ANALYSIS OF TRANSACTIONS**   Charles Chadwick began a new business called Charlie's Detective Service in January 19--. Set up T accounts for the following accounts: Cash; Accounts Receivable; Office Supplies; Computer Equipment; Office Furniture; Accounts Payable; Charles Chadwick, Capital; Charles Chadwick, Drawing; Professional Fees; Rent Expense; and Utilities Expense.

The following transactions occurred during the first month of business. Record these transactions in T accounts. After all transactions are recorded, foot and balance the accounts if necessary.

(a) Chadwick invested cash in the business, $30,000.
(b) Bought office supplies for cash, $300.
(c) Bought office furniture for cash, $5,000.
(d) Purchased computer and printer on account, $8,000.
(e) Received cash from clients for services, $3,000.
(f) Paid cash on account for computer and printer purchased in transaction (d), $4,000.
(g) Earned professional fees on account during the month, $9,000.
(h) Paid cash for office rent for January, $1,500.
(i) Paid utility bills for the month, $800.
(j) Received cash from clients billed in transaction (g), $6,000.
(k) Chadwick withdrew cash for personal use, $3,000.

5 **EXERCISE 3A8 TRIAL BALANCE**   Based on the transactions recorded in Exercise 3A7, prepare a trial balance for Charlie's Detective Service as of January 31, 19--.

5 **EXERCISE 3A9 TRIAL BALANCE**   The following accounts have normal balances. Prepare a trial balance for Juanita's Delivery Service as of September 30, 19--.

Cash	$5,000
Accounts Receivable	3,000
Supplies	800
Prepaid Insurance	600
Delivery Equipment	8,000
Accounts Payable	2,000
Juanita Raye, Capital	10,000
Juanita Raye, Drawing	1,000
Delivery Fees	9,400
Wages Expense	2,100
Rent Expense	900

EXERCISE 3A10 INCOME STATEMENT   From the information in Exercise 3A9, prepare an income statement for Juanita's Delivery Service for the month ended September 30, 19--.

EXERCISE 3A11 STATEMENT OF OWNER'S EQUITY   From the information in Exercise 3A9, prepare a statement of owner's equity for Juanita's Delivery Service for the month ended September 30, 19--.

EXERCISE 3A12 BALANCE SHEET   From the information in Exercise 3A9, prepare a balance sheet for Juanita's Delivery Service as of September 30, 19--.

2/4/5   **PROBLEM 3A1 T ACCOUNTS AND TRIAL BALANCE**   Harold Long started a business in May 19-- called Harold's Home Repair. Long hired a part-time college student as an assistant. Long has decided to use the following accounts for recording transactions:

Assets	Owner's Equity
Cash	Harold Long, Capital
Accounts Receivable	Harold Long, Drawing
Office Supplies	Revenue
Prepaid Insurance	Service Fees
Equipment	Expenses
Van	Rent Expense
Liabilities	Wages Expense
Accounts Payable	Telephone Expense
	Gas and Oil Expense

The following transactions occurred during May.

(a) Long invested cash in the business, $20,000.
(b) Purchased a used van for cash, $7,000.
(c) Purchased equipment on account, $5,000.
(d) Received cash for services rendered, $6,000.
(e) Paid cash on amount owed from transaction (c), $2,000.
(f) Paid rent for the month, $900.
(g) Paid telephone bill, $200.
(h) Earned revenue on account, $4,000.
(i) Purchased office supplies for cash, $120.
(j) Paid wages to student, $600.
(k) Purchased insurance, $1,200.
(l) Received cash from services performed in transaction (h), $3,000.
(m) Paid cash for gas and oil expense on the van, $160.
(n) Purchased additional equipment for $3,000, paying $1,000 cash and spreading the remaining payments over the next 10 months.
(o) Service fees earned for the remainder of the month amounted to $3,200: $1,800 in cash and $1,400 on account.
(p) Long withdrew cash at the end of the month, $2,800.

REQUIRED

1. Enter the transactions in T accounts, identifying each transaction with its corresponding letter.
2. Foot and balance the accounts where necessary.
3. Prepare a trial balance as of May 31, 19--.

PROBLEM 3A2 NET INCOME AND CHANGE IN OWNER'S EQUITY   Refer to the trial balance of Harold's Home Repair in Problem 3A1 to determine the following information. Use the format provided on the next page.

1. a. Total revenue for the month _____
   b. Total expenses for the month _____
   c. Net income for the month _____
2. a. Harold Long's original investment in the business _____
     + the net income for the month _____
     − owner's drawing _____
     = ending owner's equity _____
   b. End of month accounting equation:

ASSETS	=	LIABILITIES	+ OWNER'S EQUITY
_____	=	_____	+ _____

PROBLEM 3A3 FINANCIAL STATEMENTS   Refer to the trial balance in Problem 3A1 and to the analysis of the change in owner's equity in Problem 3A2.

REQUIRED
1. Prepare an income statement for Harold's Home Repair for the month ended May 31, 19--.
2. Prepare a statement of owner's equity for Harold's Home Repair for the month ended May 31, 19--.
3. Prepare a balance sheet for Harold's Home Repair as of May 31, 19--.

SERIES B EXERCISES

2 **EXERCISE 3B1 FOOT AND BALANCE A T ACCOUNT**   Foot and balance the accounts payable T account shown.

Accounts Payable

300	450
250	350
	150

3 **EXERCISE 3B2 DEBIT AND CREDIT ANALYSIS**   Complete the following questions using either "debit" or "credit."

(a) The asset account Prepaid Insurance is increased with a _____ .
(b) The owner's drawing account is increased with a _____ .
(c) The asset account Accounts Receivable is decreased with a _____ .
(d) The liability account Accounts Payable is decreased with a _____ .
(e) The owner's capital account is increased with a _____ .
(f) The revenue account Professional Fees is increased with a _____ .
(g) The expense account Repair Expense is increased with a _____ .
(h) The asset account Cash is decreased with a _____ .
(i) The asset account Accounts Receivable is increased with a _____ .

2/3/4 **EXERCISE 3B3 ANALYSIS OF T ACCOUNTS**   Roberto Alvarez began a business called Roberto's Fix-It Shop.

1. Create T accounts for Cash; Supplies; Roberto Alvarez, Capital; and Utilities Expense. Identify the following transactions by letter and place them on the proper side of the T accounts.
   (a) Alvarez invested cash in the business, $6,000.
   (b) Purchased supplies for cash, $1,200.
   (c) Paid utility bill, $900.
2. Foot the T account for Cash and enter the ending balance.

3 **EXERCISE 3B4 NORMAL BALANCE OF ACCOUNT**   Indicate the normal balance (debit or credit) for each of the following accounts.

1. Cash
2. Rent Expense
3. Notes Payable
4. Owner's Drawing
5. Accounts Receivable
6. Owner's Capital
7. Tools

4 **EXERCISE 3B5 TRANSACTION ANALYSIS**   George Atlas started a new business on June 1, 19--. Analyze the following transactions for the first month of business using T accounts. Label each T account with the title of the account affected and then place the dollar amount on the debit or credit side.

(a) Atlas invested cash in the business, $7,000.
(b) Purchased equipment for cash, $900.
(c) Purchased equipment on account, $1,500.
(d) Paid $800 on account for equipment purchased in transaction (c).
(e) Atlas withdrew cash for personal use, $1,100.

2 **EXERCISE 3B6 ANALYSIS OF T ACCOUNT**   From the transactions in Exercise 3B5, analyze the transactions affecting Cash, foot the T account, and indicate the ending balance.

2/4 **EXERCISE 3B7 ANALYSIS OF TRANSACTIONS**   Nicole Lawrence began a new business called Nickie's Neat Ideas in January 19--. Set up T accounts for the following accounts: Cash; Accounts Receivable; Office Supplies; Computer Equipment; Office Furniture; Accounts Payable; Nicole Lawrence, Capital; Nicole Lawrence, Drawing; Professional Fees; Rent Expense; and Utilities Expense.
  The following transactions occurred during the first month of business. Record these transactions in T accounts. After all transactions have been recorded, foot and balance the accounts if necessary.

(a) Lawrence invested cash in the business, $18,000.
(b) Purchased office supplies for cash, $500.

continued

(c) Purchased office furniture for cash, $8,000.
(d) Purchased computer and printer on account, $5,000.
(e) Received cash from clients for services, $4,000.
(f) Paid cash on account for computer and printer purchased in transaction (d), $2,000.
(g) Earned professional fees on account during the month, $7,000.
(h) Paid office rent for January, $900.
(i) Paid utility bills for the month, $600.
(j) Received cash from clients that were billed previously in transaction (g), $3,000.
(k) Lawrence withdrew cash for personal use, $4,000.

5   **EXERCISE 3B8 TRIAL BALANCE**   Based on the transactions recorded in Exercise 3B7, prepare a trial balance for Nickie's Neat Ideas as of January 31, 19--.

5   **EXERCISE 3B9 TRIAL BALANCE**   The following accounts have normal balances. Prepare a trial balance for Bill's Delivery Service as of September 30, 19--.

Cash	$ 7,000
Accounts Receivable	4,000
Supplies	600
Prepaid Insurance	900
Delivery Equipment	9,000
Accounts Payable	3,000
Bill Swift, Capital	12,000
Bill Swift, Drawing	2,000
Delivery Fees	12,500
Wages Expense	3,000
Rent Expense	1,000

EXERCISE 3B10 INCOME STATEMENT   From the information in Exercise 3B9, prepare an income statement for Bill's Delivery Service for the month ended September 30, 19--.

EXERCISE 3B11 STATEMENT OF OWNER'S EQUITY   From the information in Exercise 3B9, prepare a statement of owner's equity for Bill's Delivery Service for the month ended September 30, 19--.

EXERCISE 3B12 BALANCE SHEET   From the information in Exercise 3B9, prepare a balance sheet for Bill's Delivery Service as of September 30, 19--.

SERIES B   PROBLEMS

2/4/5   **PROBLEM 3B1 T ACCOUNTS AND TRIAL BALANCE**   Sue Jantz
started a business in August 19-- called Jantz Plumbing Service. Jantz hired a
part-time college student as an administrative assistant. Jantz has decided to
use the following accounts:

NAMES & NIf

Assets 100-	Owner's Equity 30
Cash	Sue Jantz, Capital
Accounts Receivable	Sue Jantz, Drawing
Office Supplies	Revenue 400
Prepaid Insurance	Service Fees
Plumbing Equipment	Expenses 500
Van	Rent Expense
200Liabilities	Wages Expense
Accounts Payable	Telephone Expense
	Advertising Expense

The following transactions occurred during August.

(a) Jantz invested cash in the business, $30,000.   INC.
(b) Purchased a used van for cash, $8,000.
(c) Purchased plumbing equipment on account, $4,000.   AC.P.
(d) Received cash for services rendered, $3,000.
(e) Paid cash on amount owed from transaction (c), $1,000. ACP-
(f) Paid rent for the month, $700.   E + Dc
(g) Paid telephone bill, $100.
(h) Earned revenue on account, $4,000. AC.
(i) Purchased office supplies for cash, $300.
(j) Paid wages to student, $500.
(k) Purchased insurance, $800.
(l) Received cash from services performed in transaction (h), $3,000.
(m) Paid cash for advertising expense, $2,000.
(n) Purchased additional plumbing equipment for $2,000, paying $500 cash
     and spreading the remaining payments over the next 6 months.
(o) Revenue earned from services for the remainder of the month amount-
     ed to $2,800: $1,100 in cash and $1,700 on account. D+ D+ C+
(p) Jantz withdrew cash at the end of the month, $3,000.

REQUIRED
1. Enter the transactions in T accounts, identifying each transaction with its
    corresponding letter.
2. Foot and balance the accounts where necessary.
3. Prepare a trial balance as of August 31, 19--.

**PROBLEM 3B2 NET INCOME AND CHANGE IN OWNER'S
EQUITY**   Refer to the trial balance of Jantz Plumbing Service in Problem
3B1 to determine the following information. Use the format provided
below.

1. a. Total revenue for the month   _____
   b. Total expenses for the month   _____
   c. Net income for the month   _____
2. a. Sue Jantz's original investment in the business   _____
        + the net income for the month   _____
        − owner's drawing   _____
        = ending owner's equity   _____
   b. End of month accounting equation:

ASSETS	=	LIABILITIES	+ OWNER'S EQUITY
_____	=	_____	+ _____

PROBLEM 3B3 FINANCIAL STATEMENTS   Refer to the trial balance in Problem 3B1 and to the analysis of the change in owner's equity in Problem 3B2.

REQUIRED

1. Prepare an income statement for Jantz Plumbing Service for the month ended August 31, 19--.
2. Prepare a statement of owner's equity for Jantz Plumbing Service for the month ended August 31, 19--.
3. Prepare a balance sheet for Jantz Plumbing Service as of August 31, 19--.

MASTERY PROBLEM

Craig Fisher started a lawn service called Craig's Quick Cut to earn money over the summer months. Fisher has decided to use the following accounts for recording transactions:

Assets
  Cash
  Accounts Receivable
  Mowing Equipment
  Lawn Tools
Liabilities
  Accounts Payable
  Notes Payable
Owner's Equity
  Craig Fisher, Capital
  Craig Fisher, Drawing

Revenue
  Lawn Fees
Expenses
  Rent Expense
  Wages Expense
  Telephone Expense
  Gas and Oil Expense
  Transportation Expense

Transactions for the month of June are listed below.

(a) Fisher invested cash in the business, $3,000.
(b) Bought mowing equipment for $1,000: paid $200 in cash and promised to pay the balance over the next four months.
(c) Paid garage rent for June, $50.
(d) Provided lawn services for customers on account, $520.
(e) Paid telephone bill, $30.

continued

(f) Borrowed cash from the bank by signing a note payable, $500.

(g) Bought lawn tools, $480.

(h) Collected cash from customers for services performed on account in transaction (d), $400.

(i) Paid associates for lawn work done during the first half of the month, $350.

(j) Paid for gas and oil for the equipment, $60.

(k) Paid cash on account for the mowing equipment purchased in transaction (b), $200.

(l) Earned lawn fees of $1,320: $600 in cash and $720 on account.

(m) Paid associates for last half of month, $700.

(n) Reimbursed associates for expenses associated with using their own vehicles for transportation, $150.

(o) Paid on note payable to bank, $100.

(p) Fisher withdrew cash for personal use, $200.

REQUIRED

1. Enter the transactions for June in T accounts. Use the accounting equation as a guide for setting up the T accounts.

2. Foot and balance the T accounts where necessary.

3. Prepare a trial balance of the accounts as of June 30, 19--.

4. Prepare an income statement for the month ended June 30, 19--.

5. Prepare a statement of owner's equity for the month ended June 30, 19--.

6. Prepare a balance sheet as of June 30, 19--.

4

Journalizing and Posting Transactions

Careful study of this chapter should enable you to:

LO1 Describe the flow of data from source documents through the trial balance.

LO2 Describe the chart of accounts as a means of classifying financial information.

LO3 Describe and explain the purpose of source documents.

LO4 Journalize transactions.

LO5 Post to the general ledger.

LO6 Explain how to find and correct errors.

"Jim, come here," called Mary. "Look at how Rob entered this transaction. What was he thinking? Why does he make these entries in ink? Do you have an ink eraser?" Should Mary try to correct Rob's error by erasing his work and reentering the transaction?

The double-entry framework of accounting was explained and illustrated in Chapter 3. To demonstrate the use of debits and credits, business transactions were entered directly into T accounts. Now we will take a more detailed look at the procedures used to account for business transactions.

FLOW OF DATA

LO1 Describe the flow of data from source documents through the trial balance.

This chapter traces the flow of financial data from the source documents through the accounting information system. This process includes the following steps:

1. Analyze what happened by using information from source documents and the firm's chart of accounts.
2. Enter business transactions in the general journal.
3. Post entries to accounts in the general ledger.
4. Prepare a trial balance.

The flow of data from the source documents through the preparation of a trial balance is shown in Figure 4-1.

FIGURE 4-1   Flow of Data from Source Documents Through Trial Balance

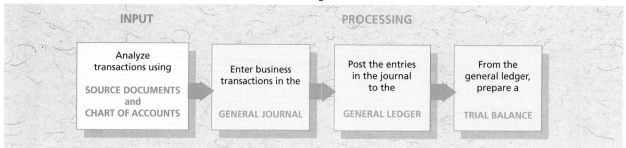

THE CHART OF ACCOUNTS

LO2 Describe the chart of accounts as a means of classifying financial information.

You learned in Chapters 2 and 3 that there are three basic questions that must be answered when analyzing transactions:

1. What happened?
2. Which accounts are affected?
3. How is the accounting equation affected?

To determine which accounts are affected (step 2), the accountant must know the accounts being used by the business. A list of all accounts used by a business is called a **chart of accounts**.

The chart of accounts includes the account titles in numeric order for all assets, liabilities, owner's equity, revenues, and expenses. The numbering should follow a consistent pattern. In Jessie Jane's Campus Delivery, asset accounts begin with "1," liability accounts begin with "2," owner's equity accounts begin with "3," revenue accounts begin with "4," and expense accounts begin with "5." Jane uses three-digit numbers for all accounts.

A chart of accounts for Jessie Jane's Campus Delivery is shown in Figure 4-2. Jane would not need many accounts initially because the business is new. Additional accounts can easily be added as needed. Note that the accounts are arranged according to the accounting equation.

FIGURE 4-2   Chart of Accounts

Jessie Jane's Campus Delivery Chart of Accounts			
Assets (100–199)		**Revenues** (400–499)	
111	Cash	411	Delivery Fees
131	Accounts Receivable		
151	Supplies	**Expenses** (500–599)	
155	Prepaid Insurance	541	Rent Expense
185	Delivery Equipment	542	Wages Expense
		545	Telephone Expense
Liabilities (200–299)			
216	Accounts Payable		
Owner's Equity (300–399)			
311	Jessica Jane, Capital		
312	Jessica Jane, Drawing		

Assets begin with 1

Liabilities begin with 2

Owner's Equity begin with 3

Revenues begin with 4

Expenses begin with 5

SOURCE DOCUMENTS

LO3 Describe and explain the purpose of source documents.

Almost any document that provides information about a business transaction can be called a **source document**. A source document triggers the analysis of what happened. It begins the process of entering transactions into the accounting system. Examples of source documents are shown in Figure 4-3. These source documents provide information that is useful in determining the effect of business transactions on specific accounts.

In addition to serving as input for transaction analysis, source documents serve as objective evidence of business transactions. If anyone questions the accounting records, these documents may be used as objective, verifiable evidence of the accuracy of the accounting records. For this reason, source documents are filed for possible future reference. *Having objective, verifiable evidence that a transaction occurred is an important accounting concept.*

FIGURE 4-3   Source Documents

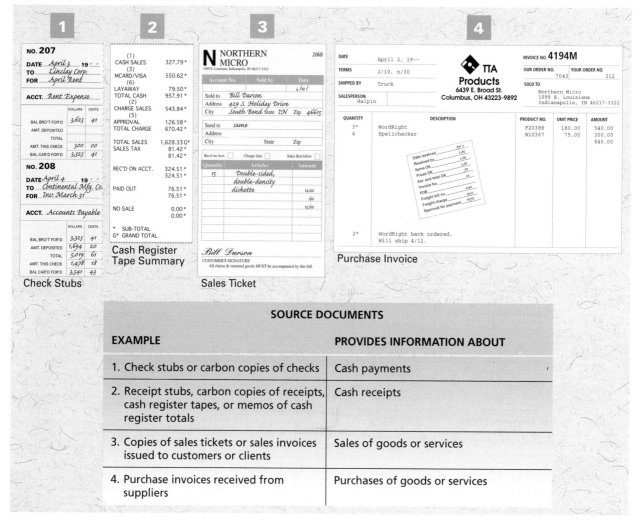

SOURCE DOCUMENTS	
EXAMPLE	**PROVIDES INFORMATION ABOUT**
1. Check stubs or carbon copies of checks	Cash payments
2. Receipt stubs, carbon copies of receipts, cash register tapes, or memos of cash register totals	Cash receipts
3. Copies of sales tickets or sales invoices issued to customers or clients	Sales of goods or services
4. Purchase invoices received from suppliers	Purchases of goods or services

THE GENERAL JOURNAL

LO4 Journalize transactions.

A day-by-day listing of the transactions of a business is called a **journal**. The purpose of a journal is to provide a record of all transactions completed by the business. The journal shows the date of each transaction, titles of the accounts to be debited and credited, and the amounts of the debits and credits.

 A journal provides a day-by-day listing of all transactions completed by the business.

A journal is commonly referred to as a **book of original entry** because it is here that the first formal accounting record of a transaction is made.

Although many types of journals are used in business, the simplest journal form is a two-column general journal (Figure 4-4). Any kind of business transaction may be entered into a general journal.

FIGURE 4-4   Two-Column General Journal

	DATE	DESCRIPTION	POST. REF.	DEBIT	CREDIT	
	19--					
1	[1]	[2]	[3]	[4]	[5]	1
2						2
3						3

GENERAL JOURNAL   PAGE **1**

A **two-column general journal** is so-named because it has only two amount columns, one for debit amounts and one for credit amounts. Journal pages are numbered in the upper right-hand corner. The five column numbers in Figure 4-4 are explained in Figure 4-5.

FIGURE 4-5   The Columns in a Two-Column General Journal

Column [1] Date	The year is entered in small figures at the top of the column immediately below the column heading. The year is repeated only at the top of each new page. The month is entered for the first entry on the page and for the first transaction of the month. The day of the month is recorded for every transaction, even if it is the same as the prior entry.
Column [2] Description	The **Description** or **Explanation** column is used to enter the titles of the accounts affected by each transaction, and to provide a very brief description of the transaction. Each transaction affects two or more accounts. The account(s) to be debited are entered first at the extreme left of the column. The account(s) to be credited are listed after the debits and indented about one-half inch. The description should be entered immediately following the last credit entry and indented an additional one-half inch.
Column [3] Posting Reference	No entries are made in the **Posting Reference column** during journalizing. Entries are made in this column when the debits and credits are copied to the proper accounts in the ledger. This process will be explained in detail later in this chapter.
Column [4] Debit Amount	The **Debit amount column** is used to enter the amount to be debited to an account. The amount should be entered on the same line as the title of that account.
Column [5] Credit Amount	The **Credit amount column** is used to enter the amount to be credited to an account. The amount should be entered on the same line as the title of that account.

Journalizing

Entering the transactions in a journal is called **journalizing.** For every transaction, the entry should include the date, the title of each account affected, the amounts, and a brief description.

To illustrate the journalizing process, transactions for the first month of operations of Jessie Jane's Campus Delivery will be journalized. The transactions are listed in Figure 4-6. Since you analyzed these transactions in Chapters 2 and 3, the journalizing process should be easier to understand. Let's start with a close look at the steps followed when journalizing the first transaction, Jane's initial investment of $2,000.

When journalizing, the exact account titles shown in the chart of accounts must be used. Refer to the chart of accounts in Figure 4-2 as you review the entries for Jessie Jane's Campus Delivery.

FIGURE 4-6   Summary of Transactions

		Summary of Transactions Jessie Jane's Campus Delivery
Transaction		
(a)	June 1	Jessica Jane invested cash in her business, $2,000.
(b)	3	Bought delivery equipment for cash, $1,200.
(c)	5	Bought delivery equipment on account from Big Red Scooters, $900.
(d)	6	Paid first installment from transaction (c) to Big Red Scooters, $300.
(e)	6	Received cash for delivery services rendered, $500.
(f)	7	Paid cash for June office rent, $200.
(g)	15	Paid telephone bill, $50.
(h)	15	Made deliveries on account for a total of $600: Accounting Department ($400) and the School of Optometry ($200).
(i)	16	Bought supplies for cash, $80.
(j)	18	Paid cash for an eight-month liability insurance policy, $200. Coverage began on June 1.
(k)	20	Received $570 in cash for services performed in transaction (h): $400 from the Accounting Department and $170 from the School of Optometry.
(l)	25	Bought a third scooter from Big Red Scooters, $1,500. Paid $300 cash, with the remaining payments expected over the next four months.
(m)	27	Paid part-time employees wages, $650.
(n)	30	Earned delivery fees for the remainder of the month amounting to $900: $430 in cash and $470 on account. Deliveries on account: Accounting Department ($100) and Athletic Ticket Office ($370).
(o)	30	Jane withdrew cash for personal use, $150.

TRANSACTION (a)

June 1   Jessica Jane opened a bank account with a deposit of $2,000 for her business.

STEP 1   **Enter the date.**   Since this is the first entry on the journal page, the year is entered on the first line of the Date column (in small print at the top of the line). The month and day are entered on the same line, below the year, in the Date column.

			GENERAL JOURNAL			PAGE 1
	DATE		**DESCRIPTION**	**POST. REF.**	**DEBIT**	**CREDIT**
1	19-- June	1				1
2						2

STEP 2 **Enter the debit.** Cash is entered on the first line at the extreme left of the Description column. The amount of the debit, $2,000, is entered on the same line in the Debit column.

			GENERAL JOURNAL			PAGE 1
	DATE		**DESCRIPTION**	**POST. REF.**	**DEBIT**	**CREDIT**
1	19-- June	1	Cash		2 0 0 0 00	1
2						2

STEP 3 **Enter the credit.** The title of the account to be credited, Jessica Jane, Capital, is entered on the second line, indented one-half inch from the left side of the Description column. The amount of the credit, $2,000, is entered on the same line in the Credit column.

6 spaces indent

			GENERAL JOURNAL			PAGE 1
	DATE		**DESCRIPTION**	**POST. REF.**	**DEBIT**	**CREDIT**
1	19-- June	1	Cash		2 0 0 0 00	1
2			Jessica Jane, Capital			2 0 0 0 00	2

STEP 4 **Enter the explanation.** The explanation of the entry is entered on the next line, indented an additional one-half inch. The second line of the explanation, if needed, is also indented the same distance as the first.

			GENERAL JOURNAL			PAGE 1
	DATE		**DESCRIPTION**	**POST. REF.**	**DEBIT**	**CREDIT**
1	19-- June	1	Cash		2 0 0 0 00	1
2			Jessica Jane, Capital			2 0 0 0 00	2
3			Owner's original investment in				3
4			delivery business				4

To enter transaction (b), the purchase of a motor scooter for $1,200 cash, we skip a line and follow the same four steps. In practice, you probably would not skip a line to prevent inappropriate changes to entries. Note that the month and year do not need to be repeated. The day of the month must, however, be entered.

GENERAL JOURNAL   PAGE 1

	DATE		DESCRIPTION	POST. REF.	DEBIT	CREDIT	
1	19-- June	1	Cash		2 0 0 0 00		1
2			Jessica Jane, Capital			2 0 0 0 00	2
3			Owner's original investment in				3
4			delivery business				4
5							5
6		3	Delivery Equipment		1 2 0 0 00		6
7			Cash			1 2 0 0 00	7
8			Purchased delivery equipment				8
9			for cash				9

Skip a line

The journal entries for the month of June are shown in Figure 4-7. Note that the entries on June 25 and June 30 affect more than two accounts. These are called **compound entries**.

FIGURE 4-7   General Journal Entries

GENERAL JOURNAL   PAGE 1

	DATE		DESCRIPTION	POST. REF.	DEBIT	CREDIT	
1	19-- June	1	Cash		2 0 0 0 00		1
2			Jessica Jane, Capital			2 0 0 0 00	2
3			Owner's original investment in				3
4			delivery business				4
5							5
6		3	Delivery Equipment		1 2 0 0 00		6
7			Cash			1 2 0 0 00	7
8			Purchased delivery equipment				8
9			for cash				9
10							10
11		5	Delivery Equipment		9 0 0 00		11
12			Accounts Payable			9 0 0 00	12
13			Purchased delivery equipment				13
14			on account from Big Red				14
15			Scooters				15

List debits first

List credits second and indented 1/2"

Explanation is third and indented another 1/2"

Space to make entries easier to read

In practice, this might not be done to prevent inappropriate changes to entries.

FIGURE 4-7   General Journal Entries (continued)

GENERAL JOURNAL   PAGE 1

	DATE	DESCRIPTION	POST. REF.	DEBIT	CREDIT	
17	6	Accounts Payable		3 0 0 00		17
18		Cash			3 0 0 00	18
19		Made partial payment to Big				19
20		Red Scooters				20
21						21
22	6	Cash		5 0 0 00		22
23		Delivery Fees			5 0 0 00	23
24		Received cash for delivery				24
25		services				25
26						26
27	7	Rent Expense		2 0 0 00		27
28		Cash			2 0 0 00	28
29		Paid office rent for June				29
30						30
31	15	Telephone Expense		5 0 00		31
32		Cash			5 0 00	32
33		Paid telephone bill for June				33
34						34
35	15	Accounts Receivable		6 0 0 00		35
36		Delivery Fees			6 0 0 00	36
37		Deliveries made on account for				37
38		Accounting Department ($400)				38
39		and School of Optometry ($200)				39
40						40

GENERAL JOURNAL   PAGE 2

	DATE	DESCRIPTION	POST. REF.	DEBIT	CREDIT	
	19--					
1	June 16	Supplies		8 0 00		1
2		Cash			8 0 00	2
3		Purchased supplies for cash				3
4						4
5	18	Prepaid Insurance		2 0 0 00		5
6		Cash			2 0 0 00	6
7		Paid premium for eight-month				7
8		insurance policy				8

FIGURE 4-7   General Journal Entries (continued)

	DATE	DESCRIPTION	POST. REF.	DEBIT	CREDIT	
	19--					
10	20	Cash		5 7 0 00		10
11		Accounts Receivable			5 7 0 00	11
12		Received cash on account from				12
13		Accounting Department ($400)				13
14		and School of Optometry ($170)				14
15						15
16	25	Delivery Equipment		1 5 0 0 00		16
17		Accounts Payable			1 2 0 0 00	17
18		Cash			3 0 0 00	18
19		Purchased scooter with down				19
20		payment; balance on account				20
21		from Big Red Scooters				21
22						22
23	27	Wages Expense		6 5 0 00		23
24		Cash			6 5 0 00	24
25		Paid employees				25
26						26
27	30	Cash		4 3 0 00		27
28		Accounts Receivable		4 7 0 00		28
29		Delivery Fees			9 0 0 00	29
30		Deliveries made for cash and				30
31		on account to Accounting				31
32		Department ($100) and				32
33		Athletic Ticket Office ($370)				33
34						34
35	30	Jessica Jane, Drawing		1 5 0 00		35
36		Cash			1 5 0 00	36
37		Owner's withdrawal				37

GENERAL JOURNAL   PAGE 2

Compound entry → (line 16)

Compound entry → (line 27)

THE GENERAL LEDGER

LO5   Post to the general ledger.

The journal provides a day-by-day record of business transactions. To determine the current balance of specific accounts, however, the information in the journal must be copied to accounts similar to the T accounts illustrated in Chapter 3.

> **LEARNING KEY**   While the journal provides a day-by-day record of business transactions, the ledger provides a record of the transactions entered in each account.

A complete set of all the accounts used by a business is known as the **general ledger**. The general ledger provides a complete record of the transactions entered in each account. The accounts are numbered and arranged in the same order as the chart of accounts. That is, accounts are numbered and grouped by classification: assets, liabilities, owner's equity, revenues, and expenses.

Four-Column Account

For purposes of illustration, the T account was introduced in Chapter 3. In practice, businesses are more likely to use a version of the account called the **four-column account**. A four-column account contains columns for the debit or credit transaction and columns for the debit or credit running balance. In addition, there are columns for the date, description of the item, and posting reference. The "Item" column is used to provide descriptions of special entries. For example, "Balance" is written in this column when the balance of an account is transferred to a new page. The "Posting Reference" column is used to indicate the journal page from which an entry was posted, or a check mark (✓) is inserted to indicate that no posting was required. Figure 4-8 compares the cash T account from Chapter 3 for Jessie Jane's Campus Delivery and a four-column cash account summarizing the same cash transactions.

FIGURE 4-8   Comparison of T Account and Four-Column Account

SUMMARY ACCOUNT

Cash

(a)	2,000	(b)	1,200
(e)	500	(d)	300
(k)	570	(f)	200
(n)	430	(g)	50
	3,500	(i)	80
		(j)	200
		(l)	300
		(m)	650
		(o)	150
			3,130
Bal.	370		

GENERAL LEDGER

ACCOUNT: **CASH**   ACCOUNT NO. **111**

DATE		ITEM	POST. REF.	DEBIT	CREDIT	BALANCE DEBIT	BALANCE CREDIT
19-- June	1			2 0 0 0 00		2 0 0 0 00	
	3				1 2 0 0 00	8 0 0 00	
	6				3 0 0 00	5 0 0 00	
	6			5 0 0 00		1 0 0 0 00	
	7				2 0 0 00	8 0 0 00	
	15				5 0 00	7 5 0 00	
	16				8 0 00	6 7 0 00	
	18				2 0 0 00	4 7 0 00	
	20			5 7 0 00		1 0 4 0 00	
	25				3 0 0 00	7 4 0 00	
	27				6 5 0 00	9 0 00	
	30			4 3 0 00		5 2 0 00	
	30				1 5 0 00	3 7 0 00	

└ Transaction Amount ┘└ Running Balances ┘

LEARNING KEY   The primary advantage of the four-column account over the T account is that the four-column account maintains a running balance.

As shown in Figure 4-8, the primary advantage of the T account is that the debit and credit sides of the account are easier to identify. Thus, for demonstration purposes and analyzing what happened, T accounts are very helpful. However, computing the balance of a T account is cumbersome. The primary advantage of the four-column account is that it maintains a running balance.

Note that the heading for the four-column account has the account title and an account number. The account number is taken from the chart of accounts and is used in the posting process.

Posting to the General Ledger

The process of copying the debits and credits from the journal to the ledger accounts is known as **posting**. All amounts entered in the journal must be posted to the general ledger accounts.

 Posting is simply the copying of the exact dates and dollar amounts from the journal to the ledger.

Posting from the journal to the ledger is done daily or at frequent intervals. There are five steps.

STEPS IN THE POSTING PROCESS

In the ledger account:

STEP 1   Enter the date of the transaction in the Date column. There is no need to repeat the month and year, but the day must be entered even if it is the same date as in the previous transaction.

STEP 2   Enter the amount of the debit or credit in the Debit or Credit column.

STEP 3   Enter the new balance in the Balance columns under Debit or Credit. If the balance of the account is zero, draw a line through the debit and credit columns.

STEP 4   Enter the journal page number from which each transaction is posted in the Posting Reference column.

In the journal:

STEP 5   Enter the ledger account number in the Posting Reference column of the journal for each transaction that is posted.

Step 5 is the last step in the posting process. After this step is completed, the posting references will indicate which journal entries have been posted to the ledger accounts. This is very helpful, particularly if you are interrupted during the posting process. The information in the posting reference columns of the journal and ledger provides a link between the journal and ledger known as a **cross-reference**.

 Posting references indicate that a journal entry has been posted to the general ledger.

To illustrate the posting process, the first journal entry for Jessie Jane's Campus Delivery will be posted step-by-step. First, let's post the debit to Cash (Figure 4-9).

FIGURE 4-9   Posting a Debit

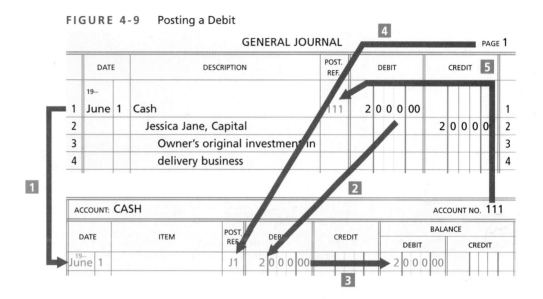

In the ledger account:

STEP 1   Enter the year, "19--," the month, "June," and the day, "1," in the Date column of the cash account.

STEP 2   Enter the amount, "$2,000," in the Debit column.

STEP 3   Enter the $2,000 balance in the Balance columns under Debit.

STEP 4   Enter "J1" in the Posting Reference column since the posting came from page 1 of the *Journal.*

In the journal:

STEP 5   Enter the account number for cash, 111 (see chart of accounts in Figure 4-2 on page 83), in the Posting Reference column of the journal on the same line as the debit to Cash for $2,000.

Now let's post the credit portion of the first entry (Figure 4-10).

In the ledger account:

STEP 1   Enter the year, "19--," the month, "June," and the day, "1," in the Date column of the Jessica Jane, capital account.

STEP 2   Enter the amount, "$2,000," in the Credit column.

STEP 3   Enter the $2,000 balance in the Balance columns under Credit.

STEP 4   Enter "J1" in the Posting Reference column since the posting came from Page 1 of the *Journal.*

FIGURE 4-10   Posting a Credit

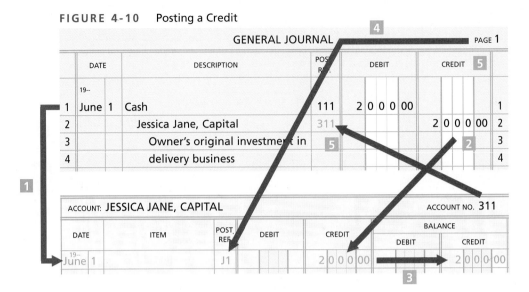

In the journal:

STEP 5   Enter the account number for Jessica Jane, Capital, 311, in the Posting Reference column.

After posting the journal entries for Jessie Jane's Campus Delivery for the month of June, the general journal and general ledger should appear as illustrated in Figures 4-11 and 4-12 on pages 94–98. *Note that the Posting Reference column of the journal has been filled in because the entries have been posted.*

FIGURE 4-11   General Journal After Posting

GENERAL JOURNAL													PAGE 1	
	DATE		DESCRIPTION	POST. REF.	DEBIT					CREDIT				
1	19-- June	1	Cash	111	2	0	0	0	00					1
2			Jessica Jane, Capital	311						2	0	0	0 00	2
3			Owner's original investment in											3
4			delivery business											4
5														5
6		3	Delivery Equipment	185	1	2	0	0	00					6
7			Cash	111						1	2	0	0 00	7
8			Purchased delivery equipment											8
9			for cash											9
10														10
11		5	Delivery Equipment	185	9	0	0		00					11
12			Accounts Payable	216						9	0	0	00	12
13			Purchased delivery equipment											13
14			on account from Big Red											14
15			Scooters											15

FIGURE 4-11   General Journal After Posting (continued)

GENERAL JOURNAL   PAGE 1

	DATE		DESCRIPTION	POST. REF.	DEBIT	CREDIT	
16							16
17		6	Accounts Payable	216	3 0 0 00		17
18			Cash	111		3 0 0 00	18
19			Made partial payment to Big				19
20			Red Scooters				20
21							21
22		6	Cash	111	5 0 0 00		22
23			Delivery Fees	411		5 0 0 00	23
24			Received cash for delivery				24
25			services				25
26							26
27		7	Rent Expense	541	2 0 0 00		27
28			Cash	111		2 0 0 00	28
29			Paid office rent for June				29
30							30
31		15	Telephone Expense	545	5 0 00		31
32			Cash	111		5 0 00	32
33			Paid telephone bill for June				33
34							34
35		15	Accounts Receivable	131	6 0 0 00		35
36			Delivery Fees	411		6 0 0 00	36
37			Deliveries made on account for				37
38			Accounting Department ($400)				38
39			and School of Optometry ($200)				39

GENERAL JOURNAL   PAGE 2

	DATE		DESCRIPTION	POST. REF.	DEBIT	CREDIT	
1	19-- June	16	Supplies	151	8 0 00		1
2			Cash	111		8 0 00	2
3			Purchased supplies for cash				3
4							4
5		18	Prepaid Insurance	155	2 0 0 00		5
6			Cash	111		2 0 0 00	6
7			Paid premium for eight-month				7
8			insurance policy				8
9							9

FIGURE 4-11   General Journal After Posting (concluded)

GENERAL JOURNAL   PAGE 2

	DATE	DESCRIPTION	POST. REF.	DEBIT	CREDIT	
10	20	Cash	111	5 7 0 00		10
11		Accounts Receivable	131		5 7 0 00	11
12		Received cash on account from				12
13		Accounting Department ($400)				13
14		and School of Optometry ($170)				14
15						15
16	25	Delivery Equipment	185	1 5 0 0 00		16
17		Accounts Payable	216		1 2 0 0 00	17
18		Cash	111		3 0 0 00	18
19		Purchased scooter with down				19
20		payment; balance on account				20
21		from Big Red Scooters				21
22						22
23	27	Wages Expense	542	6 5 0 00		23
24		Cash	111		6 5 0 00	24
25		Paid employees				25
26						26
27	30	Cash	111	4 3 0 00		27
28		Accounts Receivable	131	4 7 0 00		28
29		Delivery Fees	411		9 0 0 00	29
30		Deliveries made for cash and				30
31		on account to Accounting				31
32		Department ($100) and				32
33		Athletic Ticket Office ($370)				33
34						34
35	30	Jessica Jane, Drawing	312	1 5 0 00		35
36		Cash	111		1 5 0 00	36
37		Owner's withdrawal				37
38						38
39						39
40						40
41						41
42						42
43						43
44						44
45						45
46						46
47						47
48						48
49						49

FIGURE 4-12   General Ledger After Posting

GENERAL LEDGER

ACCOUNT: **Cash**   ACCOUNT NO. 111

DATE		ITEM	POST. REF.	DEBIT	CREDIT	BALANCE DEBIT	BALANCE CREDIT
19-- June	1		J1	2 0 0 0 00		2 0 0 0 00	
	3		J1		1 2 0 0 00	8 0 0 00	
	6		J1		3 0 0 00	5 0 0 00	
	6		J1	5 0 0 00		1 0 0 0 00	
	7		J1		2 0 0 00	8 0 0 00	
	15		J1		5 0 00	7 5 0 00	
	16		J2		8 0 00	6 7 0 00	
	18		J2		2 0 0 00	4 7 0 00	
	20		J2	5 7 0 00		1 0 4 0 00	
	25		J2		3 0 0 00	7 4 0 00	
	27		J2		6 5 0 00	9 0 00	
	30		J2	4 3 0 00		5 2 0 00	
	30		J2		1 5 0 00	3 7 0 00	

ACCOUNT: **Accounts Receivable**   ACCOUNT NO. 131

DATE		ITEM	POST. REF.	DEBIT	CREDIT	BALANCE DEBIT	BALANCE CREDIT
19-- June	15		J1	6 0 0 00		6 0 0 00	
	20		J2		5 7 0 00	3 0 00	
	30		J2	4 7 0 00		5 0 0 00	

ACCOUNT: **Supplies**   ACCOUNT NO. 151

DATE		ITEM	POST. REF.	DEBIT	CREDIT	BALANCE DEBIT	BALANCE CREDIT
19-- June	16		J2	8 0 00		8 0 00	

ACCOUNT: **Prepaid Insurance**   ACCOUNT NO. 155

DATE		ITEM	POST. REF.	DEBIT	CREDIT	BALANCE DEBIT	BALANCE CREDIT
19-- June	18		J2	2 0 0 00		2 0 0 00	

ACCOUNT: **Delivery Equipment**   ACCOUNT NO. 185

DATE		ITEM	POST. REF.	DEBIT	CREDIT	BALANCE DEBIT	BALANCE CREDIT
19-- June	3		J1	1 2 0 0 00		1 2 0 0 00	
	5		J1	9 0 0 00		2 1 0 0 00	
	25		J2	1 5 0 0 00		3 6 0 0 00	

FIGURE 4-12   General Ledger After Posting (concluded)

ACCOUNT: Accounts Payable   ACCOUNT NO. 216

DATE		ITEM	POST. REF.	DEBIT	CREDIT	BALANCE DEBIT	BALANCE CREDIT
19-- June	5		J1		9 0 0 00		9 0 0 00
	6		J1	3 0 0 00			6 0 0 00
	25		J2		1 2 0 0 00		1 8 0 0 00

ACCOUNT: Jessica Jane, Capital   ACCOUNT NO. 311

DATE		ITEM	POST. REF.	DEBIT	CREDIT	BALANCE DEBIT	BALANCE CREDIT
19-- June	1		J1		2 0 0 0 00		2 0 0 0 00

ACCOUNT: Jessica Jane, Drawing   ACCOUNT NO. 312

DATE		ITEM	POST. REF.	DEBIT	CREDIT	BALANCE DEBIT	BALANCE CREDIT
19-- June	30		J2	1 5 0 00		1 5 0 00	

ACCOUNT: Delivery Fees   ACCOUNT NO. 411

DATE		ITEM	POST. REF.	DEBIT	CREDIT	BALANCE DEBIT	BALANCE CREDIT
19-- June	6		J1		5 0 0 00		5 0 0 00
	15		J1		6 0 0 00		1 1 0 0 00
	30		J2		9 0 0 00		2 0 0 0 00

ACCOUNT: Rent Expense   ACCOUNT NO. 541

DATE		ITEM	POST. REF.	DEBIT	CREDIT	BALANCE DEBIT	BALANCE CREDIT
19-- June	7		J1	2 0 0 00		2 0 0 00	

ACCOUNT: Wages Expense   ACCOUNT NO. 542

DATE		ITEM	POST. REF.	DEBIT	CREDIT	BALANCE DEBIT	BALANCE CREDIT
19-- June	27		J2	6 5 0 00		6 5 0 00	

ACCOUNT: Telephone Expense   ACCOUNT NO. 545

DATE		ITEM	POST. REF.	DEBIT	CREDIT	BALANCE DEBIT	BALANCE CREDIT
19-- June	15		J1	5 0 00		5 0 00	

The Trial Balance

In Chapter 3, a **trial balance** was used to prove that the totals of the debit and credit balances in the T accounts were equal. In this chapter, a trial balance is used to prove the equality of the debits and credits in the ledger accounts. A trial balance can be prepared daily, weekly, monthly, or whenever desired. Before preparing a trial balance, all transactions should be journalized and posted so that the effect of all transactions will be reflected in the ledger accounts.

The trial balance for Jessie Jane's Campus Delivery shown in Figure 4-13 was prepared from the balances in the general ledger in Figure 4-12. The accounts are listed in the order used in the chart of accounts. This order is also often used when preparing financial statements. In Chapter 2, we pointed out that many firms list expenses from highest to lowest amounts. Some firms list expenses according to the chart of accounts. We will follow the latter approach in the text and assignment material.

LEARNING KEY   The chart of accounts determines the order for listing accounts in the general ledger and trial balance. This order may also be used when preparing financial statements.

FIGURE 4-13   Trial Balance

Jessie Jane's Campus Delivery
Trial Balance
June 30, 19--

ACCOUNT TITLE	ACCOUNT NO.	DEBIT BALANCE	CREDIT BALANCE
Cash	111	3 7 0 00	
Accounts Receivable	131	5 0 0 00	
Supplies	151	8 0 00	
Prepaid Insurance	155	2 0 0 00	
Delivery Equipment	185	3 6 0 0 00	
Accounts Payable	216		1 8 0 0 00
Jessica Jane, Capital	311		2 0 0 0 00
Jessica Jane, Drawing	312	1 5 0 00	
Delivery Fees	411		2 0 0 0 00
Rent Expense	541	2 0 0 00	
Wages Expense	542	6 5 0 00	
Telephone Expense	545	5 0 00	
		5 8 0 0 00	5 8 0 0 00

Even though the trial balance indicates that the ledger is in balance, the ledger can still contain errors. For example, if a journal entry was made debiting or crediting the wrong accounts, or if an item was posted to the wrong account, the ledger will still be in balance. It is important, therefore, to be very careful in preparing the journal entries and in posting them to the ledger accounts.

FINDING AND CORRECTING ERRORS IN THE TRIAL BALANCE

LO6 Explain how to find and correct errors.

Tips are available to help if your trial balance has an error. Figure 4-14 offers hints for finding the error when your trial balance does not balance.

FIGURE 4-14 Tips for Finding Errors in the Trial Balance

1. Double check your addition.

2. Find the difference between the debits and the credits.
   a. If the difference is equal to the amount of a specific transaction, perhaps you forgot to post the debit or credit portion of this transaction.
   b. Divide the difference by **2**. If the difference is evenly divisible by 2, you may have posted two debits or two credits for a transaction. If a debit was posted as a credit, it would mean that one transaction had two credits and no debits. The difference between the total debits and credits would be twice the amount of the debit that was posted as a credit.
   c. Divide the difference by **9**. If the difference is evenly divisible by 9, you may have committed a **slide error** or a **transposition error**. A slide occurs when debit or credit amounts "slide" a digit or two to the left or right when entered. For example, if **$250** was entered as **$25**:

      $250 − 25 = $225

      $225 ÷ **9** = $25

      The difference is evenly divisible by 9.

      A transposition occurs when two digits are reversed. For example, if **$250** was entered as **$520**:

      $520 − 250 = $270

      $270 ÷ **9** = $30

      Again, the difference is evenly divisible by 9.

Profiles in Accounting

JEFF CLIFTON, Account Supervisor

Jeff Clifton maintained a 4.0 GPA with nearly perfect attendance while earning an Associate Degree in Accounting Automation. He performed an externship with Brooke County Taxing Authority and then began working as an accounts receivable clerk with the DeBartolo Properties Management, Inc., in Youngstown, OH.

He was promoted and is now an account supervisor where duties include management of accounts receivable for 20 development properties across the United States, supervising five employees and interviewing prospective employees.

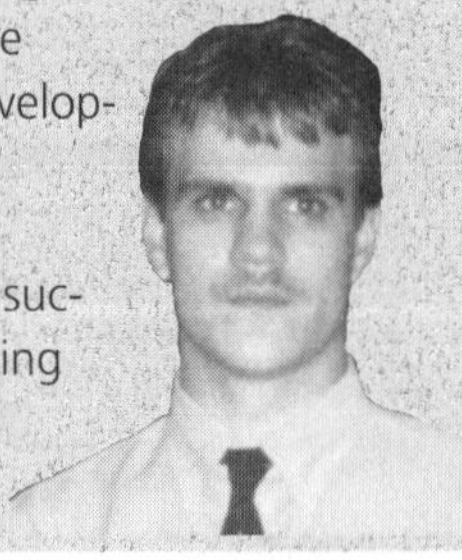

According to Jeff, being self motivated is the main key to success. You need to work hard and success will come. Accounting interested Jeff because he enjoys working with numbers and considers himself to be very analytical.

If the tips in Figure 4-14 don't work, you must retrace your steps through the accounting process. Double check your addition for the ledger accounts. Also trace all postings. Be patient as you search for your error. Use this process as an opportunity to reinforce your understanding of the flow of information through the accounting system. Much can be learned while looking for an error.

Once you have found an error, there are two methods of making the correction. Although you may want to erase when correcting your homework, this is not acceptable in practice. An erasure may suggest that you are trying to hide something. Instead you should use the ruling method or make a correcting entry.

Ruling Method

The **ruling method** should be used to correct two types of errors:

1. When an incorrect journal entry has been made, but not yet posted.
2. When a proper entry has been made but posted incorrectly.

When using the ruling method, draw a line through the incorrect account title or amount and write the correct information directly above the line. Corrections should be initialed so the source and reason for the correction can be traced. This type of correction may be made in the journal or ledger accounts, as shown in Figure 4-15.

FIGURE 4-15   Ruling Method of Making a Correction

GENERAL JOURNAL   PAGE 2

	DATE		DESCRIPTION	POST. REF.	DEBIT	CREDIT	
1	19— Sept.	17	*Wages Expense* **RP** ~~Entertainment Expense~~		6 5 0 00		1
2			Cash			6 5 0 00	2
3			Paid employees				3
4					**RP**		4
5		18	Prepaid Insurance		*2 0 0 00* ~~2 0 00~~	**RP**	5
6			Cash			*2 0 0 00* ~~2 0 00~~	6
7			Paid premium for eight-month				7
8			insurance policy				8
9							9

Slide

GENERAL LEDGER

ACCOUNT: **Accounts Payable**   ACCOUNT NO. **216**

DATE		ITEM	POST. REF.	DEBIT	CREDIT	BALANCE DEBIT	BALANCE CREDIT
19— Sept.	8		J1		7 0 0 00		9 0 0 00
	15		J1	2 0 0 00	*1 2 0 0 00* **RP**		**RP** *1 2 0 0 00* ~~5 0 0 00~~
	25		J2		~~2 1 0 0 00~~		~~2 6 0 0 00~~

Transposition

Correcting Entry Method

If an incorrect entry has been journalized and posted to the wrong account, a **correcting entry** should be made. For example, assume that a $400 payment for Rent Expense was incorrectly debited to Repair Expense and correctly credited to Cash. This requires a correcting entry and explanation as shown in Figure 4-16. Figure 4-17 shows the effects of the correcting entry on the ledger accounts.

FIGURE 4-16   Correcting Entry Method

GENERAL JOURNAL   PAGE **6**

	DATE	DESCRIPTION	POST. REF.	DEBIT	CREDIT	
1	19-- Sept. 25	Rent Expense	541	4 0 0 00		1
2		Repair Expense	565		4 0 0 00	2
3		To correct error in which				3
4		payment for rent was debited				4
5		to Repair Expense				5

FIGURE 4-17   Effects of Correcting Entry on Ledger Accounts

GENERAL LEDGER

ACCOUNT: **Rent Expense**   ACCOUNT NO. **541**

DATE	ITEM	POST. REF.	DEBIT	CREDIT	BALANCE DEBIT	BALANCE CREDIT
19-- Sept. 25		J6	4 0 0 00		4 0 0 00	

ACCOUNT: **Repair Expense**   ACCOUNT NO. **565**

DATE	ITEM	POST. REF.	DEBIT	CREDIT	BALANCE DEBIT	BALANCE CREDIT
19-- Sept. 10		J5	5 0 00		5 0 00	
15		J5	4 0 0 00		4 5 0 00	
25		J6		4 0 0 00	5 0 00	

KEY POINTS

1   The flow of data from the source documents through the trial balance is:

1. Analyze business transactions.
2. Journalize transactions in the general journal.
3. Post journal entries to the general ledger.
4. Prepare a trial balance.

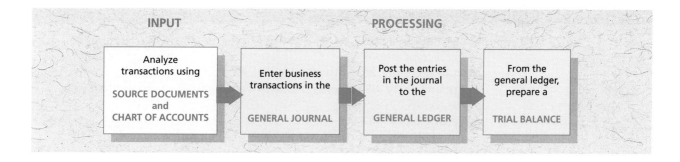

2 The chart of accounts includes the account titles in numeric order for all assets, liabilities, owner's equity, revenues, and expenses. The chart of accounts is used in classifying information about transactions.

3 Source documents trigger the analysis of business transactions and the entries into the accounting system.

4 A journal provides a day-by-day listing of transactions. The journal shows the date, titles of the accounts to be debited or credited, and the amounts of the debits and credits. The steps in the journalizing process are:

1. Enter the date.
2. Enter the debit. Accounts to be debited are entered first.
3. Enter the credit. Accounts to be credited are entered after the debits and are indented one-half inch.
4. Enter the explanation. A brief explanation of the transaction should be entered in the description column on the line following the last credit. The explanation should be indented an additional one-half inch.

5 The general ledger is a complete set of all accounts used by the business. The steps in posting from the general journal to the general ledger are:

In the general ledger:
1. Enter the date of each transaction.
2. Enter the amount of each debit or credit in the Debit or Credit column.
3. Enter the new balance.
4. Enter the journal page number from which each transaction is posted in the Posting Reference column.

In the journal:
5. Enter the account number in the Posting Reference column for each transaction that is posted.

6 When an error is discovered, use the ruling method or the correcting entry method to correct the error.

KEY TERMS

book of original entry 84 The journal or the first formal accounting record of a transaction.

chart of accounts 82 A list of all accounts used by a business.

compound entry 88 A general journal entry that affects more than two accounts.

correcting entry 102 An entry to correct an incorrect entry that has been journalized and posted to the wrong account.

cross-reference 92 The information in the Posting Reference columns of the journal and ledger that provides a link between the journal and ledger.

four-column account 91 An account with columns for the debit or credit transaction and columns for the debit or credit running balance.

general ledger 91 A complete set of all the accounts used by a business.

journal 84 A day-by-day listing of the transactions of a business.

journalizing 85 Entering the transactions in a journal.

posting 92 Copying the debits and credits from the journal to the ledger accounts.

ruling method 101 A method of correcting an entry in which a line is drawn through the error and the correct information is placed above it.

slide error 100 An error that occurs when debit or credit amounts "slide" a digit or two to the left or right.

source document 83 Any document that provides information about a business transaction.

transposition error 100 Occurs when two digits are reversed.

trial balance 99 A list used to prove that the totals of the debit and credit balances in the ledger accounts are equal.

two-column general journal 85 A journal with only two amount columns, one for debit amounts and one for credit amounts.

REVIEW QUESTIONS

1. Trace the flow of accounting information through the accounting system.
2. Explain the purpose of a chart of accounts.
3. Name the five types of financial statement classifications for which it is ordinarily desirable to keep separate accounts.
4. Name a source document that provides information about each of the following types of business transactions:
   a. Cash payment
   b. Cash receipt
   c. Sale of goods or services
   d. Purchase of goods or services
5. Where is the first formal accounting record of a business transaction usually made?
6. Describe the four steps required to journalize a business transaction in a general journal.
7. In what order are the accounts customarily placed in the ledger?
8. Explain the primary advantage of a four-column ledger account.

9. Explain the five steps required when posting the journal to the ledger.
10. What information is entered in the Posting Reference column of the journal as an amount is posted to the proper account in the ledger?
11. Explain why the ledger can still contain errors even though the trial balance is in balance. Give examples of two such types of errors.
12. What is a slide error?
13. What is a transposition error?
14. What is the ruling method of correcting an error?
15. What is the correcting entry method?

MANAGING YOUR WRITING

You are a public accountant with many small business clients. During a recent visit to a client's business, the bookkeeper approached you with a problem. The columns of the trial balance were not equal. You helped the bookkeeper find and correct the error, but believe you should go one step further. Write a memo to all of your clients that explains the purpose of the double-entry framework, the importance of maintaining the equality of the accounting equation, the errors that might cause an inequality, and suggestions for finding the errors.

DEMONSTRATION PROBLEM

George Fielding is a financial planning consultant. He provides budgeting, estate planning, tax planning, and investing advice for professional golfers. He developed the following chart of accounts for his business.

Assets	Revenues
111 Cash	411 Professional Fees
152 Office Supplies	

Liabilities	Expenses
216 Accounts Payable	541 Rent Expense
	542 Wages Expense
Owner's Equity	545 Telephone Expense
311 George Fielding, Capital	546 Automobile Expense
312 George Fielding, Drawing	555 Utilities Expense
	557 Charitable Contributions Expense

The following transactions took place during the month of December of the current year.

Dec. 1   Fielding invested cash to start the business, $20,000.
      3   Paid Bollhorst Real Estate for December office rent, $1,000.
      4   Received cash from Aaron Patton, a client, for services, $2,500.

Dec.   6 Paid T. Z. Anderson Electric for December heating and light, $75.

      7 Received cash from Andrew Conder, a client, for services, $2,000.

   12 Paid Fichter's Super Service for gasoline and oil purchases, $60.

   14 Paid Hillenburg Staffing for temporary secretarial services during the past two weeks, $600.

   17 Bought office supplies from Bowers Office Supply on account, $280.

   20 Paid Mitchell Telephone Co. for business calls during the past month, $100.

   21 Fielding withdrew cash for personal use, $1,100.

   24 Made donation to the National Multiple Sclerosis Society, $100.

   27 Received cash from Billy Walters, a client, for services, $2,000.

   28 Paid Hillenburg Staffing for temporary secretarial services during the past two weeks, $600.

   29 Made payment on account to Bowers Office Supply, $100.

REQUIRED

1. Record the preceding transactions in a general journal.
2. Post the entries to the general ledger.
3. Prepare a trial balance.

SOLUTION

1.

GENERAL JOURNAL
PAGE 1

	DATE		DESCRIPTION	POST. REF.	DEBIT	CREDIT	
1	19-- Dec.	1	Cash	111	20 0 0 0 00		1
2			George Fielding, Capital	311		20 0 0 0 00	2
3			Owner's original investment in				3
4			consulting business				4
5							5
6		3	Rent Expense	541	1 0 0 0 00		6
7			Cash	111		1 0 0 0 00	7
8			Paid rent for December				8
9							9
10		4	Cash	111	2 5 0 0 00		10
11			Professional Fees	411		2 5 0 0 00	11
12			Received cash for services				12
13			rendered				13
14							14

1. continued

	DATE		DESCRIPTION	POST. REF.	DEBIT	CREDIT	
15		6	Utilities Expense	555	7 5 00		15
16			Cash	111		7 5 00	16
17			Paid utilities				17
18							18
19		7	Cash	111	2 0 0 0 00		19
20			Professional Fees	411		2 0 0 0 00	20
21			Received cash for services				21
22			rendered				22
23							23
24		12	Automobile Expense	546	6 0 00		24
25			Cash	111		6 0 00	25
26			Paid for gas and oil				26
27							27
28		14	Wages Expense	542	6 0 0 00		28
29			Cash	111		6 0 0 00	29
30			Paid temporary secretaries				30
31							31
32		17	Office Supplies	152	2 8 0 00		32
33			Accounts Payable	216		2 8 0 00	33
34			Purchased office supplies on				34
35			account from Bowers Office				35
36			Supply				36

GENERAL JOURNAL — PAGE 1

	DATE		DESCRIPTION	POST. REF.	DEBIT	CREDIT	
1	Dec.	20	Telephone Expense	545	1 0 0 00		1
2			Cash	111		1 0 0 00	2
3			Paid telephone bill				3
4							4
5		21	George Fielding, Drawing	312	1 1 0 0 00		5
6			Cash	111		1 1 0 0 00	6
7			Owner's withdrawal				7
8							8

GENERAL JOURNAL — PAGE 2

1. continued

GENERAL JOURNAL   PAGE 2

	DATE	DESCRIPTION	POST. REF.	DEBIT	CREDIT	
9	24	Charitable Contributions Expense	557	1 0 0 00		9
10		Cash	111		1 0 0 00	10
11		Contribution to National				11
12		Multiple Sclerosis Society				12
13						13
14	27	Cash	111	2 0 0 0 00		14
15		Professional Fees	411		2 0 0 0 00	15
16		Received cash for services				16
17		rendered				17
18						18
19	28	Wages Expense	542	6 0 0 00		19
20		Cash	111		6 0 0 00	20
21		Paid temporary secretaries				21
22						22
23	29	Accounts Payable	216	1 0 0 00		23
24		Cash	111		1 0 0 00	24
25		Payment on account to Bowers				25
26		Office Supply				26

2.

GENERAL LEDGER

ACCOUNT: **Cash**   ACCOUNT NO. 111

DATE		ITEM	POST. REF.	DEBIT	CREDIT	BALANCE DEBIT	BALANCE CREDIT
Dec.	1		J1	20 0 0 0 00		20 0 0 0 00	
	3		J1		1 0 0 0 00	19 0 0 0 00	
	4		J1	2 5 0 0 00		21 5 0 0 00	
	6		J1		7 5 00	21 4 2 5 00	
	7		J1	2 0 0 0 00		23 4 2 5 00	
	12		J1		6 0 00	23 3 6 5 00	
	14		J1		6 0 0 00	22 7 6 5 00	
	20		J2		1 0 0 00	22 6 6 5 00	
	21		J2		1 1 0 0 00	21 5 6 5 00	
	24		J2		1 0 0 00	21 4 6 5 00	
	27		J2	2 0 0 0 00		23 4 6 5 00	
	28		J2		6 0 0 00	22 8 6 5 00	
	29		J2		1 0 0 00	22 7 6 5 00	

ACCOUNT: Office Supplies ACCOUNT NO. 152

DATE	ITEM	POST. REF.	DEBIT	CREDIT	BALANCE DEBIT	BALANCE CREDIT
19-- Dec. 17		J1	2 8 0 00		2 8 0 00	

ACCOUNT: Accounts Payable ACCOUNT NO. 216

DATE	ITEM	POST. REF.	DEBIT	CREDIT	BALANCE DEBIT	BALANCE CREDIT
19-- Dec. 17		J1		2 8 0 00		2 8 0 00
29		J2	1 0 0 00			1 8 0 00

ACCOUNT: George Fielding, Capital ACCOUNT NO. 311

DATE	ITEM	POST. REF.	DEBIT	CREDIT	BALANCE DEBIT	BALANCE CREDIT
19-- Dec. 1		J1		20 0 0 0 00		20 0 0 0 00

ACCOUNT: George Fielding, Drawing ACCOUNT NO. 312

DATE	ITEM	POST. REF.	DEBIT	CREDIT	BALANCE DEBIT	BALANCE CREDIT
19-- Dec. 21		J2	1 1 0 0 00		1 1 0 0 00	

ACCOUNT: Professional Fees ACCOUNT NO. 411

DATE	ITEM	POST. REF.	DEBIT	CREDIT	BALANCE DEBIT	BALANCE CREDIT
19-- Dec. 4		J1		2 5 0 0 00		2 5 0 0 00
7		J1		2 0 0 0 00		4 5 0 0 00
27		J2		2 0 0 0 00		6 5 0 0 00

ACCOUNT: Rent Expense ACCOUNT NO. 541

DATE	ITEM	POST. REF.	DEBIT	CREDIT	BALANCE DEBIT	BALANCE CREDIT
19-- Dec. 3		J1	1 0 0 0 00		1 0 0 0 00	

ACCOUNT: Wages Expense ACCOUNT NO. 542

DATE	ITEM	POST. REF.	DEBIT	CREDIT	BALANCE DEBIT	BALANCE CREDIT
19-- Dec. 14		J1	6 0 0 00		6 0 0 00	
28		J2	6 0 0 00		1 2 0 0 00	

ACCOUNT: Telephone Expense ACCOUNT NO. 545

DATE	ITEM	POST. REF.	DEBIT	CREDIT	BALANCE DEBIT	BALANCE CREDIT
19-- Dec. 20		J2	1 0 0 00		1 0 0 00	

ACCOUNT: Automobile Expense					ACCOUNT NO. 546	
DATE	ITEM	POST. REF.	DEBIT	CREDIT	BALANCE	
					DEBIT	CREDIT
19– Dec. 12		J1	6 0 00		6 0 00	

ACCOUNT: Utilities Expense					ACCOUNT NO. 555	
DATE	ITEM	POST. REF.	DEBIT	CREDIT	BALANCE	
					DEBIT	CREDIT
19– Dec. 6		J1	7 5 00		7 5 00	

ACCOUNT: Charitable Contributions Expense					ACCOUNT NO. 557	
DATE	ITEM	POST. REF.	DEBIT	CREDIT	BALANCE	
					DEBIT	CREDIT
19– Dec. 24		J2	1 0 0 00		1 0 0 00	

3.

George Fielding, Financial Planning Consultant
Trial Balance
December 31, 19--

ACCOUNT TITLE	ACCOUNT NO.	DEBIT BALANCE	CREDIT BALANCE
Cash	111	22 7 6 5 00	
Office Supplies	152	2 8 0 00	
Accounts Payable	216		1 8 0 00
George Fielding, Capital	311		20 0 0 0 00
George Fielding, Drawing	312	1 1 0 0 00	
Professional Fees	411		6 5 0 0 00
Rent Expense	541	1 0 0 0 00	
Wages Expense	542	1 2 0 0 00	
Telephone Expense	545	1 0 0 00	
Automobile Expense	546	6 0 00	
Utilities Expense	555	7 5 00	
Charitable Contributions Expense	557	1 0 0 00	
		26 6 8 0 00	26 6 8 0 00

SERIES A   EXERCISES

3 **EXERCISE 4A1 SOURCE DOCUMENTS**   Source documents trigger the analysis of events requiring an accounting entry. Match the following source documents with the type of information they provide.

1. Check stubs or check register
2. Purchase invoice from suppliers (vendors)
3. Sales tickets or invoices to customers
4. Receipts or cash register tapes

a. A good or service has been sold.
b. Cash has been received by the business.
c. Cash has been paid by the business.
d. Goods or services have been purchased by the business.

4 **EXERCISE 4A2 GENERAL JOURNAL ENTRIES**   For each of the following transactions, list the account to be debited and the account to be credited in the general journal.

1. Invested cash in the business, $5,000
2. Paid office rent, $500.
3. Purchased office supplies on account, $300.
4. Received cash for services rendered (fees), $400.
5. Paid cash on account, $50.
6. Rendered services on account, $300.
7. Received cash for an amount owed by a customer, $100.

5 **EXERCISE 4A3 GENERAL LEDGER ACCOUNTS**   Set up T accounts for each of the general ledger accounts needed for Exercise 4A2 and post debits and credits to the accounts.

4 **EXERCISE 4A4 GENERAL JOURNAL ENTRIES**   Jean Jones has opened Jones Consulting. Journalize the following transactions that occurred during January of the current year. Use the following journal pages: January 1–10, page 1 and January 11–29, page 2. Use the chart of accounts provided below.

Chart of Accounts

Assets
111   Cash
121   Office Supplies
131   Office Equipment

Liabilities
211   Accounts Payable

Owner's Equity
311   Jean Jones, Capital
312   Jean Jones, Drawing

Revenues
411   Consulting Fees

Expenses
511   Rent Expense
521   Wages Expense
531   Telephone Expense
541   Utilities Expense
551   Miscellaneous Expense

Jan.   1 Invested cash in the business, $10,000.
        2 Paid office rent, $500.
        3 Purchased office equipment on account, $1,500.
        5 Received cash for services rendered, $750.
        8 Paid telephone bill, $65.
       10 Paid for a magazine subscription, $15 (miscellaneous expense).
       11 Purchased office supplies on account, $300.
       15 Made a payment on account, $150 (see Jan. 3 transaction).
       18 Paid part-time employee, $500.
       21 Received cash for services rendered, $350.
       25 Paid utilities bill, $85.
       27 Withdrew cash for personal use, $100.
       29 Paid part-time employee, $500.

5 **EXERCISE 4A5 GENERAL LEDGER ACCOUNTS; TRIAL BALANCE** Set up four-column general ledger accounts using the chart of accounts provided in Exercise 4A4. Post the transactions from Exercise 4A4 to the general ledger accounts and prepare a trial balance.

EXERCISE 4A6 FINANCIAL STATEMENTS From the information in Exercises 4A4 and 4A5, prepare an income statement, a statement of owner's equity, and a balance sheet.

EXERCISE 4A7 FINANCIAL STATEMENTS From the following trial balance taken after one month of operation, prepare an income statement, a statement of owner's equity, and a balance sheet. Assume that TJ Ulza made no additional investments in the business during the month.

TJ's Paint Service
Trial Balance
July 31, 19--

ACCOUNT TITLE	ACCOUNT NO.	DEBIT BALANCE	CREDIT BALANCE
Cash	101	4 3 0 0 00	
Accounts Receivable	111	1 1 0 0 00	
Supplies	121	8 0 0 00	
Paint Equipment	131	9 0 0 00	
Accounts Payable	201		2 1 5 0 00
TJ Ulza, Capital	311		3 2 0 5 00
TJ Ulza, Drawing	312	5 0 0 00	
Painting Fees	411		3 6 0 0 00
Rent Expense	511	2 5 0 00	
Telephone Expense	521	5 0 00	
Utilities Expense	531	7 0 00	
Transportation Expense	541	6 0 00	
Wages Expense	551	9 0 0 00	
Miscellaneous Expense	561	2 5 00	
		8 9 5 5 00	8 9 5 5 00

6 **EXERCISE 4A8 FINDING AND CORRECTING ERRORS** Joe Adams bought $500 worth of office supplies on account. The following entry was recorded on May 17. Find the error(s) and correct it (them) using the ruling method.

14							14
15	May	17	Office Equipment	4 0 0 00			15
16			Cash		4 0 0 00		16
17			Purchased copy paper				17

On May 25, after the transactions had been posted, Adams discovered that the following entry contains an error. The cash received represents a collection on account, rather than new service fees. Correct the error in the general journal using the correcting entry method.

22																	22
23	¹⁹⁻ May	23	Cash	111	1	0	0	0	00								23
24			Service Fees	411						1	0	0	0	00			24
25			Received cash for services														25
26			previously earned														26

SERIES A PROBLEMS

4/5   **PROBLEM 4A1 JOURNALIZING AND POSTING TRANSACTIONS**
Jim Andrews opened a delivery business in March. He rented a small office and has a part-time assistant. His trial balance (shown on the next page) shows accounts for the first three months of business. Andrews' transactions for the month of June are as follows:

June 1 Paid rent, $300.
      2 Performed delivery service: $100 in cash and $200 on account.
      4 Paid for newspaper advertising, $15.
      6 Purchased office supplies on account, $180.
      7 Received cash for delivery services rendered, $260.
      9 Paid cash on account (truck payment), $200.
     10 Purchased a copier (office equipment): paid $100 in cash and put $600 on account.
     11 Made a contribution to the Red Cross (charitable contributions), $20.
     12 Received cash for delivery services rendered, $380.
     13 Received cash on account for services previously rendered, $100.
     15 Paid a part-time worker, $200.
     16 Paid electric bill, $36.
     18 Paid telephone bill, $46.
     19 Received cash on account for services previously rendered, $100.
     20 Andrews withdrew cash for personal use, $200.
     21 Paid for gas and oil, $32.
     22 Made payment on account (for office supplies), $40.
     24 Received cash for services rendered, $340.
     26 Paid for a magazine subscription (miscellaneous expense), $15.
     27 Received cash for services rendered, $180.
     27 Received cash on account for services previously rendered, $100.
     29 Paid for gasoline, $24.
     30 Paid a part-time worker, $200.

REQUIRED

1. Journalize the transactions for June in a two-column general journal. Use the following journal pages: June 1–10: page 7; June 11–20: page 8; June 21–30: page 9.

Jim's Quick Delivery
Trial Balance
May 31, 19--

ACCOUNT TITLE	ACCOUNT NO.	DEBIT BALANCE	CREDIT BALANCE
Cash	101	3 8 2 6 00	
Accounts Receivable	111	1 2 1 2 00	
Office Supplies	121	6 4 8 00	
Office Equipment	131	2 1 0 0 00	
Delivery Truck	151	8 0 0 0 00	
Accounts Payable	211		6 0 0 0 00
Jim Andrews, Capital	311		4 4 7 8 00
Jim Andrews, Drawing	312	1 8 0 0 00	
Delivery Fees	411		9 8 8 0 00
Rent Expense	511	9 0 0 00	
Wages Expense	523	1 2 0 0 00	
Telephone Expense	542	1 2 6 00	
Electricity Expense	546	9 8 00	
Gas and Oil Expense	551	1 8 6 00	
Advertising Expense	562	9 0 00	
Charitable Contributions Expense	571	6 0 00	
Miscellaneous Expense	592	1 1 2 00	
		20 3 5 8 00	20 3 5 8 00

2. Set up four-column general ledger accounts, entering the balances as of June 1. Post the entries from the general journal.

3. Prepare a trial balance.

4/5 **PROBLEM 4A2 JOURNALIZING AND POSTING TRANSACTIONS**
Annette Creighton opened Creighton Consulting. She rented a small office space and paid a part-time worker to answer the telephone and make deliveries. Her chart of accounts is as follows:

Chart of Accounts

Assets
101 Cash
111 Office Supplies
121 Office Equipment

Liabilities
211 Accounts Payable

Owner's Equity
311 Annette Creighton, Capital
312 Annette Creighton, Drawing

Revenues
411 Consulting Fees

Expenses
511 Rent Expense
522 Wages Expense
524 Telephone Expense
531 Utilities Expense
533 Transportation Expense
542 Advertising Expense
568 Miscellaneous Expense

Creighton's transactions for the first month of business are as follows:

Jan. 1 Creighton invested cash in the business, $10,000.
      1 Paid rent, $500.
      2 Purchased office supplies on account, $300.
      4 Purchased office equipment on account, $1,500.
      6 Received cash for services rendered, $580.
      7 Paid telephone bill, $42.
      8 Paid utilities bill, $38.
     10 Received cash for services rendered, $360.
     12 Made payment on account, $50.
     13 Paid for car rental while visiting an out-of-town client (transportation expense), $150.
     15 Paid part-time worker, $360.
     17 Received cash for services rendered, $420.
     18 Withdrew cash for personal use, $100.
     20 Paid for a newspaper ad, $26.
     22 Reimbursed part-time employee for cab fare incurred delivering materials to clients (transportation expense), $35.
     24 Paid for books on consulting practices (miscellaneous expense), $28.
     25 Received cash for services rendered, $320.
     27 Made payment on account for office equipment purchased, $150.
     29 Paid part-time worker, $360.
     30 Received cash for services rendered, $180.

REQUIRED

1. Journalize the transactions for January in a two-column general journal. Use the following journal page numbers: Jan 1–10, page 1; Jan 12–24, page 2; Jan 25–30, page 3.
2. Set up four-column general ledger accounts from the chart of accounts and post the transactions from the general journal.
3. Prepare a trial balance.
4. Prepare an income statement and a statement of owner's equity for the month of January, and a balance sheet as of January 31, 19--.

6 **PROBLEM 4A3 CORRECTING ERRORS**   Assuming that all entries have been posted, prepare correcting entries for each of the following errors:

1. The following entry was made to record the purchase of $500 in supplies on account:

Supplies	500	
Cash		500

2. The following entry was made to record the payment of $300 in wages:

Rent Expense	300	
Cash		300

3. The following entry was made to record a $200 payment to a supplier on account:

Supplies	100	
Cash		100

SERIES B EXERCISES

3 **EXERCISE 4B1 SOURCE DOCUMENTS** What type of information is found on each of the following source documents?

1. Cash register tape
2. Sales ticket (issued to customer)
3. Purchase invoice (received from supplier or vendor)
4. Check stub

4 **EXERCISE 4B2 GENERAL JOURNAL ENTRIES** For each of the following transactions, list the account to be debited and the account to be credited in the general journal.

1. Invested cash in the business, $1,000.
2. Performed services on account, $200.
3. Purchased office equipment on account, $500.
4. Received cash on account for services previously rendered, $200.
5. Made a payment on account, $100.

5 **EXERCISE 4B3 GENERAL LEDGER ACCOUNTS** Set up T accounts for each general ledger account needed for Exercise 4B2 and post debits and credits to the accounts. Foot the accounts and enter the balances. Prove that total debits equal total credits.

4 **EXERCISE 4B4 GENERAL JOURNAL ENTRIES** Sengel Moon opened The Bike Doctor. Journalize the following transactions that occurred during the month of October of the current year. Use the following journal pages: October 1–12, page 1 and October 14–29, page 2. Use the chart of accounts provided below.

Chart of Accounts

Assets
111 Cash
121 Office Supplies
131 Bicycle Parts

Liabilities
211 Accounts Payable

Owner's Equity
311 Sengel Moon, Capital
312 Sengel Moon, Drawing

Revenues
411 Repair Fees

Expenses
511 Rent Expense
521 Wages Expense
531 Telephone Expense
541 Utilities Expense
551 Miscellaneous Expense

Oct. 1 Moon invested cash in the business, $15,000.
2 Paid shop rental for the month, $300.
3 Purchased bicycle parts on account, $2,000.
5 Purchased office supplies on account, $250.
8 Paid telephone bill, $38.
9 Received cash for services, $140.

continued

Oct. 11 Paid a sports magazine subscription (miscellaneous expense), $15.
12 Made payment on account (see Oct. 3 transaction), $100.
14 Paid part-time employee, $300.
15 Received cash for services, $350.
16 Paid utilities bill, $48.
19 Received cash for services, $250.
23 Moon withdrew cash for personal use, $50.
25 Made payment on account (see Oct. 5 transaction), $50.
29 Paid part-time employee, $300.

5   **EXERCISE 4B5 GENERAL LEDGER ACCOUNTS; TRIAL BALANCE**
Set up four-column general ledger accounts. Post the transactions from Exercise 4B4 to the general ledger accounts and prepare a trial balance.

EXERCISE 4B6 FINANCIAL STATEMENTS   From the information in Exercises 4B4 and 4B5, prepare an income statement, a statement of owner's equity, and a balance sheet.

EXERCISE 4B7 FINANCIAL STATEMENTS   From the following trial balance taken after one month of operation, prepare an income statement, a statement of owner's equity, and a balance sheet. Assume that no additional investments were made during the month.

AT's Speaker's Bureau
Trial Balance
March 31, 19--

ACCOUNT TITLE	ACCOUNT NO.	DEBIT BALANCE	CREDIT BALANCE
Cash	101	6 6 0 0 00	
Accounts Receivable	111	2 8 0 0 00	
Office Supplies	121	1 0 0 0 00	
Office Equipment	131	1 5 0 0 00	
Accounts Payable	211		3 0 0 0 00
AT Speaker, Capital	311		6 0 9 8 00
AT Speaker, Drawing	312	8 0 0 00	
Speaking Fees	411		4 8 0 0 00
Rent Expense	511	2 0 0 00	
Telephone Expense	521	3 5 00	
Wages Expense	531	4 0 0 00	
Utilities Expense	541	8 8 00	
Travel Expense	551	4 5 0 00	
Miscellaneous Expense	561	2 5 00	
		13 8 9 8 00	13 8 9 8 00

6   **EXERCISE 4B8 FINDING AND CORRECTING ERRORS**   Mary Smith purchased $350 worth of office equipment on account. The following entry was recorded on April 6. Find the error(s) and correct it (them) using the ruling method.

9	19-- Apr.	6	Office Supplies			5 3 0 00			9
10			Cash				5 3 0 00	10
11			Purchased office equipment					11

On April 25, after the transactions had been posted, Smith discovered the following entry contains an error. When her customer received services, Cash was debited, but no cash was received. Correct the error in the journal using the correcting entry method.

28	19-- Apr.	21	Cash	111	3 0 0 00		28
29			Service Fees	411		3 0 0 00	29
30			Revenue earned from services				30

SERIES B PROBLEMS

4/5 **PROBLEM 4B1 JOURNALIZING AND POSTING TRANSACTIONS**
Ann Tailor owns a suit tailoring shop. She opened business in September. She rented a small work space and has an assistant to receive job orders and process claim tickets. Her trial balance shows her account balances for the first two months of business.

Tailor Tailoring
Trial Balance
October 31, 19--

ACCOUNT TITLE	ACCOUNT NO.	DEBIT BALANCE	CREDIT BALANCE
Cash	101	6 2 1 1 00	
Accounts Receivable	111	4 8 4 00	
Tailoring Supplies	121	1 0 0 0 00	
Tailoring Equipment	131	3 8 0 0 00	
Accounts Payable	211		4 1 2 5 00
Ann Tailor, Capital	311		6 1 3 0 00
Ann Tailor, Drawing	312	8 0 0 00	
Tailoring Fees	411		3 6 0 0 00
Rent Expense	511	6 0 0 00	
Wages Expense	522	8 0 0 00	
Telephone Expense	533	6 0 00	
Electricity Expense	555	4 4 00	
Advertising Expense	566	3 4 00	
Miscellaneous Expense	588	2 2 00	
		13 8 5 5 00	13 8 5 5 00

Tailor's transactions for November are as follows:

Nov.   1   Paid rent, $300.
2   Purchased tailoring supplies on account, $150.
3   Purchased a new button hole machine on account, $300.
5   Earned first week's revenue: $100 in cash and $300 on account.
8   Paid for newspaper advertising, $13.
9   Paid telephone bill, $28.
10   Paid electric bill, $21.
11   Received cash on account from customers, $200.
12   Earned second week's revenue: $200 in cash and $250 on account.
15   Paid assistant, $400.
16   Made payment on account, $100.
17   Paid for magazine subscription (miscellaneous expense), $12.
19   Earned third week's revenue: $300 in cash, $150 on account.
23   Received cash on account from customers, $300.
24   Paid for newspaper advertising, $13.
26   Paid for postage (miscellaneous expense), $12.
27   Earned fourth week's revenue: $200 in cash and $400 on account.
30   Received cash on account from customers, $400.

REQUIRED

1. Journalize the transactions for November in a two-column general journal. Use the following journal page numbers: Nov. 1–11, page 7; Nov. 12–24, page 8; Nov. 26–30, page 9.
2. Set up four-column general ledger accounts, entering the balances as of November 1, 19--. Post the entries from the general journal.
3. Prepare a trial balance.

4/5 **PROBLEM 4B2 JOURNALIZING AND POSTING TRANSACTIONS**
Benito Mendez opened Mendez Appraisals. He rented office space and has a part-time secretary to answer the telephone and make appraisal appointments. His chart of accounts is as follows:

Assets
111   Cash
122   Accounts Receivable
133   Office Supplies
146   Office Equipment

Liabilities
211   Accounts Payable

Owner's Equity
311   Benito Mendez, Capital
312   Benito Mendez, Drawing

Revenues
411   Appraisal Fees

Expenses
512   Rent Expense
532   Advertising Expense
544   Telephone Expense
555   Electricity Expense
562   Wages Expense
577   Transportation Expense
592   Miscellaneous Expense

Mendez's transactions for the first month of business are as follows:

May   1   Invested cash in the business, $5,000.
2   Paid rent, $500.

continued

May 3 Purchased office supplies, $100.
      4 Purchased office equipment on account, $2,000.
      5 Received cash for services rendered, $280.
      8 Paid telephone bill, $38.
      9 Paid electric bill, $42.
     10 Received cash for services rendered, $310.
     13 Paid part-time employee, $500.
     14 Paid car rental for out-of-town trip, $200.
     15 Paid for newspaper ad, $30.
     18 Received cash for services rendered, $620.
     19 Paid mileage reimbursement for part-time employee's use of personal car for business deliveries (transportation expense), $22.
     21 Withdrew cash for personal use, $50.
     23 Made payment on account for office equipment purchased earlier, $200.
     24 Earned appraisal fee, which will be paid in a week, $500.
     26 Paid for newspaper ad, $30.
     27 Paid for local softball team sponsorship (miscellaneous expense), $15.
     28 Paid part-time employee, $500.
     29 Received cash on account, $250.
     30 Received cash for services rendered, $280.
     31 Paid cab fare (transportation expense), $13.

REQUIRED

1. Journalize the transactions for May in a two-column general journal. Use the following journal page numbers: May 1–10, page 1; May 13–24, page 2; May 26–31, page 3.
2. Set up four-column general ledger accounts from the chart of accounts and post the transactions from the general journal.
3. Prepare a trial balance.
4. Prepare an income statement and a statement of owner's equity for the month of May, and a balance sheet as of May 31, 19--.

6 | **PROBLEM 4B3 CORRECTING ERRORS** Assuming that all entries have been posted, prepare correcting entries for each of the following errors:

1. The following entry was made to record the purchase of $400 in equipment on account:

Supplies	400	
Cash		400

2. The following entry was made to record the payment of $200 for advertising:

Repair Expense	200	
Cash		200

3. The following entry was made to record a $600 payment to a supplier on account:

Prepaid Insurance	400	
Cash		400

MASTERY PROBLEM

Barry Bird opened the Barry Bird Basketball Camp for children ages 10 through 18. Campers typically register for one week in June or July, arriving on Sunday and returning home the following Saturday. College players serve as cabin counselors and assist the local college and high school coaches who run the practice sessions. The registration fee includes a room, meals at a nearby restaurant, and basketball instruction. In the off-season, the facilities are used for weekend retreats and coaching clinics. Bird developed the following chart of accounts for his service business.

Assets
111 Cash
152 Office Supplies
182 Athletic Equipment
183 Basketball Facilities

Liabilities
216 Accounts Payable

Owner's Equity
311 Barry Bird, Capital
312 Barry Bird, Drawing

Revenues
411 Registration Fees

Expenses
532 Advertising Expense
542 Wages Expense
544 Food Expense
545 Telephone Expense
555 Utilities Expense
564 Postage Expense

The following transactions took place during the month of June.

June 1 Bird invested cash in business, $10,000.
      1 Purchased basketballs and other athletic equipment, $3,000.
      2 Paid Hite Advertising for fliers that had been mailed to prospective campers, $5,000.
      2 Collected registration fees, $15,000.
      2 Rogers Construction completed work on a new basketball court that cost $12,000. Arrangements were made to pay the bill in July.
      5 Purchased Office Supplies on account from Gordon Office Supplies, $300.
      6 Received bill from Magic's Restaurant for meals served to campers on account, $5,800.
      7 Collected registration fees, $16,200.
     10 Paid wages to camp counselors, $500.
     14 Collected registration fees, $13,500.
     14 Received bill from Magic's Restaurant for meals served to campers on account, $6,200.
     17 Paid wages to camp counselors, $500.
     18 Paid postage, $85.
     21 Collected registration fees, $15,200.
     22 Received bill from Magic's Restaurant for meals served to campers on account, $6,500.
     24 Paid wages to camp counselors, $500.
     28 Collected registration fees, $14,000.

continued

June   30   Received bill from Magic's Restaurant for meals served to campers on account, $7,200.
      30   Paid wages to camp counselors, $500.
      30   Paid Magic's Restaurant on account, $25,700.
      30   Paid utility bill, $500.
      30   Paid telephone bill, $120.
      30   Barry Bird withdrew cash for personal use, $2,000.

REQUIRED

1. Enter the above transactions in a general journal. Use the following journal pages: June 1–6, page 1; June 7–22, page 2; June 24–30, page 3.
2. Post the entries to the general ledger.
3. Prepare a trial balance.

5

Adjusting Entries and the Work Sheet

After reviewing the trial balance, Betsy Ray, Quick Dunk's controller commented, "These accounts don't look right. Let's make a few adjustments before we issue the financial statements." Does it seem appropriate to make adjustments prior to issuing financial statements?

Up to this point, you have learned how to journalize business transactions, post to the ledger, and prepare a trial balance. Now, it is time to learn how to make end-of-period adjustments to the accounts listed in the trial balance. This chapter explains the need for adjustments and illustrates how they are made using a work sheet.

END-OF-PERIOD ADJUSTMENTS

LO1   Prepare end-of-period adjustments.

Throughout the accounting period, business transactions are entered in the accounting system. These transactions are based on exchanges between the business and other firms and individuals. During the accounting period, other changes occur that affect the firm's financial condition. For example, equipment is wearing out, prepaid insurance and supplies are being used up, and employees are earning wages that have not yet been paid.

> Matching revenues earned with expenses incurred as a result of efforts to produce those revenues offers the best measure of net income.

The **matching principle** in accounting requires the matching of revenues earned during an accounting period with the expenses incurred to produce the revenues. This approach offers the best measure of net income. The income statement reports earnings for a specific period of time and the balance sheet reports the assets, liabilities, and owner's equity on a specific date. Thus, to follow the matching principle, the accounts must be brought up to date before financial statements are prepared. This requires adjusting some of the accounts listed in the trial balance. Figure 5-1 lists reasons to adjust the trial balance.

FIGURE 5-1   Reasons to Adjust the Trial Balance

1. To report all revenues earned during the accounting period.
2. To report all expenses incurred to produce the revenues earned in this accounting period.
3. To accurately report the assets on the balance sheet date. Some may have been used up during the accounting period.
4. To accurately report the liabilities on the balance sheet date. Expenses may have been incurred but not yet paid.

Generally, adjustments are made and financial statements prepared at the end of a twelve-month period called a **fiscal year**. This period does not need to be the same as a calendar year. In fact, some businesses schedule their fiscal year-end for a time when business is slow. In this chapter we continue the illustration of Jessie Jane's Campus Delivery and will prepare adjustments at the end of the first month of operations. We will focus on the following accounts: Supplies, Prepaid Insurance, Delivery Equipment, and Wages Expense.

Supplies

Since it is not practical to make a journal entry for supplies expense each time a supply, such as an envelope is used, one adjusting entry is made at the end of the accounting period.

During June, Jane purchased supplies consisting of paper, pens, and delivery envelopes for $80. *Since these supplies were expected to provide future benefits, Supplies, an asset, was debited at the time of the purchase.* No other entries were made to the supplies account during June. As reported on the trial balance in Figure 5-2, the $80 balance remains in the supplies account at the end of the month.

FIGURE 5-2   Trial Balance

Jessie Jane's Campus Delivery
Trial Balance
June 30, 19--

ACCOUNT TITLE	ACCOUNT NO.	DEBIT BALANCE	CREDIT BALANCE
Cash	111	3 7 0 00	
Accounts Receivable	131	5 0 0 00	
Supplies	151	8 0 00	
Prepaid Insurance	155	2 0 0 00	
Delivery Equipment	185	3 6 0 0 00	
Accounts Payable	216		1 8 0 0 00
Jessica Jane, Capital	311		2 0 0 0 00
Jessica Jane, Drawing	312	1 5 0 00	
Delivery Fees	411		2 0 0 0 00
Rent Expense	541	2 0 0 00	
Wages Expense	542	6 5 0 00	
Telephone Expense	545	5 0 00	
		5 8 0 0 00	5 8 0 0 00

As supplies are used, an expense is incurred. However, it is not practical to make a journal entry to recognize this expense and the reduction in the supplies account every time someone uses an envelope. It is more efficient to wait until the end of the accounting period to make one adjusting entry to reflect the expense incurred for the use of supplies for the entire month.

At the end of the month, an inventory, or physical count, of the remaining supplies is taken. The inventory shows that supplies costing $20 were still unused at the end of June. Since Jane bought supplies costing $80, and only $20 worth remain, supplies costing $60 must have been used ($80 – $20 = $60). Thus, supplies expense for the month is $60. (Trial balance is abbreviated TB in Figure 5-3 and other T account illustrations.)

LEARNING KEY

Abbreviations: Often debit and credit are abbreviated as:

Dr. = Debit
Cr. = Credit
(based on the Latin terms
"debere" and "credere").

FIGURE 5-3   Adjustment for Supplies

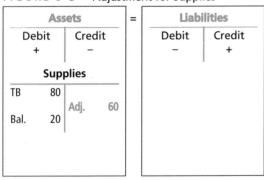

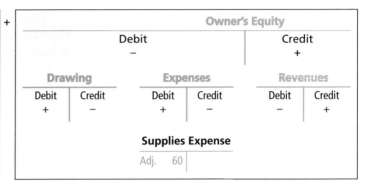

Since $60 worth of supplies have been used, Supplies Expense is debited and Supplies (asset) is credited for $60. Thus, as shown in Figure 5-4, supplies with a cost of $20 will be reported as an asset on the balance sheet and a supplies expense of $60 will be reported on the income statement. The adjusting entry affected an income statement account (Supplies Expense) and a balance sheet account (Supplies).

LEARNING KEY

By making an adjusting entry that debits Supplies Expense and credits Supplies, you are taking the amount of supplies used out of the Supplies account and putting it in Supplies Expense.

FIGURE 5-4   Effect of Adjusting Entry for Supplies on Financial Statements

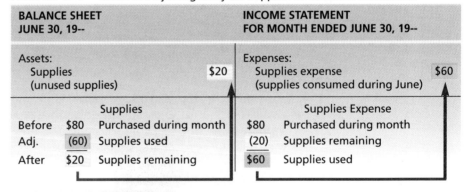

Prepaid Insurance

On June 18, Jane paid $200 for an eight-month liability insurance policy with coverage beginning on June 1. *Prepaid Insurance, an asset, was debit-*

ed because the insurance policy is expected to provide future benefits. The $200 balance is reported on the trial balance. As the insurance policy expires with the passage of time, the asset should be reduced and an expense recognized.

> **LEARNING KEY**   The $200 premium covers eight months. The cost for June is $25 ($200 ÷ 8 months).

Since the $200 premium covers eight months, the cost of the expired coverage for June is $25 ($200 ÷ 8 months). As shown in Figure 5-5, the adjusting entry is to debit Insurance Expense for $25 and credit Prepaid Insurance for $25. Figure 5-6 shows that the unexpired portion of the insurance premium will be reported on the balance sheet as Prepaid Insurance of $175. The expired portion will be reported on the income statement as Insurance Expense of $25.

FIGURE 5-5   Adjustment for Expired Insurance

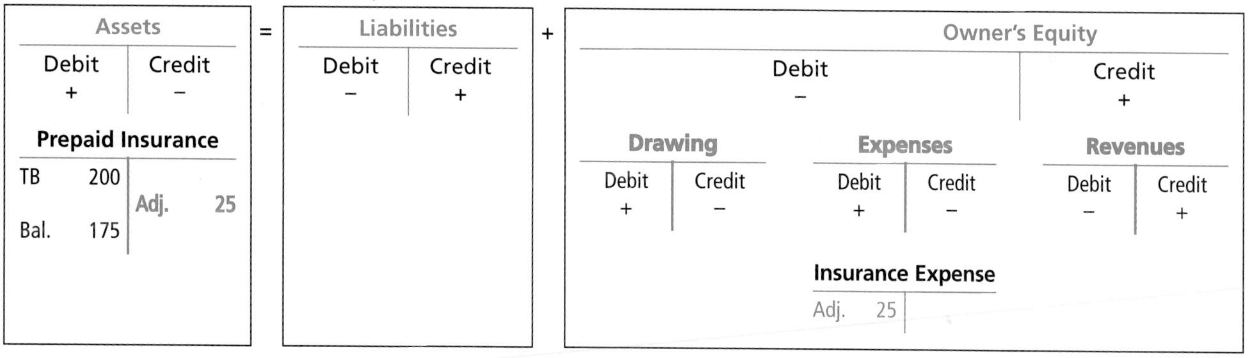

FIGURE 5-6   Effect of Adjusting Entry for Prepaid Insurance on Financial Statements

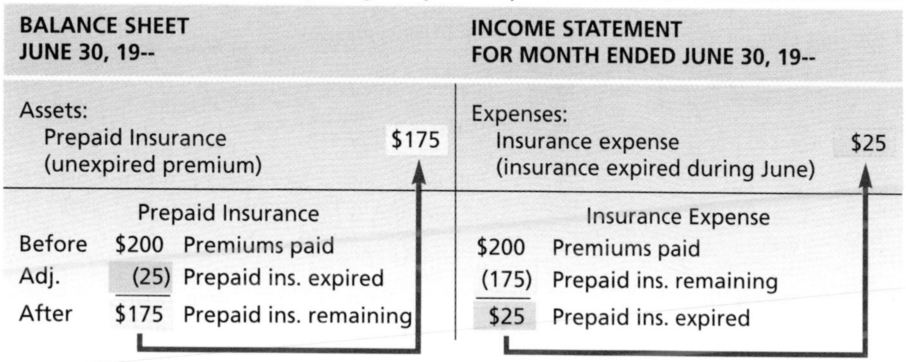

Wages Expense

Jane paid her part-time employees $650 on June 26. Since then, they have earned an additional $50, but have not yet been paid. The additional wages expense must be recognized.

Since the employees have not been paid, Wages Payable, a liability, should be established. Thus, Wages Expense is debited and Wages Payable is credited for $50 in Figure 5-7. Note in Figure 5-8 that Wages Expense of $700 is reported on the income statement and Wages Payable of $50 is reported on the balance sheet.

FIGURE 5-7 Adjustment for Unpaid Wages

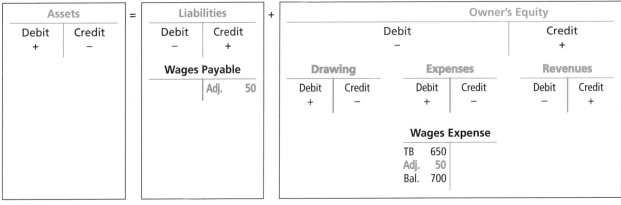

FIGURE 5-8 Effect of Adjusting Entry for Wages on Financial Statements

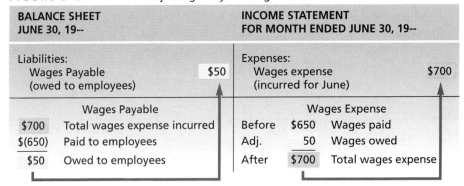

Depreciation Expense

The historical cost principle is an important accounting concept. Assets are recorded at their actual cost. This historical cost is not adjusted for changes in market values.

During the month of June, Jane purchased three motor scooters. Since the scooters will provide future benefits, they were recorded as assets in the delivery equipment account. Under the **historical cost principle**, assets are recorded at their actual cost, in this case $3,600. This cost remains on the books as long as the business owns the asset. No adjustments are made for changes in the market value of the asset. It does not matter whether the firm got a "good buy" or paid "too much" when the asset was purchased.

The period of time that an asset is expected to help produce revenues is called its **useful life**. The asset's useful life expires as a result of wear and tear or because it no longer satisfies the needs of the business. For example, as Jane adds miles to her scooters, they will become less reliable and will eventually fail to run. As this happens, depreciation expense should be recognized and the value of the asset should be reduced. **Depreciation** is a method of *matching* an asset's original cost against the revenues produced over its useful life. There are many depreciation methods. In our example, we will use the **straight-line method**.

Let's assume that Jane's motor scooters have useful lives of three years and will have no salvage value at the end of that time period. **Salvage value** is the expected **market value** or selling price of the asset at the end of its useful life. Let's also assume that a full month's depreciation is recognized in the month in which an asset is purchased. The cost of the scooters that is subject to depreciation, called **depreciable cost**, is $3,600.

The depreciable cost is spread over 36 months (3 years x 12 months). Thus, the straight-line depreciation expense for the month of June is $100 ($3,600 ÷ 36 months).

Straight-Line Depreciation

Original Cost – Salvage Value = Depreciable Cost

$$\frac{\text{Depreciable Cost}}{\text{Estimated Useful Life}} = \frac{\$3,600}{36 \text{ months}} = \$100 \text{ per month}$$

LEARNING KEY Depreciable assets provide benefits over more than one year. Therefore, rather than directly crediting the asset to show that it has been depreciated, a *contra-asset* account is used.

When we made adjustments for supplies and prepaid insurance, the asset accounts were credited to show that they had been consumed. Assets expected to provide benefits over a longer period of time, called **plant assets**, require a different approach. The business maintains a record of the original cost and the amount of depreciation taken since the asset was acquired. By comparing these two amounts, the reader can estimate the relative age of the assets. Thus, instead of crediting Delivery Equipment for the amount of depreciation, a contra-asset account, Accumulated Depreciation—Delivery Equipment, is credited. A **contra-asset** has a credit balance and is deducted from the related asset account on the balance sheet.

As shown in Figure 5-9, the appropriate adjusting entry consists of a debit to Depreciation Expense—Delivery Equipment and a credit to Accumulated Depreciation—Delivery Equipment. Note the position of the accumulated depreciation account in the accounting equation. It is shown in the asset section, directly beneath Delivery Equipment. Contra-asset accounts should always be shown along with the related asset account. Therefore, Delivery Equipment and Accumulated Depreciation—Delivery Equipment are shown together.

The same concept is used on the balance sheet. Note in Figure 5-10 that Accumulated Depreciation is reported immediately beneath Delivery Equipment as a deduction. The difference between these accounts is known as the **book value**, or **undepreciated cost**, of the delivery equipment. Book value simply means the value carried on the books or in the accounting

FIGURE 5-9   Adjustment for Depreciation of Delivery Equipment

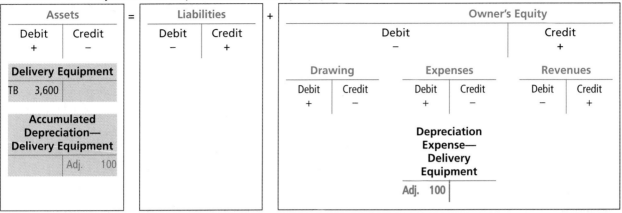

FIGURE 5-10   Effect of Adjusting Entry for Depreciation on Financial Statements for June

BALANCE SHEET JUNE 30, 19--			INCOME STATEMENT FOR MONTH ENDED JUNE 30, 19--	
Assets:			Expenses:	
Delivery equipment	$3,600		Depreciation expense	$100
Less: Accumulated depreciation	100	$3,500	(Expired cost for June)	
		(Book value)		

records. It does *not* represent the **market value**, or selling price, of the asset.

LEARNING KEY   Cost of Plant Assets – Accumulated Depreciation = Book Value

If no delivery equipment is bought or sold during the next month, the same adjusting entry would be made at the end of July. If an income statement for the month of July and a balance sheet as of July 31 were prepared, the amounts shown in Figure 5-11 would be reported for the delivery equipment.

FIGURE 5-11   Effect of Adjusting Entry for Depreciation on Financial Statements for July

BALANCE SHEET JULY 31, 19--			INCOME STATEMENT FOR MONTH ENDED JULY 31, 19--	
Assets:			Expenses:	
Delivery equipment	$3,600		Depreciation expense	$100
Less: Accumulated depreciation	200	$3,400	(Expired cost for July)	
		(Book value)		

The cost ($3,600) remains unchanged, but the accumulated depreciation has increased to $200. This represents *the depreciation that has accumulated* since the delivery equipment was purchased ($100 in June and $100 in

July). The depreciation expense for July is $100, the same as reported for June. Depreciation expense is reported for a specific time period. It does not accumulate across reporting periods.

Expanded Chart of Accounts

Several new accounts were needed to make the adjusting entries. New accounts are easily added to the chart of accounts, as shown in Figure 5-12. Note the close relationship between assets and contra-assets in the numbering of the accounts. Contra-accounts carry the same number as the related asset account with a ".1" suffix. For example, Delivery Equipment is account number 185 and the contra-asset account, Accumulated Depreciation—Delivery Equipment, is account number 185.1.

FIGURE 5-12 Expanded Chart of Accounts

Jessie Jane's Campus Delivery Chart of Accounts				
Assets			**Revenue**	
111	Cash		411	Delivery Fees
131	Accounts Receivable			
151	Supplies		**Expenses**	**(500–599)**
155	Prepaid Insurance		541	Rent Expense
185	Delivery Equipment		542	Wages Expense
185.1	Accumulated Depr.—		543	Supplies Expense
	Delivery Equipment		545	Telephone Expense
			547	Depr. Expense—
Liabilities				Delivery Equipment
216	Accounts Payable		559	Insurance Expense
219	Wages Payable			
Owner's Equity				
311	Jessica Jane, Capital			
312	Jessica Jane, Drawing			

THE WORK SHEET

LO2 Prepare a work sheet.

A **work sheet** pulls together all of the information needed to enter adjusting entries and prepare the financial statements. Work sheets are not financial statements and are not a formal part of the accounting system. Ordinarily, only the accountant uses a work sheet. For this reason, a work sheet is usually prepared in pencil or as a spreadsheet on a computer.

The Ten-Column Work Sheet

Although a work sheet can take several forms, a common format has a column for account titles and ten amount columns grouped into five pairs. The work sheet format and the five steps in preparing the work sheet are illustrated in Figure 5-13. As with financial statements, the work sheet has a heading consisting of the name of the company, name of the working paper, and the date of the accounting period just ended. The five major column headings for the work sheet are: Trial Balance, Adjustments, Adjusted Trial Balance, Income Statement, and Balance Sheet.

Preparing the Work Sheet

Let's apply the five steps required for the preparation of a work sheet to Jessie Jane's Campus Delivery.

STEP 1   **Prepare the Trial Balance.**   As shown in Figure 5-14, the first pair of amount columns is for the trial balance. The trial balance assures the equality of the debits and credits before the adjustment process begins. The columns should be double ruled to show that they are equal.

You are already familiar with a trial balance. Here we are simply copying a trial balance to a different form, called a work sheet.

Note that all accounts listed in the expanded chart of accounts are included in the Trial Balance columns of the work sheet. This is done even though some accounts have zero balances. The accounts with zero balances could be added to the bottom of the list as they are needed for adjusting entries. However, it is easier to include them now, especially if preparing the work sheet on an electronic spreadsheet. Listing the accounts within their proper classifications (assets, liabilities, etc.) also makes it easier to extend the amounts to the proper columns.

STEP 2   **Prepare the Adjustments.**   As shown in Figure 5-15, the second pair of amount columns is used to prepare the adjusting entries. Enter the adjustments directly in these columns. When an account is debited or credited, the amount is entered on the same line as the name of the account and in the appropriate Adjustments Debit or Credit column. Each adjusting entry made on the work sheet is identified by a small letter in parentheses.

For adjustments (a), (b), and (d), we are simply recognizing that assets have been used. When this happens, the asset must be decreased and an expense recognized. Note that the reported amount for delivery equipment is reduced by crediting a contra-asset.

FIGURE 5-13 Steps in Preparing the Work Sheet

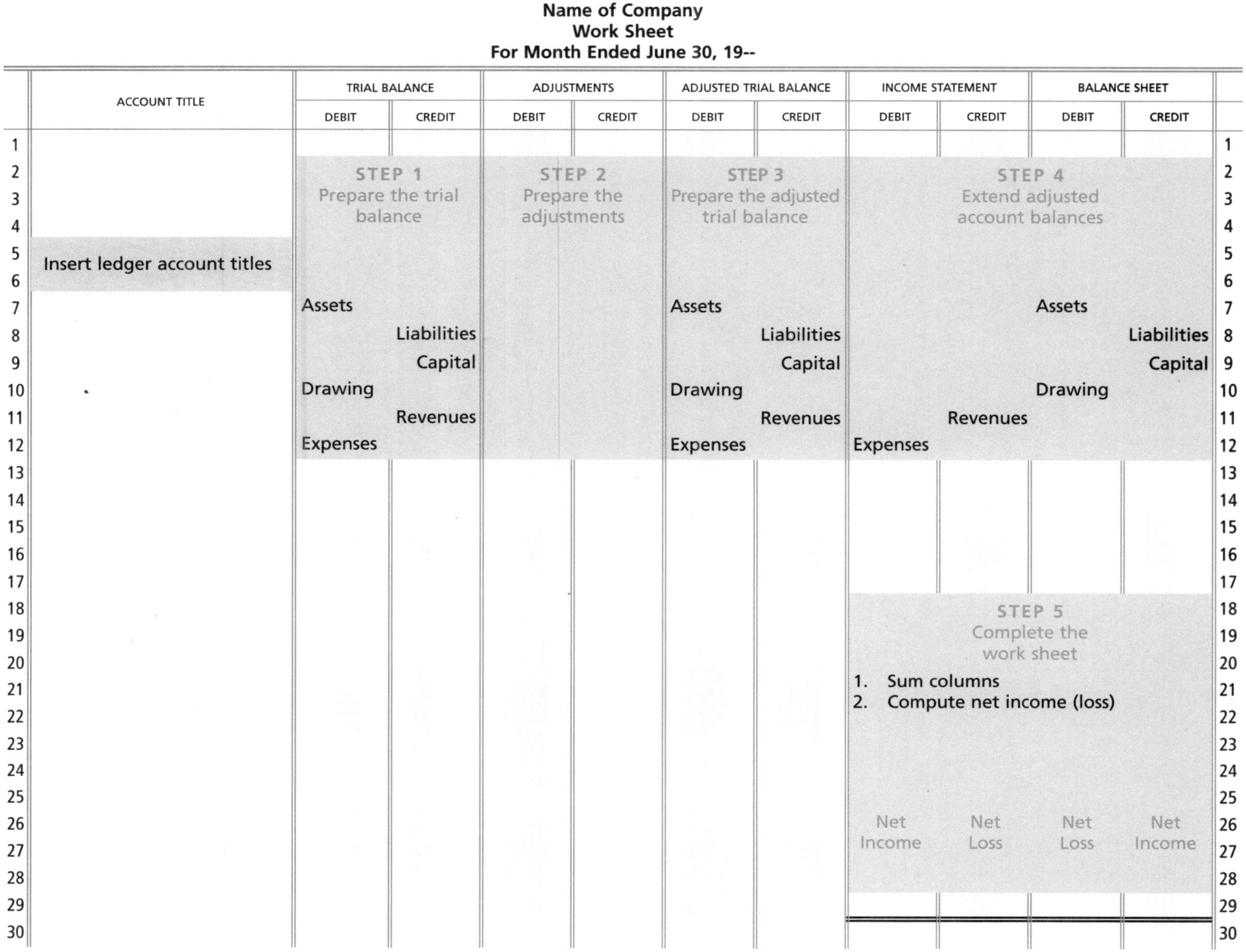

Name of Company
Work Sheet
For Month Ended June 30, 19--

ACCOUNT TITLE	TRIAL BALANCE		ADJUSTMENTS		ADJUSTED TRIAL BALANCE		INCOME STATEMENT		BALANCE SHEET	
	DEBIT	CREDIT	DEBIT	CREDIT	DEBIT	CREDIT	DEBIT	CREDIT	DEBIT	CREDIT

Insert ledger account titles

STEP 1 — Prepare the trial balance: Assets, Drawing, Expenses (Debit); Liabilities, Capital, Revenues (Credit)

STEP 2 — Prepare the adjustments

STEP 3 — Prepare the adjusted trial balance: Assets, Drawing, Expenses (Debit); Liabilities, Capital, Revenues (Credit)

STEP 4 — Extend adjusted account balances: Assets, Drawing (Balance Sheet Debit); Liabilities, Capital (Balance Sheet Credit); Expenses (Income Statement Debit); Revenues (Income Statement Credit)

STEP 5 — Complete the work sheet
1. Sum columns
2. Compute net income (loss)
Net Income / Net Loss

FIGURE 5-14   Step 1—Prepare the Trial Balance

Jessie Jane's Campus Delivery
Work Sheet
For Month Ended June 30, 19--

	ACCOUNT TITLE	TRIAL BALANCE		ADJUSTMENTS		ADJUSTED TRIAL BALANCE		INCOME STATEMENT		BALANCE SHEET	
		DEBIT	CREDIT	DEBIT	CREDIT	DEBIT	CREDIT	DEBIT	CREDIT	DEBIT	CREDIT
1	Cash	3700.00									
2	Accounts Receivable	500.00									
3	Supplies	80.00									
4	Prepaid Insurance	200.00									
5	Delivery Equipment	3600.00									
6	Accum. Depr.—Del. Equip.										
7	Accounts Payable		1800.00								
8	Wages Payable										
9	Jessica Jane, Capital		2000.00								
10	Jessica Jane, Drawing	150.00									
11	Delivery Fees		2000.00								
12	Rent Expense	200.00									
13	Wages Expense	650.00									
14	Supplies Expense										
15	Telephone Expense	50.00									
16	Depr. Expense—Del. Equip.										
17	Insurance Expense										
18		5800.00	5800.00								
19											
20											
21											
22											
23											
24											
25											
26											
27											
28											
29											
30											

STEP 1

Preparing the Work Sheet

STEP 1 **Prepare the Trial Balance.**

- Write the heading, account titles, and the debit and credit amounts from the general ledger.
- Place a single rule across the Trial Balance columns and total the debit and credit amounts.
- Place a double rule under the columns to show that they are equal.

STEP 2 **Prepare the Adjustments.**

- Record the adjustments.
  Hint: Make certain that each adjustment is on the same line as the account name and in the appropriate column.
  Hint: Identify each adjusting entry by a letter in parentheses.
- Rule the Adjusted Trial Balance columns.
- Total the debit and credit columns and double rule the columns to show equality.

STEP 3 **Prepare the Adjusted Trial Balance.**

- Extend those debits and credits that are not adjusted directly to the appropriate Adjusted Trial Balance column.
- Enter the adjusted balances in the appropriate Adjusted Trial Balance column.
  Hint: If an account has a debit and a credit, subtract the adjustment. If an account has two debits or two credits, add the adjustment.
- Single rule the Adjusted Trial Balance columns. Total and double rule the debit and credit columns.

STEP 4 **Extend Adjusted Balances to the Income Statement and Balance Sheet Columns.**

- Extend all revenue accounts to the Income Statement Credit column.
- Extend all expense accounts to the Income Statement Debit column.
- Extend the asset and drawing accounts to the Balance Sheet Debit column.
- Extend the liability and owner's capital accounts to the Balance Sheet Credit column.

STEP 5 **Complete the Work Sheet.**

- Rule and total the Income Statement and Balance Sheet columns.
- Calculate the difference between the Income Statement Debit and Credit columns. Calculate the difference between the Balance Sheet Debit and Credit columns.
  Hint: If the Income Statement credits exceed debits, net income has occurred; otherwise a net loss has occurred. If the Balance Sheet debits exceed the credits, the difference is net income; otherwise a net loss has occurred.
  Hint: The difference between the Balance Sheet columns and the difference between the Income Statement columns should be the same.
- Add the net income to the Income Statement Debit column or add the net loss to the Income Statement Credit column. Add the net income to the Balance Sheet Credit column or the net loss to the Balance Sheet Debit column.
- Total and double rule the columns.

ADJUSTMENT (a):

Supplies costing $60 were used during June.

	Debit	Credit
Supplies Expense	60	
Supplies		60

ADJUSTMENT (b):

One month's insurance premium has expired.

Insurance Expense	25	
Prepaid Insurance		25

ADJUSTMENT (c):

Employees earned $50 that has not yet been paid.

Wages Expense	50	
Wages Payable		50

> Adjustment (c) recognizes an economic event that has not required an actual transaction yet. Employees earned wages, but have not been paid. The adjustment recognizes an expense and a liability.

ADJUSTMENT (d):

Depreciation on the motor scooters is recognized.

Depreciation Expense—Delivery Equipment	100	
Accumulated Depreciation—Delivery Equipment		100

When all adjustments have been entered on the work sheet, each column should be totaled to assure that the debits equal the credits for all entries. After balancing the columns, they should be double ruled.

STEP 3   **Prepare the Adjusted Trial Balance.**   As shown in Figure 5-16, the third pair of amount columns of the work sheet are the **Adjusted Trial Balance Columns**. When an account balance is not affected by entries in the Adjustments columns, the amount in the Trial Balance columns is extended directly to the Adjusted Trial Balance columns. *When affected by an entry in the Adjustments columns, the balance to be entered in the Adjusted Trial Balance columns increases or decreases by the amount of the adjusting entry.*

For example, in Jessica Jane's business, Supplies is listed in the Trial Balance Debit column as $80. Since the entry of $60 is in the Adjustments Credit column, the amount extended to the Adjusted Trial Balance Debit column is $20 ($80 − $60).

Wages Expense is listed in the Trial Balance Debit column as $650. Since $50 is in the Adjustments Debit column, the amount extended to the Adjusted Trial Balance Debit column is $700 ($650 + $50).

After all extensions have been made, the Adjusted Trial Balance columns are totaled to prove the equality of the debits and the credits. Once balanced, the columns are double ruled.

STEP 4   **Extend Adjusted Balances to the Income Statement and Balance Sheet Columns.**   As shown in Figure 5-17, each account listed in the Adjusted Trial Balance must be extended to either the Income Statement or Balance Sheet columns. The **Income Statement columns** show the amounts that will be reported in the income statement. All revenue accounts are extended to the Income Statement Credit column and expense accounts are extended to the Income Statement Debit column.

> The Balance Sheet columns show the amounts in both the balance sheet and the statement of owner's equity.

The asset, liability, drawing, and capital accounts are extended to the **Balance Sheet columns**. Although called the Balance Sheet columns, these columns of the work sheet show the amounts that will be reported in the balance sheet and the statement of owner's equity. The asset and drawing accounts are extended to the Balance Sheet Debit column. The liability and owner's capital accounts are extended to the Balance Sheet Credit column.

STEP 5   **Complete the Work Sheet.**   To complete the work sheet, first total the Income Statement columns. If the total of the credits (revenues) exceeds the total of the debits (expenses), the difference represents net income. If the total of the debits exceeds the total of the credits, the difference represents a net loss.

The Income Statement columns of Jane's work sheet in Figure 5-18 show total credits of $2,000 and total debits of $1,135. The difference, $865, is the net income for the month of June. This amount should be added to the debit column to balance the Income Statement columns and "Net Income" should be written on the same line in the Account Title column. If the business had a net loss, the amount of the loss would be added to the Income Statement Credit column and the words "Net Loss" would be written in the Account Title column. Once balanced, the columns should be double ruled.

Finally, the Balance Sheet columns are totaled. The difference between the totals of these columns also is the amount of net income or net loss for the accounting period. If the total debits exceed the total credits, the difference is net income. If the total credits exceed the total debits, the difference is a net loss. This difference should be the same as the difference we found for the Income Statement columns.

The Balance Sheet columns of Jane's work sheet show total debits of $4,815 and total credits of $3,950. The difference of $865 represents the amount of net income for the month. This amount is added to the credit column to balance the Balance Sheet columns. If the business had a net loss, this amount would be added to the Balance Sheet Debit column. Once balanced, the columns should be double ruled.

A trick for remembering the appropriate placement of the net income and net loss is the following: Net Income *apart*; Net Loss *together*. Figure 5-19 illustrates this learning aid.

FIGURE 5-19   Net Income Apart, Net Loss Together

	Income Statement		Balance Sheet				Income Statement		Balance Sheet	
	Debit	Credit	Debit	Credit			Debit	Credit	Debit	Credit
	1,135	2,000	4,815	3,950			2,500	2,000	5,015	5,515
Net Income	865			865		Net Loss		500	500	
	2,000	2,000	4,815	4,815			2,500	2,500	5,515	5,515
		Apart						Together		

FINDING ERRORS ON THE WORK SHEET

LO3   Describe methods for finding errors on the work sheet.

If any of the columns on the work sheet do not balance, you must find the error before you continue. Once you are confident that the work sheet is accurate, you are ready to journalize the adjusting entries and prepare financial statements. Figure 5-20 offers tips for finding errors on the work sheet.

FIGURE 5-20   Finding Errors on the Work Sheet

TIPS FOR FINDING ERRORS ON THE WORK SHEET
1. Check the addition of all columns.
2. Check the addition and subtraction required when extending to the Adjusted Trial Balance columns.
3. Make sure the adjusted account balances have been extended to the appropriate columns.
4. Make sure that the net income or net loss has been added to the appropriate columns.

JOURNALIZING ADJUSTING ENTRIES

LO4   Journalize adjusting entries.

Keep in mind that the work sheet simply helps the accountant organize the end-of-period work. Writing the adjustments on the work sheet has no effect on the ledger accounts in the accounting system. The only way to change the balance of a ledger account is to make a journal entry. Once the adjustments have been entered on the work sheet, simply copy the adjustments from the work sheet to the journal.

Jane's adjusting entries are illustrated in Figure 5-21 as they would appear in a general journal. Note that the last day of the accounting period, June 30, has been entered in the date column and *"Adjusting Entries"* is written in the Description column prior to the first adjusting entry. No explanation is required in the Description column for individual adjusting entries. We simply label them as adjusting entries.

POSTING ADJUSTING ENTRIES

LO5   Post adjusting entries to the general ledger.

Adjusting entries are posted to the general ledger in the same manner as all other entries, except that *"Adjusting"* is written in the Item column of the general ledger. Figure 5-22 shows the posting of the adjusting entry for supplies.

FIGURE 5-21   Adjusting Entries

	DATE		DESCRIPTION	POST. REF.	DEBIT	CREDIT	
1			**Adjusting Entries**				1
2	June	30	Supplies Expense	543	6 0 00		2
3			Supplies	151		6 0 00	3
4							4
5		30	Insurance Expense	548	2 5 00		5
6			Prepaid Insurance	155		2 5 00	6
7							7
8		30	Wages Expense	542	5 0 00		8
9			Wages Payable	219		5 0 00	9
10							10
11		30	Depr. Expense—Delivery Equip.	547	1 0 0 00		11
12			Accum. Depr.—Delivery Equip.	185.1		1 0 0 00	12

Note: GENERAL JOURNAL — PAGE 3, 19--

FIGURE 5-22   Posting the Adjusting Entry for Supplies

GENERAL LEDGER

ACCOUNT: **Supplies**   ACCOUNT NO. **151**

DATE		ITEM	POST. REF.	DEBIT	CREDIT	BALANCE DEBIT	BALANCE CREDIT
June	16		J1	8 0 00		8 0 00	
	30	Adjusting	J3		6 0 00	2 0 00	

Note: 19--

ACCOUNT: **Supplies Expense**   ACCOUNT NO. **543**

DATE		ITEM	POST. REF.	DEBIT	CREDIT	BALANCE DEBIT	BALANCE CREDIT
June	30	Adjusting	J3	6 0 00		6 0 00	

Note: 19--

KEY POINTS

1   End-of-period adjustments are necessary to bring the general ledger accounts up to date prior to preparing financial statements. Reasons to adjust the trial balance are:

1. To report all revenues earned during the accounting period.
2. To report all expenses incurred to produce the revenues.
3. To accurately report the assets on the balance sheet date. Some may have been used during the accounting period.
4. To accurately report the liabilities on the balance sheet date. Expenses may have been incurred, but not yet paid.

2 Steps in preparing the work sheet are:

1. Prepare the trial balance.
2. Prepare the adjustments.
3. Prepare the adjusted trial balance.
4. Extend the adjusted account balances to the Income Statement and Balance Sheet columns.
5. Total the Income Statement and Balance Sheet columns to compute the net income or net loss.

3 Tips for finding errors on the work sheet include:

1. Check the addition of all columns.
2. Check the addition and subtraction required when extending to the Adjusted Trial Balance columns.
3. Make sure the adjusted account balances have been extended to the appropriate columns.
4. Make sure that the net income or net loss has been added to the appropriate columns.

4 The adjustments are copied from the work sheet to the journal. The last day of the accounting period is entered in the Date column and "Adjusting Entries" is written in the Description column.

5 Adjusting entries are posted to the general ledger in the same manner as all other entries, except that "Adjusting" is written in the Item column of the general ledger.

KEY TERMS

Adjusted Trial Balance columns 132H   The third pair of amount columns of the work sheet.

Balance Sheet columns 133   The work sheet columns that show the amounts that will be reported in the balance sheet and the statement of owner's equity.

book value 129   The difference between the asset account and its related accumulated depreciation account. The value reflected by the accounting records.

contra-asset 129   An account with a credit balance that is deducted from the related asset account on the balance sheet.

depreciable cost 129   The cost of an asset that is subject to depreciation.

depreciation 129   A method of matching an asset's original cost against the revenues produced over its useful life.

fiscal year 124   A twelve-month period for which financial reports are prepared.

historical cost principle 128   Under this principle, assets are recorded at their actual cost.

Income Statement columns 133   The work sheet columns that show the amounts that will be reported in the income statement.

market value 129   The amount an item can be sold for under normal economic conditions.

matching principle 124   A principle that requires the matching of revenues earned during an accounting period with the expenses incurred to produce the revenues.

plant assets 129   Assets expected to provide benefits over a long period of time.

salvage value 129   The expected market value of an asset at the end of its useful life.

straight-line method 129   A depreciation method in which the depreciable cost is divided by the estimated useful life.

undepreciated cost 129   The difference between the asset account and its related accumulated depreciation account. Also known as book value.

useful life 128   The period of time that an asset is expected to help produce revenues.

work sheet 131   A form used to pull together all of the information needed to enter adjusting entries and prepare the financial statements.

REVIEW QUESTIONS

1. Explain the matching principle.
2. Explain the historical cost principle.
3. Describe a plant asset.
4. What is a contra-asset?
5. What is the useful life of an asset?
6. What is the purpose of depreciation?
7. What is an asset's depreciable cost?
8. What is the book value of an asset?
9. Explain the purpose of the work sheet.
10. Identify the five major column headings on a work sheet.
11. List the five steps taken in preparing a work sheet.
12. Describe four tips for finding errors on the work sheet.

MANAGING YOUR WRITING

Delia Alvarez, owner of Delia's Lawn Service, wants to borrow money to buy new lawn equipment. A local bank has asked for financial statements. Alvarez has asked you to prepare financial statements for the year ended December 31, 19--. You have been given the unadjusted trial balance shown on the next page and suspect that Alvarez expects you to base your statements on this information. You are concerned, however, that some of the account balances may need to be adjusted. Write a memo to Alvarez explaining what additional information you need before you can prepare the financial statements. Alvarez is not familiar with accounting issues.

Therefore, explain in your memo why you need this information, the potential impact of this information on the financial statements, and the importance of making these adjustments before approaching the bank for a loan.

Delia's Lawn Service
Trial Balance
December 31, 19--

ACCOUNT TITLE	ACCOUNT NO.	DEBIT BALANCE	CREDIT BALANCE
Cash		7 7 0 00	
Accounts Receivable		1 7 0 0 00	
Supplies		2 8 0 00	
Prepaid Insurance		4 0 0 00	
Lawn Equipment		13 8 0 0 00	
Accounts Payable			2 2 0 0 00
Delia Alvarez, Capital			3 0 0 0 00
Delia Alvarez, Drawing		3 5 0 00	
Lawn Cutting Fees			52 4 0 0 00
Rent Expense		1 2 0 0 00	
Wages Expense		35 8 5 0 00	
Gas and Oil Expense		3 2 5 0 00	
		57 6 0 0 00	57 6 0 0 00

DEMONSTRATION PROBLEM

Justin Park is a lawyer specializing in corporate tax law. He began his practice on January 1. A chart of accounts and trial balance taken on December 31, 19-1 are provided below.

Information for year-end adjustments:

(a) Office supplies on hand at year end amounted to $300.
(b) On January 1, 19-1, Park purchased office equipment costing $15,000 with an expected life of five years and no salvage value.
(c) Computer equipment costing $6,000 with an expected life of three years and no salvage value was purchased on July 1, 19-1. Assume that Park computes depreciation to the nearest full month.
(d) A premium of $1,200 for a one-year insurance policy was paid on December 1, 19-1.
(e) Wages earned by Park's part-time secretary, which have not yet been paid, amount to $300.

REQUIRED
1. Prepare the work sheet for the year ended December 31, 19-1.
2. Prepare adjusting entries in a general journal.

Justin Park Legal Services
Chart of Accounts

Assets		Revenues	
111	Cash	411	Client Fees
152	Office Supplies		
155	Prepaid Insurance	**Expenses**	
181	Office Equipment	541	Rent Expense
181.1	Accum. Depr.—	542	Wages Expense
	Office Equip.	543	Office Supp. Exp.
194	Computer Equip.	545	Telephone Expense
194.1	Accum. Depr.—	547	Depr. Expense—
	Computer Equip.		Office Equip.
		548	Depr. Expense—
Liabilities			Computer Equip.
216	Accounts Payable	555	Utilities Expense
218	Notes Payable	559	Insurance Expense
219	Wages Payable		
Owner's Equity			
311	Justin Park, Capital		
312	Justin Park, Drawing		

Justin Park Legal Services
Trial Balance
December 31, 19-1

ACCOUNT TITLE	ACCOUNT NO.	DEBIT BALANCE	CREDIT BALANCE
Cash		7 0 0 0 00	
Office Supplies		8 0 0 00	
Prepaid Insurance		1 2 0 0 00	
Office Equipment		15 0 0 0 00	
Computer Equipment		6 0 0 0 00	
Accounts Payable			5 0 0 00
Notes Payable			5 0 0 0 00
Justin Park, Capital			11 4 0 0 00
Justin Park, Drawing		5 0 0 0 00	
Client Fees			40 0 0 0 00
Rent Expense		5 0 0 0 00	
Wages Expense		12 0 0 0 00	
Telephone Expense		1 0 0 0 00	
Utilities Expense		3 9 0 0 00	
		56 9 0 0 00	56 9 0 0 00

SOLUTION 1.

Justin Park Legal Services
Work Sheet
For Year Ended December 31, 19-1

	ACCOUNT TITLE	TRIAL BALANCE DEBIT	TRIAL BALANCE CREDIT	ADJUSTMENTS DEBIT	ADJUSTMENTS CREDIT	ADJUSTED TRIAL BALANCE DEBIT	ADJUSTED TRIAL BALANCE CREDIT	INCOME STATEMENT DEBIT	INCOME STATEMENT CREDIT	BALANCE SHEET DEBIT	BALANCE SHEET CREDIT	
1	Cash	7 0 0 0 00				7 0 0 0 00				7 0 0 0 00		1
2	Office Supplies	8 0 0 00			(a) 5 0 0 00	3 0 0 00				3 0 0 00		2
3	Prepaid Insurance	1 2 0 0 00			(d) 1 0 0 00	1 1 0 0 00				1 1 0 0 00		3
4	Office Equipment	15 0 0 0 00				15 0 0 0 00				15 0 0 0 00		4
5	Accum. Depr.—Office Equip.				(b) 3 0 0 0 00		3 0 0 0 00				3 0 0 0 00	5
6	Computer Equipment	6 0 0 0 00				6 0 0 0 00				6 0 0 0 00		6
7	Accum. Depr.—Computer Equip.				(c) 1 0 0 0 00		1 0 0 0 00				1 0 0 0 00	7
8	Accounts Payable		5 0 0 00				5 0 0 00				5 0 0 00	8
9	Notes Payable		5 0 0 0 00				5 0 0 0 00				5 0 0 0 00	9
10	Wages Payable				(e) 3 0 0 00		3 0 0 00				3 0 0 00	10
11	Justin Park, Capital		11 4 0 0 00				11 4 0 0 00				11 4 0 0 00	11
12	Justin Park, Drawing	5 0 0 0 00				5 0 0 0 00				5 0 0 0 00		12
13	Client Fees		40 0 0 0 00				40 0 0 0 00		40 0 0 0 00			13
14	Rent Expense	5 0 0 0 00				5 0 0 0 00		5 0 0 0 00				14
15	Wages Expense	12 0 0 0 00		(e) 3 0 0 00		12 3 0 0 00		12 3 0 0 00				15
16	Office Supplies Expense			(a) 5 0 0 00		5 0 0 00		5 0 0 00				16
17	Telephone Expense	1 0 0 0 00				1 0 0 0 00		1 0 0 0 00				17
18	Depr. Expense—Office Equip.			(b) 3 0 0 0 00		3 0 0 0 00		3 0 0 0 00				18
19	Depr. Expense—Computer Equip.			(c) 1 0 0 0 00		1 0 0 0 00		1 0 0 0 00				19
20	Utilities Expense	3 9 0 0 00				3 9 0 0 00		3 9 0 0 00				20
21	Insurance Expense			(d) 1 0 0 00		1 0 0 00		1 0 0 00				21
22		56 9 0 0 00	56 9 0 0 00	4 9 0 0 00	4 9 0 0 00	61 2 0 0 00	61 2 0 0 00	26 8 0 0 00	40 0 0 0 00	34 4 0 0 00	21 2 0 0 00	22
23	Net Income							13 2 0 0 00			13 2 0 0 00	23
24								40 0 0 0 00	40 0 0 0 00	34 4 0 0 00	34 4 0 0 00	24
25												25

2.

				GENERAL JOURNAL												PAGE 11	
	DATE		DESCRIPTION			POST. REF.		DEBIT					CREDIT					
1			Adjusting Entries															1
2	Dec.¹⁹⁻¹	31	Office Supplies Expense					5	0	0	00							2
3			Office Supplies										5	0	0	00		3
4																		4
5		31	Depr. Expense—Office Equip.					3	0	0	0	00						5
6			Accum. Depr.—Office Equip.										3	0	0	0	00	6
7																		7
8		31	Depr. Expense—Computer Equip.					1	0	0	0	00						8
9			Accum. Depr.—Computer Equip.										1	0	0	0	00	9
10																		10
11		31	Insurance Expense						1	0	0	00						11
12			Prepaid Insurance											1	0	0	00	12
13																		13
14		31	Wages Expense						3	0	0	00						14
15			Wages Payable											3	0	0	00	15

SERIES A   EXERCISES

1   **EXERCISE 5A1 ADJUSTMENT FOR SUPPLIES**   On December 31, the trial balance indicates that the supplies account has a balance, prior to the adjusting entry, of $320. A physical count of the supplies inventory shows that $90 of supplies remain. Analyze this adjustment for supplies using T accounts, and them formally enter this adjustment in the general journal.

1   **EXERCISE 5A2 ADJUSTMENT FOR INSURANCE**   On December 1, a six-month liability insurance policy was purchased for $900. Analyze the required adjustment as of December 31 using T accounts, and then formally enter this adjustment in the general journal.

1   **EXERCISE 5A3 ADJUSTMENT FOR WAGES**   On December 31, the trial balance shows wages expense of $600. An additional $200 of wages was earned by the employees, but has not yet been paid. Analyze this adjustment for wages, and then formally enter this adjustment in the general journal.

1   **EXERCISE 5A4 ADJUSTMENT FOR DEPRECIATION OF ASSET**   On December 1, delivery equipment was purchased for $7,200. The delivery equipment has an estimated useful life of 4 years (48 months) and no salvage value. Using the straight-line depreciation method, prepare the necessary adjusting entry as of December 31 (one month), and then formally enter this adjustment in the general journal.

1 **EXERCISE 5A5 CALCULATION OF BOOK VALUE** One June 1, 19--, a depreciable asset was acquired for $5,400. The asset has an estimated useful life of 5 years (60 months) and no salvage value. Using the straight-line depreciation method, calculate the book value as of December 31, 19--.

1 **EXERCISE 5A6 ANALYSIS OF ADJUSTING ENTRY FOR SUPPLIES** Analyze each situation and indicate the correct dollar amount for the adjusting entry. (Trial balance is abbreviated as TB.)

1. Ending inventory of supplies is $130.

(Balance Sheet) Supplies	(Income Statement) Supplies Expense
TB 460	
Adj. _____	Adj. _____
Bal. _____	

2. Amount of supplies used is $320.

(Balance Sheet) Supplies	(Income Statement) Supplies Expense
TB 545	
Adj. _____	Adj. _____
Bal. _____	

1 **EXERCISE 5A7 ANALYSIS OF ADJUSTING ENTRY FOR INSURANCE** Analyze each situation and indicate the correct dollar amount for the adjusting entry.

1. Amount of insurance expired is $900.

(Balance Sheet) Prepaid Insurance	(Income Statement) Insurance Expense
TB 1,300	
Adj. _____	Adj. _____
Bal. _____	

2. Amount of unexpired insurance is $185.

(Balance Sheet) Prepaid Insurance	(Income Statement) Insurance Expense
TB 860	
Adj. _____	Adj. _____
Bal. _____	

2 **EXERCISE 5A8 WORK SHEET AND ADJUSTING ENTRIES** A partial work sheet for Jim Jacob's Furniture Repair is shown as follows. The work sheet contains four adjusting entries. Indicate by letters (a) through (d) the four adjustments of the work sheet, properly matching each debit and credit. Complete the Adjustments columns.

Jim Jacob's Furniture Repair
Work Sheet (Partial)
For Year Ended December 31, 19--

	ACCOUNT TITLE	TRIAL BALANCE		ADJUSTMENTS		ADJUSTED TRIAL BALANCE		
		DEBIT	CREDIT	DEBIT	CREDIT	DEBIT	CREDIT	
1	Cash	1 0 0 00				1 0 0 00		1
2	Supplies	8 5 0 00				2 0 0 00		2
3	Prepaid Insurance	9 0 0 00				3 0 0 00		3
4	Delivery Equipment	3 6 0 0 00				3 6 0 0 00		4
5	Accum. Depr.—Del. Equip.		6 0 0 00				8 0 0 00	5
6	Wages Payable						1 0 0 00	6
7	Jim Jacobs, Capital		4 0 0 0 00				4 0 0 0 00	7
8	Repair Fees		1 6 5 0 00				1 6 5 0 00	8
9	Wages Expense	6 0 0 00				7 0 0 00		9
10	Advertising Expense	2 0 0 00				2 0 0 00		10
11	Supplies Expense					6 5 0 00		11
12	Depr. Exp.—Del. Equip.					2 0 0 00		12
13	Insurance Expense					6 0 0 00		13
14		6 2 5 0 00	6 2 5 0 00			6 5 5 0 00	6 5 5 0 00	14

4 **EXERCISE 5A9 JOURNALIZING ADJUSTING ENTRIES** From the Adjustments columns from Exercise 5A8, journalize the four adjusting entries, on December 31, in proper general journal format.

5 **EXERCISE 5A10 POSTING ADJUSTING ENTRIES** Two adjusting entries are in the following general journal. Post these adjusting entries to the four general ledger accounts. The following account numbers were taken from the chart of accounts: 151, Supplies; 219, Wages Payable; 542, Wages Expense; and 543, Supplies Expense. If you are not using the working papers that accompany this text, enter the following balances before posting the entries: Supplies, $200 Dr.; Wages Expense, $1,200 Dr.

		GENERAL JOURNAL						PAGE 9	
	DATE	DESCRIPTION	POST. REF.	DEBIT		CREDIT			
1		Adjusting Entries							1
2	Dec. 31	Supplies Expense		8 5 00					2
3		Supplies				8 5 00			3
4									4
5	31	Wages Expense		2 2 0 00					5
6		Wages Payable				2 2 0 00			6

2 **EXERCISE 5A11 EXTENDING ADJUSTED BALANCES TO THE INCOME STATEMENT AND BALANCE SHEET COLUMNS** Indicate with an "x" whether each account total should be extended to the Income

Statement Debit or Credit or to the Balance Sheet Debit or Credit columns on the work sheet.

	Income Statement		Balance Sheet	
	Debit	Credit	Debit	Credit
Cash	_____	_____	_____	_____
Accounts Receivable	_____	_____	_____	_____
Supplies	_____	_____	_____	_____
Prepaid Insurance	_____	_____	_____	_____
Delivery Equipment	_____	_____	_____	_____
Accum. Depr.—Delivery Equip.	_____	_____	_____	_____
Accounts Payable	_____	_____	_____	_____
Wages Payable	_____	_____	_____	_____
Owner, Capital	_____	_____	_____	_____
Owner, Drawing	_____	_____	_____	_____
Delivery Fees	_____	_____	_____	_____
Rent Expense	_____	_____	_____	_____
Wages Expense	_____	_____	_____	_____
Supplies Expense	_____	_____	_____	_____
Insurance Expense	_____	_____	_____	_____
Depr. Exp.—Delivery Equip.	_____	_____	_____	_____

2 **EXERCISE 5A12 ANALYSIS OF NET INCOME OR NET LOSS ON THE WORK SHEET**   Indicate with an "x" in which columns, Income Statement Debit or Credit or Balance Sheet Debit or Credit, a net income or a net loss would appear on a work sheet.

	Income Statement		Balance Sheet	
	Debit	Credit	Debit	Credit
Net Income	_____	_____	_____	_____
Net Loss	_____	_____	_____	_____

SERIES A   PROBLEMS

1/2   **PROBLEM 5A1 ADJUSTMENTS AND WORK SHEET SHOWING NET INCOME**   The trial balance after one month of operation for Mason's Delivery Service as of September 30, 19--, is shown on the next page.

Data to complete the adjustments are as follows:
(a) Supplies inventory as of September 30, $165.
(b) Insurance expired, $800.
(c) Depreciation on delivery equipment, $400.
(d) Wages earned by employees, but not paid as of September 30, $225.

REQUIRED
1. Enter the adjustments in the Adjustments columns of the work sheet.
2. Complete the work sheet.

Mason's Delivery Service
Work Sheet
For Month Ended September 30, 19--

	ACCOUNT TITLE	TRIAL BALANCE		ADJUSTMENTS		
		DEBIT	CREDIT	DEBIT	CREDIT	
1	Cash	1 6 0 0 00				1
2	Accounts Receivable	9 4 0 00				2
3	Supplies	6 3 5 00				3
4	Prepaid Insurance	1 2 0 0 00				4
5	Delivery Equipment	6 4 0 0 00				5
6	Accum. Depr.—Del. Equip.					6
7	Accounts Payable		1 2 2 0 00			7
8	Wages Payable					8
9	Jill Mason, Capital		8 0 0 0 00			9
10	Jill Mason, Drawing	1 4 0 0 00				10
11	Delivery Fees		6 2 0 0 00			11
12	Rent Expense	8 0 0 00				12
13	Wages Expense	1 5 0 0 00				13
14	Supplies Expense					14
15	Telephone Expense	1 6 5 00				15
16	Oil and Gas Expense	9 0 00				16
17	Depr. Exp.—Del. Equip.					17
18	Insurance Expense					18
19	Advertising Expense	4 6 0 00				19
20	Repair Expense	2 3 0 00				20
21		15 4 2 0 00	15 4 2 0 00			21
22						22
23						23
24						24
25						25
26						26
27						27

2   **PROBLEM 5A2 ADJUSTMENTS AND WORK SHEET SHOWING A NET LOSS**   Jason Armstrong started a business called Campus Escort Service. After the first month of operations, the trial balance as of November 30, 19--, is shown on the next page.

REQUIRED
1. Analyze the following adjustments and enter them on the work sheet.
   (a) Ending inventory of supplies on November 30, $185.
   (b) Unexpired insurance as of November 30, $800.
   (c) Depreciation expense on van, $300.
   (d) Wages earned, but not paid as of November 30, $190.
2. Complete the work sheet.

Campus Escort Service
Work Sheet
For Month Ended November 30, 19--

| | ACCOUNT TITLE | TRIAL BALANCE | | ADJUSTMENTS | | |
		DEBIT	CREDIT	DEBIT	CREDIT	
1	Cash	9 8 0 00				1
2	Accounts Receivable	5 9 0 00				2
3	Supplies	5 7 5 00				3
4	Prepaid Insurance	1 3 0 0 00				4
5	Van	5 8 0 0 00				5
6	Accum. Depr.—Van					6
7	Accounts Payable		9 6 0 00			7
8	Wages Payable					8
9	Jason Armstrong, Capital		10 0 0 0 00			9
10	Jason Armstrong, Drawing	6 0 0 00				10
11	Escort Fees		2 6 0 0 00			11
12	Rent Expense	9 0 0 00				12
13	Wages Expense	1 8 0 0 00				13
14	Supplies Expense					14
15	Telephone Expense	2 2 0 00				15
16	Oil and Gas Expense	1 0 0 00				16
17	Depr. Exp.—Van					17
18	Insurance Expense					18
19	Advertising Expense	3 8 0 00				19
20	Repair Expense	3 1 5 00				20
21		13 5 6 0 00	13 5 6 0 00			21
22						22
23						23
24						24
25						25

4/5 **PROBLEM 5A3 JOURNALIZE AND POST ADJUSTING ENTRIES FROM THE WORK SHEET** Refer to Problem 5A2 and the following additional information.

Account Name	Account Number	Balance in Account Before Adjusting Entry
Supplies	151	$ 575
Prepaid Insurance	155	1,300
Accum. Depr.—Van	185.1	0
Wages Payable	219	0
Wages Expense	542	1,800
Supplies Expense	543	0
Depr. Expense—Van	547	0
Insurance Expense	548	0

REQUIRED

1. Journalize the adjusting entries on page 5 of the general journal.
2. Post the adjusting entries to the general ledger. (If you are not using the working papers that accompany this text, enter the balances provided on page 146 before posting adjusting entries.)

3 **PROBLEM 5A4 CORRECTING WORK SHEET WITH ERRORS**   A beginning accounting student tried to complete a work sheet for Joyce Lee's Tax Service. The following adjusting entries were to have been analyzed and entered onto the work sheet. The worksheet is shown on page 148.

(a) Ending inventory of supplies as of March 31, $160.
(b) Unexpired insurance as of March 31, $520.
(c) Depreciation of office equipment, $275.
(d) Wages earned, but not paid as of March 31, $110.

REQUIRED

The accounting student made a number of errors. Review the work sheet for addition mistakes, transpositions, and other errors and make all necessary corrections.

SERIES B EXERCISES

1 **EXERCISE 5B1 ADJUSTMENT FOR SUPPLIES**   On July 31, the trial balance indicates that the supplies account has a balance, prior to the adjusting entry, of $430. A physical count of the supplies inventory shows that $120 of supplies remain. Analyze the adjustment for supplies using T accounts, and then formally enter this adjustment in the general journal.

1 **EXERCISE 5B2 ADJUSTMENT FOR INSURANCE**   On July 1, a six-month liability insurance policy was purchased for $750. Analyze the required adjustment as of July 31 using T accounts, and then formally enter this adjustment in the general journal.

1 **EXERCISE 5B3 ADJUSTMENT FOR WAGES**   On July 31, the trial balance shows wages expense of $800. An additional $150 of wages was earned by the employees but has not yet been paid. Analyze the required adjustment using T accounts, and then formally enter this adjustment in the general journal.

1 **EXERCISE 5B4 ADJUSTMENT FOR DEPRECIATION OF ASSET**   On July 1, delivery equipment was purchased for $4,320. The delivery equipment has an estimated useful life of 3 years (36 months) and no salvage value. Using the straight-line depreciation method, prepare the necessary adjusting entry as of July 31 (one month), and then formally enter this adjustment in the general journal.

Joyce Lee's Tax Service
Work Sheet
For Month Ended March 31, 19--

#	ACCOUNT TITLE	TRIAL BALANCE Debit	TRIAL BALANCE Credit	ADJUSTMENTS Debit	ADJUSTMENTS Credit	ADJUSTED TRIAL BALANCE Debit	ADJUSTED TRIAL BALANCE Credit	INCOME STATEMENT Debit	INCOME STATEMENT Credit	BALANCE SHEET Debit	BALANCE SHEET Credit
1	Cash	1725 00				1725 00				1725 00	
2	Accounts Receivable	960 00				960 00				96 00	
3	Supplies	525 00			(a) 160 00	365 00				365 00	
4	Prepaid Insurance	930 00			(b) 410 00	540 00				540 00	
5	Office Equipment	5450 00				5175 00				5175 00	
6	Accum. Depr.—Office Equip.				(c) 275 00		480 00				
7	Accounts Payable		480 00				110 00		110 00		480 00
8	Wages Payable				(d) 110 00						
9	Joyce Lee, Capital		7500 00				7500 00				7500 00
10	Joyce Lee, Drawing	1125 00				1125 00		1125 00			
11	Professional Fees		5700 00				5700 00		5700 00		
12	Rent Expense	700 00				700 00		700 00			
13	Wages Expense	1420 00		(d) 110 00		1420 00		1420 00			1580 00
14	Supplies Expense			(a) 160 00		160 00		160 00			
15	Telephone Expense	130 00				130 00		130 00			
16	Depr. Expense—Office Equip.			(c) 275 00		275 00		275 00			
17	Insurance Expense			(b) 410 00		410 00		410 00			
18	Utilities Expense	190 00				190 00		190 00			
19	Advertising Expense	350 00				350 00		350 00			
20	Miscellaneous Expense	175 00				175 00		175 00			
21		13680 00	13680 00	955 00	955 00	13160 00	13790 00	4566 00	5810 00	9508 00	7980 00
22								1244 00			1528 00
23								5810 00	5810 00	9508 00	9508 00

This worksheet contains errors

1 **EXERCISE 5B5 CALCULATION OF BOOK VALUE**   On January 1, 19--, a depreciable asset was acquired for $5,760. The asset has an estimated useful life of 4 years (48 months) and no salvage value. Use the straight-line depreciation method to calculate the book value as of July 1, 19--.

1 **EXERCISE 5B6 ANALYSIS OF ADJUSTING ENTRY FOR SUPPLIES**   Analyze each situation and indicate the correct dollar amount for the adjusting entry.

1. Ending inventory of supplies is $95.

(Balance Sheet) Supplies		(Income Statement) Supplies Expense	
TB 540	Adj. _____	Adj. _____	
Bal. _____			

2. Amount of supplies used is $280.

(Balance Sheet) Supplies		(Income Statement) Supplies Expense	
TB 330	Adj. _____	Adj. _____	
Bal. _____			

1 **EXERCISE 5B7 ANALYSIS OF ADJUSTING ENTRY FOR INSURANCE**   Analyze each situation and indicate the correct dollar amount for the adjusting entry.

1. Amount of insurance expired is $830.

(Balance Sheet) Prepaid Insurance		(Income Statement) Insurance Expense	
TB 960	Adj. _____	Adj. _____	
Bal. _____			

2. Amount of unexpired insurance is $340.

(Balance Sheet) Prepaid Insurance		(Income Statement) Insurance Expense	
TB 1,135	Adj. _____	Adj. _____	
Bal. _____			

2 **EXERCISE 5B8 WORK SHEET AND ADJUSTING ENTRIES**   The following shows a partial work sheet for Jasmine Kah's Auto Detailing. The work sheet contains four adjusting entries. Indicate by letters (a) through (d) the four adjustments in the adjustment columns of the work sheet, properly matching each debit and credit. Complete the Adjustments columns.

Jasmine Kah's Auto Detailing
Work Sheet (Partial)
For Month Ended June 30, 19--

	ACCOUNT TITLE	TRIAL BALANCE		ADJUSTMENTS		ADJUSTED TRIAL BALANCE		
		DEBIT	CREDIT	DEBIT	CREDIT	DEBIT	CREDIT	
1	Cash	1 5 0 00				1 5 0 00		1
2	Supplies	5 2 0 00				9 0 00		2
3	Prepaid Insurance	7 5 0 00				2 0 0 00		3
4	Cleaning Equipment	5 4 0 0 00				5 4 0 0 00		4
5	Accum. Depr.—Clean. Equip.		8 5 0 00				1 1 5 0 00	5
6	Wages Payable						2 5 0 00	6
7	Jasmine Kah, Capital		4 6 0 0 00				4 6 0 0 00	7
8	Detailing Fees		2 2 2 0 00				2 2 2 0 00	8
9	Wages Expense	7 0 0 00				9 5 0 00		9
10	Advertising Expense	1 5 0 00				1 5 0 00		10
11	Supplies Expense					4 3 0 00		11
12	Depr. Exp—Clean. Equip.					3 0 0 00		12
13	Insurance Expense					5 5 0 00		13
14		7 6 7 0 00	7 6 7 0 00			8 2 2 0 00	8 2 2 0 00	14

4   **EXERCISE 5B9 JOURNALIZING ADJUSTING ENTRIES**   From the Adjustments columns in Exercise 5B8, journalize the four adjusting entries as of June 30, in proper general journal format.

5   **EXERCISE 5B10 POSTING ADJUSTING ENTRIES**   Two adjusting entries are shown in the following general journal. Post these adjusting entries to the four general ledger accounts. The following account numbers were taken from the chart of accounts: 155, Prepaid Insurance; 186.1, Accumulated Depreciation—Cleaning Equipment; 547, Depreciation Expense—Cleaning Equipment; and 548, Insurance Expense. If you are not using the working papers that accompany this text, enter the following balances before posting the entries: Prepaid Insurance, $960 Dr.; Accumulated Depr.—Cleaning Equip., $870 Cr.

			GENERAL JOURNAL				PAGE 7	
	DATE		DESCRIPTION	POST. REF.	DEBIT		CREDIT	
1			Adjusting Entries					1
2	July	31	Insurance Expense		3 2 0 00			2
3			Prepaid Insurance				3 2 0 00	3
4								4
5		31	Depr. Expense—Cleaning Equip.		1 4 5 00			5
6			Accum. Depr.—Cleaning Equip.				1 4 5 00	6
7								7

(Date column note: 19-1)

2   **EXERCISE 5B11 EXTENDING ADJUSTED BALANCES TO THE INCOME STATMENT AND BALANCE SHEET COLUMNS**   Indicate with an "x" whether each account total should be extended to the Income Statement Debit or Credit or to the Balance Sheet Debit or Credit columns on the work sheet.

	Income Statement		Balance Sheet	
	Debit	Credit	Debit	Credit
Cash	_____	_____	_____	_____
Accounts Receivable	_____	_____	_____	_____
Supplies	_____	_____	_____	_____
Prepaid Insurance	_____	_____	_____	_____
Automobile	_____	_____	_____	_____
Accum. Depr.—Automobile	_____	_____	_____	_____
Accounts Payable	_____	_____	_____	_____
Wages Payable	_____	_____	_____	_____
Owner, Capital	_____	_____	_____	_____
Owner, Drawing	_____	_____	_____	_____
Service Fees	_____	_____	_____	_____
Utilities Expense	_____	_____	_____	_____
Wages Expense	_____	_____	_____	_____
Supplies Expense	_____	_____	_____	_____
Insurance Expense	_____	_____	_____	_____
Depr. Exp.—Automobile	_____	_____	_____	_____

2   **EXERCISE 5B12 ANALYSIS OF NET INCOME OR NET LOSS ON THE WORK SHEET**   Insert the dollar amounts where the net income or net loss would appear on the work sheet.

	Income Statement		Balance Sheet	
	Debit	Credit	Debit	Credit
Net Income: $2,500	_____	_____	_____	_____
Net Loss: $1,900	_____	_____	_____	_____

SERIES B   PROBLEMS

2   **PROBLEM 5B1 ADJUSTMENTS AND WORK SHEET SHOWING NET INCOME**   Louie Long started a business called Louie's Lawn Service. After the first month of operation, the trial balance as of March 31 is shown on the next page.

REQUIRED

1. Analyze the following adjustments and enter them on a work sheet.
   (a) Ending supplies inventory as of March 31, $165.
   (b) Insurance expired, $100.
   (c) Depreciation of lawn equipment, $200.
   (d) Wages earned, but not paid as of March 31, $180.
2. Complete the work sheet.

Louie's Lawn Service
Work Sheet
For Month Ended March 31, 19--

	ACCOUNT TITLE	TRIAL BALANCE DEBIT	TRIAL BALANCE CREDIT	ADJUSTMENTS DEBIT	ADJUSTMENTS CREDIT	
1	Cash	1 3 7 5 00				1
2	Accounts Receivable	8 8 0 00				2
3	Supplies	4 9 0 00				3
4	Prepaid Insurance	8 0 0 00				4
5	Lawn Equipment	5 7 0 0 00				5
6	Accum. Depr.—Lawn Equip.					6
7	Accounts Payable		7 8 0 00			7
8	Wages Payable					8
9	Louie Long, Capital		6 5 0 0 00			9
10	Louie Long, Drawing	1 2 5 0 00				10
11	Lawn Service Fees		6 1 0 0 00			11
12	Rent Expense	7 2 5 00				12
13	Wages Expense	1 1 4 5 00				13
14	Supplies Expense					14
15	Telephone Expense	1 6 0 00				15
16	Miscellaneous Expense	6 5 00				16
17	Depr. Exp.—Lawn Equip.					17
18	Insurance Expense					18
19	Advertising Expense	5 4 0 00				19
20	Repair Expense	2 5 0 00				20
21		13 3 8 0 00	13 3 8 0 00			21
22						22
23						23
24						24
25						25
26						26
27						27

2 **PROBLEM 5B2 ADJUSTMENTS AND WORK SHEET SHOWING A NET LOSS**   Val Nolan started a business called Nolan's Home Appraisals. After the first month of operations, the trial balance as of October 31 is shown on the following page.

REQUIRED
1. Analyze the following adjustments and enter them on the work sheet.
    (a) Supplies inventory as of October 31, $210.
    (b) Unexpired insurance as of October 31, $800.
    (c) Depreciation of automobile, $250.
    (d) Wages earned, but not paid as of October 31, $175.
2. Complete the work sheet.

Nolan's Home Appraisals
Work Sheet
For Month Ended October 31, 19--

	ACCOUNT TITLE	TRIAL BALANCE		ADJUSTMENTS		
		DEBIT	CREDIT	DEBIT	CREDIT	
1	Cash	8 3 0 00				1
2	Accounts Receivable	7 6 0 00				2
3	Supplies	6 2 5 00				3
4	Prepaid Insurance	9 5 0 00				4
5	Automobile	6 5 0 0 00				5
6	Accum. Depr.—Automobile					6
7	Accounts Payable		1 5 0 0 00			7
8	Wages Payable					8
9	Val Nolan, Capital		9 9 0 0 00			9
10	Val Nolan, Drawing	1 1 0 0 00				10
11	Appraisal Fees		3 0 0 0 00			11
12	Rent Expense	1 0 5 0 00				12
13	Wages Expense	1 5 6 0 00				13
14	Supplies Expense					14
15	Telephone Expense	2 5 5 00				15
16	Oil and Gas Expense	8 0 00				16
17	Depr. Exp.—Automobile					17
18	Insurance Expense					18
19	Advertising Expense	4 2 0 00				19
20	Repair Expense	2 7 0 00				20
21		14 4 0 0 00	14 4 0 0 00			21
22						22
23						23
24						24
25						25

4/5   **PROBLEM 5B3 JOURNALIZE AND POST ADJUSTING ENTRIES FROM THE WORK SHEET**   Refer to Problem 5B2 and the following additional information.

Account Name	Account Number	Balance in Account Before Adjusting Entry
Supplies	151	$ 625
Prepaid Insurance	155	950
Accum. Depr.—Automobile	185.1	0
Wages Payable	219	0
Wages Expense	542	1,560
Supplies Expense	543	0
Depr. Expense—Automobile	547	0
Insurance Expense	548	0

1. Journalize the adjusting entries on page 3 of the general journal.
2. Post the adjusting entries to the general ledger. (If you are not using the working papers that accompany this text, enter the balances provided on page 153 before posting adjusting entries.)

3 **PROBLEM 5B4 CORRECTING WORK SHEET WITH ERRORS**   A beginning accounting student tried to complete a work sheet for Dick Ady's Bookkeeping Service. The following adjusting entries were to have been analyzed and entered in the work sheet.

(a) Ending inventory of supplies on July 31, $130.
(b) Unexpired insurance on July 31, $420.
(c) Depreciation of office equipment, $325.
(d) Wages earned, but not paid as of July 31, $95.

Review the work sheet shown on page 155 for addition mistakes, transpositions, and other errors and make all necessary corrections.

MASTERY PROBLEM

Kristi Williams offers family counseling services specializing in financial and marital problems. A chart of accounts and a trial balance taken on December 31, 19-1, are provided below.

Kristi Williams Family Counseling Services Chart of Accounts			
Assets		**Revenue**	
111	Cash	411	Client Fees
152	Office Supplies		
155	Prepaid Insurance	**Expenses**	
181	Office Equipment	541	Rent Expense
181.1	Accum. Depr.—	542	Wages Expense
	Office Equip.	543	Office Supp. Exp.
194	Computer Equip.	547	Depr. Expense—
194.1	Accum. Depr.—		Office Equip.
	Computer Equip.	548	Depr. Expense—
			Computer Equip.
Liabilities		555	Utilities Expense
216	Accounts Payable	559	Insurance Expense
218	Notes Payable	592	Miscellaneous Exp.
Owner's Equity			
311	Kristi Williams, Capital		
312	Kristi Williams, Drawing		

Dick Ady's Bookkeeping Service
Work Sheet
For Month Ended July 31, 19--

| | TRIAL BALANCE | | ADJUSTMENTS | | ADJUSTED TRIAL BALANCE | | INCOME STATEMENT | | BALANCE SHEET | | |
ACCOUNT TITLE	DEBIT	CREDIT	DEBIT	CREDIT	DEBIT	CREDIT	DEBIT	CREDIT	DEBIT	CREDIT	
1 Cash	1365 00				1365 00				1365 00		1
2 Accounts Receivable	845 00				845 00			845 00			2
3 Supplies	620 00			(a) 490 00	130 00				130 00		3
4 Prepaid Insurance	1150 00			(b) 420 00	730 00				730 00		4
5 Office Equipment	6400 00			(c) 325 00	6725 00				6725 00		5
6 Accum. Depr.—Office Equip.											6
7 Accounts Payable		735 00				735 00				735 00	7
8 Wages Payable				(d) 95 00		95 00				59 00	8
9 Dick Ady, Capital		7800 00				7800 00				7800 00	9
10 Dick Ady, Drawing	1200 00				1200 00				1200 00		10
11 Professional Fees		6350 00				6350 00		6350 00			11
12 Rent Expense	850 00				850 00		850 00				12
13 Wages Expense	1495 00		(d) 95 00		1590 00		1590 00				13
14 Supplies Expense			(a) 490 00		490 00		490 00				14
15 Telephone Expense	205 00				205 00		250 00				15
16 Depr. Expense—Office Equip.			(c) 325 00		325 00		325 00				16
17 Insurance Expense			(b) 420 00		420 00		420 00				17
18 Utilities Expense	285 00				285 00		285 00				18
19 Advertising Expense	380 00				380 00		380 00				19
20 Miscellaneous Expense	90 00				90 00		90 00				20
21	14885 00	14885 00	1330 00	1330 00	15630 00	14980 00	4880 00	7195 00	10141 00	8594 00	21
22 Net Income							2315 00			1547 00	22
23							7195 00	7195 00	10141 00	10141 00	23

This worksheet contains errors

Kristi Williams Family Counseling Services
Trial Balance
December 31, 19-1

ACCOUNT TITLE	ACCOUNT NO.	DEBIT BALANCE	CREDIT BALANCE
Cash	111	8 7 3 0 00	
Office Supplies	152	7 0 0 00	
Prepaid Insurance	155	6 0 0 00	
Office Equipment	181	18 0 0 0 00	
Computer Equipment	194	6 0 0 0 00	
Accounts Payable	216		5 0 0 00
Notes Payable	218		8 0 0 0 00
Kristi Williams, Capital	311		11 4 0 0 00
Kristi Williams, Drawing	312	3 0 0 0 00	
Client Fees	411		35 8 0 0 00
Rent Expense	541	6 0 0 0 00	
Wages Expense	542	9 5 0 0 00	
Utilities Expense	555	2 1 7 0 00	
Miscellaneous Expense	592	1 0 0 0 00	
		55 7 0 0 00	55 7 0 0 00

Information for year-end adjustments:
(a) Office supplies on hand at year end amounted to $100.
(b) On January 1, 19-1, Williams purchased office equipment that cost $18,000. It has an expected useful life of ten years and no salvage value.
(c) On July 1, 19-1, Williams purchased computer equipment costing $8,000. It has an expected useful life of four years and no salvage value. Assume that Williams computes depreciation to the nearest full month.
(d) On December 1, 19-1, Williams paid a premium of $600 for a six-month insurance policy.

REQUIRED
1. Prepare the work sheet for the year ended December 31, 19-1.
2. Prepare adjusting entries in a general journal.

CHAPTER 5 APPENDIX

Depreciation Methods

Careful study of this appendix should enable you to:

LO1 Prepare a depreciation schedule using the straight-line method.

LO2 Prepare a depreciation schedule using the sum-of-the-years'-digits method.

LO3 Prepare a depreciation schedule using the double-declining-balance method.

LO4 Prepare a depreciation schedule for tax purposes using the Modified Accelerated Cost Recovery System.

In Chapter 5, we introduced the straight-line method of depreciation. Here, we will review this method and illustrate three others: sum-of-the-year's-digits; double-declining-balance; and, for tax purposes, the Modified Accelerated Cost Recovery System. For all illustrations, we will assume that a delivery van was purchased for $18,000. It has a five-year useful life and salvage value of $3,000.

STRAIGHT-LINE METHOD

LO1   Prepare a depreciation schedule using the straight-line method.

Under the straight-line method, an equal amount of depreciation will be taken each period. First, compute the depreciable cost by subtracting the salvage value from the cost of the asset. This is done because we expect to sell the asset for $3,000 at the end of its useful life. Thus, the total cost to be recognized as an expense over the five years is $15,000, not $18,000.

$$\text{Cost} \quad - \text{Salvage Value} = \text{Depreciable Cost}$$
$$\$18,000 - \quad \$3,000 \quad = \quad \$15,000$$

Next, we divide the depreciable cost by the expected life of the asset, 5 years.

$$\text{Depreciation Expense per Year} = \frac{\text{Depreciable Cost}}{\text{Years of Life}}$$

$$\$3,000 \text{ per year} \quad = \quad \frac{\$15,000}{5 \text{ years}}$$

When preparing a depreciation schedule, it is often convenient to use a depreciation rate per year. In this case it would be 20% (1 year ÷ 5 years of life). Figure 5A-1 shows the depreciation expense, accumulated depreciation, and book value for each of the five years.

FIGURE 5A-1   Depreciation Schedule Using Straight-Line Method

| | | | | | | ACCUMULATED | |
| | DEPRECIABLE | | | | DEPRECIATION | DEPRECIATION | BOOK VALUE^c |
YEAR	COST^a	x	RATE^b	=	EXPENSE	(END OF YEAR)	(END OF YEAR)
1	$15,000		20%		$3,000	$ 3,000	$15,000
2	15,000		20%		3,000	6,000	12,000
3	15,000		20%		3,000	9,000	9,000
4	15,000		20%		3,000	12,000	6,000
5	15,000		20%		3,000	15,000	3,000

^aDepreciable Cost = Cost − Salvage Value ($18,000 − $3,000 = $15,000).
^bRate = 1 year ÷ 5 years of life x 100 = 20%.
^cBook Value = Cost ($18,000) − Accumulated Depreciation.

SUM-OF-THE-YEARS'-DIGITS

LO2   Prepare a depreciation schedule using the sum-of-the-years'-digits method.

Under the sum-of-the-years'-digits method, depreciation is determined by multiplying the depreciable cost by a schedule of fractions. The numerator of the fraction for a specific year is the number of years of remaining useful life for the asset, measured from the beginning of the year. The denominator for all fractions is determined by adding the digits that represent the years of the estimated life of the asset. The calculation for our delivery van with a five-year useful life is shown below.

Sum-of-the-Years'-Digits = 5 + 4 + 3 + 2 + 1 = 15

A depreciation schedule using these fractions is shown in Figure 5A-2.

DOUBLE-DECLINING-BALANCE METHOD

LO3   Prepare a depreciation schedule using the double-declining-balance method.

Under this method, the book value is multiplied by a fixed rate, often double the straight-line rate. The van has a five year life, so the straight-line rate is 1 ÷ 5, or 20%. Double the straight-line rate is 2 ÷ 5, or 40%. The double-declining-balance depreciation schedule is shown in Figure 5A-3. Note that the rate is applied to the book value of the asset. Once the book value is reduced to the expected salvage value, $3,000, no more depreciation may be recognized.

FIGURE 5A-2   Depreciation Schedule Using Sum-of-the-Years'-Digits Method

SUM-OF-THE-YEARS'-DIGITS

YEAR	DEPRECIABLE COST[a]	x	RATE[b]	=	DEPRECIATION EXPENSE	ACCUMULATED DEPRECIATION (END OF YEAR)	BOOK VALUE[c] (END OF YEAR)
1	$15,000		5/15		$5,000	$ 5,000	$13,000
2	15,000		4/15		4,000	9,000	9,000
3	15,000		3/15		3,000	12,000	6,000
4	15,000		2/15		2,000	14,000	4,000
5	15,000		1/15		1,000	15,000	3,000

[a]Depreciable Cost = Cost − Salvage Value ($18,000 − $3,000 = $15,000).
[b]Rate = Number of Years of Remaining Useful Life ÷ Sum-of-the-Years'-Digits.
[c]Book Value = Cost ($18,000) − Accumulated Depreciation.

FIGURE 5A-3   Depreciation Schedule for Double-Declining-Balance Method

DOUBLE-DECLINING-BALANCE METHOD

YEAR	BOOK VALUE[a] (BEGINNING OF YEAR)	x	RATE[b]	=	DEPRECIATION EXPENSE	ACCUMULATED DEPRECIATION (END OF YEAR)	BOOK VALUE (END OF YEAR)
1	$18,000		40%		$7,200	$ 7,200	$10,800
2	10,800		40%		4,320	11,520	6,480
3	6,480		40%		2,592	14,112	3,888
4	3,888				888	15,000	3,000
5	3,000				0	15,000	3,000

[a]Book Value = Cost ($18,000) − Accumulated Depreciation.
[b]Rate = Double the straight-line rate (1/5 x 2 = 2/5 or 40%).

LEARNING KEY

Double means double the straight-line rate. Declining-balance means that the rate is multiplied by the *book value* (not depreciable cost) at the beginning of each year. This amount is *declining* each year.

MODIFIED ACCELERATED COST RECOVERY SYSTEM

LO4   Prepare a depreciation schedule for tax purposes using the Modified Accelerated Cost Recovery System.

For assets purchased since 1986, many firms use the Modified Accelerated Cost Recovery System (MACRS) for tax purposes. Under this method, the Internal Revenue Service (IRS) classifies various assets according to useful life and sets depreciation rates for each year of the asset's life. These rates are then multiplied by the cost of the asset. Even though the van is expected to have a useful life of five years, and a salvage value of $3,000, the IRS schedule, shown in Figure 5A-4, spreads the depreciation over a six-year period and assumes no salvage value.

FIGURE 5A-4 Depreciation Schedule for Modified Accelerated Cost Recovery System

YEAR	COST	x	RATE[a]	=	DEPRECIATION EXPENSE	ACCUMULATED DEPRECIATION (END OF YEAR)	BOOK VALUE[b] (END OF YEAR)
			MODIFIED ACCELERATED COST RECOVERY SYSTEM				
1	$18,000		20.00%		$3,600	$ 3,600	$14,400
2	18,000		32.00%		5,760	9,360	8,640
3	18,000		19.20%		3,456	12,816	5,184
4	18,000		11.52%		2,074	14,890	3,110
5	18,000		11.52%		2,074	16,964	1,036
6	18,000		5.76%		1,036	18,000	0

[a]Rates set by IRS.
[b]Book Value = Cost ($18,000) – Accumulated Depreciation.

SERIES A EXERCISES

1 **EXERCISE 5ApxA1 STRAIGHT-LINE DEPRECIATION** A small delivery truck was purchased on January 1 at a cost of $25,000. It has an estimated useful life of 4 years and an estimated salvage value of $5,000. Prepare a depreciation schedule showing the depreciation expense, accumulated depreciation, and book value for each year under the straight-line method.

2 **EXERCISE 5ApxA2 SUM-OF-THE-YEARS'-DIGITS DEPRECIATION** Using the information given in Exercise 5ApxA1, prepare a depreciation schedule showing the depreciation expense, accumulated depreciation, and book value for each year under the sum-of-the-years'-digits method.

3 **EXERCISE 5ApxA3 DOUBLE-DECLINING BALANCE DEPRECIATION** Using the information given in Exercise 5ApxA1, prepare a depreciation schedule showing the depreciation expense, accumulated depreciation, and book value for each year under the double-declining-balance method.

4 **EXERCISE 5ApxA4 MODIFIED ACCELERATED COST RECOVERY SYSTEM** Using the information given in Exercise 5ApxA1 and the rates shown in Figure 5A-4, prepare a depreciation schedule showing the depreciation expense, accumulated depreciation, and book value for each year under the Modified Accelerated Cost Recovery System. For tax purposes, assume that the truck has a useful life of 5 years.

SERIES B EXERCISES

1 **EXERCISE 5ApxB1 STRAIGHT-LINE DEPRECIATION** A computer was purchased on January 1 at a cost of $5,000. It has an estimated useful life of 5 years and an estimated salvage value of $500. Prepare a depreciation schedule showing the depreciation expense, accumulated depreciation, and book value for each year under the straight-line method.

2   **EXERCISE 5ApxB2 SUM-OF-THE-YEARS'-DIGITS DEPRECIATION**
Using the information given in Exercise 5ApxB1, prepare a depreciation schedule showing the depreciation expense, accumulated depreciation, and book value for each year under the sum-of-the-years'-digits method.

3   **EXERCISE 5ApxB3 DOUBLE-DECLINING BALANCE DEPRECIA-TION**   Using the information given in Exercise 5ApxB1, prepare a depreciation schedule showing the depreciation expense, accumulated depreciation, and book value for each year under the double-declining-balance method.

4   **EXERCISE 5ApxB4 MODIFIED ACCELERATED COST RECOVERY SYSTEM**   Using the information given in Exercise 5ApxB1 and the rates shown in Figure 5A-4, prepare a depreciation schedule showing the depreciation expense, accumulated depreciation, and book value for each year under the Modified Accelerated Cost Recovery System. For tax purposes, assume that the truck has a useful life of 5 years.

6

Financial Statements and the Closing Process

Careful study of this chapter should enable you to:

LO1 Prepare financial statements with the aid of a work sheet.

LO2 Journalize and post closing entries.

LO3 Prepare a post-closing trial balance.

LO4 List and describe the steps in the accounting cycle.

"Come on Carlota, let's get busy. We have to close the books before we go to the New Year's Eve party," said Ramon. But after seeing the disappointed look on Carlota's face, Ramon changed his mind. "What the heck. Let's do it on the 2nd, while we recover from watching all of those bowl games." "Great," said Carlota, "let's get out of here." Will Ramon and Carlota be in trouble for not closing the books before the end of the year?

The work sheet, introduced in Chapter 5, is used for three major end-of-period activities:

1. journalizing adjusting entries,
2. preparing financial statements, and
3. journalizing closing entries.

This chapter illustrates the use of the work sheet for preparing financial statements and closing entries. In addition, the post-closing trial balance will be explained and illustrated. All of these activities take place at the end of the firm's fiscal year. However, to continue our illustration of Jessie Jane's Campus Delivery, we will demonstrate these activities at the end of the first month of operations.

THE FINANCIAL STATEMENTS

LO1   Prepare financial statements with the aid of a work sheet.

Since Jane made no additional investments, the work sheet prepared in Chapter 5 supplies all of the information needed to prepare an income statement, a statement of owner's equity, and a balance sheet. The statements and work sheet columns from which they are derived for Jessie Jane's Campus Delivery are shown in Figures 6-1 and 6-2.

As you refer to the financial statements in Figures 6-1 and 6-2, notice the placement of dollar signs, single rulings, and double rulings. Dollar signs are placed at the top of each column and beneath rulings. Single rulings indicate addition or subtraction, and double rulings are placed under totals. Notice that each statement heading contains three lines: (1) company name, (2) statement title, and (3) period ended or date.

Working Together to Understand the Income Statement

In 1980, SRC, an engine remanufacturing subsidiary of International Harvester, was facing crippling financial difficulties. The company was taken private in a leveraged buyout organized by plant manager Jack Stack. Jack set out to "teach anyone who moved a broom or operated a grinder everything a bank lender knew. That way they could really understand how every nickel saved could make a difference."

Today, after extensive financial training, every employee can interpret the business' income statement. Weekly, employees meet in small groups to study the most current financial statements. Since their yearly bonus is based on meeting goals measured by numbers in these statements, employees take a keen interest in the numbers. Employees know how much it costs to make a photocopy or shut down a machine for repairs. They also look for ways to reduce costs and improve net income, the company's bottom line. One group of machinists recently chose to work overtime to cover an increased work load, rather than pay for the training of new employees. After studying the numbers, they decided the overtime would cost the company less.

Source: Jaclyn Fierman, "Winning Ideas from Maverick Managers" *Fortune* (February 6, 1995): 67–68.

FIGURE 6-1 The Work Sheet and the Income Statement

Jessie Jane's Campus Delivery
Work Sheet (Partial)
For Month Ended June 30, 19--

	ACCOUNT TITLE	INCOME STATEMENT DEBIT	INCOME STATEMENT CREDIT	BALANCE SHEET DEBIT	BALANCE SHEET CREDIT	
1	Cash					1
2	Accounts Receivable					2
3	Supplies					3
4	Prepaid Insurance					4
5	Delivery Equipment					5
6	Accum. Depr.—Del. Equip.					6
7	Accounts Payable					7
8	Wages Payable					8
9	Jessica Jane, Capital					9
10	Jessica Jane, Drawing					10
11	Delivery Fees		2 0 0 0 00			11
12	Rent Expense	2 0 0 00				12
13	Wages Expense	7 0 0 00				13
14	Supplies Expense	6 0 00				14
15	Telephone Expense	5 0 00				15
16	Depr. Exp.—Del. Equip.	1 0 0 00				16
17	Insurance Expense	2 5 00				17
18		1 1 3 5 00	2 0 0 0 00			18
19	Net Income	8 6 5 00				19
20		2 0 0 0 00	2 0 0 0 00			20
21						21
22						22

Dollar signs are not used on the work sheet

The Income Statement

Figure 6-1 shows how the Income Statement columns of the work sheet provide the information needed to prepare an income statement. Revenue is shown first, followed by an itemized and totaled list of expenses. Then, net income is calculated to double check the accuracy of the work sheet. It is presented with a double ruling as the last item in the statement.

The expenses could be listed in the same order that they appear in the chart of accounts or in descending order by dollar amount. The second approach helps the reader identify the most important expenses.

 LEARNING KEY Multiple columns are used on the financial statements to make them easier to read. There are no debit or credit columns on the financial statements.

FIGURE 6-1   The Work Sheet and the Income Statement (continued)

Jessie Jane's Campus Delivery Income Statement For Month Ended June 30, 19--			Name of company Title of statement Accounting period ended
Revenue:			**Revenues** listed first
Delivery fees		$2 0 0 0 00	**Expenses** listed second by amount (largest to smallest) or in chart of accounts order; amounts are itemized in left column, subtotaled in right column
Expenses:			
Rent expense	$ 2 0 0 00		
Wages expense	7 0 0 00		
Supplies expense	6 0 00		
Telephone expense	5 0 00		**Dollar signs** used at top of columns and under rulings
Depreciation expense—delivery equipment	1 0 0 00		
Insurance expense	2 5 00		**Single rulings** indicate addition or subtraction
Total expenses		1 1 3 5 00	
Net income		$ 8 6 5 00	**Double rulings** indicate totals

The Statement of Owner's Equity

Figure 6-2 shows that the Balance Sheet columns of the work sheet provide the information needed to prepare a statement of owner's equity. Jane's capital account balance and the drawing account balance are in the Balance Sheet columns of the work sheet. The net income for the year can be found either on the work sheet at the bottom of the Balance Sheet columns or on the income statement. With these three items of information, the statement of owner's equity can be prepared.

Be careful when using the capital account balance reported in the balance sheet columns of the work sheet. This account balance is the beginning balance *plus any additional investments made during the period.* Since Jane made no additional investments during June, the $2,000 balance may be used as the beginning balance on the statement of owner's equity.

 LEARNING KEY   The owner's capital account in the general ledger must be reviewed to determine if additional investments were made during the accounting period.

What if the owner of a business made additional investments during the accounting period? Then, we must review the owner's capital account in the general ledger to get the information needed to prepare the statement of owner's equity. Figure 6-3 illustrates this situation for another business, Ramon's Shopping Service. The $5,000 balance on July 1, 19--, in Ramon Balboa's general ledger capital account is used as the beginning balance on the statement of owner's equity. The additional investment of $3,000 made on July 5 and posted to Balboa's general ledger capital account is reported by writing "Add additional investments" on the line immediately after the beginning balance. The beginning balance plus the additional investment equals the total investment by the owner in the business. From this point,

FIGURE 6-2 Using the Balance Sheet Columns of the Work Sheet to Prepare Statements

Jessie Jane's Campus Delivery
Work Sheet (Partial)
For Month Ended June 30, 19--

	ACCOUNT TITLE	BALANCE SHEET		
		DEBIT	CREDIT	
1	Cash	3 7 0 00		1
2	Accounts Receivable	5 0 0 00		2
3	Supplies	2 0 00		3
4	Prepaid Insurance	1 7 5 00		4
5	Delivery Equipment	3 6 0 0 00		5
6	Accum. Depr.—Del. Equip.		1 0 0 00	6
7	Accounts Payable		1 8 0 0 00	7
8	Wages Payable		5 0 00	8
9	Jessica Jane, Capital		2 0 0 0 00	9
10	Jessica Jane, Drawing	1 5 0 00		10
11	Delivery Fees			11
12	Rent Expense			12
13	Wages Expense			13
14	Supplies Expense			14
15	Telephone Expense			15
16	Depr. Exp.—Del. Equip.			16
17	Insurance Expense			17
18		4 8 1 5 00	3 9 5 0 00	18
19	Net Income		8 6 5 00	19
20		4 8 1 5 00	4 8 1 5 00	20
21				21
22				22

the preparation of the statement is the same as for businesses without additional investments.

The Balance Sheet

As shown in Figure 6-2, the work sheet and the statement of owner's equity are used to prepare Jane's balance sheet. The asset and liability amounts can be found in the Balance Sheet columns of the work sheet. The ending balance in Jessica Jane, Capital has been computed on the statement of owner's equity. This amount should be copied from the statement of owner's equity to the balance sheet.

Two important features of the balance sheet in Figure 6-2 should be noted. First, it is a **report form of balance sheet,** which means that the liabilities and owner's equity sections are shown below the assets section. It differs from an **account form of balance sheet** in which the assets are on the left and the liabilities and owner's equity sections on the right. (See Jane's balance sheet illustrated in Figure 2-2 on page 28 in Chapter 2.)

FIGURE 6-2   Using the Balance Sheet Columns of the Work Sheet to Prepare Statements (concluded)

Jessie Jane's Campus Delivery Statement of Owner's Equity For Month Ended June 30, 19--				Name of company Title of statement Accounting period ended
Jessica Jane, capital, June 1, 19--			$2 0 0 0 00	Dollar signs used at top of columns and beneath rulings
Net income for June	$ 8 6 5 00			
Less withdrawals for June	1 5 0 00			Single rulings indicate addition or subtraction
Increase in capital		7 1 5 00		
Jessica Jane, capital, June 30, 19--		$2 7 1 5 00		Double rulings indicate totals

Jessie Jane's Campus Delivery Balance Sheet June 30, 19--				Name of company Title of statement Date of statement
Assets				Report form of balance sheet
Current assets:				
Cash	$ 3 7 0 00			Current assets: cash and items that will be converted to cash or used up within a year
Accounts receivable	5 0 0 00			
Supplies	2 0 00			
Prepaid insurance	1 7 5 00			
Total current assets		$1 0 6 5 00		
Property, plant, and equipment:				Property, plant, and equipment: assets that will help produce revenues for more than a year
Delivery equipment	$3 6 0 0 00			
Less accumulated depreciation	1 0 0 00	3 5 0 0 00		
Total assets		$4 5 6 5 00		
Liabilities				Current liabilities: amounts owed that will be paid within a year (will require the use of current assets)
Current liabilities:				
Accounts payable	$1 8 0 0 00			
Wages payable	5 0 00			
Total current liabilities		$1 8 5 0 00		
Owner's Equity				Ending capital is not taken from work sheet; it is computed on the statement of owner's equity
Jessica Jane, capital		2 7 1 5 00		
Total liabilities and owner's equity		$4 5 6 5 00		

Second, it is a **classified balance sheet,** which means that similar items are grouped together on the balance sheet. Assets are classified as current assets and property, plant, and equipment. Similarly, liabilities are broken down into current and long-term sections. The following major balance sheet classifications are generally used.

Current Assets.   **Current assets** include cash and assets that will be converted into cash or consumed within either one year or the normal operating cycle of the business, whichever is longer. An **operating cycle** is the period of time required to purchase supplies and services and convert them back into cash.

FIGURE 6-3   Statement of Owner's Equity with Additional Investment

GENERAL LEDGER

ACCOUNT: **Ramon Balboa, Capital**   ACCOUNT NO. **311**

DATE	ITEM	POST. REF.	DEBIT	CREDIT	BALANCE DEBIT	BALANCE CREDIT
19-- July 1				5 0 0 0 00		5 0 0 0 00
5				3 0 0 0 00		8 0 0 0 00

Amount invested July 1

Amount reported on work sheet

Ramon's Shopping Service
Statement of Owner's Equity
For Month Ended July 31, 19--

From general ledger

From work sheet

Ramon Balboa, capital, July 1, 19--		$5 0 0 0 00
Add additional investments		3 0 0 0 00
Total investment		$8 0 0 0 00
Net income for July	$2 1 0 0 00	
Less withdrawals for July	2 5 0 00	
Increase in capital		1 8 5 0 00
Ramon Balboa, capital, July 31, 19--		$9 8 5 0 00

Property, Plant, and Equipment.   **Property, plant and equipment,** also called **plant assets** or **long-term assets,** represent assets that are expected to serve the business for many years.

Current Liabilities.   **Current liabilities** are liabilities that are due within either one year or the normal operating cycle of the business, whichever is longer, and that are to be paid out of current assets. Accounts payable and wages payable are classified as current liabilities.

Long-Term Liabilities.   **Long-term liabilities,** or **long-term debt,** are obligations that are not expected to be paid within a year and do not require the use of current assets. A mortgage on an office building is an example of a long-term liability. Jane has no long-term debts. If she did, they would be listed on the balance sheet in the long-term liabilities section immediately following the current liabilities.

THE CLOSING PROCESS

LO2   Journalize and post closing entries.

Assets, liabilities, and the owner's capital account accumulate information across accounting periods. Their balances are brought forward for each new period. For example, the amount of cash at the end of one accounting period must be the same as the amount of cash at the beginning of the next. Thus, the balance reported for Cash is a result of all cash transactions since the business first opened. This is true for all accounts reported on the balance sheet. For this reason, they are called **permanent accounts.**

 Permanent accounts contain the results of all transactions since the business started. Their balances are carried forward to each new accounting period.

Revenue, expense, and drawing accounts accumulate information *for a specific accounting period.* At the end of the fiscal year, these accounts must be *closed.* The **closing process** gives these accounts zero balances so they are prepared to accumulate new information for the next accounting period. Since these accounts do not accumulate information across accounting periods, they are called **temporary accounts.** The drawing account and all accounts reported on the income statement are temporary accounts and must be closed at the end of each accounting period.

 Temporary accounts contain information for one accounting period. These accounts are closed at the end of each accounting period.

The closing process is most clearly demonstrated by returning to the accounting equation and T accounts. As shown in Figure 6-4, revenues, expenses, and drawing impact owner's equity and should be considered "under the umbrella" of the capital account. The effect of these accounts on owner's equity is formalized at the end of the accounting period when the balances of the temporary accounts are transferred to the owner's capital account (a permanent account) during the closing process.

The four basic steps in the closing process are illustrated in Figure 6-4. As you can see, a new account, **Income Summary,** is used in the closing

FIGURE 6-4　The Closing Process

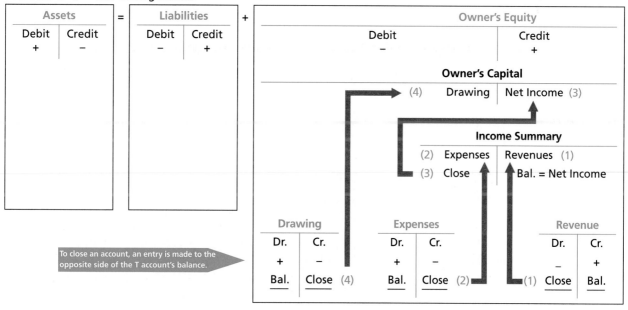

process. This account may also be called *Expense and Revenue Summary*. This temporary account summarizes the effects of all revenue and expense accounts. Income Summary is opened during the closing process. Then it is closed to the owner's capital account. It does not appear on any financial statement. The four steps in the closing process are explained below.

STEPS IN THE CLOSING PROCESS

STEP 1   **Close Revenue Accounts to Income Summary.**   Revenues have credit balances and increase owner's equity. Therefore, the revenue account is debited to create a zero balance. Income Summary is credited for the same amount.

STEP 2   **Close Expense Accounts to Income Summary.**   Expenses have debit balances and reduce owner's equity. Therefore, the expense accounts are credited to create a zero balance. Income Summary must be debited for the total of the expenses.

STEP 3   **Close Income Summary to Capital.**   The balance in Income Summary represents the net income (credit balance) or net loss (debit balance) for the period. This balance is transferred to the owner's capital account. If net income has been earned, Income Summary is debited to create a zero balance, and the owner's capital account is credited. If a net loss has been incurred, the owner's capital account is debited and Income Summary is credited to create a zero balance Figure 6-5 shows examples of Step 3 for net income and net loss.

FIGURE 6-5   Step 3: Closing Net Income and Closing Net Loss

NET INCOME				NET LOSS			
Capital				**Capital**			
	1,000	STEP 3		STEP 3	2,000		
	(Net Income)			(Net Loss)			
Income Summary				**Income Summary**			
(Exp.)	4,000	5,000	(Rev.)	(Exp.)	6,000	4,000	(Rev.)
STEP 3	1,000					2,000	STEP 3

STEP 4   **Close Drawing to Capital.**   Drawing has a debit balance and reduces owner's equity. Therefore, it is credited to create a zero balance. The owner's capital account is debited.

 LEARNING KEY   The owner can make withdrawals from the business for any amount and at any time, as long as the assets are available. These withdrawals are for personal reasons and have nothing to do with measuring the profitability of the firm. Thus, they are closed directly to the owner's capital account.

Upon completion of these four steps, all temporary accounts have zero balances as indicated by the rules at the bottom of the T accounts. The earnings and withdrawals for the period have been transferred to the owner's capital account.

Journalize Closing Entries

Of course, to actually change the ledger accounts, the closing entries must be journalized and posted to the general ledger. As shown in Figure 6-6, the balances of the accounts to be closed are readily available from the Income Statement and Balance Sheet columns of the work sheet. These balances are used to illustrate the closing entries for Jessie Jane's Campus Delivery, in T account and general journal form, in Figures 6-7 and 6-8 respectively. Remember: closing entries are made at the end of the *fiscal year*. Closing entries at the end of June are illustrated here so you can see the completion of the accounting cycle for Jessie Jane's Campus Delivery.

FIGURE 6-6   Role of the Work Sheet in the Closing Process

Jessie Jane's Campus Delivery
Work Sheet (Partial)
For Month Ended June 30, 19--

	ACCOUNT TITLE	INCOME STATEMENT DEBIT	INCOME STATEMENT CREDIT	BALANCE SHEET DEBIT	BALANCE SHEET CREDIT	
1	Cash			3 7 0 00		1
2	Accounts Receivable			5 0 0 00		2
3	Supplies			2 0 00		3
4	Prepaid Insurance			1 7 5 00		4
5	Delivery Equipment			3 6 0 0 00		5
6	Accum. Depr.—Del. Equip.				1 0 0 00	6
7	Accounts Payable				1 8 0 0 00	7
8	Wages Payable				5 0 00	8
9	Jessica Jane, Capital				2 0 0 0 00	9
10	Jessica Jane, Drawing			1 5 0 00		10
11	Delivery Fees		2 0 0 0 00			11
12	Rent Expense	2 0 0 00				12
13	Wages Expense	7 0 0 00				13
14	Supplies Expense	6 0 00				14
15	Telephone Expense	5 0 00				15
16	Depr. Exp.—Del. Equip.	1 0 0 00				16
17	Insurance Expense	2 5 00				17
18		1 1 3 5 00	2 0 0 0 00	4 8 1 5 00	3 9 5 0 00	18
19	Net Income	8 6 5 00			8 6 5 00	19
20		2 0 0 0 00	2 0 0 0 00	4 8 1 5 00	4 8 1 5 00	20

STEP 1 Close revenue accounts to Income Summary.

STEP 2 Close expense accounts to Income Summary.

STEP 3 Close Income Summary to the owner's capital account.

STEP 4 Close Drawing to the owner's capital account.

Like adjusting entries, the closing entries are made on the last day of the accounting period. "Closing Entries" is written in the description column before the first entry and no explanations are required. Note that it is best to make one compound entry to close the expense accounts.

FIGURE 6-7 Closing Entries in T Account Form

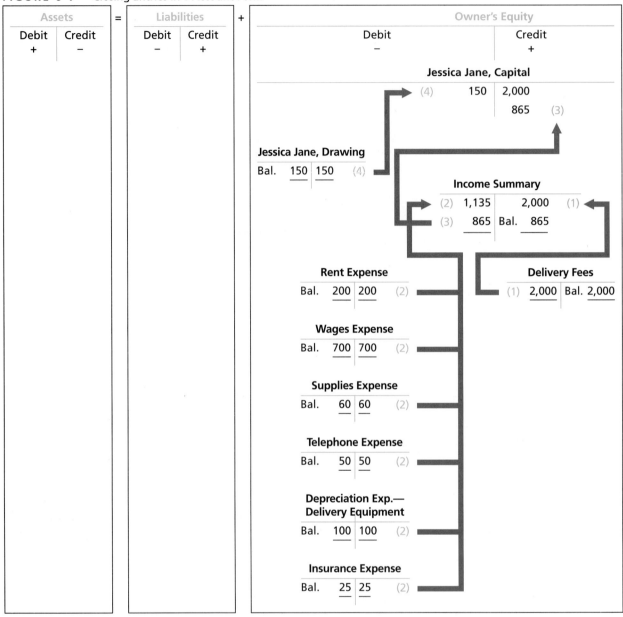

 LEARNING KEY Each individual revenue, expense, and drawing account must be closed.

Post the Closing Entries

The account numbers have been entered in the Posting Reference column of the journal to show that the entries have been posted to the ledger

FIGURE 6-8 Closing Entries in General Journal

GENERAL JOURNAL   PAGE **4**

	DATE		DESCRIPTION	POST. REF.	DEBIT	CREDIT	
1			Closing Entries				1
2	June	30	Delivery Fees	411	2 0 0 0 00		2
3			Income Summary	313		2 0 0 0 00	3
4							4
5		30	Income Summary	313	1 1 3 5 00		5
6			Rent Expense	541		2 0 0 00	6
7			Wages Expense	542		7 0 0 00	7
8			Supplies Expense	543		6 0 00	8
9			Telephone Expense	545		5 0 00	9
10			Depr. Exp.—Del. Equip.	547		1 0 0 00	10
11			Insurance Expense	559		2 5 00	11
12							12
13		30	Income Summary	313	8 6 5 00		13
14			Jessica Jane, Capital	311		8 6 5 00	14
15							15
16		30	Jessica Jane, Capital	311	1 5 0 00		16
17			Jessica Jane, Drawing	312		1 5 0 00	17
18							18
19							19

STEP 1 (row 2)
STEP 2 (row 5)
Compound entry
STEP 3 (row 13)
STEP 4 (row 16)
No explanations are necessary

accounts illustrated in Figure 6-9. Note that "Closing" has been written in the Item column of each account to identify the closing entries. Zero account balances are recorded by drawing a line through both the debit and credit Balance columns.

LEARNING KEY Once the closing entries are posted, the general ledger account balances will agree with the amounts reported on the balance sheet.

FIGURE 6-9 Closing Entries Posted to the General Ledger

GENERAL LEDGER

ACCOUNT: Jessica Jane, Capital   ACCOUNT NO. **311**

DATE		ITEM	POST. REF.	DEBIT	CREDIT	BALANCE DEBIT	BALANCE CREDIT
June	1		J1		2 0 0 0 00		2 0 0 0 00
	30	Closing	J4		8 6 5 00		2 8 6 5 00
	30	Closing	J4	1 5 0 00			2 7 1 5 00

FIGURE 6-9 Closing Entries Posted to the General Ledger (continued)

ACCOUNT: Jessica Jane, Drawing ACCOUNT NO. 312

DATE	ITEM	POST. REF.	DEBIT	CREDIT	BALANCE DEBIT	BALANCE CREDIT
19-- June 30		J2	1 5 0 00		1 5 0 00	
30	Closing	J4		1 5 0 00	——	——

ACCOUNT: Income Summary ACCOUNT NO. 313

DATE	ITEM	POST. REF.	DEBIT	CREDIT	BALANCE DEBIT	BALANCE CREDIT
19-- June 30	Closing	J4		2 0 0 0 00		2 0 0 0 00
30	Closing	J4	1 1 3 5 00			8 6 5 00
30	Closing	J4	8 6 5 00		——	——

ACCOUNT: Delivery Fees ACCOUNT NO. 411

DATE	ITEM	POST. REF.	DEBIT	CREDIT	BALANCE DEBIT	BALANCE CREDIT
19-- June 6		J1		5 0 0 00		5 0 0 00
15		J1		6 0 0 00		1 1 0 0 00
30		J2		9 0 0 00		2 0 0 0 00
30	Closing	J4	2 0 0 0 00		——	——

ACCOUNT: Rent Expense ACCOUNT NO. 541

DATE	ITEM	POST. REF.	DEBIT	CREDIT	BALANCE DEBIT	BALANCE CREDIT
19-- June 7		J1	2 0 0 00			2 0 0 00
30	Closing	J4		2 0 0 00	——	——

ACCOUNT: Wages Expense ACCOUNT NO. 542

DATE	ITEM	POST. REF.	DEBIT	CREDIT	BALANCE DEBIT	BALANCE CREDIT
19-- June 27		J2	6 5 0 00		6 5 0 00	
30	Adjusting	J3	5 0 00		7 0 0 00	
30	Closing	J4		7 0 0 00	——	——

ACCOUNT: Supplies Expense ACCOUNT NO. 543

DATE	ITEM	POST. REF.	DEBIT	CREDIT	BALANCE DEBIT	BALANCE CREDIT
19-- June 30	Adjusting	J3	6 0 00		6 0 00	
30	Closing	J4		6 0 00	——	——

FIGURE 6-9   Closing Entries Posted to the General Ledger (concluded)

ACCOUNT: **Telephone Expense**   ACCOUNT NO. 545

DATE		ITEM	POST. REF.	DEBIT	CREDIT	BALANCE DEBIT	BALANCE CREDIT
19-- June	15		J1	5 0 00		5 0 00	
	30	Closing	J4		5 0 00	——	——

ACCOUNT: **Depreciation Expense**   ACCOUNT NO. 547

DATE		ITEM	POST. REF.	DEBIT	CREDIT	BALANCE DEBIT	BALANCE CREDIT
19-- June	30	Adjusting	J3	1 0 0 00		1 0 0 00	
	30	Closing	J4		1 0 0 00	——	——

ACCOUNT: **Insurance Expense**   ACCOUNT NO. 559

DATE		ITEM	POST. REF.	DEBIT	CREDIT	BALANCE DEBIT	BALANCE CREDIT
19-- June	30	Adjusting	J3	2 5 00		2 5 00	
	30	Closing	J4		2 5 00	——	——

POST-CLOSING TRIAL BALANCE

LO3   Prepare a post-closing trial balance.

After posting the closing entries, a **post-closing trial balance** should be pre-pared to prove the equality of the debit and credit balances in the general ledger accounts. The ending balance of each general ledger account that remains open at the end of the year is listed. Remember: only the perma-nent accounts remain open after the closing process is completed. Figure 6-10 shows the post-closing trial balance for Jane's ledger.

THE ACCOUNTING CYCLE

LO4   List and describe the steps in the accounting cycle.

The steps involved in accounting for all of the business activities during an accounting period are called the **accounting cycle.** The cycle begins with the analysis of source documents and ends with a post-closing trial balance. A brief summary of the steps in the cycle follows.

FIGURE 6-10   Post-Closing Trial Balance

Jessie Jane's Campus Delivery
Post-Closing Trial Balance
June 30, 19--

ACCOUNT TITLE	ACCOUNT NO.	DEBIT BALANCE	CREDIT BALANCE
Cash	111	3 7 0 00	
Accounts Receivable	131	5 0 0 00	
Supplies	151	2 0 00	
Prepaid Insurance	155	1 7 5 00	
Delivery Equipment	185	3 6 0 0 00	
Accumulated Depreciation—Delivery Equipment	185.1		1 0 0 00
Accounts Payable	216		1 8 0 0 00
Wages Payable	219		5 0 00
Jessica Jane, Capital	311		2 7 1 5 00
		4 6 6 5 00	4 6 6 5 00

STEPS IN THE ACCOUNTING CYCLE

During Accounting Period

STEP 1   Analyze source documents.

STEP 2   Journalize the transactions.

STEP 3   Post to the ledger accounts.

End of Accounting Period

STEP 4   Prepare a trial balance.

STEP 5   Determine and prepare the needed adjustments on the work sheet.

STEP 6   Complete an end-of-period work sheet.

STEP 7   Prepare an income statement, statement of owner's equity, and balance sheet.

STEP 8   Journalize and post the adjusting entries.

STEP 9   Journalize and post the closing entries.

STEP 10   Prepare a post-closing trial balance.

> Properly analyzing and journalizing transactions is very important. A mistake made in Step 1 is carried through the entire accounting cycle.

Steps (4) through (10) in the preceding list are performed *as of* the last day of the accounting period. This does not mean that they are actually done on the last day. The accountant may not be able to do any of these things until the first few days (sometimes weeks) of the next period. Nevertheless, the work sheet, statements, and entries are prepared as of the closing date.

KEY POINTS

1 The work sheet is a very useful tool. It is used as an aid in preparing the:

1. adjusting entries,
2. financial statements, and
3. closing entries.

The following classifications are used for accounts reported on the balance sheet.

- **Current assets** include cash and assets that will be converted into cash or consumed within either one year or the normal operating cycle of the business, whichever is longer. An **operating cycle** is the time required to purchase supplies and services and convert them back into cash.
- **Property, plant, and equipment,** also called **plant assets** or **long-term assets,** represent assets that are expected to serve the business for many years.
- **Current liabilities** are liabilities that are due within either one year or the normal operating cycle of the business, whichever is longer, and that are to be paid out of current assets.
- **Long-term liabilities,** or **long-term debt,** are obligations that are not expected to be paid within a year and do not require the use of current assets.

2 Steps in the closing process are:

1. Close revenue accounts to Income Summary.
2. Close expense accounts to Income Summary.
3. Close Income Summary to Capital.
4. Close Drawing to Capital.

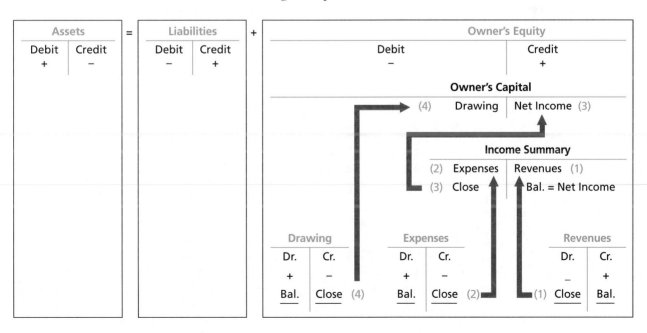

3 After posting the closing entries, a post-closing trial balance should be prepared to prove the equality of the debit and credit balances in the general ledger accounts. The accounts shown in the post-closing trial balance are the permanent accounts.

4 Steps in the accounting cycle are:

During Accounting Period

1. Analyze source documents.
2. Journalize the transactions.
3. Post to the ledger accounts.

End of Accounting Period

4. Prepare a trial balance.
5. Determine and prepare the needed adjustments on the work sheet.
6. Complete an end-of-period work sheet.
7. Prepare an income statement, statement of owner's equity, and balance sheet.
8. Journalize and post the adjusting entries.
9. Journalize and post the closing entries.
10. Prepare a post-closing trial balance.

KEY TERMS

account form of balance sheet 166   The assets are on the left and the liabilities and the owner's equity sections are on the right.

accounting cycle 175   The steps involved in accounting for all of the business activities during an accounting period.

classified balance sheet 167   Similar items are grouped together on the balance sheet.

closing process 169   The process of giving zero balances to the temporary accounts so that they can accumulate information for the next accounting period.

current assets 167   Cash and assets that will be converted into cash or consumed within either one year or the normal operating cycle of the business, whichever is longer.

current liabilities 168   Liabilities that are due within either one year or the normal operating cycle of the business, whichever is longer, and that are to be paid out of current assets.

Income Summary 169   A temporary account used in the closing process to summarize the effects of all revenue and expense accounts.

long-term assets 168   See property, plant, and equipment.

long-term debt 168   See long-term liabilities.

long-term liabilities 168   Obligations that are not expected to be paid within a year and do not require the use of current assets.

operating cycle 167   The period of time required to purchase supplies and services and convert them back into cash.

permanent accounts 169   All accounts reported on the balance sheet.

plant assets 168   See property, plant, and equipment.

post-closing trial balance 175   Prepared after posting the closing entries to prove the equality of the debit and credit balances in the general ledger accounts.

property, plant, and equipment 168   Assets that are expected to serve the business for many years. Also called plant assets or long-term assets.

report form of balance sheet 166   The liabilities and the owner's equity sections are shown below the assets section.

temporary accounts 169   Accounts that do not accumulate information across accounting periods but are closed, such as the drawing account and all income statement accounts.

REVIEW QUESTIONS

1. Identify the source of the information needed to prepare the income statement.
2. Describe two approaches to listing the expenses in the income statement.
3. Identify the sources of the information needed to prepare the statement of owner's equity.
4. If additional investments were made during the year, what information in addition to the work sheet would be needed to prepare the statement of owner's equity?
5. Identify the sources of the information needed to prepare the balance sheet.
6. What is a permanent account? On which financial statement are permanent accounts reported?
7. Name three types of temporary accounts.
8. List the four steps for closing the temporary accounts.
9. Describe the net effect of the four closing entries on the balance of the owner's capital account. Where else is this same amount calculated?
10. What is the purpose of the post-closing trial balance?
11. List the ten steps in the accounting cycle.

MANAGING YOUR WRITING

At lunch, two bookkeepers got into a heated discussion about whether closing entries should be made before or after preparing the financial statements. They have come to you to resolve this issue and have agreed to accept your position. Write a memo explaining the purpose of closing entries and whether they should be made before or after preparing the financial statements.

DEMONSTRATION PROBLEM

Timothy Chang owns and operates Hard Copy Printers. A work sheet for the year ended December 31, 19--, is provided on the next page. Chang made no additional investments during the year.

REQUIRED

1. Prepare financial statements.
2. Prepare closing entries.

Hard Copy Printers
Work Sheet
For Year Ended December 31, 19—

	ACCOUNT TITLE	TRIAL BALANCE Debit	TRIAL BALANCE Credit	ADJUSTMENTS Debit	ADJUSTMENTS Credit	ADJUSTED TRIAL BALANCE Debit	ADJUSTED TRIAL BALANCE Credit	INCOME STATEMENT Debit	INCOME STATEMENT Credit	BALANCE SHEET Debit	BALANCE SHEET Credit
1	Cash	1 1 8 0 00				1 1 8 0 00				1 1 8 0 00	
2	Paper Supplies	3 6 0 0 00			(a) 3 5 5 0 00	5 0 00				5 0 00	
3	Prepaid Insurance	1 0 0 0 00			(b) 5 0 5 00	4 9 5 00				4 9 5 00	
4	Printing Equipment	5 8 0 0 00				5 8 0 0 00				5 8 0 0 00	
5	Accum. Depr.—Printing Equip.				(d) 1 2 0 0 00		1 2 0 0 00				1 2 0 0 00
6	Accounts Payable		5 0 0 00				5 0 0 00				5 0 0 00
7	Wages Payable				(c) 3 0 00		3 0 00				3 0 00
8	Timothy Chang, Capital		1 0 0 0 0 00				1 0 0 0 0 00				1 0 0 0 0 00
9	Timothy Chang, Drawing	1 3 0 0 0 00				1 3 0 0 0 00				1 3 0 0 0 00	
10	Printing Fees		3 5 1 0 0 00				3 5 1 0 0 00		3 5 1 0 0 00		
11	Rent Expense	7 5 0 0 00				7 5 0 0 00		7 5 0 0 00			
12	Wages Expense	1 1 9 7 0 00		(c) 3 0 00		1 2 0 0 0 00		1 2 0 0 0 00			
13	Paper Supplies Expense			(a) 3 5 5 0 00		3 5 5 0 00		3 5 5 0 00			
14	Telephone Expense	5 5 0 00				5 5 0 00		5 5 0 00			
15	Depr. Expense—Printing Equip.			(d) 1 2 0 0 00		1 2 0 0 00		1 2 0 0 00			
16	Utilities Expense	1 0 0 0 00				1 0 0 0 00		1 0 0 0 00			
17	Insurance Expense			(b) 5 0 5 00		5 0 5 00		5 0 5 00			
18		4 5 6 0 0 00	4 5 6 0 0 00	5 2 8 5 00	5 2 8 5 00	4 6 8 3 0 00	4 6 8 3 0 00	2 6 3 0 5 00	3 5 1 0 0 00	2 0 5 2 5 00	1 1 7 3 0 00
19	Net Income							8 7 9 5 00			8 7 9 5 00
20								3 5 1 0 0 00	3 5 1 0 0 00	2 0 5 2 5 00	2 0 5 2 5 00

SOLUTION

1.

Hard Copy Printers
Income Statement
For Year Ended December 31, 19--

Revenue:			
Printing fees			$35 1 0 0 00
Expenses:			
Rent expense	$ 7 5 0 0 00		
Wages expense	12 0 0 0 00		
Paper supplies expense	3 5 5 0 00		
Telephone expense	5 5 0 00		
Depreciation expense—printing equipment	1 2 0 0 00		
Utilities expense	1 0 0 0 00		
Insurance expense	5 0 5 00		
Total expenses			26 3 0 5 00
Net income			$ 8 7 9 5 00

Hard Copy Printers
Statement of Owner's Equity
For Year Ended December 31, 19--

Timothy Chang, capital, Jan. 1, 19--			$10 0 0 0 00
Net income for 19--	$ 8 7 9 5 00		
Less withdrawals for 19--	13 0 0 0 00		
Decrease in capital			(4 2 0 5 00)
Timothy Chang, capital, Dec. 31, 19--			$ 5 7 9 5 00

Hard Copy Printers
Balance Sheet
December 31, 19--

<div align="center">Assets</div>			
Current assets:			
Cash	$1 1 8 0 00		
Paper supplies	5 0 00		
Prepaid insurance	4 9 5 00		
Total current assets			$1 7 2 5 00
Property, plant, and equipment:			
Printing equipment	$5 8 0 0 00		
Less accumulated depreciation	1 2 0 0 00	4 6 0 0 00	
Total assets			$6 3 2 5 00
<div align="center">Liabilities</div>			
Current liabilities:			
Accounts payable	$ 5 0 0 00		
Wages payable	3 0 00		
Total current liabilities			$ 5 3 0 00
<div align="center">Owner's Equity</div>			
Timothy Chang, capital			5 7 9 5 00
Total liabilities and owner's equity			$6 3 2 5 00

2.

			GENERAL JOURNAL				PAGE 4	
	DATE		DESCRIPTION	POST. REF.	DEBIT	CREDIT	
1			Closing Entries				1
2	Dec.¹⁹⁻⁻	31	Printing Fees		35 1 0 0 00		2
3			Income Summary			35 1 0 0 00	3
4							4
5		31	Income Summary		26 3 0 5 00		5
6			Rent Expense			7 5 0 0 00	6
7			Wages Expense			12 0 0 0 00	7
8			Paper Supplies Expense			3 5 5 0 00	8
9			Telephone Expense			5 5 0 00	9
10			Depr. Expense—Printing Equip.			1 2 0 0 00	10
11			Utilities Expense			1 0 0 0 00	11
12			Insurance Expense			5 0 5 00	12
13							13
14		31	Income Summary		8 7 9 5 00		14
15			Timothy Chang, Capital			8 7 9 5 00	15
16							16
17		31	Timothy Chang, Capital		13 0 0 0 00		17
18			Timothy Chang, Drawing			13 0 0 0 00	18
19							19
20							20
21							21
22							22

SERIES A EXERCISES

1 **EXERCISE 6A1 INCOME STATEMENT** From the partial work sheet for Case Advising on page 183, prepare an income statement.

1 **EXERCISE 6A2 STATEMENT OF OWNER'S EQUITY** From the partial work sheet in Exercise 6A1, prepare a statement of owner's equity, assuming no additional investment was made by the owner.

1 **EXERCISE 6A3 BALANCE SHEET** From the partial work sheet in Exercise 6A1, prepare a balance sheet.

2 **EXERCISE 6A4 CLOSING ENTRIES (NET INCOME)** Set up T accounts for Case Advising based on the work sheet and chart of accounts provided on page 183. Enter the existing balance for each account. Prepare closing entries in general journal form. Then post the closing entries to the T accounts.

Case Advising
Work Sheet (Partial)
For Month Ended January 31, 19--

	ACCOUNT TITLE	INCOME STATEMENT		BALANCE SHEET		
		DEBIT	CREDIT	DEBIT	CREDIT	
1	Cash			1 2 1 2 00		1
2	Accounts Receivable			8 9 6 00		2
3	Supplies			4 8 2 00		3
4	Prepaid Insurance			9 0 0 00		4
5	Office Equipment			3 0 0 0 00		5
6	Accum. Depr.—Off. Equip.				1 0 0 00	6
7	Accounts Payable				1 0 0 0 00	7
8	Wages Payable				2 0 0 00	8
9	Bill Case, Capital				4 0 0 0 00	9
10	Bill Case, Drawing			8 0 0 00		10
11	Advising Fees		3 7 9 3 00			11
12	Rent Expense	5 0 0 00				12
13	Wages Expense	8 0 0 00				13
14	Supplies Expense	1 2 0 00				14
15	Telephone Expense	5 8 00				15
16	Depr. Exp.—Off. Equip.	1 0 0 00				16
17	Insurance Expense	3 0 00				17
18	Electricity Expense	4 4 00				18
19	Advertising Expense	8 0 00				19
20	Gas and Oil Expense	3 8 00				20
21	Miscellaneous Expense	3 3 00				21
22		1 8 0 3 00	3 7 9 3 00	7 2 9 0 00	5 3 0 0 00	22
23	Net Income	1 9 9 0 00			1 9 9 0 00	23
24		3 7 9 3 00	3 7 9 3 00	7 2 9 0 00	7 2 9 0 00	24

Chart of Accounts

Assets
111	Cash
131	Accounts Receivable
151	Supplies
155	Prepaid Insurance
181	Office Equipment
181.1	Accum. Depr.—Office Equip.

Liabilities
| 216 | Accounts Payable |
| 219 | Wages Payable |

Owner's Equity
311	Bill Case, Capital
312	Bill Case, Drawing
313	Income Summary

Revenues
| 411 | Advising Fees |

Expenses
541	Rent Expense
542	Wages Expense
543	Supplies Expense
545	Telephone Expense
547	Depr. Exp.—Office Equip.
548	Insurance Expense
549	Electricity Expense
551	Advertising Expense
552	Gas and Oil Expense
572	Miscellaneous Expense

2 **EXERCISE 6A5 CLOSING ENTRIES (NET LOSS)** Using the following T accounts, prepare closing entries in general journal form dated January 31, 19--. Then post the closing entries to the T accounts.

Accum. Depr.— Del. Equip. 185.1		Rent Expense 541		Insurance Expense 548
Bal. 100		Bal. 500		Bal. 30

Wages Payable 219		Wages Expense 542		Electricity Expense 549
Bal. 200		Bal. 1,800		Bal. 44

Saburo Goto, Capital 311		Supplies Expense 543		Advertising Expense 551
Bal. 4,000		Bal. 120		Bal. 80

Saburo Goto, Drawing 312		Telephone Expense 545		Gas and Oil Expense 552
Bal. 800		Bal. 58		Bal. 38

Income Summary 313		Depr. Exp.— Del. Equip. 547		Miscellaneous Expense 572
		Bal. 100		Bal. 33

Delivery Fees 411
Bal. 2,200

SERIES A PROBLEMS

1 **PROBLEM 6A1 FINANCIAL STATEMENTS** The following page shows a work sheet for Monte's Repairs. No additional investments were made by the owner during the month.

REQUIRED

1. Prepare an income statement.
2. Prepare a statement of owner's equity.
3. Prepare a balance sheet.

1 **PROBLEM 6A2 STATEMENT OF OWNER'S EQUITY** The capital account for Autumn Chou, with an additional investment, and a partial work sheet are shown on page 186.

Monte's Repairs
Work Sheet
For Month Ended January 31, 19--

	ACCOUNT TITLE	TRIAL BALANCE DEBIT	TRIAL BALANCE CREDIT	ADJUSTMENTS DEBIT	ADJUSTMENTS CREDIT	ADJUSTED TRIAL BALANCE DEBIT	ADJUSTED TRIAL BALANCE CREDIT	INCOME STATEMENT DEBIT	INCOME STATEMENT CREDIT	BALANCE SHEET DEBIT	BALANCE SHEET CREDIT	
1	Cash	3 1 5 0 00				3 1 5 0 00				3 1 5 0 00		1
2	Accounts Receivable	1 2 0 0 00				1 2 0 0 00				1 2 0 0 00		2
3	Supplies	8 0 0 00			(a) 2 0 0 00	6 0 0 00				6 0 0 00		3
4	Prepaid Insurance	9 0 0 00			(b) 1 0 0 00	8 0 0 00				8 0 0 00		4
5	Delivery Equipment	3 0 0 0 00				3 0 0 0 00				3 0 0 0 00		5
6	Accum. Depr.—Delivery Equip.				(d) 3 0 00		3 0 00				3 0 00	6
7	Accounts Payable		1 1 0 0 00				1 1 0 0 00				1 1 0 0 00	7
8	Wages Payable				(c) 1 5 0 00		1 5 0 00				1 5 0 00	8
9	Monte Eli, Capital		7 0 0 0 00				7 0 0 0 00				7 0 0 0 00	9
10	Monte Eli, Drawing	1 0 0 0 00				1 0 0 0 00				1 0 0 0 00		10
11	Repair Fees		4 2 3 0 00				4 2 3 0 00		4 2 3 0 00			11
12	Rent Expense	4 2 0 00				4 2 0 00		4 2 0 00				12
13	Wages Expense	1 6 5 0 00		(c) 1 5 0 00		1 8 0 0 00		1 8 0 0 00				13
14	Supplies Expense			(a) 2 0 0 00		2 0 0 00		2 0 0 00				14
15	Telephone Expense	4 9 00				4 9 00		4 9 00				15
16	Depr. Exp.—Delivery Equip.			(d) 3 0 00		3 0 00		3 0 00				16
17	Insurance Expense			(b) 1 0 0 00		1 0 0 00		1 0 0 00				17
18	Advertising Expense	1 0 0 00				1 0 0 00		1 0 0 00				18
19	Gas and Oil Expense	3 3 00				3 3 00		3 3 00				19
20	Miscellaneous Expense	2 8 00				2 8 00		2 8 00				20
21		1 2 3 3 0 00	1 2 3 3 0 00	4 8 0 00	4 8 0 00	1 2 5 1 0 00	1 2 5 1 0 00	2 7 6 0 00	4 2 3 0 00	9 7 5 0 00	8 2 8 0 00	21
22	Net Income							1 4 7 0 00			1 4 7 0 00	22
23								4 2 3 0 00	4 2 3 0 00	9 7 5 0 00	9 7 5 0 00	23
24												24
25												25
26												26
27												27
28												28
29												29
30												30
31												31
32												32

REQUIRED

Prepare a statement of owner's equity.

GENERAL LEDGER

ACCOUNT: Autumn Chou, Capital   ACCOUNT NO. 311

DATE		ITEM	POST. REF.	DEBIT	CREDIT	BALANCE DEBIT	BALANCE CREDIT
19-- Jan.	1	Balance	✔				4 8 0 0 00
	18		J1		1 2 0 0 00		6 0 0 0 00

Autumn's Home Designs
Work Sheet (Partial)
For Month Ended January 31, 19--

	ACCOUNT TITLE	INCOME STATEMENT DEBIT	INCOME STATEMENT CREDIT	BALANCE SHEET DEBIT	BALANCE SHEET CREDIT	
1	Cash			3 2 0 0 00		1
2	Accounts Receivable			1 6 0 0 00		2
3	Supplies			8 0 0 00		3
4	Prepaid Insurance			9 0 0 00		4
5	Office Equipment			2 5 0 0 00		5
6	Accum. Depr.—Office Equip.				5 0 00	6
7	Accounts Payable				1 9 5 0 00	7
8	Wages Payable				1 8 0 00	8
9	Autumn Chou, Capital				6 0 0 0 00	9
10	Autumn Chou, Drawing			1 0 0 0 00		10
11	Design Fees		4 8 6 6 00			11
12	Rent Expense	6 0 0 00				12
13	Wages Expense	1 9 0 0 00				13
14	Supplies Expense	2 0 0 00				14
15	Telephone Expense	8 5 00				15
16	Depr. Exp.—Office Equip.	5 0 00				16
17	Insurance Expense	6 0 00				17
18	Electricity Expense	4 8 00				18
19	Advertising Expense	2 1 00				19
20	Gas and Oil Expense	3 2 00				20
21	Miscellaneous Expense	5 0 00				21
22		3 0 4 6 00	4 8 6 6 00	1 0 0 0 0 00	8 1 8 0 00	22
23	Net Income	1 8 2 0 00			1 8 2 0 00	23
24		4 8 6 6 00	4 8 6 6 00	1 0 0 0 0 00	1 0 0 0 0 00	24

1/2/3   **PROBLEM 6A3 FINANCIAL STATEMENTS, CLOSING ENTRIES, POST-CLOSING TRIAL BALANCE**   Refer to the work sheet in Problem 6A1 for Monte's Repairs. The trial balance amounts (before adjustments) have been entered in the ledger accounts provided in the working papers. If you are not using the working papers that accompany this book, set up ledger accounts and enter these balances as of January 31, 19--. A chart of accounts is provided below.

Monte's Repairs
Chart of Accounts

Assets

111	Cash
131	Accounts Receivable
151	Supplies
155	Prepaid Insurance
185	Delivery Equipment
185.1	Accum. Depr.—Delivery Equip.

Liabilities

216	Accounts Payable
219	Wages Payable

Owner's Equity

311	Monte Eli, Capital
312	Monte Eli, Drawing
313	Income Summary

Revenues

411	Repair Fees

Expenses

541	Rent Expense
542	Wages Expense
543	Supplies Expense
545	Telephone Expense
547	Depr. Exp.—Delivery Equip.
548	Insurance Expense
551	Advertising Expense
552	Gas and Oil Expense
572	Miscellaneous Expense

REQUIRED

1. Journalize (page 10) and post the adjusting entries.
2. Journalize (page 11) and post the closing entries.
3. Prepare a post-closing trial balance.

SERIES B   EXERCISES

1 **EXERCISE 6B1 INCOME STATEMENT**   From the partial work sheet for Adams' Shoe Shine shown on the next page, prepare an income statement.

1 **EXERCISE 6B2 STATEMENT OF OWNER'S EQUITY**   From the partial work sheet in Exercise 6B1, prepare a statement of owner's equity, assuming no additional investment was made by the owner.

1 **EXERCISE 6B3 BALANCE SHEET**   From the partial work sheet in Exercise 6B1, prepare a balance sheet for Adams' Shoe Shine.

2 **EXERCISE 6B4 CLOSING ENTRIES (NET INCOME)**   Set up T accounts for Adams' Shoe Shine based on the work sheet and chart of accounts provided on page 188. Enter the existing balance for each account. Prepare closing entries in general journal form. Then, post the closing entries to the T accounts.

Adams' Shoe Shine
Work Sheet (Partial)
For Month Ended June 30, 19--

	ACCOUNT TITLE	INCOME STATEMENT DEBIT	INCOME STATEMENT CREDIT	BALANCE SHEET DEBIT	BALANCE SHEET CREDIT	
1	Cash			3 2 6 2 00		1
2	Accounts Receivable			1 2 4 4 00		2
3	Supplies			8 0 0 00		3
4	Prepaid Insurance			6 4 0 00		4
5	Office Equipment			2 1 0 0 00		5
6	Accum. Depr.—Office Equip.				1 1 0 00	6
7	Accounts Payable				1 8 5 0 00	7
8	Wages Payable				2 6 0 00	8
9	Mary Adams, Capital				6 0 0 0 00	9
10	Mary Adams, Drawing			2 0 0 0 00		10
11	Service Fees		4 8 1 3 00			11
12	Rent Expense	9 0 0 00				12
13	Wages Expense	1 0 8 0 00				13
14	Supplies Expense	3 2 2 00				14
15	Telephone Expense	1 3 3 00				15
16	Depr. Exp.—Office Equip.	1 1 0 00				16
17	Insurance Expense	1 2 0 00				17
18	Utilities Expense	1 0 2 00				18
19	Advertising Expense	3 4 00				19
20	Gas and Oil Expense	8 8 00				20
21	Miscellaneous Expense	9 8 00				21
22		2 9 8 7 00	4 8 1 3 00	1 0 0 4 6 00	8 2 2 0 00	22
23	Net Income	1 8 2 6 00			1 8 2 6 00	23
24		4 8 1 3 00	4 8 1 3 00	1 0 0 4 6 00	1 0 0 4 6 00	24

Chart of Accounts

Assets
111   Cash
131   Accounts Receivable
151   Supplies
155   Prepaid Insurance
191   Office Equipment
191.1   Accum. Depr.—Office Equip.

Liabilities
216   Accounts Payable
219   Wages Payable

Owner's Equity
311   Mary Adams, Capital
312   Mary Adams, Drawing
313   Income Summary

Revenues
411   Service Fees

Expenses
541   Rent Expense
542   Wages Expense
543   Supplies Expense
545   Telephone Expense
547   Depr. Exp.—Office Equip.
548   Insurance Expense
549   Utilities Expense
551   Advertising Expense
552   Gas and Oil Expense
572   Miscellaneous Expense

2 **EXERCISE 6B5 CLOSING ENTRIES (NET LOSS)**   From the T accounts shown below, prepare closing entries in general journal form dated June 30, 19--. Then, post the closing entries to the T accounts.

Accum. Depr.—Office Equip. 191.1		Rent Expense 541		Insurance Expense 548	
	Bal. 110	Bal. 900		Bal. 120	

Wages Payable 219		Wages Expense 542		Utilities Expense 549	
	Bal. 260	Bal. 1,080		Bal. 102	

Raquel Zapata, Capital 311		Supplies Expense 543		Advertising Expense 551	
	Bal. 6,000	Bal. 322		Bal. 34	

Raquel Zapata, Drawing 312		Telephone Expense 545		Gas and Oil Expense 552	
Bal. 2,000		Bal. 133		Bal. 88	

Income Summary 313		Depr. Exp.—Office Equip. 547		Miscellaneous Expense 572	
		Bal. 110		Bal. 98	

Referral Fees 411	
	Bal. 2,813

SERIES B   PROBLEMS

1 **PROBLEM 6B1 FINANCIAL STATEMENTS**   A work sheet for Juanita's Consulting is shown on page 190. No additional investments were made by the owner this month.

REQUIRED

1. Prepare an income statement.
2. Prepare a statement of owner's equity.
3. Prepare a balance sheet.

Juanita's Consulting
Work Sheet
For Month Ended June 30, 19--

	TRIAL BALANCE		ADJUSTMENTS		ADJUSTED TRIAL BALANCE		INCOME STATEMENT		BALANCE SHEET		
ACCOUNT TITLE	DEBIT	CREDIT	DEBIT	CREDIT	DEBIT	CREDIT	DEBIT	CREDIT	DEBIT	CREDIT	
1 Cash	5285 00				5285 00				5285 00		1
2 Accounts Receivable	1075 00				1075 00				1075 00		2
3 Supplies	750 00			(a) 250 00	500 00				500 00		3
4 Prepaid Insurance	500 00			(b) 100 00	400 00				400 00		4
5 Office Equipment	2200 00				2200 00				2200 00		5
6 Accum. Depr.—Office Equip.				(d) 110 00		110 00				110 00	6
7 Accounts Payable		1500 00				1500 00				1500 00	7
8 Wages Payable				(c) 200 00		200 00				200 00	8
9 Juanita Alvarez, Capital		7000 00				7000 00				7000 00	9
10 Juanita Alvarez, Drawing	800 00				800 00				800 00		10
11 Consulting Fees		4204 00				4204 00		4204 00			11
12 Rent Expense	500 00				500 00		500 00				12
13 Wages Expense	1400 00		(c) 200 00		1600 00		1600 00				13
14 Supplies Expense			(a) 250 00		250 00		250 00				14
15 Telephone Expense	46 00				46 00		46 00				15
16 Depr. Exp.—Office Equip.			(d) 110 00		110 00		110 00				16
17 Insurance Expense			(b) 100 00		100 00		100 00				17
18 Electricity Expense	39 00				39 00		39 00				18
19 Advertising Expense	60 00				60 00		60 00				19
20 Gas and Oil Expense	28 00				28 00		28 00				20
21 Miscellaneous Expense	21 00				21 00		21 00				21
22	12704 00	12704 00	660 00	660 00	13014 00	13014 00	2754 00	4204 00	10260 00	8810 00	22
23 Net Income							1450 00			1450 00	23
24							4204 00	4204 00	10260 00	10260 00	24

1 **PROBLEM 6B2 STATEMENT OF OWNER'S EQUITY** The capital account for Minta's Editorial Services, with an additional investment and a partial work sheet are shown below.

GENERAL LEDGER

ACCOUNT: Minta Berry, Capital   ACCOUNT NO. 311

DATE		ITEM	POST. REF.	DEBIT	CREDIT	BALANCE DEBIT	BALANCE CREDIT
19-- Jan.	1	Balance	✔				3 6 0 0 00
	22		J1		2 9 0 0 00		6 5 0 0 00

Minta's Editorial Services
Work Sheet (Partial)
For Month Ended January 31, 19--

	ACCOUNT TITLE	INCOME STATEMENT DEBIT	INCOME STATEMENT CREDIT	BALANCE SHEET DEBIT	BALANCE SHEET CREDIT	
1	Cash			3 8 0 0 00		1
2	Accounts Receivable			2 2 0 0 00		2
3	Supplies			1 0 0 0 00		3
4	Prepaid Insurance			9 5 0 00		4
5	Comp. Equipment			4 5 0 0 00		5
6	Accum. Depr.—Comp. Equip.				2 2 5 00	6
7	Accounts Payable				2 1 0 0 00	7
8	Wages Payable				1 5 0 00	8
9	Minta Berry, Capital				6 5 0 0 00	9
10	Minta Berry, Drawing			1 7 0 0 00		10
11	Editing Fees		7 0 1 2 00			11
12	Rent Expense	4 5 0 00				12
13	Wages Expense	6 0 0 00				13
14	Supplies Expense	2 8 8 00				14
15	Telephone Expense	4 4 00				15
16	Depr. Exp.—Comp. Equip.	2 2 5 00				16
17	Insurance Expense	1 2 5 00				17
18	Utilities Expense	3 8 00				18
19	Advertising Expense	4 9 00				19
20	Miscellaneous Expense	1 8 00				20
21		1 8 3 7 00	7 0 1 2 00	14 1 5 0 00	8 9 7 5 00	21
22	Net Income	5 1 7 5 00			5 1 7 5 00	22
23		7 0 1 2 00	7 0 1 2 00	14 1 5 0 00	14 1 5 0 00	23
24						24

REQUIRED

Prepare a statement of owner's equity.

1/2/3

PROBLEM 6B3 FINANCIAL STATEMENTS, CLOSING ENTRIES, AND POST-CLOSING TRIAL BALANCE   Refer to the work sheet for Juanita's Consulting in Problem 6B1. The trial balance amounts (before adjustments) have been entered in the ledger accounts provided in the working papers. If you are not using the working papers that accompany this book, set up ledger accounts and enter these balances as of June 30, 19--. A chart of accounts is provided below.

Juanita's Consulting
Chart of Accounts

Assets
111	Cash
131	Accounts Receivable
151	Supplies
155	Prepaid Insurance
191	Office Equipment
191.1	Accum. Depr.—Office Equip.

Liabilities
216	Accounts Payable
219	Wages Payable

Owner's Equity
311	Juanita Alvarez, Capital
312	Juanita Alvarez, Drawing
313	Income Summary

Revenues
411	Consulting Fees

Expenses
541	Rent Expense
542	Wages Expense
543	Supplies Expense
545	Telephone Expense
547	Depr. Exp.—Office Equip.
548	Insurance Expense
549	Electricity Expense
551	Advertising Expense
552	Gas and Oil Expense
572	Miscellaneous Expense

REQUIRED

1. Journalize (page 10) and post the adjusting entries.
2. Journalize (page 11) and post the closing entries.
3. Prepare a post-closing trial balance.

MASTERY PROBLEM

Elizabeth Soltis owns and operates Aunt Ibby's Styling Salon. A year-end work sheet is provided on the next page. Using this information, prepare financial statements and closing entries. Soltis made no additional investments during the year.

Aunt Ibby's Styling Salon
Work Sheet
For Year Ended December 31, 19--

	ACCOUNT TITLE	TRIAL BALANCE DEBIT	TRIAL BALANCE CREDIT	ADJUSTMENTS DEBIT	ADJUSTMENTS CREDIT	ADJUSTED TRIAL BALANCE DEBIT	ADJUSTED TRIAL BALANCE CREDIT	INCOME STATEMENT DEBIT	INCOME STATEMENT CREDIT	BALANCE SHEET DEBIT	BALANCE SHEET CREDIT	
1	Cash	940.00				940.00				940.00		1
2	Styling Supplies	1 500.00			(a) 1 450.00	50.00				50.00		2
3	Prepaid Insurance	800.00			(b) 650.00	150.00				150.00		3
4	Salon Equipment	4 500.00				4 500.00				4 500.00		4
5	Accum. Depr.—Salon Equip.				(d) 900.00		900.00				900.00	5
6	Accounts Payable		225.00				225.00				225.00	6
7	Wages Payable				(c) 40.00		40.00				40.00	7
8	Elizabeth Soltis, Capital		2 765.00				2 765.00				2 765.00	8
9	Elizabeth Soltis, Drawing	12 000.00				12 000.00				12 000.00		9
10	Styling Fees		32 000.00				32 000.00		32 000.00			10
11	Rent Expense	6 000.00				6 000.00		6 000.00				11
12	Wages Expense	8 000.00		(c) 40.00		8 040.00		8 040.00				12
13	Styling Supplies Expense			(a) 1 450.00		1 450.00		1 450.00				13
14	Telephone Expense	450.00				450.00		450.00				14
15	Depr. Expense—Salon Equip.			(d) 900.00		900.00		900.00				15
16	Utilities Expense	800.00				800.00		800.00				16
17	Insurance Expense			(b) 650.00		650.00		650.00				17
18		34 990.00	34 990.00	3 040.00	3 040.00	35 930.00	35 930.00	18 290.00	32 000.00	17 640.00	3 930.00	18
19	Net Income							13 710.00			13 710.00	19
20								32 000.00	32 000.00	17 640.00	17 640.00	20
21												21
22												22
23												23
24												24
25												25
26												26
27												27
28												28
29												29
30												30
31												31
32												32
33												33
34												34
35												35
36												36
37												37
38												38
39												39
40												40
41												41

Statement of Cash Flows

Careful study of this appendix should enable you to:

LO1 Classify business transactions as operating, investing, or financing.

LO2 Prepare a statement of cash flows by analyzing and categorizing a series of business transactions.

Thus far, we have discussed three financial statements: the income statement, the statement of owner's equity, and the balance sheet. A fourth statement, the statement of cash flows, is also very important. It explains what the business did to generate cash and how the cash was used. This is done by categorizing all cash transactions into three types of activities: operating, investing, and financing.

TYPES OF BUSINESS ACTIVITIES

LO1   Classify business transactions as operating, investing, or financing.

There are three types of business activities: operating, investing, and financing.

Cash flows from **operating activities** are related to the revenues and expenses reported on the income statement. Examples include cash received for services performed and the payment of cash for expenses.

Investing activities are those transactions involving the purchase and sale of long-term assets, lending money, and collecting the principal on the related loans.

Financing activities are those transactions dealing with the exchange of cash between the business and its owners and creditors. Examples include cash received from the owner to finance the operations and cash paid to the owner as withdrawals. Financing activities also include borrowing cash and repaying the loan.

Lending money to another entity is an outflow of cash from investing activities. The collection of the principal when the loan is due is an inflow of cash from investing activities. Borrowing cash is an inflow from financing activities. Repayment of the loan is an outflow from financing activities.

Figure 6A-1 provides a review of the transactions for Jessie Jane's Campus Delivery for the month of June. The transactions are classified as operating, investing, or financing, and an explanation for the classification is provided.

FIGURE 6A-1   Summary of Transactions for Jessie Jane's Campus Delivery

SUMMARY OF TRANSACTIONS JESSIE JANE'S CAMPUS DELIVERY	TYPE OF TRANSACTION	EXPLANATION
(a) Jessica Jane invested cash in her business, $2,000.	Financing	Cash received from the owner is an inflow from financing activities. Don't be fooled by the word "invested." From Jane's point of view, this is an investment. From the firm's point of view, this is a way to *finance* the business.
(b) Purchased delivery equipment for cash, $1,200.	Investing	Purchases of long-term assets are investments.
(c) Purchased delivery equipment on account from Big Red Scooters, $900. (Note: Big Red has loaned Jane $900.)	No cash involved	This transaction will not affect the statement of cash flows.
(d) Paid first installment to Big Red Scooters, $300. (See transaction (c).)	Financing	Repayments of loans are financing activities.
(e) Received cash for delivery services rendered, $500.	Operating	Cash received as a result of providing services is classified as an operating activity.
(f) Paid cash for June office rent, $200.	Operating	Cash payments for expenses are classified as operating activities.
(g) Paid telephone bill, $50.	Operating	Cash payments for expenses are classified as operating activities.
(h) Made deliveries on account for a total of $600: $400 for the Accounting Department and $200 for the School of Optometry.	No cash involved	This transaction will not affect the statement of cash flows.
(i) Purchased supplies for cash, $80.	Operating	Cash payments for expenses are classified as operating activities. Most of these supplies were used up. Those that remain will be used in the near future. These are not long-term assets and, thus, do not qualify as investments.
(j) Paid for an eight-month liability insurance policy, $200. Coverage began on June 1.	Operating	Cash payments for expenses are classified as operating activities. Prepaid Insurance is not considered a long-term asset and, thus, does not qualify as an investment.
(k) Received $570 in cash for services performed earlier in transaction (h): $400 from the Accounting Department and $170 from the School of Optometry.	Operating	Cash received as a result of providing services is classified as an operating activity.

FIGURE 6A-1   Summary of Transactions for Jessie Jane's Campus Delivery (concluded)

SUMMARY OF TRANSACTIONS JESSIE JANE'S CAMPUS DELIVERY	TYPE OF TRANSACTION	EXPLANATION
(l) Purchased a third scooter from Big Red Scooters, $1,500. A down payment of $300 was made with the remaining payments expected over the next four months.	Investing	Purchases of long-term assets are investments. Only the $300 cash paid will be reported on the statement of cash flows.
(m) Paid part-time employees wages, $650.	Operating	Cash payments for expenses are classified as operating activities.
(n) Earned delivery fees for the remainder of the month amounting to $900: $430 for cash and $470 on account. Deliveries on account: $100 for the Accounting Department, and $370 for the Athletic Ticket Office.	Operating	Cash received ($430) as a result of providing services is classified as an operating activity.
(o) Jane withdrew cash for personal use, $150.	Financing	Cash payments to owners are classified as a financing activity.

PREPARING THE STATEMENT OF CASH FLOWS

LO2   Prepare a statement of cash flows by analyzing and categorizing a series of business transactions.

The classifications of the cash transactions for Jessie Jane's Campus Delivery are summarized in the expanded cash T account shown in Figure 6A-2. Using this information, we can prepare a statement of cash flows. As shown in Figure 6A-3, the heading is similar to that used for the income statement. Since the statement of cash flows reports on the flow of cash for a period of time, the statement is dated for the month ended June 30, 19--.

FIGURE 6A-2   Cash T Account for Jessie Jane's Campus Delivery with Classifications for Cash Transactions

Cash

Event	Classification	Amount	Amount	Classification	Event	
(a) Investment by Jane.	Financing	2,000	1,200	Investing	Purchased delivery equipment.	(b)
(e) Cash received for services.	Operating	500	300	Financing	Made payment on loan.	(d)
(k) Cash received for services.	Operating	570	200	Operating	Paid office rent.	(f)
(n) Cash received for services.	Operating	430	50	Operating	Paid telephone bill.	(g)
		_3,500_	80	Operating	Purchased supplies.	(i)
			200	Operating	Paid for insurance.	(j)
			300	Investing	Purchased delivery equipment.	(l)
			650	Operating	Paid wages.	(m)
			150	Financing	Withdrawal by owner.	(o)
			_3,130_			
	Bal.	370				

The main body of the statement is arranged in three sections: operating, investing, and financing activities. First, cash received from customers is listed under operating activities. Then, cash payments for operating activities are listed and totaled. The net amount is reported as net cash provided by operating activities. Since this is the main purpose of the business, it is important to be able to generate positive cash flows from operating activities.

The next two sections list the inflows and outflows from investing and financing activities. Debits to the cash account are inflows and credits are outflows. Note that there was an outflow from investing activities resulting from the purchase of the motor scooters. In addition, the business had a net inflow from financing activities because Jane's initial investment more than covered her withdrawal and the payment on the loan. These investing and financing activities are typical for a new business.

> **LEARNING KEY** To prove the accuracy of the statement of cash flows, compare the net increase or decrease reported on the statement with the change in the balance of the cash account.

The sum of the inflows and outflows from operating, investing, and financing activities equals the net increase (or decrease) in the cash account during the period. Since this is a new business, the cash account had a beginning balance of zero. The ending balance is $370. This agrees with the net increase in cash reported on the statement of cash flows of $370.

FIGURE 6A-3   Statement of Cash Flows for Jessie Jane's Campus Delivery

Jessie Jane's Campus Delivery
Statement of Cash Flows
For Month Ended June 30, 19--

Cash flows from operating activities:		
Cash received from customers for		
delivery services		$ 1 5 0 0 00
Cash paid for rent	$ (2 0 0 00)	
Cash paid for telephone	(5 0 00)	
Cash paid for supplies	(8 0 00)	
Cash paid for insurance	(2 0 0 00)	
Cash paid for wages	(6 5 0 00)	
Total cash paid for operations		(1 1 8 0 00)
Net cash provided by operating activities		$ 3 2 0 00
Cash flows from investing activities:		
Cash paid for delivery equipment	$(1 5 0 0 00)	
Net cash used for investing activities		(1 5 0 0 00)
Cash flows from financing activities:		
Cash investment by owner	$ 2 0 0 0 00	
Cash withdrawal by owner	(1 5 0 00)	
Payment made on loan	(3 0 0 00)	
Net cash provided by financing activities		1 5 5 0 00
Net increase in cash		$ 3 7 0 00

The purpose of this appendix was to introduce you to the purpose and format of the statement of cash flows. Here, we classified entries made to the cash account as operating, investing, or financing. These classifications were then used to prepare the statement. Large businesses have thousands of entries to the cash account. Thus, this approach to preparing the statement is not practical for large businesses. Other approaches to preparing the statement will be discussed in Chapter 24. However, the purpose and format of the statements are the same.

KEY POINTS

1 The purpose of the statement of cash flows is to report what the firm did to generate cash and how the cash was used. Business transactions are classified as operating, investing, and financing activities.

Operating activities are related to the revenues and expenses reported on the income statement.

Investing activities are those transactions involving the purchase and sale of long-term assets, lending money, and collecting the principal on the related loans.

Financing activities are those transactions dealing with the exchange of cash between the business and its owners and creditors.

2 The main body of the statement of cash flows consists of three sections: operating, investing, and financing activities.

Name of Business
Statement of Cash Flows
For Period Ended Date

Cash flows from operating activities:		
Cash received from customers		$ x x x x xx
List cash paid for various expenses	$ (x x x xx)	
Total cash paid for operations		(x x x x xx)
Net cash provided by (used for) operating activities		$ x x x xx
Cash flows from investing activities:		
List cash received from the sale of long-term assets		
and other investing activities	$ x x x x x xx	
List cash paid for the purchase of long-term assets		
and other investing activities	x x x x x xx	
Net cash provided by (used for) investing		
activities		x x x x xx
Cash flows from financing activities:		
List cash received from owners and creditors	$ x x x x x xx	
List cash paid to owners and creditors	(x x x xx)	
Net cash provided by (used for) financing activities		x x x x xx
Net increase (decrease) in cash		$ x x x xx

KEY TERMS

financing activities 194   Those transactions dealing with the exchange of cash between the business and its owners and creditors.

investing activities 194   Those transactions involving the purchase and sale of long-term assets, lending money, and collecting the principal on the related loans.

operating activities 194   Those transactions related to the revenues and expenses reported on the income statement.

REVIEW QUESTIONS

1. Explain the purpose of the statement of cash flows.
2. Define and provide examples of the three types of business activities.

SERIES A   EXERCISE

1 **EXERCISE 6ApxA1 CLASSIFYING BUSINESS TRANSACTIONS** Dolores Lopez opened a new consulting business. The following transactions occurred during January of the current year. Classify each transaction as an operating, investing, or financing activity.

(a) Invested cash in the business, $10,000.
(b) Paid office rent, $500.
(c) Purchased office equipment. Paid $1,500 cash and agreed to pay the balance of $2,000 in four monthly installments.
(d) Received cash for services rendered, $900.
(e) Paid telephone bill, $65.
(f) Made payment on loan in transaction c, $500.
(g) Paid wages to part-time employee, $500.
(h) Received cash for services rendered, $800.
(i) Paid electricity bill, $85.
(j) Withdrew cash for personal use, $100.
(k) Paid wages to part-time employee, $500.

SERIES A   PROBLEM

2 **PROBLEM 6ApxA1 PREPARING A STATEMENT OF CASH FLOWS**   Prepare a statement of cash flows based on the transactions reported in Exercise A-1.

SERIES B   EXERCISE

1 **EXERCISE 6ApxB1 CLASSIFYING BUSINESS TRANSACTIONS** Bob Jacobs opened an advertising agency. The following transactions occurred during January of the current year. Classify each transaction as an operating, investing, or financing activity.

(a) Invested cash in the business, $5,000.
(b) Purchased office equipment. Paid $2,500 cash and agreed to pay the balance of $2,000 in four monthly installments.
(c) Paid office rent, $400.
(d) Received cash for services rendered, $600.
(e) Paid telephone bill, $95.
(f) Received cash for services rendered, $700.
(g) Made payment on loan in transaction b, $500.
(h) Paid wages to part-time employee, $800.
(i) Paid electricity bill, $100.
(j) Withdrew cash for personal use, $500.
(k) Paid wages to part-time employee, $600.

SERIES B PROBLEM

2 **PROBLEM 6ApxB1 PREPARING A STATEMENT OF CASH FLOWS** Prepare a statement of cash flows based on the transactions reported in Exercise B-1.

COMPREHENSIVE PROBLEM 1: THE ACCOUNTING CYCLE

Bob Night opened "The General's Favorite Fishing Hole." The fishing camp is open from April through September and attracts many famous college basketball coaches during the off-season. Guests typically register for one week, arriving on Sunday afternoon and returning home the following Saturday afternoon. The registration fee includes room and board, the use of fishing boats, and professional instruction in fishing techniques. The chart of accounts for the camping operations is provided below.

The General's Favorite Fishing Hole
Chart of Accounts

Assets		Revenues	
111	Cash	411	Registration Fees
152	Office Supplies		
154	Food Supplies		Expenses
155	Prepaid Insurance	541	Rent Expense
185	Fishing Boats	542	Wages Expense
185.1	Accum. Depr.—Fishing Boats	543	Office Supplies Expense
		545	Telephone Expense
Liabilities		547	Depr. Exp.—Fishing Boats
216	Accounts Payable	548	Insurance Expense
219	Wages Payable	555	Utilities Expense
		556	Food Supplies Expense
Owner's Equity		564	Postage Expense
311	Bob Night, Capital		
312	Bob Night, Drawing		
313	Income Summary		

The following transactions took place during April 19--.

Apr. 1 Night invested cash in business, $90,000.

1 Paid insurance premium for camping season, $9,000.

2 Paid rent on lodge and campgrounds for the month of April, $40,000.

2 Deposited registration fees, $35,000.

2 Purchased ten fishing boats on account for $60,000. The boats have estimated useful lives of five years, at which time they will be donated to a local day camp. Arrangements were made to pay for the boats in July.

3 Purchased food supplies from Acme Super Market on account, $7,000.

5 Purchased office supplies from Gordon Office Supplies on account, $500.

7 Deposited registration fees, $38,600.

10 Purchased food supplies from Acme Super Market on account, $8,200.

10 Paid wages to fishing guides, $10,000.

14 Deposited registration fees, $30,500.

Apr.   16 Purchased food supplies from Acme Super Market on account, $9,000.
       17 Paid wages to fishing guides, $10,000.
       18 Paid postage, $150.
       21 Deposited registration fees, $35,600.
       24 Purchased food supplies from Acme Super Market on account, $8,500.
       24 Paid wages to fishing guides, $10,000.
       28 Deposited registration fees, $32,000.
       29 Paid wages to fishing guides, $10,000.
       30 Purchased food supplies from Acme Super Market on account, $6,000.
       30 Paid Acme Super Market on account, $32,700.
       30 Paid utility bill, $2,000.
       30 Paid telephone bill, $1,200.
       30 Bob Night withdrew cash for personal use, $6,000.

Adjustment information for the end of April is provided below:

(a) Office supplies remaining on hand, $100.
(b) Food supplies remaining on hand, $8,000.
(c) Insurance expired during the month of April, $1,500.
(d) Depreciation on the fishing boats for the month of April, $1,000.
(e) Wages earned, but not yet paid at the end of April, $500.

REQUIRED
  1. Enter the above transactions in a general journal.
  2. Post the entries to the general ledger. (If you are not using the working papers that accompany this text, you will need to enter the account titles and account numbers in the general ledger accounts.)
  3. Prepare a trial balance on a work sheet.
  4. Complete the work sheet.
  5. Prepare the income statement.
  6. Prepare the statement of owner's equity.
  7. Prepare the balance sheet.
  8. Journalize the adjusting entries.
  9. Post the adjusting entries to the general ledger.
  10. Journalize the closing entries.
  11. Post the closing entries to the general ledger.
  12. Prepare a post-closing trial balance.

PART 2

Specialized Accounting Procedures for Service Businesses and Proprietorships

7

Accounting for a Professional Service Business: The Combination Journal

Careful study of this chapter should enable you to:

LO1   Explain the cash, modified cash, and accrual bases of accounting.

LO2   Describe special records for a professional service business using the modified cash basis.

LO3   Use the combination journal to record transactions of a professional service business.

LO4   Post from the combination journal to the general ledger.

LO5   Prepare a work sheet, financial statements, and adjusting and closing entries for a professional service business.

You have just been hired to work in a doctor's office as a bookkeeper. You have been observing general office procedures and are a bit confused about when to record revenues. Some patients pay cash as they leave the office. Others submit forms that are filed with insurance companies. Sometimes the insurance companies pay the entire amount. Other times, only a portion of the bill is paid, with the balance being billed to the patient. Generally, the patients pay the balance, but occasionally they don't. Finally, there are some patients that never seem to pay. This all seems very confusing. When should revenues be recognized?

Throughout the first six chapters, the accrual basis of accounting for a service business was demonstrated. For simplicity, we used a general journal as the book of original entry. Not all businesses use the accrual basis of accounting and many use specialized journals. In this chapter we explain the cash basis and modified cash basis of accounting. In addition, we demonstrate the advantages of using a combination journal as the book of original entry.

ACCRUAL BASIS VERSUS CASH BASIS

LO1   Explain the cash, modified cash, and accrual bases of accounting.

Under the **accrual basis of accounting**, revenues are recorded when earned. Revenues are earned when a service is provided or a product sold, regardless of whether cash is received. If cash is not received, a receivable is set up. The accrual basis also assumes that expenses are recorded when incurred. Expenses are incurred when a service is received or an asset consumed, regardless of when cash is paid. If cash is not paid when a service is received, a payable is set up. When assets are consumed, prepaid assets are decreased or long-term assets are depreciated. Since the accrual basis accounts for long-term assets, prepaid assets, receivables, and payables, it is the best method of measuring income for the vast majority of businesses.

Accrual Basis	
Accounting for Revenues and Expenses	**Assets and Liabilities**
Record revenue when earned.	Accounts receivable: Yes
Record expenses when incurred.	Accounts payable: Yes
	Prepaid assets: Yes
	Long-term assets: Yes

However, the **cash basis of accounting** is used by some small businesses and by most individuals for tax purposes. Under the cash basis of accounting, revenues are recorded when cash is received and expenses are recorded when cash is paid. This method does not account for long-term assets, prepaid assets, receivables, or payables. As shown in Figure 7-1, the cash and accrual bases can result in very different measures of net income.

Cash Basis	
Accounting for Revenues and Expenses	**Assets and Liabilities**
Record revenue when cash is received.	Accounts receivable: No
Record expenses when cash is paid.	Accounts payable: No
	Prepaid assets: No
	Long-term assets: No

Accrual Basis:

Revenues recorded when earned

Expenses recorded when incurred

Cash Basis:

Revenues recorded when cash is received

Expenses recorded when cash is paid

FIGURE 7-1 Cash Versus Accrual Accounting

Entries Made for Expenses and Revenues

| | METHOD OF ACCOUNTING | | | |
| | ACCRUAL BASIS | | CASH BASIS | |
TRANSACTION	EXPENSE	REVENUE	EXPENSE	REVENUE
(a) Sold merchandise on account, $600.		600		
(b) Paid wages, $300.	300		300	
(c) Received cash for merchandise sold on account, $200.				200
(d) Received cleaning bill for month, $250	250			
(e) Paid on account for last month's advertising, $100			100	
	550	600	400	200

	ACCRUAL BASIS	CASH BASIS
Revenue	$600	$200
Expense	550	400
Net Income (Loss)	$ 50	($200)

	ACCRUAL BASIS	CASH BASIS
Revenues are recognized when:	earned	cash is received
Expenses are recognized when:	incurred	cash is paid

A third method of accounting combines aspects of the cash and accrual methods. With the **modified cash basis**, a firm uses the cash basis for recording revenues and most expenses. Exceptions are made when cash is paid for assets with useful lives greater than one accounting period. For example, under a strict cash basis, if cash is paid for equipment, buildings, supplies, or insurance, the amount is immediately recorded as an expense. This approach would cause major distortions when measuring net income. Under the modified cash basis, cash payments like these are recorded as assets, and adjustments are made each period as under the accrual basis.

Although similar to the accrual basis, the modified cash basis does not account for receivables or for payables for services received. Thus, the modified cash basis is a combination of the cash and accrual methods of accounting. The differences and similarities among the cash, modified cash, and accrual methods of accounting are demonstrated in Figure 7-2.

Modified Cash Basis

Accounting for Revenues and Expenses	Assets and Liabilities

Record revenue when cash is received. Record expenses when paid, except for assets with useful lives greater than one accounting period. Accrual accounting is used for prepaid assets (insurance and supplies) and long-term assets.	Accounts receivable: No
	Accounts payable
	  for purchase of assets: Yes
	  for services received: No
	Prepaid assets: Yes
	Long-term assets: Yes

LEARNING KEY

Shaded area shows that sometimes the modified cash basis is the same as the cash basis and sometimes it is the same as the accrual basis. For some transactions, all methods are the same.

FIGURE 7-2   Comparison of Cash, Modified Cash, and Accrual Methods

Entries Made Under Each Accounting Method

EVENT	CASH	MODIFIED CASH	ACCRUAL
Revenues: Perform services for cash	Cash Professional fees	Cash Professional fees	Cash Professional fees
Perform services on account	No entry	No entry	Accounts Receivable Professional fees
Expenses: Pay cash for operating expenses: wages advertising, rent, telephone, etc.	Expense Cash	Expense Cash	Expense Cash
Pay cash for prepaid items: insurance, supplies, etc.	Expense Cash	Prepaid Asset Cash	Prepaid Asset Cash
Pay cash for property, plant, and equipment (PP & E)	Expense Cash	PP & E Asset Cash	PP & E Asset Cash
End-of-period adjustments: Wages earned but not paid	No entry	No entry	Wages Expense Wages Payable
Prepaid items used	No entry	Expense Prepaid Asset	Expense Prepaid Asset
Depreciation on property, plant, and equipment	No entry	Depreciation Expense Accumulated Depreciation	Depreciation Expense Accumulated Depreciation
Other: Purchase of assets on account	No entry	Asset Accounts Payable	Asset Accounts Payable

ACCOUNTING FOR A PROFESSIONAL SERVICE BUSINESS

LO2   Describe special records for a professional service business using the modified cash basis.

Many small professional service businesses use the modified cash basis of accounting. Professional service businesses include law, dentistry, medicine, optometry, architecture, engineering, and accounting.

Look again at Figure 7-2. There are two primary differences between the accrual basis and the modified cash basis. First, under the modified cash basis, no adjusting entries are made for accrued wages expense. Second, under the modified cash basis, revenues from services performed on account are not recorded until cash is received. Thus, no accounts receivable are entered in the accounting system. This means that other records must be maintained to keep track of amounts owed by clients and patients. These records generally include an appointment record and a client or patient ledger record. These records are illustrated in Figures 7-3 and 7-4.

The appointment record is used to schedule appointments and to maintain a record of the services rendered, fees charged, and payments received. This information is copied to the patient ledger records, which show the amount owed by each client or patient for services performed. A copy of this record may also be used for billing purposes.

THE COMBINATION JOURNAL

LO3   Use the combination journal to record transactions of a professional service business.

The two-column general journal illustrated in Chapter 4 can be used to enter every transaction of a business. However, in most businesses, there are many similar transactions that involve the same account or accounts. Cash receipts and payments are good examples. Suppose that in a typical

Quality

Continuing education for professionals is one way to help improve the quality of service to consumers. Regulatory agencies now require continuing education for a wide variety of professionals including certified public accountants.

Requiring professionals to continue their education is one way to encourage professionals to keep up on changes in their profession. A specific number of continuing education hours is usually required every year or two years. Depending on the profession, CE credits can be earned in several ways. Professionals can take classes offered by colleges, universities, and professional organizations. There are also companies that are in business solely to provide continuing education through lectures, videotape presentations, and correspondence courses.

Reading professional journals is another avenue for earning continuing education credits. For example, members of the American Institute of CPAs can earn credits by reading selected articles in the *Journal of Accountancy*, completing study guides, and passing examinations.

In addition to continuing education required for licensing and certification, some professional organizations require CE to maintain membership. Some companies routinely provide continuing education for all levels of employees.

Whether it is a warehouse employee learning new techniques for handling hazardous chemicals, a surgeon learning new ways to use lasers, or an accountant learning about new accounting standards, continuing education is a key to quality.

FIGURE 7-3   Appointment Record

Date: 6/4/--

Time	Patient	Medical Service	Fees	Payments
8:00	Dennis Rogan	OV	40.00	40.00
15				
30	Rick Cosier	OV;EKG	120.00	
45				
9:00	George Hettenhouse	OV;MISC	50.00	
15				
30	Sam Frumer	OV;LAB	75.00	75.00
45				
10:00	Dan Dalton	OV	40.00	
15				
30	Louis Biagioni	OV;X	65.00	
45				
11:00	Mike Groomer	X	40.00	40.00
15				
30				
45				
12:00				
15				
30				
45				
1:00	Mike Tiller	OV;LAB	80.00	
15				
30	Peggy Hite	OV;PHYS	190.00	
45				
2:00				
15				
30				
45				
3:00	Vivian Winston	OV;MISC	40.00	
15				
30				
45				
4:00	Hank Davis	OV	40.00	40.00
15				
30				
45				
	Bill Sharp			150.00
	Phil Jones			80.00
	Diane Gallagher			200.00
			780.00	625.00

FIGURE 7-4 Client or Patient Ledger Account

Patient Name __Dennis Rogan__
Address __1542 Hamilton Avenue Cincinnati, OH 45240__
Phone Number __555-1683__

Date	Service Rendered	Time	Debit	Credit	Balance
19-- June 4	Office visit	8:00	40.00		
4				40.00	----

month there are 30 transactions that result in an increase in cash and 40 transactions that cause a decrease in cash. In a two-column general journal, this would require entering the account "Cash" 70 times, using a journal line each time.

A considerable amount of time and space is saved if a journal contains **special columns** for cash debits and cash credits. At the end of the month, the special columns for cash debits and credits are totaled. The total of the Cash Debit column is posted as one amount to the debit side of the cash account and the total of the Cash Credit column is posted as one amount to the credit side of the cash account. Thus, instead of receiving 70 postings, Cash receives only two: one debit and one credit. This method requires much less time and reduces the risk of making posting errors.

 LEARNING KEY The totals of special journal columns are posted as one amount to the account. This saves time and reduces the possibility of posting errors.

If other accounts are used frequently, special columns can be added for these accounts. When accounts are used infrequently, the only columns necessary are a **General Debit column** and a **General Credit column**. A journal with such special and general columns is called a **combination journal**.

Many small professional enterprises use a combination journal to record business transactions. To demonstrate the use of a combination journal, let's consider the medical practice of Dr. Ray Bonita. Bonita uses the modified cash basis of accounting. The chart of accounts for his medical practice is shown in Figure 7-5. The transactions for the month of June, his first month in practice, are provided in Figure 7-6.

 LEARNING KEY Set up special columns for the most frequently used accounts.

A combination journal for Bonita's medical practice is illustrated in Figure 7-7 on page 213. Note that special columns were set up for Cash (Debit and Credit), Medical Fees (Credit), Wages Expense (Debit), Laboratory Expense (Debit), Medical Supplies (Debit), and Office Supplies (Debit). Special columns were set up for these accounts because they will be used frequently in this business. Other businesses might set up special

FIGURE 7-5   Chart of Accounts

Ray Bonita, M.D. Chart of Accounts				
Assets		**Revenues**		
111	Cash	411	Medical Fees	
151	Medical Supplies			
152	Office Supplies	**Expenses**		
155	Prepaid Insurance	541	Rent Expense	
185	Medical Equipment	542	Wages Expense	
185.1	Accum. Depr.–Med. Equip.	543	Office Supplies Exp.	
192	Office Furniture	544	Med. Supplies Exp.	
192.1	Accum. Depr.—Office Furn.	545	Telephone Expense	
Liabilities		546	Laboratory Expense	
216	Accounts Payable	547	Depr. Exp.—Med. Equip.	
		548	Depr. Exp.—Off. Furn.	
Owner's Equity		559	Insurance Expense	
311	Ray Bonita, Capital			
312	Ray Bonita, Drawing			
313	Income Summary			

columns for different accounts depending on the frequency of their use. Of course, General Debit and Credit columns for transactions affecting other accounts are also needed.

Journalizing in a Combination Journal

The following procedures were used to enter the transactions for Bonita for June.

General Columns.   Enter transactions in the *general columns* in a manner similar to that used for the *general journal*. Look at the entry for June 5 in Figure 7-7.

a. Enter the name of the debited account (Office Furniture) first at the extreme left of the Description column.
b. Enter the amount in the General Debit column.
c. Enter the name of the account credited (Accounts Payable—Bittle's Furniture) on the next line, indented about ½ inch.
d. Enter the amount in the General Credit column.

FIGURE 7-6   Summary of Transactions for Ray Bonita's Medical Practice

June	1	Ray Bonita invested cash to start a medical practice, $50,000.
	2	Paid for a one-year liability insurance policy, $6,000. Coverage began on June 1.
	3	Purchased medical equipment for cash, $22,000.
	4	Paid bill for laboratory work, $300.
	5	Purchased office furniture on credit from Bittle's Furniture, $9,000.
	6	Received cash from patients and insurance companies for medical services rendered, $5,000.
	7	Paid June office rent, $2,000.
	8	Paid part-time wages, $3,000.
	9	Purchased medical supplies for cash, $250.
	15	Paid telephone bill, $150.
	15	Received cash from patients and insurance companies for medical services rendered, $10,000.
	16	Paid bill for laboratory work, $280.
	17	Paid part-time wages, $3,000.
	19	Purchased office supplies for cash, $150.
	20	Received cash from patients and insurance companies for medical services rendered, $3,000.
	22	Paid the first installment to Bittle's Furniture, $3,000.
	23	Purchased medical supplies for cash, $200.
	24	Paid bill for laboratory work, $400.
	25	Purchased additional furniture from Bittle's Furniture, $3,500. A down payment of $500 was made, with the remaining payments expected over the next four months.
	27	Paid part-time wages, $2,500.
	30	Received cash from patients and insurance companies for medical services rendered, $7,000.
	30	Bonita withdrew cash for personal use, $10,000.

General and Special Accounts.   Some transactions affect both a *general account and a special account.* Look at the entry for June 1 in Figure 7-7.

a. Enter the name of the general account in the Description column.
b. Enter the amount in the General Debit or Credit column.
c. Enter the amount of the debit or credit for the special account in the appropriate special column.

Enter all of this information on the same line.

FIGURE 7-7   Combination Journal

COMBINATION JOURNAL

PAGE 1

Date (19-- June)	Description	Post. Ref.	Cash Debit	Cash Credit	General Debit	General Credit	Medical Fees Credit	Wages Expense Debit	Laboratory Expense Debit	Medical Supplies Debit	Office Supplies Debit
1	Ray Bonita, Capital	311	50000.00			50000.00					
2	Prepaid Insurance	155		6000.00	6000.00						
3	Medical Equipment	185		22000.00	22000.00						
4	—	—		300.00					300.00		
5	Office Furniture	192			9000.00						
6	Accounts Payable—Bittle's Furn.	216				9000.00					
7	—	—	5000.00				5000.00				
8	Rent Expense	541		2000.00	2000.00						
9	—	—		3000.00				3000.00			
15	—	—		280.00					280.00		
15	—	—		250.00						250.00	
16	Telephone Expense	545		150.00	150.00						
16	—	—	10000.00				10000.00				
17	—	—		3000.00				3000.00			
19	—	—		150.00							150.00
20	—	—	3000.00				3000.00				
22	Accounts Payable—Bittle's Furn.	216		3000.00	3000.00						
23	—	—		200.00						200.00	
24	—	—		400.00					400.00		
25	Office Furniture	192		500.00	3500.00						
25	Accounts Payable—Bittle's Furn.	216				3000.00					
27	—	—		2500.00				2500.00			
30	—	—	7000.00				7000.00				
30	Ray Bonita, Drawing	312		10000.00	10000.00						
			75000.00	53730.00	55650.00	62000.00	25000.00	8500.00	980.00	450.00	150.00
			(111)	(111)	(√)	(√)	(411)	(542)	(546)	(151)	(152)

Proving the Combination Journal

Debit Columns		Credit Columns	
Cash	75,000	Cash	53,730
General	55,650	General	62,000
Wages Expense	8,500	Medical Fees	25,000
Laboratory Expense	980		140,730
Medical Supplies	450		
Office Supplies	150		
	140,730		

Special Accounts.   Many transactions affect only *special accounts*. Look at the entry for June 6 in Figure 7-7.

a. Enter the amounts in the appropriate special debit and credit columns.
b. Do not enter anything in the Description column.
c. Place a dash in the Posting Reference column to indicate that this amount is not posted individually. It will be posted as part of the total of the special column at the end of the month. (The posting process is described later in this chapter.)

Description Column.   In general, the **Description column** is used for the following:

a. To enter the account titles for the General Debit and General Credit columns.
b. To identify specific creditors when assets are purchased on account (see entry for June 5).
    NOTE: For firms using the accrual basis of accounting, this column also would be used to identify specific customers receiving services on account.
c. To identify amounts forwarded. When more than one page is required during an accounting period, amounts from the previous page are brought forward. In this situation, "Amounts Forwarded" is entered in the Description column on the first line.

Proving the Combination Journal

At the end of the accounting period, all columns of the combination journal should be totaled and ruled. The sum of the debit columns should be compared with the sum of the credit columns to verify that they are equal. The proving of Bonita's combination journal for the month of June is shown at the bottom of Figure 7-7 on page 213.

POSTING FROM THE COMBINATION JOURNAL

LO4   Post from the combination journal to the general ledger.

The procedures for posting a special column are different from the procedures used when posting a general column. Accounts debited or credited in the general columns are posted individually in the same manner as that followed for the general journal. A different procedure is used for special columns. Figure 7-8 describes the procedures to follow in posting from the combination journal.

Amounts in the General column are posted individually. Only the totals of the special columns are posted.

The general ledger accounts for Cash, Accounts Payable, and Medical Fees are shown in Figure 7-9 to illustrate the effects of this posting process.

FIGURE 7-8   Posting from a Combination Journal

GENERAL COLUMNS	Since a combination journal is being used, enter "CJ" and the page number in each general ledger account's Posting Reference column. Once the amount has been posted to the general ledger account, the account number is entered in the **Posting Reference column** of the combination journal. Accounts in the general column should be posted daily. The check marks at the bottom of the General Debit and Credit columns indicate that these totals should not be posted.
SPECIAL COLUMNS	1. Post the totals of the special columns to the appropriate general ledger accounts. 2. Once posted, enter the account number (in parentheses) beneath the column.

FIGURE 7-9   The General Ledger After Posting

GENERAL LEDGER

ACCOUNT: **Cash**   ACCOUNT NO. **111**

DATE	ITEM	POST. REF.	DEBIT	CREDIT	BALANCE DEBIT	BALANCE CREDIT
19-- June 30		CJ1	75 0 0 0 00		75 0 0 0 00	
30		CJ1		53 7 3 0 00	21 2 7 0 00	

ACCOUNT: **Accounts Payable**   ACCOUNT NO. **216**

DATE	ITEM	POST. REF.	DEBIT	CREDIT	BALANCE DEBIT	BALANCE CREDIT
19-- June 5		CJ1		9 0 0 0 00		9 0 0 0 00
22		CJ1	3 0 0 0 00			6 0 0 0 00
25		CJ1		3 0 0 0 00		9 0 0 0 00

ACCOUNT: **Medical Fees**   ACCOUNT NO. **411**

DATE	ITEM	POST. REF.	DEBIT	CREDIT	BALANCE DEBIT	BALANCE CREDIT
19-- June 30		CJ1		25 0 0 0 00		25 0 0 0 00

To see the advantages of posting a combination journal compared with the general journal, simply compare the accounts in Figure 7-9 with the same accounts in Chapter 4, Figure 4-12. Note the number of postings required for the general journal and combination journal.

Number of Postings

	General Journal	Combination Journal	
Cash	13	2	(Special columns for cash)
Accounts Payable	3	3	(No special column)
Delivery/Medical Fees	3	1	(Special column for Medical Fees)

Clearly, using the combination journal can be quite efficient.

Determining the Cash Balance

	Beginning cash balance
+	Cash debits to date
–	Cash credits to date
	Current cash balance

The debits and credits to Cash are not posted until the end of the accounting period. Therefore, the cash balance must be computed when this information is needed. The cash balance may be computed at any time during the month by taking the beginning balance, adding total cash debits and subtracting total cash credits to date. Figure 7-10 shows the calculation of Bonita's cash balance on June 15.

PERFORMING END-OF-PERIOD WORK FOR A PROFESSIONAL SERVICE BUSINESS

LO5   Prepare a work sheet, financial statements, and adjusting and closing entries for a professional service business.

Once the combination journal has been posted to the general ledger, the end-of-period work sheet is prepared in the same way as described in Chapter 5. Recall that financial statements are prepared and end-of-period work is normally performed at the end of the fiscal year. For illustration purposes, we will perform these activities at the end of Bonita's first month of operations.

Preparing the Work Sheet

Bonita's work sheet is illustrated in Figure 7-11. Adjustments were made for the following items:

(a) Medical supplies remaining on June 30, $350.
(b) Office supplies remaining on June 30, $100.
(c) Prepaid insurance expired during June, $500.
(d) Depreciation on medical equipment for June, $300.
(e) Depreciation on office furniture for June, $200.

Preparing Financial Statements

No additional investment was made by Bonita during June. Thus, as we saw in Chapter 6, the financial statements can be prepared directly from the

FIGURE 7-10 Determining the Cash Balance

COMBINATION JOURNAL

PAGE 1

	DATE		CASH DEBIT	CASH CREDIT	DESCRIPTION	POST. REF.	GENERAL DEBIT	GENERAL CREDIT	MEDICAL FEES CREDIT	WAGES EXPENSE DEBIT	LABORATORY EXPENSE DEBIT	MEDICAL SUPPLIES DEBIT	OFFICE SUPPLIES DEBIT	
1	19-- June	1	50 000 00		Ray Bonita, Capital	311		50 000 00						1
2		2		6 000 00	Prepaid Insurance	155	6 000 00							2
3		3		22 000 00	Medical Equipment	185	22 000 00							3
4		4		300 00		—					300 00			4
5		5			Office Furniture	192	9 000 00							5
6					Accounts Payable—Bittle's Furn.	216		9 000 00						6
7		6	5 000 00			—			5 000 00					7
8		7		2 000 00	Rent Expense	541	2 000 00							8
9		8		3 000 00		—				3 000 00				9
10		9		250 00		—						250 00		10
11		15		150 00	Telephone Expense	545	150 00							11
12		15	10 000 00			—			10 000 00					12
13			65 000 00	33 700 00										13

Beginning balance	$ 0
Add cash debits	65,000
Total	65,000
Less cash credits	33,700
Cash balance, June 15	$31,300

FIGURE 7-11 Work Sheet for Ray Bonita, M.D.

Ray Bonita, M.D.
Work Sheet
For Month Ended June 30, 19--

	ACCOUNT TITLE	TRIAL BALANCE		ADJUSTMENTS		ADJUSTED TRIAL BALANCE		INCOME STATEMENT		BALANCE SHEET		
		DEBIT	CREDIT	DEBIT	CREDIT	DEBIT	CREDIT	DEBIT	CREDIT	DEBIT	CREDIT	
1	Cash	21 270 00				21 270 00				21 270 00		1
2	Medical Supplies	450 00			(a) 100 00	350 00				350 00		2
3	Office Supplies	150 00			(b) 50 00	100 00				100 00		3
4	Prepaid Insurance	6 000 00			(c) 500 00	5 500 00				5 500 00		4
5	Medical Equipment	22 000 00				22 000 00				22 000 00		5
6	Accum. Depr.—Medical Equip.				(d) 300 00		300 00				300 00	6
7	Office Furniture	12 500 00				12 500 00				12 500 00		7
8	Accum. Depr.—Office Furniture				(e) 200 00		200 00				200 00	8
9	Accounts Payable		9 000 00				9 000 00				9 000 00	9
10	Ray Bonita, Capital		50 000 00				50 000 00				50 000 00	10
11	Ray Bonita, Drawing	10 000 00				10 000 00				10 000 00		11
12	Medical Fees		25 000 00				25 000 00		25 000 00			12
13	Rent Expense	2 000 00				2 000 00		2 000 00				13
14	Wages Expense	8 500 00				8 500 00		8 500 00				14
15	Office Supplies Expense			(b) 50 00		50 00		50 00				15
16	Medical Supplies Expense			(a) 100 00		100 00		100 00				16
17	Telephone Expense	150 00				150 00		150 00				17
18	Laboratory Expense	980 00				980 00		980 00				18
19	Depr. Expense—Medical Equip.			(d) 300 00		300 00		300 00				19
20	Depr. Expense—Office Furniture			(e) 200 00		200 00		200 00				20
21	Insurance Expense			(c) 500 00		500 00		500 00				21
22		84 000 00	84 000 00	1 150 00	1 150 00	84 500 00	84 500 00	12 780 00	25 000 00	71 720 00	59 500 00	22
23	Net Income							12 220 00			12 220 00	23
24								25 000 00	25 000 00	71 720 00	71 720 00	24
25												25
26												26
27												27
28												28
29												29
30												30
31												31
32												32
33												33
34												34
35												35
36												36
37												37
38												38
39												39
40												40

Profiles in Accounting

AMY BUTLER, Office Manager

Amy Butler earned an Associate Degree in Travel/Hospitality Management. After completing her externship with the Clubhouse Inn, Amy worked for Design Coatings as a receptionist. After eight months, she accepted an office manager's position with EMI, a database consulting firm.

Amy's duties include accounts payable and receivable, payroll, word processing, filing, and supervising and training eight employees.

She considers being professional at all times the key to success.

work sheet. Recall that if Bonita had made an additional investment, this amount would be identified by reviewing Bonita's capital account and would need to be reported in the statement of owner's equity. Bonita's financial statements are illustrated in Figure 7-12.

FIGURE 7-12   Financial Statements for Ray Bonita, M.D.

Ray Bonita, M.D.
Income Statement
For Month Ended June 30, 19--

Revenue:		
Medical fees		$25 0 0 0 00
Expenses:		
Rent expense	$2 0 0 0 00	
Wages expense	8 5 0 0 00	
Office supplies expense	5 0 00	
Medical supplies expense	1 0 0 00	
Telephone expense	1 5 0 00	
Laboratory expense	9 8 0 00	
Depreciation expense—medical equipment	3 0 0 00	
Depreciation expense—office furniture	2 0 0 00	
Insurance expense	5 0 0 00	
Total expenses		12 7 8 0 00
Net income		$12 2 2 0 00

Ray Bonita, M.D.
Statement of Owner's Equity
For Month Ended June 30, 19--

Ray Bonita, capital, June 1, 19--		$50 0 0 0 00
Net income for June	$12 2 2 0 00	
Less withdrawals for June	10 0 0 0 00	
Increase in capital		2 2 2 0 00
Ray Bonita, capital, June 30, 19--		$52 2 2 0 00

FIGURE 7-12   Financial Statements for Ray Bonita, M.D. (continued)

Ray Bonita, M.D. Balance Sheet June 30, 19--			
Assets			
Current assets:			
Cash	$21 2 7 0 00		
Medical supplies	3 5 0 00		
Office supplies	1 0 0 00		
Prepaid insurance	5 5 0 0 00		
Total current assets		$27 2 2 0 00	
Property, plant, and equipment:			
Medical equipment	$22 0 0 0 00		
Less accumulated depreciation	3 0 0 00	21 7 0 0 00	
Office furniture	$12 5 0 0 00		
Less accumulated depreciation	2 0 0 00	12 3 0 0 00	
Total assets		$61 2 2 0 00	
Liabilities			
Current liabilities:			
Accounts payable		$ 9 0 0 0 00	
Owner's Equity			
Ray Bonita, capital		52 2 2 0 00	
Total liabilities and owner's equity		$61 2 2 0 00	

Preparing Adjusting and Closing Entries

Adjusting and closing entries are made in the combination journal in the same manner demonstrated for the general journal in Chapter 6. We simply use the Description and General Debit and Credit columns. These posted entries are illustrated in Figures 7-13 and 7-14.

FIGURE 7-13   Adjusting Entries

COMBINATION JOURNAL

	DATE		CASH DEBIT	CASH CREDIT	DESCRIPTION	POST. REF.	GENERAL DEBIT	GENERAL CREDIT	
1					Adjusting Entries				1
2	19-- June	30			Medical Supplies Expense	544	1 0 0 00		2
3					Medical Supplies	151		1 0 0 00	3
4		30			Office Supplies Expense	543	5 0 00		4
5					Office Supplies	152		5 0 00	5
6		30			Insurance Expense	559	5 0 0 00		6
7					Prepaid Insurance	155		5 0 0 00	7
8		30			Depreciation Expense—Medical Equipment	547	3 0 0 00		8
9					Accumulated Depreciation—Medical Equipment	185.1		3 0 0 00	9
10		30			Depreciation Expense—Office Furniture	548	2 0 0 00		10
11					Accumulated Depreciation—Office Furniture	192.1		2 0 0 00	11

FIGURE 7-14   Closing Entries

COMBINATION JOURNAL

	DATE		CASH		DESCRIPTION	POST. REF.	GENERAL		
			DEBIT	CREDIT			DEBIT	CREDIT	
12									12
13					Closing Entries				13
14	June	30			Medical Fees	411	25 0 0 0 00		14
15					Income Summary	313		25 0 0 0 00	15
16		30			Income Summary	313	12 7 8 0 00		16
17					Rent Expense	541		2 0 0 0 00	17
18					Wages Expense	542		8 5 0 0 00	18
19					Office Supplies Expense	543		5 0 00	19
20					Medical Supplies Expense	544		1 0 0 00	20
21					Telephone Expense	545		1 5 0 00	21
22					Laboratory Expense	546		9 8 0 00	22
23					Depreciation Expense—Medical Equipment	547		3 0 0 00	23
24					Depreciation Expense—Office Furniture	548		2 0 0 00	24
25					Insurance Expense	559		5 0 0 00	25
26		30			Income Summary	313	12 2 2 0 00		26
27					Ray Bonita, Capital	311		12 2 2 0 00	27
28		30			Ray Bonita, Capital	311	10 0 0 0 00		28
29					Ray Bonita, Drawing	312		10 0 0 0 00	29

KEY POINTS

1 There are three bases of accounting: cash, modified cash, and accrual. Differences in the recording of revenues, expenses, assets, and liabilities are listed below.

Recording revenues

Cash:	when cash is received
Modified cash:	when cash is received
Accrual:	when earned

Recording expenses

Cash:	when cash is paid
Modified cash:	when cash is paid, except for property, plant and equipment and prepaid items
Accrual:	when incurred

Recording assets and liabilities

	Cash Basis	Modified Cash Basis	Accrual Basis
Accounts receivable	No	No	Yes
Payables			
for purchase of assets	No	Yes	Yes
for services received (wages payable)	No	No	Yes
Prepaid assets	No	Yes	Yes
Long-term assets	No	Yes	Yes

2 Special records are required for a professional service business using the modified cash basis. Since accounts receivable are not entered in the accounting system, other records must be maintained to keep track of amounts owed by clients and patients. These records generally include an appointment record and a client or patient ledger record.

3 A combination journal is used by some businesses to improve the efficiency of recording and posting transactions. It includes general and special columns. The headings for a typical combination journal for a doctor's office are shown below.

COMBINATION JOURNAL PAGE 1

DATE	CASH DEBIT	CASH CREDIT	DESCRIPTION	POST. REF.	GENERAL DEBIT	GENERAL CREDIT	MEDICAL FEES CREDIT	WAGES EXPENSE DEBIT	LABORATORY EXPENSE DEBIT	MEDICAL SUPPLIES DEBIT	OFFICE SUPPLIES DEBIT

4 Rules for posting a combination journal:

1. Amounts entered in the general columns are posted individually to the general ledger on a daily basis.

2. The totals of the special columns are posted to the general ledger at the end of the month.

5 The work sheet, financial statements, adjusting entries, and closing entries are prepared in the same manner as discussed in Chapters 5 and 6. Remember, however, that under the modified cash basis, adjustments are made only for prepaid items and depreciation of plant and equipment.

KEY TERMS

accrual basis of accounting 205 A method of accounting under which revenues are recorded when earned and expenses are recorded when incurred.

cash basis of accounting 205 A method of accounting under which revenues are recorded when cash is received and expenses are recorded when cash is paid.

combination journal 210   A journal with special and general columns.

Description column 214   In the combination journal, this column is used to enter the account titles for the General Debit and General Credit columns, to identify specific creditors when assets are purchased on account, and to identify amounts forwarded.

General Credit column 210   In the combination journal, this column is used to credit accounts that are used infrequently.

General Debit column 210   In the combination journal, this column is used to debit accounts that are used infrequently.

modified cash basis 206   A method of accounting that combines aspects of the cash and accrual methods. It uses the cash basis for recording revenues and most expenses. Exceptions are made when cash is paid for assets with useful lives greater than one accounting period.

Posting Reference column 215   In the combination journal, the account number is entered in this column after posting.

special columns 210   Columns in journals for frequently used accounts.

REVIEW QUESTIONS

1. Explain when revenues are recorded under the cash basis, modified cash basis, and accrual basis of accounting.
2. Explain when expenses are recorded under the cash basis, modified cash basis, and accrual basis of accounting.
3. Explain the purpose of an appointment record.
4. Explain the purpose of a patient ledger account.
5. Explain the purpose of a special column in the combination journal.
6. Explain the purpose of the General columns in the combination journal.
7. How does the use of the combination journal save time and space in entering cash transactions?
8. Explain the purpose of the Description column in the combination journal.
9. What is the purpose of proving the totals in the combination journal?
10. When an entry is posted from the combination journal to a ledger account, what information is entered in the Posting Reference column of the combination journal? In the Posting Reference column of the ledger account?

MANAGING YOUR WRITING

Your friend is planning to start her own business and has asked you for advice. In particular, she is concerned about which method of accounting she should use. She has heard about the cash, modified cash, and accrual methods of accounting. However, she does not really understand the differences. Write a memo that explains each method and the type of business for which each method is most appropriate.

DEMONSTRATION PROBLEM

Maria Vietor is a financial planning consultant. She developed the following chart of accounts for her business.

Vietor Financial Planning
Chart of Accounts

Assets	Revenues
111 Cash	411 Professional Fees
152 Office Supplies	
	Expenses
Liabilities	541 Rent Expense
216 Accounts Payable	542 Wages Expense
	543 Office Supplies Expense
Owner's Equity	545 Telephone Expense
311 Maria Vietor, Capital	546 Automobile Expense
312 Maria Vietor, Drawing	555 Utilities Expense
313 Income Summary	557 Charitable Contributions Expense

Vietor completed the following transactions during the month of December of the current year:

Dec. 1 Vietor invested cash to start a consulting business, $20,000.
3 Paid December office rent, $1,000.
4 Received a check from Aaron Bisno, a client, for services, $2,500.
6 Paid Union Electric for December heating and light, $75.
7 Received a check from Will Carter, a client, for services $2,000.
12 Paid Smith's Super Service for gasoline and oil purchases, $60.
14 Paid Comphelp for temporary secretarial services obtained through them during the past two weeks, $600.
17 Purchased office supplies from Cleat Office Supply on account, $280.
20 Paid Cress Telephone Co. for local and long-distance business calls during the past month, $100.
21 Vietor withdrew cash for personal use, $1,100.
24 Made donation to the National Multiple Sclerosis Society, $100.
27 Received a check from Ellen Thaler, a client, for services, $2,000.
28 Paid Comphelp for temporary secretarial services obtained through them during the past two weeks, $600.
29 Made payment on account to Cleat Office Supply, $100.

REQUIRED

1. Enter the transactions in a combination journal. Establish special columns for Professional Fees, Wages Expense, and Automobile Expense. Vietor uses the modified cash basis of accounting. (Refer to the Chapter 4 Demonstration Problem to see how similar transactions were recorded in a general journal. Notice that the combination journal is much more efficient.)
2. Prove the combination journal.
3. Post these transactions to a general ledger.
4. Prepare a trial balance.

SOLUTION

1, 2 See page 226.

3.

GENERAL LEDGER

ACCOUNT: **Cash** ACCOUNT NO. 111

DATE	ITEM	POST. REF.	DEBIT	CREDIT	BALANCE DEBIT	BALANCE CREDIT
19-- Dec. 31		CJ1	26 500 00		26 500 00	
31		CJ1		3 735 00	22 765 00	

ACCOUNT: **Office Supplies** ACCOUNT NO. 152

DATE	ITEM	POST. REF.	DEBIT	CREDIT	BALANCE DEBIT	BALANCE CREDIT
19-- Dec. 17		CJ1	2 80 00		2 80 00	

ACCOUNT: **Accounts Payable** ACCOUNT NO. 216

DATE	ITEM	POST. REF.	DEBIT	CREDIT	BALANCE DEBIT	BALANCE CREDIT
19-- Dec. 17		CJ1		2 80 00		2 80 00
29		CJ1	1 00 00			1 80 00

ACCOUNT: **Maria Vietor, Capital** ACCOUNT NO. 311

DATE	ITEM	POST. REF.	DEBIT	CREDIT	BALANCE DEBIT	BALANCE CREDIT
19-- Dec. 1		CJ1		20 000 00		20 000 00

ACCOUNT: **Maria Vietor, Drawing** ACCOUNT NO. 312

DATE	ITEM	POST. REF.	DEBIT	CREDIT	BALANCE DEBIT	BALANCE CREDIT
19-- Dec. 21		CJ1	1 100 00		1 100 00	

ACCOUNT: **Income Summary** ACCOUNT NO. 313

DATE	ITEM	POST. REF.	DEBIT	CREDIT	BALANCE DEBIT	BALANCE CREDIT
19--						

COMBINATION JOURNAL

PAGE 1

DATE	CASH DEBIT	CASH CREDIT	DESCRIPTION	POST. REF.	GENERAL DEBIT	GENERAL CREDIT	PROFESSIONAL FEES CREDIT	WAGES EXPENSE DEBIT	AUTOMOBILE EXPENSE DEBIT	
19-- Dec. 1	20000 00		Maria Vietor, Capital	311		20000 00				1
3		1000 00	Rent Expense	541	1000 00					2
4	2500 00			—			2500 00			3
6		75 00	Utilities Expense	555	75 00					4
6	2000 00			—			2000 00			5
		60 00		—					60 00	6
		60 00		—				600 00		7
12			Office Supplies	152	280 00					8
14			Accounts Payable—Cleat Office Supply	216		280 00				9
17		100 00	Telephone Expense	545	100 00					10
20		1100 00	Maria Vietor, Drawing	312	1100 00					11
21		100 00	Charitable Contributions Expense	557	100 00					12
24	2000 00			—			2000 00			13
27		600 00		—				600 00		14
29		100 00	Accounts Payable—Cleat Office Supply	216	100 00					15
	26500 00	3735 00			2755 00	20280 00	6500 00	1200 00	60 00	16
	(111)	(111)			(✓)	(✓)	(411)	(542)	(546)	17

Proving the Combination Journal

Debit Columns		Credit Columns	
Cash	26,500	Cash	3,735
General	2,755	General	20,280
Wages Expense	1,200	Professional Fees	6,500
Auto. Expense	60		30,515
	30,515		

ACCOUNT: Professional Fees   ACCOUNT NO. 411

DATE	ITEM	POST. REF.	DEBIT	CREDIT	BALANCE	
					DEBIT	CREDIT
Dec. 31 (19--)		CJ1		6 5 0 0 00		6 5 0 0 00

ACCOUNT: Rent Expense   ACCOUNT NO. 541

DATE	ITEM	POST. REF.	DEBIT	CREDIT	BALANCE	
					DEBIT	CREDIT
Dec. 3 (19--)		CJ1	1 0 0 0 00		1 0 0 0 00	

ACCOUNT: Wages Expense   ACCOUNT NO. 542

DATE	ITEM	POST. REF.	DEBIT	CREDIT	BALANCE	
					DEBIT	CREDIT
Dec. 31 (19--)		CJ1	1 2 0 0 00		1 2 0 0 00	

ACCOUNT: Office Supplies Expense   ACCOUNT NO. 543

DATE	ITEM	POST. REF.	DEBIT	CREDIT	BALANCE	
					DEBIT	CREDIT
19--						

ACCOUNT: Telephone Expense   ACCOUNT NO. 545

DATE	ITEM	POST. REF.	DEBIT	CREDIT	BALANCE	
					DEBIT	CREDIT
Dec. 20 (19--)		CJ1	1 0 0 00		1 0 0 00	

ACCOUNT: Automobile Expense   ACCOUNT NO. 546

DATE	ITEM	POST. REF.	DEBIT	CREDIT	BALANCE	
					DEBIT	CREDIT
Dec. 31 (19--)		CJ1	6 0 00		6 0 00	

ACCOUNT: Utilities Expense   ACCOUNT NO. 555

DATE	ITEM	POST. REF.	DEBIT	CREDIT	BALANCE	
					DEBIT	CREDIT
Dec. 6 (19--)		CJ1	7 5 00		7 5 00	

ACCOUNT: Charitable Contributions Expense   ACCOUNT NO. 557

DATE	ITEM	POST. REF.	DEBIT	CREDIT	BALANCE	
					DEBIT	CREDIT
Dec. 24 (19--)		CJ1	1 0 0 00		1 0 0 00	

4.

Vietor Financial Planning
Trial Balance
December 31, 19--

ACCOUNT TITLE	ACCOUNT NO.	DEBIT BALANCE	CREDIT BALANCE
Cash	111	22 7 6 5 00	
Office Supplies	152	2 8 0 00	
Accounts Payable	216		1 8 0 00
Maria Vietor, Capital	311		20 0 0 0 00
Maria Vietor, Drawing	312	1 1 0 0 00	
Professional Fees	411		6 5 0 0 00
Rent Expense	541	1 0 0 0 00	
Wages Expense	542	1 2 0 0 00	
Telephone Expense	545	1 0 0 00	
Automobile Expense	546	6 0 00	
Utilities Expense	555	7 5 00	
Charitable Contributions Expense	557	1 0 0 00	
		26 6 8 0 00	26 6 8 0 00

SERIES A EXERCISES

1 **EXERCISE 7A1 CASH, MODIFIED CASH, AND ACCRUAL BASES OF ACCOUNTING**   Prepare the entry for each of the following transactions, using the (a) cash basis, (b) modified cash basis, and (c) accrual basis of accounting.

1. Purchase supplies on account.
2. Make payment on asset previously purchased.
3. Purchase supplies for cash.
4. Purchase insurance for cash.
5. Pay cash for wages.
6. Pay cash for telephone expense.
7. Pay cash for new equipment.

End-of-Period Adjusting Entries:

8. Wages earned but not paid.
9. Prepaid item purchased, partly used.
10. Depreciation on long-term assets.

1 **EXERCISE 7A2 JOURNAL ENTRIES**   Jean Akins opened a consulting business. Journalize the following transactions that occurred during the month of January of the current year using the modified cash basis and a combination journal. Set up special columns for consulting fees (credit) and wages expense (debit).

Jan. 1 Invested cash in the business, $10,000.
2 Paid office rent, $500.
3 Purchased office equipment from Business Machines, Inc., on account, $1,500.
5 Received cash for services rendered, $750.
8 Paid telephone bill, $65.
10 Paid for a magazine subscription (miscellaneous expense), $15.
11 Purchased office supplies from Leo's Office Supplies on account, $300.
15 Paid for one-year liability insurance policy, $150.
18 Paid part-time help, $500.
21 Received cash for services rendered, $350.
25 Paid electricity bill, $85.
27 Withdrew cash for personal use, $100.
29 Paid part-time help, $500.

1/3   **EXERCISE 7A3 JOURNAL ENTRIES**   Bill Rackes opened a bicycle repair shop. Journalize the following transactions that occurred during the month of October of the current year. Use the modified cash basis and a combination journal with special columns for Repair Fees (credit) and Wages Expense (debit). Prove the combination journal.

Oct. 1 Invested cash in the business, $15,000.
2 Paid shop rental for the month, $300.
3 Purchased bicycle parts from Tracker's Bicycle Parts on account, $2,000.
5 Purchased office supplies from Downtown Office Supplies on account, $250.
8 Paid telephone bill, $38.
9 Received cash for services, $140.
11 Paid for a sports magazine subscription (miscellaneous expense), $15.
12 Made payment on account for parts previously purchased, $100.
14 Paid part-time help, $300.
15 Received cash for services, $350.
16 Paid electricity bill, $48.
19 Received cash for services, $250.
23 Withdrew cash for personal use, $50.
25 Made payment on account for office supplies previously purchased, $50.
29 Paid part-time help, $300.

SERIES A PROBLEMS

3/4/5   **PROBLEM 7A1 JOURNALIZING AND POSTING TRANS-ACTIONS AND PREPARING FINANCIAL STATEMENTS**   Angela McWharton opened an on-call nursing services business. She rented a small office space and pays a part-time worker to answer the telephone. Her chart of accounts is shown on the next page.

Angela McWharton Nursing Services
Chart of Accounts

Assets
101   Cash
111   Office Supplies
121   Office Equipment

Liabilities
211   Accounts Payable

Owner's Equity
311   Angela McWharton, Capital
312   Angela McWharton, Drawing
313   Income Summary

Revenues
411   Nursing Care Fees

Expenses
511   Rent Expense
522   Wages Expense
524   Telephone Expense
531   Electricity Expense
533   Transportation Expense
542   Advertising Expense
568   Miscellaneous Expense

McWharton's transactions for the first month of business are as follows:

Jan.   1 Invested cash in the business, $10,000.
        1 Paid January rent, $500.
        2 Purchased office supplies from Crestline Office Supplies on account, $300.
        4 Purchased office equipment from Office Technology, Inc., on account, $1,500.
        6 Received cash for nursing services rendered, $580.
        7 Paid telephone bill, $42.
        8 Paid electricity bill, $38.
       10 Received cash for nursing services rendered, $360.
       12 Made payment on account for office supplies previously purchased, $50.
       13 Reimbursed part-time worker for use of personal automobile (transportation expense), $150.
       15 Paid part-time worker, $360.
       17 Received cash for nursing services rendered, $420.
       18 Withdrew cash for personal use, $100.
       20 Paid for newspaper advertising, $26.
       22 Paid for gas and oil, $35.
       24 Paid subscription for journal on nursing care practices (miscellaneous expense), $28.
       25 Received cash for nursing services rendered, $320.
       27 Made payment on account for office equipment previously purchased, $150.
       29 Paid part-time worker, $360.
       30 Received cash for nursing services rendered, $180.

REQUIRED

1. Journalize the transactions for January using the modified cash basis and page 1 in a combination journal. Set up special columns for Nursing Care Fees (credit), Wages Expense (debit), and Transportation Expense (debit).

2. Determine the cash balance as of January 12 (using the combination journal).
3. Prove the combination journal.
4. Set up four-column general ledger accounts from the chart of accounts and post the transactions from the combination journal.
5. Prepare a trial balance.

3/4/5 **PROBLEM 7A2 JOURNALIZING AND POSTING TRANS-ACTIONS AND PREPARING FINANCIAL STATEMENTS** Sue Reyton owns a suit tailoring shop. She opened business in September. She rented a small work space and has an assistant to receive job orders and process claim tickets. Her trial balance shows her account balances for the first two months of business (September and October).

Sue Reyton Tailors
Trial Balance
October 31, 19--

ACCOUNT TITLE	ACCOUNT NO.	DEBIT BALANCE	CREDIT BALANCE
Cash	101	6 2 1 1 50	
Office Supplies	111	4 8 4 50	
Tailoring Supplies	121	1 0 0 0 00	
Prepaid Insurance	131	1 0 0 00	
Tailoring Equipment	141	3 8 0 0 00	
Accumulated Depreciation—Tailoring Equipment	141.1		8 0 0 00
Accounts Payable	211		4 1 2 5 00
Sue Reyton, Capital	311		5 4 3 0 00
Sue Reyton, Drawing	312	8 0 0 00	
Tailoring Fees	411		3 6 0 0 00
Rent Expense	511	6 0 0 00	
Wages Expense	522	8 0 0 00	
Telephone Expense	533	6 0 00	
Electricity Expense	555	4 4 00	
Advertising Expense	566	3 3 00	
Miscellaneous Expense	588	2 2 00	
		13 9 5 5 00	13 9 5 5 00

Reyton's transactions for November are as follows:

Nov. 1 Paid November rent, $300.
      2 Purchased tailoring supplies from Sew Easy Supplies on account, $150.
      3 Purchased a new button hole machine from Seam's Sewing Machines on account, $3,000.
      5 Earned first week's revenue: $400 in cash.
      8 Paid for newspaper advertising, $13.

Nov.   9 Paid telephone bill, $28.
        10 Paid electricity bill, $21.
        12 Earned second week's revenue: $200 in cash, $300 on account.
        15 Paid part-time worker, $400.
        16 Made payment on account for tailoring supplies, $100.
        17 Paid for magazine subscription (miscellaneous expense), $12.
        19 Earned third week's revenue: $450 in cash.
        21 Paid for prepaid insurance for the year, $500.
        23 Received cash from customers (previously owed), $300.
        24 Paid for newspaper advertising, $13.
        26 Paid for special delivery fee (miscellaneous expense), $12.
        29 Earned fourth week's revenue: $600 in cash.

Additional accounts needed are:

313 Income Summary
541 Tailoring Supplies Expense
542 Office Supplies Expense
543 Insurance Expense
544 Depreciation Expense—Tailoring Equipment

Nov. 30 Adjustments:

(a) Tailoring supplies on hand, $450.
(b) Office supplies on hand, $284.50.
(c) Prepaid insurance expired over past three months, $150.
(d) Depreciation on tailoring equipment for past three months, $300.

REQUIRED

1. Journalize the transactions for November using the modified cash basis
   and page 5 in a combination journal. Set up special columns for
   Tailoring Fees (credit), Wages Expense (debit), and Advertising Expense
   (debit).
2. Determine the cash balance as of November 12.
3. Prove the combination journal.
4. Set up four-column general ledger accounts, including the additional
   accounts listed above, entering the balances as of November 1, 19--. Post
   the entries from the combination journal.
5. Prepare a work sheet for the three months ended November 30, 19--.
6. Prepare an income statement, statement of owner's equity, and balance
   sheet as of November 30, 19--. (Assume that Reyton made an investment
   of $5,430 on September 1, 19--.)
7. Record the adjusting and closing entries on page 6 of the combination
   journal and post to the general ledger accounts.

SERIES B EXERCISES

1 **EXERCISE 7B1 CASH, MODIFIED CASH, AND ACCRUAL BASES
OF ACCOUNTING**   For each journal entry shown below, indicate the
accounting method(s) for which the entry would be appropriate. If the jour-

nal entry is not appropriate for a particular accounting method, explain the proper accounting treatment for that method.

1. Office Equipment
      Cash
         Purchased equipment for cash
2. Office Equipment
      Accounts Payable
         Purchased equipment on account
3. Cash
      Revenue
         Cash receipts for week
4. Accounts Receivable
      Revenue
         Services performed on account
5. Prepaid Insurance
      Cash
         Purchased prepaid asset
6. Supplies
      Accounts Payable
         Purchased prepaid asset
7. Telephone Expense
      Cash
         Paid telephone bill
8. Wages Expense
      Cash
         Paid wages for month
9. Accounts Payable
      Cash
         Payment on account

Adjusting Entries:

10. Supplies Expense
       Supplies
11. Wages Expense
       Wages Payable
12. Depreciation Expense—Office Equipment
       Accumulated Depreciation—Office Equipment

3   **EXERCISE 7B2 JOURNAL ENTRIES**   Bill Miller opened a bookkeeping service business. Journalize the following transactions that occurred during the month of March of the current year. Use the modified cash basis and a combination journal with special columns for Bookkeeping Fees (credit) and Wages Expense (debit).

Mar.   1 Invested cash in the business, $7,500.
        3 Paid March office rent, $500.

Mar. 5 Purchased office equipment from Desk Top Office Equipment on account, $800.
      6 Received cash for services rendered, $400.
      8 Paid telephone bill, $48.
      10 Paid for a magazine subscription (miscellaneous expense), $25.
      11 Purchased office supplies, $200.
      14 Received cash for services rendered, $520.
      16 Paid for a one-year insurance policy, $200.
      18 Paid part-time worker, $400.
      21 Received cash for services rendered, $380.
      22 Made payment on account for office equipment previously purchased, $100.
      24 Paid electricity bill, $56.
      27 Withdrew cash for personal use, $200.
      29 Paid part-time worker, $400.
      30 Received cash for services rendered, $600.

3 **EXERCISE 7B3 JOURNAL ENTRIES**   Amy Anjelo opened a delivery service. Journalize the following transactions that occurred in January of the current year. Use the modified cash basis and a combination journal with special columns for Delivery Fees (credit) and Wages Expense (debit). Prove the combination journal.

Jan. 1 Invested cash in the business, $10,000.
      2 Paid shop rental for the month, $400.
      3 Purchased a delivery cart from Walt's Wheels on account, $1,000.
      5 Purchased office supplies, $250.
      6 Paid telephone bill, $51.
      8 Received cash for delivery services, $428.
      11 Paid electricity bill, $37.
      12 Paid part-time employee, $480.
      13 Paid for postage stamps (miscellaneous expense), $29.
      15 Received cash for delivery services, $382.
      18 Made payment on account for delivery cart previously purchased, $90.
      21 Withdrew cash for personal use, $250.
      24 Paid for a one-year liability insurance policy, $180.
      26 Received cash for delivery services, $292.
      29 Paid part-time employee, $480.

SERIES B PROBLEMS

3/4/5 **PROBLEM 7B1 JOURNALIZING AND POSTING TRANSACTIONS AND PREPARING FINANCIAL STATEMENTS**   J.B. Hoyt opened a training center at the marina where he provides private waterskiing lessons. He rented a small building at the marina and has a part-time worker to assist him. His chart of accounts is shown on the next page.

Water Walking by Hoyt
Chart of Accounts

Assets
101   Cash
111   Office Supplies
121   Skiing Equipment

Liabilities
211   Accounts Payable

Owner's Equity
311   J.B. Hoyt, Capital
312   J.B. Hoyt, Drawing
313   Income Summary

Revenues
411   Training Fees

Expenses
511   Rent Expense
522   Wages Expense
524   Telephone Expense
531   Repair Expense
538   Electricity Expense
542   Transportation Expense
568   Miscellaneous Expense

Transactions for the first month of business are as follows:

July   1 Invested cash in the business, $5,000.
       2 Paid rent for the month, $250.
       3 Purchased office supplies, $150.
       4 Purchased skiing equipment from Water Fun, Inc., on account,
          $2,000.
       6 Paid telephone bill, $36.
       7 Received cash for skiing lessons, $200.
      10 Paid electricity bill, $28.
      12 Paid part-time worker, $250.
      14 Received cash for skiing lessons, $300.
      16 Paid for gas and oil (transportation expense), $60.
      17 Received cash for skiing lessons, $250.
      20 Paid for repair to ski rope, $20.
      21 Made payment on account for skiing equipment previously pur-
          chased, $100.
      24 Received cash for skiing lessons, $310.
      26 Paid for award certificates (miscellaneous expense), $18.
      28 Paid part-time worker, $250.
      30 Received cash for skiing lessons, $230.
      31 Paid for repair to life jacket, $20.

REQUIRED
1. Journalize the transactions for July using the modified cash basis and
   page 1 in a combination journal. Set up special columns for Training
   Fees (credit), Wages Expense (debit), and Repair Expense (debit).
2. Determine the cash balance as of July 14, 19--.
3. Prove the combination journal.
4. Set up four-column general ledger accounts from the chart of accounts
   and post the transactions from the combination journal.
5. Prepare a trial balance.

3/4/5   **PROBLEM 7B2 JOURNALIZING AND POSTING TRANS-ACTIONS AND PREPARING FINANCIAL STATEMENTS**   Molly Claussen owns a lawn care business. She opened her business in April. She rented a small shop area where she stores her equipment and has an assistant to receive orders and process accounts. Her trial balance shows her account balances for the first two months of business (April and May).

Transactions for June are as follows:

June   1   Paid shop rent, $200.
      2   Purchased office supplies, $230.
      3   Purchased new landscaping equipment from Earth Care, Inc., on account, $1,000.
      5   Paid telephone bill, $31.
      6   Received cash for lawn care fees, $640.
      8   Paid electricity bill, $31.
    10   Paid part-time worker, $300.
    11   Received cash for lawn care fees, $580.
    12   Paid for a one-year insurance policy, $200.
    14   Made payment on account for landscaping equipment previously purchased, $100.
    15   Paid for gas and oil, $40.
    19   Paid for mower repairs, $25.
    21   Received $310 cash for lawn care fees and earned $480 on account.
    24   Withdrew cash for personal use, $100.
    26   Paid for edging equipment repairs, $20.
    28   Received cash from customers (previously owed), $480.
    29   Paid part-time worker, $300.

Additional accounts needed are:

313   Income Summary
541   Lawn Care Supplies Expense
542   Office Supplies Expense
543   Insurance Expense
544   Depreciation Expense—Lawn Care Equipment

June 30 Adjustments:

(a)   Office supplies on hand, $273.
(b)   Lawn care supplies on hand, $300.
(c)   Prepaid insurance expired over past three months, $100.
(d)   Depreciation on lawn care equipment for past three months, $260.

REQUIRED

1. Journalize the transactions for June using the modified cash basis and page 5 in a combination journal. Set up special columns for Lawn Care Fees (credit), Repair Expense (debit), and Wages Expense (debit).
2. Determine the cash balance as of June 12.
3. Prove the combination journal.

Molly Claussen's Green Thumb
Trial Balance
May 31, 19--

ACCOUNT TITLE	ACCOUNT NO.	DEBIT BALANCE	CREDIT BALANCE
Cash	101	4 8 4 4 00	
Office Supplies	111	2 4 3 00	
Lawn Care Supplies	121	5 8 8 00	
Prepaid Insurance	131	1 5 0 00	
Lawn Care Equipment	144	2 4 0 8 00	
Accumulated Depreciation—Lawn Care Equip.	144.1		2 4 0 00
Accounts Payable	211		1 0 8 0 00
Molly Claussen, Capital	311		5 0 0 0 00
Molly Claussen, Drawing	312	8 0 0 00	
Lawn Care Fees	411		4 0 3 3 00
Rent Expense	511	4 0 0 00	
Wages Expense	522	6 0 0 00	
Telephone Expense	533	8 8 00	
Electricity Expense	555	6 2 00	
Gas and Oil Expense	566	1 2 0 00	
Repair Expense	588	5 0 00	
		10 3 5 3 00	10 3 5 3 00

4. Set up four-column general ledger accounts including the additional accounts listed above, entering balances as of June 1, 19--. Post the entries from the combination journal.
5. Prepare a work sheet for the three months ended June 30, 19--.
6. Prepare an income statement, statement of owner's equity, and balance sheet as of June 30, 19--. Assume that Claussen invested $5,000 on April 1, 19--.
7. Record the adjusting and closing entries on page 6 of the combination journal and post to the general ledger accounts.

MASTERY PROBLEM

John McRoe opened a tennis resort in June 19--. Most guests register for one week, arriving on Sunday afternoon and returning home the following Saturday afternoon. Guests stay at an adjacent hotel. Lunch and dinner are provided by the tennis resort. Dining and exercise facilities are provided in a building rented by McRoe. A dietitian, masseuse, physical therapist, and athletic trainers are on call to assure the proper combination of diet and exercise. The chart of accounts and transactions for the month of June are provided on the next page. McRoe uses the modified cash basis of accounting.

McRoe Tennis Resort
Chart of Accounts

Assets

111	Cash
152	Office Supplies
154	Food Supplies
183	Tennis Facilities
183.1	Accum. Depr.—Tennis Facilities
184	Exercise Equipment
184.1	Accum. Depr.—Exercise Equip.

Liabilities

| 216 | Accounts Payable |

Owner's Equity

311	John McRoe, Capital
312	John McRoe, Drawing
313	Income Summary

Revenues

| 411 | Registration Fees |

Expenses

541	Rent Expense
542	Wages Expense
543	Office Supplies Expense
544	Food Supplies Expense
545	Telephone Expense
547	Depr. Exp.—Tennis Facilities
548	Depr. Exp.—Exercise Equip.
555	Utilities Expense
559	Insurance Expense
564	Postage Expense

June 1 McRoe invested cash in the business, $90,000.
1 Paid for new exercise equipment, $9,000.
2 Deposited registration fees in the bank, $15,000.
2 Paid rent for month of June on building and land, $2,000.
2 Rogers Construction completed work on new tennis courts that cost $70,000. The estimated useful life of the facility is five years, at which time the courts will have to be resurfaced. Arrangements were made to pay the bill in July.
3 Purchased food supplies from Au Naturel Foods on account, $5,000.
5 Purchased office supplies on account from Gordon Office Supplies, $300.
7 Deposited registration fees in the bank, $16,200.
10 Purchased food supplies from Au Naturel Foods on account, $6,200.
10 Paid wages to staff, $500.
14 Deposited registration fees in the bank, $13,500.
16 Purchased food supplies from Au Naturel Foods on account, $4,000.
17 Paid wages to staff, $500.
18 Paid postage, $85.
21 Deposited registration fees in the bank, $15,200.
24 Purchased food supplies from Au Naturel Foods on account for $5,500.
24 Paid wages to staff, $500.
28 Deposited registration fees in the bank, $14,000.
30 Purchased food supplies from Au Naturel Foods on account, $6,000.
30 Paid wages to staff, $500.
30 Paid Au Naturel Foods on account, $28,700.

June 30 Paid utility bill, $500.
      30 Paid telephone bill, $120.
      30 McRoe withdrew cash for personal use, $2,000.

REQUIRED

1. Enter the transactions in a combination journal. Establish special columns for Registration Fees (credit), Wages Expense (debit), and Food Supplies (debit).
2. Prove the combination journal.
3. Post these transactions to a general ledger.
4. Prepare a trial balance as of June 30.

8

Accounting for Cash

Careful study of this chapter should enable you to:

LO1 Describe how to open and use a checking account.

LO2 Prepare a bank reconciliation.

LO3 Describe how to operate a petty cash fund.

LO4 Use the cash short and over account.

Do you want to be able to pay your bills by mail? Then you need a checking account, because it is unsafe to mail cash. Do you want to avoid being fined for writing a check for more than you have in your account? Then you need to know how to keep track of your checking account balance. Do you want to know why your checkbook balance does not agree with the one on the bank statement? Then you need to know how to prepare a bank reconciliation.

Cash is an asset that is quite familiar and important to all of us. We generally think of **cash** as the currency and coins in our pockets and the money we have in our checking accounts. To a business, cash also includes checks received from customers, money orders, and bank cashier's checks.

Because it plays such a central role in operating a business, cash must be carefully managed and controlled. A business should have a system of **internal control**—a set of procedures designed to ensure proper accounting for transactions. For good internal control of cash transactions, all cash received should be deposited daily in a bank. All disbursements, except for payments from petty cash, should be made by check.

CHECKING ACCOUNT

LO1   Describe how to open and use a checking account.

The key documents and forms required in opening and using a checking account are the signature card, deposit tickets, checks, and bank statements.

Opening a Checking Account

To open a checking account, each person authorized to sign checks must complete and sign a **signature card** (Figure 8-1). The bank uses this card to verify the depositor's signature on any banking transactions. The depositor's social security number or employer identification number (EIN) is shown on the card to identify the depositor. An EIN can be obtained from the Internal Revenue Service.

FIGURE 8-1   Signature Card

LAST NAME, FIRST NAME, MIDDLE INITIAL	ACCT #
	TYPE
	DATE	INIT.
STREET ADDRESS TOWN	STATE ZIP

I CERTIFY THAT THE NUMBER SHOWN ON THIS FORM IS MY CORRECT TAXPAYER IDENTIFICATION NUMBER AND THAT I AM NOT SUBJECT TO BACKUP WITHHOLDING.

SIGNATURE 1	DATE OF BIRTH	SOCIAL SECURITY NO.
SIGNATURE 2		
SIGNATURE 3		

Making Deposits

A **deposit ticket** (Figure 8-2) is a detailed listing of items being deposited. Currency, coins, and checks are listed separately. Sometimes each check is identified by its **ABA (American Bankers Association) Number.** This number is the small fraction printed in the upper right hand corner of each check. The number is used to sort and route checks throughout the banking system. Normally, only the numerator of the fraction is used in identifying checks on the deposit ticket.

FIGURE 8-2   Deposit Ticket

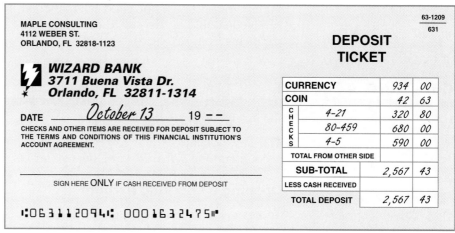

The depositor delivers or mails the deposit ticket and all items being deposited to the bank. The bank then gives or mails a receipt to the depositor.

Endorsements.   Each check being deposited must be endorsed by the depositor. The **endorsement** consists of stamping or writing the depositor's name and sometimes other information on the back of the check, near the left end. There are two basic types of endorsements.

Profiles in Accounting

LISA DAVIS, Legal Coordinator

Lisa Davis began working as a part-time legal secretary with Zegarelli Associates. Lisa continued her career with this company after earning an Associate Degree in Legal Office Management.

After graduation Lisa was hired as a legal assistant and later promoted to legal coordinator. Her duties include budgeting, accounts receivable, supervising two employees, coordinating schedules, researching, and dealing with clients on a daily basis.

According to Lisa, dependability, initiative, and loyalty lead to success. Lisa chose the legal field because she always had an interest in law and wanted to work in a fast-paced environment.

1. **Blank endorsement**—the depositor simply signs the back of the check. This makes the check payable to any bearer.
2. **Restrictive endorsement**—the depositor adds words such as "For deposit," "Pay to any bank," or "Pay to Daryl Beck only" to restrict the payment of the check.

Businesses commonly use a rubber stamp to endorse checks for deposit. The check shown in Figure 8-3 has been stamped with a restrictive endorsement.

FIGURE 8-3   Restrictive Endorsement

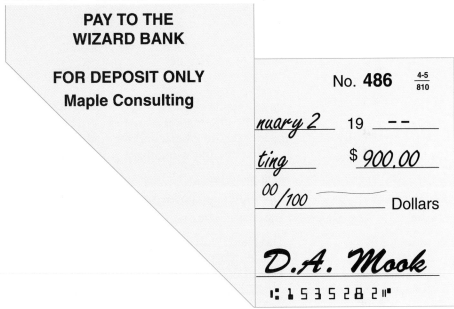

Automated Teller Machines.   Many banks now make **automated teller machines (ATM)** available at all times to depositors for making deposits or withdrawals. Each depositor has a plastic card (Figure 8-4) and a personal identification number (PIN). The depositor inserts the card into the machine and keys in the PIN, whether the transaction is a withdrawal or a deposit, and the amount. The machine has a drawer or door for the withdrawal or deposit.

Writing Checks

A **check** is a document ordering a bank to pay cash from a depositor's account. There are three parties to every check:

1. **Drawer**—the depositor who orders the bank to pay the cash.
2. **Drawee**—the bank on which the check is drawn.
3. **Payee**—the person being paid the cash.

Checks used by businesses are usually bound in the form of a book. In some checkbooks, each check is attached to a **check stub** (Figure 8-5) that contains space to record all relevant information about the check. Other

FIGURE 8-4   Automated Teller Machine Card

times the checkbook is accompanied by a small register book in which the relevant information is noted. If a financial computer software package is used, both the check and the register can be prepared electronically.

Use the following three steps in preparing a check.

STEP 1   Complete the check stub or register.

STEP 2   Enter the date, payee name, and amount on the check.

STEP 3   Sign the check.

The check stub should be completed first so that the drawer retains a record of each check issued. This information is needed to determine the proper journal entry for the transaction.

The payee name is entered on the first long line on the check, followed by the amount in figures. The amount in words is then entered on the second long line. If the amount in figures does not agree with the amount in words, the bank will either pay the amount in words, contact the drawer for the correct amount, or return the check unpaid.

The most critical point in preparing a check is signing it, and this should be done last. The signature authorizes the bank to pay cash from the drawer's account. The check signer should make sure that all other aspects of the check are correct before signing it.

Figure 8-5 shows properly completed checks and stubs.

Bank Statement

A statement of account issued by a bank to each depositor once a month is called a **bank statement**. Figure 8-6 is a bank statement for a checking account. The statement shows:

1. The balance at the beginning of the period.
2. Deposits and other amounts added during the period.
3. Checks and other amounts subtracted during the period.
4. The balance at the end of the period.

FIGURE 8-5 Checks and Check Stubs

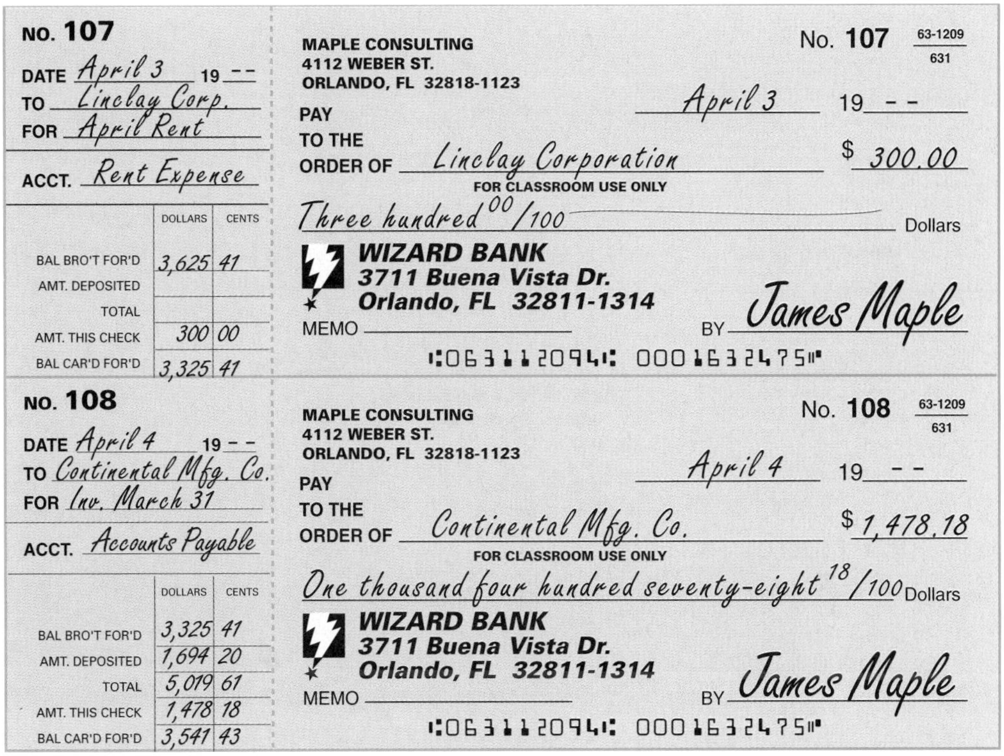
NO. 107
DATE April 3 19 --
TO Linclay Corp.
FOR April Rent
ACCT. Rent Expense

	DOLLARS	CENTS
BAL BRO'T FOR'D	3,625	41
AMT. DEPOSITED		
TOTAL		
AMT. THIS CHECK	300	00
BAL CAR'D FOR'D	3,325	41

MAPLE CONSULTING
4112 WEBER ST.
ORLANDO, FL 32818-1123
No. 107 63-1209/631
April 3 19 --
PAY TO THE ORDER OF Linclay Corporation $ 300.00
FOR CLASSROOM USE ONLY
Three hundred 00/100 Dollars
WIZARD BANK
3711 Buena Vista Dr.
Orlando, FL 32811-1314
MEMO
BY James Maple
⑆063112094⑆ 0001632475⑈

NO. 108
DATE April 4 19 --
TO Continental Mfg. Co.
FOR Inv. March 31
ACCT. Accounts Payable

	DOLLARS	CENTS
BAL BRO'T FOR'D	3,325	41
AMT. DEPOSITED	1,694	20
TOTAL	5,019	61
AMT. THIS CHECK	1,478	18
BAL CAR'D FOR'D	3,541	43

MAPLE CONSULTING
4112 WEBER ST.
ORLANDO, FL 32818-1123
No. 108 63-1209/631
April 4 19 --
PAY TO THE ORDER OF Continental Mfg. Co. $ 1,478.18
FOR CLASSROOM USE ONLY
One thousand four hundred seventy-eight 18/100 Dollars
WIZARD BANK
3711 Buena Vista Dr.
Orlando, FL 32811-1314
MEMO
BY James Maple
⑆063112094⑆ 0001632475⑈

Along with the bank statement, the bank sends to the depositor:

1. **Cancelled checks** (the depositor's checks paid by the bank during the period).
2. Any other forms representing items added to or subtracted from the account.

RECONCILING THE BANK STATEMENT

LO2 Prepare a bank reconciliation.

On any given day, the balance in the cash account on the depositor's books (the book balance) is unlikely to be the same as that on the bank's books (the bank balance). Although this may be the result of errors, it is most likely because of differences in when the transactions are recorded by the business and the bank.

Deposits

Suppose there are cash receipts of $600 on April 30. These cash receipts would be recorded on the depositor's books on April 30 and a deposit of $600 would be taken to the bank. The deposit would not be recognized by the bank, however, until at least the following day, May 1. This timing difference in recording the $600 of cash receipts is illustrated in Figure 8-7.

FIGURE 8-6   Bank Statement

Statement				𝗪 WIZARD BANK		

Maple Consulting	Reference Number	16 3247 5	Page Number	1

Maple Consulting
4112 Weber St.
Orlando, FL 32818-1123

Reference Number	16 3247 5	Page Number	1
Statement Date	Nov. 21, 19--		
Statement Instructions			

Beginning Balance	No. of Deposits and Credits	We have added these deposits and credits totaling	No. of withdrawals and charges	We have subtracted these withdrawals and charges totaling	Resulting in a statement balance of
$2,721.51	2	$2,599.31	17	$3,572.73	$1,748.09
Document Count	Average daily balance this statement period		Minimum balance this statement period	Date	Amount

If your account does not balance, please see reverse side and report any discrepancy to our Customer Service Department.

Date	Description	Amount	Balance
10/20	Beginning Balance		2,721.51
10/27	Check No. 207	-242.00	2,479.51
10/28	Check No. 212	-68.93	2,410.58
10/28	Check No. 213	-58.00	2,352.58
10/29	Deposit	867.00	3,219.58
11/3	Deposit	1,732.31	4,951.89
11/3	Check No. 214	-18.98	4,932.91
11/3	Check No. 215	-229.01	4,703.90
11/3	Check No. 216	-452.13	4,251.77
11/3	Check No. 217	-94.60	4,157.17
11/10	Check No. 218	-1,800.00	2,357.17
11/10	DM: NSF	-200.00	2,157.17
11/10	Check No. 220	-32.42	2,124.75
11/10	Check No. 221	-64.08	2,060.67
11/10	Check No. 222	-110.87	1,949.80
11/13	ATM Withdrawal	-100.00	1,849.80
11/18	Check No. 223	-18.00	1,831.80
11/18	Check No. 225	-23.31	1,808.49
11/18	Check No. 226	-58.60	1,749.89
11/19	DM: Service Charge	-1.80	1,748.09

EC - Error Correction	NSF - Not Sufficient Funds	TR - Wire Transfer
CM - Credit Memo	ATM - Automated Teller Machine	
DM - Debit Memo		

Notice that on April 30, the balances in the depositor's books and in the bank's books differ.

Cash Payments

Similar timing differences occur with cash payments. Suppose a check for $350 is written on April 30. This cash payment would be recorded on the depositor's books on April 30 and the check mailed to the payee. The check probably would not be received by the payee until May 3. If the payee deposited the check promptly, it still would not clear the bank until May 4. This timing difference in recording the $350 cash payment is illustrated in Figure 8-8. Notice once again that on April 30, the balances in the depositor's books and the bank's books differ.

Reasons for Differences Between Bank and Book Balances

When the bank statement is received, the depositor examines the records to identify the items that explain the difference between the book and bank

FIGURE 8-7   Depositor and Bank Records—Deposits

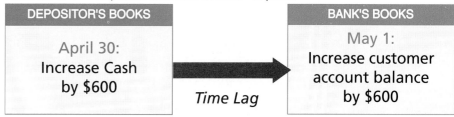

FIGURE 8-8   Depositor and Bank Records—Cash Payments

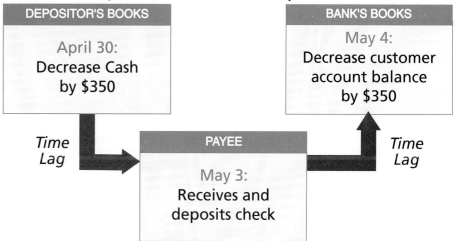

balances. This process of bringing the book and bank balances into agreement is called preparing a **bank reconciliation.**

The most common reasons for differences between the book and bank balances are the following:

1. **Outstanding checks.** Checks issued during the period that have not been presented to the bank for payment before the statement is prepared.
2. **Deposits in transit.** Deposits that have not reached or been recorded by the bank before the statement is prepared.
3. **Service charges.** Bank charges for services such as check printing and processing.
4. **Collections.** Collections of promissory notes or charge accounts made by the bank on behalf of the depositor.
5. **Not sufficient funds (NSF) checks.** Checks deposited by the depositor that are not paid because the drawer did not have sufficient funds.
6. **Errors.** Errors made by the bank or the depositor in recording cash transactions.

Steps in Preparing the Bank Reconciliation

Use the following three steps in preparing the bank reconciliation.

STEP 1   Identify deposits in transit and any related errors.

STEP 2   Identify outstanding checks and any related errors.

STEP 3   Identify additional reconciling items.

Deposits in Transit and Related Errors.   Follow these steps:

STEP 1   Compare deposits listed on the bank statement with deposits in transit on last month's bank reconciliation. All of last month's deposits in transit should appear on the current month's bank statement.

STEP 2   Compare the remaining deposits on the bank statement with deposits listed in the accounting records. Any deposits listed in the accounting records but not on the bank statement are deposits in transit on the current bank reconciliation.

STEP 3   Compare the individual deposit amounts on the bank statement and in the accounting records. If they differ, the error needs to be corrected.

Outstanding Checks and Related Errors.   Follow these steps:

STEP 1   Compare cancelled checks with the bank statement and the accounting records. If the amounts differ, the error needs to be corrected.

STEP 2   As each cancelled check is compared with the accounting records, place a check mark on the check stub or other accounting record to indicate that the check has cleared.

STEP 3   Any checks written that have not been checked off represent outstanding checks on the bank reconciliation.

Additional Reconciling Items.   Compare any additions and deductions on the bank statement that are not deposits or checks with the accounting records. Items that the bank adds to the account are called **credit memos**. Items that the bank deducts from the account are called **debit memos**. Any of these items not appearing in the accounting records represent additional items on the bank reconciliation.

Illustration of a Bank Reconciliation

A general format for a bank reconciliation is shown in Figure 8-9. Not every item shown in this illustration would be in every bank reconciliation, but this format is helpful in determining where to put items.

To illustrate the preparation of a bank reconciliation, we will use the Maple Consulting bank statement shown in Figure 8-6. That statement shows a balance of $1,748.09 as of November 21, 19--. The balance in Maple's check stubs and general ledger cash account is $2,393.23. The three steps listed at the top of this page were used to identify the following items, and the reconciliation in Figure 8-10 was prepared.

FIGURE 8-9   Bank Reconciliation Format

BANK RECONCILIATION		
Bank statement balance		$xxxx
Add: Deposits in transit	$xxxx	
Bank errors	xxxx	xxxx
Subtotal		$xxxx
Deduct: Outstanding checks	$xxxx	
Bank errors	xxxx	xxxx
Adjusted bank balance		$xxxx
Book balance		
Add: Bank credit memos	$xxxx	
Book errors	xxxx	xxxx
Subtotal		$xxxx
Deduct: Bank debit memos	$xxxx	
Book errors	xxxx	xxxx
Adjusted book balance		$xxxx

1. A deposit of $637.02 on November 21 on the books had not been received by the bank. The deposit in transit is added to the bank statement balance. Maple has received the funds, but the amount has not yet been counted by the bank.
2. Check numbers 219, 224, and 227 are outstanding. The amount of these outstanding checks is subtracted from the bank statement balance. The funds have been disbursed by Maple, but have not yet been paid out by the bank.
3. Check number 214 was written for $18.98, but was entered on the check stub and on the books as $19.88. This $.90 error is added to the book balance because $.90 too much had been deducted from the book balance.
4. Maple made the ATM withdrawal of $100 on November 13 for personal use. This amount is deducted from the book balance. The bank has reduced Maple's balance by this amount but Maple had neglected to record the withdrawal.
5. The bank returned an NSF check of $200. This amount is deducted from the book balance. The bank has reduced Maple's balance by this amount but Maple has not yet recorded it.
6. The bank service charge was $1.80. This amount is deducted from the book balance. The bank has reduced Maple's balance by this amount, but Maple has not yet recorded it.

Journal Entries

LEARNING KEY | Errors in the books and bank additions and deductions that are not in the accounting records require journal entries.

Only two kinds of items appearing on a bank reconciliation require journal entries:

FIGURE 8-10 Bank Reconciliation

Maple Consulting Bank Reconciliation November 21, 19--		
Bank statement balance, November 21		$1 7 4 8 09
Add deposit in transit		6 3 7 02
		$2 3 8 5 11
Deduct outstanding checks:		
No. 219	$2 0 0 00	
No. 224	2 5 00	
No. 227	6 7 78	2 9 2 78
Adjusted bank balance		$2 0 9 2 33
Book balance, November 21		$2 3 9 3 23
Add error on check no. 214		90
		$2 3 9 4 13
Deduct:		
Unrecorded ATM withdrawal	$1 0 0 00	
NSF check	2 0 0 00	
Bank service charge	1 80	3 0 1 80
Adjusted book balance		$2 0 9 2 33

Reconciled balances

Requires journal entry

Require journal entries

1. Errors in the books.
2. Bank additions and deductions that do not already appear in the accounting records.

Note the four items in the lower portion of the bank reconciliation in Figure 8-10. A journal entry always is required for each item in this portion of the bank reconciliation.

The $.90 item is an error in the accounting records that occurred when the check amount was incorrectly entered. Assuming the $18.98 was in payment of an account payable, the entry to correct this error is:

4		Cash		90			4
5		Accounts Payable			90		5
6		Error in recording check					6

The $100 ATM withdrawal has been deducted from Maple's account by the bank. Maple has not yet recorded the withdrawal. Maple withdrew the funds for personal use, so the following journal entry is required.

8		James Maple, Drawing		1 0 0 00			8
9		Cash			1 0 0 00		9
10		Unrecorded ATM withdrawal					10

The $200 NSF check is a bank charge for a check deposited by Maple that proved to be worthless. This amount must be deducted from the book balance. Assuming the $200 check was received from a customer on account, the following journal entry is required.

12		Accounts Receivable		2 0 0 00			12
13		Cash			2 0 0 00		13
14		Record NSF check					14

The $1.80 bank service charge is a fee for bank services received by Maple. The bank has deducted this amount from Maple's account. Bank service charges are usually small and are charged to Miscellaneous Expense.

16		Miscellaneous Expense		1 80			16
17		Cash			1 80		17
18		Bank service charge					18

Electronic Funds Transfer

Electronic funds transfer (EFT) uses a computer rather than paper checks to complete transactions with the bank. This technique is being used increasingly today. Applications of EFT include payrolls, social security payments, retail purchases, and the ATM transactions described earlier in the chapter.

Heavy use of EFT can present a challenge in preparing bank reconciliations. Many of the documents handled in a purely manual environment disappear when EFT is used. Bank accounts are just one of many areas where computers require accountants to think in new ways. Regardless of what system is used, the key point to remember is that the accounting records must be correctly updated.

THE PETTY CASH FUND

LO3 Describe how to operate a petty cash fund.

For good control over cash, payments generally should be made by check. Unfortunately, payments of very small amounts by check can be both inconvenient and inefficient. For example, the time and cost required to write a check for $.70 to mail a letter might be greater than the cost of the postage. Therefore, businesses customarily establish a **petty cash fund** to pay for small items with cash. "Petty" means small, and both the amount of the fund and the maximum amount of any bill that can be paid from the fund are small.

Establishing a Petty Cash Fund

To establish a petty cash fund, a check is written to the petty cash custodian for the amount to be set aside in the fund. The amount may be $50, $100, $200, or any amount considered necessary. The journal entry to establish a petty cash fund of $100 would be as follows.

4			Petty Cash		1 0 0 00		4
5			Cash			1 0 0 00	5
6			Establish petty cash fund				6

Petty cash is an asset that is listed immediately below Cash on the balance sheet.

The custodian cashes the check and places the money in a petty cash box. For good control, the custodian should be the only person authorized to make payments from the fund. The custodian should be able to account for the full amount of the fund at any time.

Making Payments from a Petty Cash Fund

A receipt called a **petty cash voucher** (Figure 8-11) should be prepared for every payment from the fund. The voucher shows the name of the payee, the purpose of the payment, and the account to be charged for the payment. Each voucher should be signed by the custodian and by the person receiving the cash. The vouchers should be numbered consecutively so that all vouchers can be accounted for.

FIGURE 8-11 Petty Cash Voucher

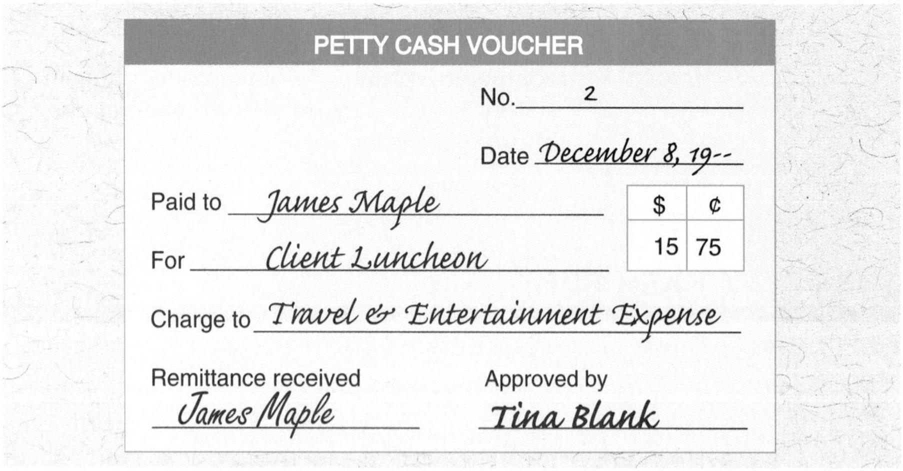
PETTY CASH VOUCHER

No. 2

Date *December 8, 19--*

Paid to *James Maple* $ 15 ¢ 75

For *Client Luncheon*

Charge to *Travel & Entertainment Expense*

Remittance received *James Maple*

Approved by *Tina Blank*

Petty Cash Payments Record

When a petty cash fund is maintained, a formal record is often kept of all payments from the fund. The **petty cash payments record** (Figure 8-12) is a special multicolumn record that supplements the regular accounting records. It is not a journal. The headings of the Distribution of Payments columns may vary, depending on the types of expenditures.

The petty cash payments record of Maple Consulting is shown in Figure 8-12 on page 254. A narrative of the petty cash transactions shown in Figure 8-12 follows.

Dec. 1 Maple issued a check for $200.00 payable to Tina Blank, Petty Cash Custodian. Blank cashed the check and placed the money in a secure cash box.

A notation of the amount received is made in the Description column of the petty cash payments record. In addition, this transaction is entered in the journal as follows:

8	19-- Dec. 1	Petty Cash		2 0 0 00		8
9		Cash			2 0 0 00	9
10		Establish petty cash fund				10

During the month of December, the following payments were made from the petty cash fund:

Dec. 5 Paid $32.80 to Jerry's Auto for servicing the company automobile. Voucher No. 1.

8 Reimbursed Maple $15.75 for the amount spent for lunch with a client. Voucher No. 2.

9 Gave Maple $30.00 for personal use. Voucher No. 3.

There is no special Distribution column for entering amounts withdrawn by the owner for personal use. Therefore this $30.00 payment is entered in the Amount column at the extreme right of the petty cash payments record.

15 Paid $28.25 for typewriter repairs. Voucher No. 4.

17 Reimbursed Maple $14.50 for travel expenses. Voucher No. 5.

19 Paid $8.00 to Big Red Car Care for washing the company automobile. Voucher No. 6.

22 Paid $9.50 for mailing a package. Voucher No. 7.

29 Paid $30.00 for postage stamps. Voucher No. 8.

Replenishing the Petty Cash Fund

The petty cash fund should be replenished whenever the fund runs low, and at the end of each accounting period, so that the accounts are brought up to date. The amount columns of the petty cash payments record are totaled to verify that the total of the Total Amount column equals the total of the Distribution columns. The amount columns are then ruled as shown in Figure 8-12.

The information in the petty cash payments record is used to replenish the petty cash fund. On December 31, a check for $168.80 is issued to the petty cash custodian. The journal entry to record the replenishment of the fund is as follows:

FIGURE 8-12 Maple Consulting's Petty Cash Payments Record

PETTY CASH PAYMENTS FOR THE MONTH OF December 19-- PAGE 1

	DAY	DESCRIPTION		VOU. NO.	TOTAL AMOUNT	DISTRIBUTION OF PAYMENTS AUTO. EXP.	POST. EXP.	TRAVEL/ ENTERT. EXP	MISC. EXP.	ACCOUNT	AMOUNT	
1	1	Received in fund	200.00									1
2	5	Automobile repairs		1	32 80	32 80						2
3	8	Client luncheon		2	15 75			15 75				3
4	9	James Maple, personal use		3	30 00					James Maple, Drawing	30 00	4
5	15	Typewriter repairs		4	28 25				28 25			5
6	17	Traveling expenses		5	14 50			14 50				6
7	19	Washing automobile		6	8 00	8 00						7
8	22	Postage expense		7	9 50		9 50					8
9	29	Postage stamps		8	30 00		30 00					9
10					168 80	40 80	39 50	30 25	28 25		30 00	10
11	31	Balance	31.20									11
12	31	Replenished fund	168.80									12
13		Total	200.00									13

Credit to replenish petty cash fund

Debits to replenish petty cash fund

18	Dec. 31	Automobile Expense				4 0 80						18
19		Postage Expense				3 9 50						19
20		Travel and Entertainment Expense				3 0 25						20
21		Miscellaneous Expense				2 8 25						21
22		James Maple, Drawing				3 0 00						22
23		Cash							1 6 8 80			23
24		Replenishment of petty cash fund										24
25												25

> **LEARNING KEY** Once the petty cash fund is established, no further entries are made to Petty Cash unless the amount of the fund is being changed. No posting is done from the petty cash payments record.

Note two important aspects of the functioning of a petty cash fund.

1. Once the fund is established by debiting Petty Cash and crediting Cash, no further entries are made to Petty Cash. Notice in the journal entry to replenish the fund that the debits are to appropriate expense accounts and the credit is to the cash account. Only if the amount of the fund itself is being changed would there be a debit or credit to Petty Cash.
2. The petty cash payments record is strictly a supplement to the regular accounting records. Because it is not a journal, no posting is done from this record.

CASH SHORT AND OVER

LO4   Use the cash short and over account.

Businesses generally must be able to make change when customers pay for goods or services received. An unavoidable part of this change-making process is that errors can occur. It is important to know whether such errors have occurred and how to account for them.

Businesses commonly use cash registers with tapes that accumulate a record of the day's receipts. The amount of cash according to the tapes can be compared with the amount of cash in the register to determine the existence and amount of any error. For example, assume a cash shortage is identified for June 19.

Receipts per register tapes	$963
Cash count	961
Cash shortage	$ 2

Similarly, assume a cash overage is identified for June 20.

Receipts per register tapes	$814
Cash count	815
Cash overage	$ 1

We account for such errors by using an account called Cash Short and Over. The register tapes on June 19 showed receipts of $963, but only $961 in cash was counted. The journal entry on June 19 to record the revenues and cash shortage would be:

18	19–– June	19	Cash			9 6 1	00					18
19			Cash Short and Over			2	00					19
20			Service Fees						9 6 3	00		20
21			Record cash shortage									21

The entry on June 20 to record the revenues and cash overage would be:

23		20	Cash			8 1 5	00					23
24			Service Fees						8 1 4	00		24
25			Cash Short and Over						1	00		25
26			Record cash overage									26

The cash short and over account is used to accumulate cash shortages and overages throughout the accounting period. At the end of the period, a debit balance in the account (a net shortage) is treated as an expense. A credit balance in the account (a net overage) is treated as revenue.

KEY POINTS

1 Three steps to follow in preparing a check are:

1. Complete the check stub or register.
2. Enter the date, payee name, and amount on the check.
3. Sign the check.

2 The most common reasons for differences between the book and bank cash balances are:

1. Outstanding checks
2. Deposits in transit
3. Bank service charges
4. Bank collections for the depositor
5. NSF checks
6. Errors by the bank or the depositor

Three steps to follow in preparing a bank reconciliation are:

1. Identify deposits in transit and any related errors.
2. Identify outstanding checks and any related errors.
3. Identify additional reconciling items.

Only two kinds of items on a bank reconciliation require journal entries:

1. Errors on the depositor's books.
2. Bank additions and deductions that do not already appear in the accounting records.

3 Two important aspects of the functioning of a petty cash fund are:

1. Once the fund is established, subsequent entries do not affect the petty cash account balance, unless the size of the fund itself is being changed.
2. The petty cash payments record is supplemental to the regular accounting records. No posting is done from this record.

4 Cash shortages and overages are accounted for using the cash short and over account. A debit balance in this account represents expense; a credit balance represents revenue.

KEY TERMS

ABA (American Bankers Association) Number 242   The small fraction printed in the upper right hand corner of each check.
automated teller machines (ATM) 243   Machines used by depositors to make withdrawals or deposits at any time.
bank reconciliation 247   Bringing the book and bank balances into agreement.
bank statement 244   A statement of account issued by a bank to each depositor once a month.
blank endorsement 243   The depositor signs on the back of the check, making the check payable to any bearer.
cancelled checks 245   The depositor's checks paid by the bank during the period.
cash 241   To a business, cash includes currency, coins, checks received from customers, money orders, and bank cashier's checks.
check 243   A document ordering a bank to pay cash from a depositor's account.
check stub 243   In some checkbooks, each check is attached to a stub that contains space for relevant information.
credit memos 248   Items that the bank adds to the account.
debit memos 248   Items that the bank deducts from the account.
deposit ticket 241   A detailed listing of items being deposited.
deposits in transit 247   Deposits that have not reached or been recorded by the bank before the statement is prepared.
drawee 243   The bank on which the check is drawn.
drawer 243   The depositor who orders the bank to pay the cash.
electronic funds transfer (EFT) 251   Using a computer rather than paper checks to complete transactions with the bank.
endorsement 242   Stamping or writing the depositor's name and sometimes other information on the back of the check.
internal control 241   A set of procedures designed to ensure proper accounting for transactions.

not sufficient funds (NSF) checks 247   Checks deposited by the depositor that are not paid because the drawer did not have sufficient funds.

outstanding checks 247   Checks issued during the period that have not been presented to the bank for payment before the statement is prepared.

payee 243   The person being paid the cash.

petty cash fund 251   A fund established to pay for small items.

petty cash payments record 252   A special multicolumn record that supplements the regular accounting records.

petty cash voucher 252   A receipt that is prepared for every payment from the petty cash fund.

restrictive endorsement 243   The depositor adds words such as "For deposit" to restrict the payment of the check.

service charges 247   Bank charges for services such as check printing and processing.

signature card 241   A card that is completed and signed by each person authorized to sign checks.

REVIEW QUESTIONS

1. Why must a signature card be filled out and signed to open a checking account?
2. Explain the difference between a blank endorsement and a restrictive endorsement.
3. Who are the three parties to every check?
4. What are the three steps to follow in preparing a check?
5. What are the most common reasons for differences between the book and bank cash balances?
6. What are the three steps to follow in preparing a bank reconciliation?
7. What two kinds of items on a bank reconciliation require journal entries?
8. Name four applications of electronic funds transfer in current use.
9. What is the purpose of a petty cash fund?
10. What should be prepared every time a petty cash payment is made?
11. At what two times should the petty cash fund be replenished?
12. From what source is the information obtained for issuing a check to replenish the petty cash fund?
13. What does a debit balance in the cash short and over account represent? What does a credit balance in this account represent?

MANAGING YOUR WRITING

The current month's bank statement for your account arrives in the mail. In reviewing the statement, you notice a deposit listed for $400 that you did not make. It has been credited in error to your account. Write a memo discussing whether you have an ethical or legal obligation to inform the bank of the error. What action should you take?

DEMONSTRATION PROBLEM

Jason Kuhn's check stubs for Kuhn's Wilderness Outfitters indicated a balance of $4,673.12 on March 31, 19--. This included a record of a deposit of $926.10 mailed to the bank on March 30, but not credited to Kuhn's account until April 1. In addition, the following checks were outstanding on March 31.

No. 462, $524.26
No. 465, $213.41
No. 473, $543.58
No. 476, $351.38
No. 477, $197.45

The bank statement showed a balance of $5,419.00 as of March 31. The bank statement included a service charge of $4.10 dated March 29. In matching the cancelled checks and record of deposits with the stubs, you discovered that check no. 456, to Office Suppliers, Inc., for $93 was erroneously recorded on the stub for $39. This caused the bank balance on that stub and those following to be $54 too large. You also discovered that an ATM withdrawal of $100 for personal use was not recorded on the books.

Kuhn maintains a $200.00 petty cash fund. His petty cash payments record showed the following totals at the end of March of the current year.

Automobile expense	$ 32.40
Postage expense	27.50
Charitable contributions expense	35.00
Telephone expense	6.20
Travel and entertainment expense	38.60
Miscellaneous expense	17.75
Jason Kuhn, Drawing	40.00
Total	$197.45

This left a balance of $2.55 in the petty cash fund.

REQUIRED
1. Prepare a bank reconciliation for Kuhn's Wilderness Outfitters as of March 31, 19--.
2. Journalize the entries that should be made for Kuhn's Wilderness Outfitters on the books as of March 31, 19--: (a) as a result of the bank reconciliation and (b) to replenish the petty cash fund.
3. Show proof that, after these entries, the total of the cash and petty cash account balances equals $4,715.02.

SOLUTION

1.

Kuhn's Wilderness Outfitters
Bank Reconciliation
March 31, 19--

Bank statement balance, March 31		$5 4 1 9 00
Add deposit in transit		9 2 6 10
		$6 3 4 5 10
Deduct outstanding checks:		
No. 462	$ 5 2 4 26	
No. 465	2 1 3 41	
No. 473	5 4 3 58	
No. 476	3 5 1 38	
No. 477	1 9 7 45	1 8 3 0 08
Adjusted bank balance		$4 5 1 5 02
Book balance, March 31		$4 6 7 3 12
Deduct: Bank service charge	$ 4 10	
Error on check no. 456	5 4 00	
Unrecorded ATM withdrawal	1 0 0 00	1 5 8 10
Adjusted book balance		$4 5 1 5 02

3						3
4	19-- Mar.	31	Miscellaneous Expense	4 10		4
5			Accounts Payable—Office Supp., Inc.	5 4 00		5
6			Jason Kuhn, Drawing	1 0 0 00		6
7			Cash		1 5 8 10	7
8			Bank transactions for March			8
9						9
10		31	Automobile Expense	3 2 40		10
11			Postage Expense	2 7 50		11
12			Charitable Contributions Expense	3 5 00		12
13			Telephone Expense	6 20		13
14			Travel and Entertainment Expense	3 8 60		14
15			Miscellaneous Expense	1 7 75		15
16			Jason Kuhn, Drawing	4 0 00		16
17			Cash		1 9 7 45	17
18			Replenishment of petty cash			18
19			fund			19
20						20
21						21

2.a. (lines 4–8)

b. (lines 10–19)

3. Cash in bank:

Check stub balance, March 31	$4,673.12
Less bank charges	158.10
Adjusted cash in bank	$4,515.02

Cash on hand:	
Petty cash fund	$ 2.55
Add replenishment	197.45
Adjusted cash on hand	$ 200.00
Total cash in bank and petty cash on hand	$4,715.02

SERIES A   EXERCISES

1 **EXERCISE 8A1 CHECKING ACCOUNT TERMS**   Match the following words with their definitions.

1. An endorsement where the depositor simply signs on the back of the check
2. An endorsement that contains words like "For Deposit Only" together with the signature
3. A card filled out and signed by each person authorized to sign checks on an account
4. The depositor who orders the bank to pay cash from the depositor's account
5. The bank on which the check is drawn
6. The person being paid the cash
7. A check that has been paid by the bank and is being returned to the depositor

a. signature card
b. cancelled check
c. blank endorsement
d. drawer
e. restrictive endorsement
f. drawee
g. payee

1 **EXERCISE 8A2 PREPARE DEPOSIT TICKET**   Based on the following information, prepare a deposit ticket.

Date:		January 15, 19--
Currency:		$334.00
Coin:		26.00
Checks:	No. 4-11	311.00
	No. 80-322	108.00
	No. 3-9	38.00

1 **EXERCISE 8A3 PREPARE CHECK AND STUB** Based on the following information, prepare a check and stub.

Date:	January 15, 19--
Balance brought forward:	$2,841.50
Deposit:	(From Exercise 8A2)
Check to:	J.M. Suppliers
Amount:	$150.00
For:	Office Supplies
Signature:	Sign your name

2 **EXERCISE 8A4 BANK RECONCILIATION TERMINOLOGY** In a format similar to the following, indicate whether the action at the left will result in an addition to (+) or subtraction from (−) the ending bank balance or the ending checkbook balance.

	Ending Bank Balance	Ending Checkbook Balance
1. Deposits in transit to the bank	_____	_____
2. Error in checkbook: check recorded as $32 but was actually for $23	_____	_____
3. Service fee charged by bank	_____	_____
4. Outstanding checks	_____	_____
5. NSF check deposited earlier	_____	_____
6. Error in checkbook: check recorded as $22 but was actually for $220	_____	_____
7. Bank credit memo advising they collected a note for us	_____	_____

2 **EXERCISE 8A5 PREPARE JOURNAL ENTRIES FOR BANK RECONCILIATION** Based on the bank reconciliation information shown on the next page, prepare the journal entries.

3 **EXERCISE 8A6 PETTY CASH JOURNAL ENTRIES** Based on the following petty cash information, prepare (a) the journal entry to establish a petty cash fund, and (b) the journal entry to replenish the petty cash fund.

On January 1, 19--, a check was written in the amount of $200 to establish a petty cash fund. During January, the following vouchers were written for cash removed from the petty cash drawer:

Voucher No.	Account Debited	Amount
1	Telephone Expense	$17.50
2	Automobile Expense	33.00
3	Joseph Levine, Drawing	70.00
4	Postage Expense	12.50
5	Charitable Contributions Expense	15.00
6	Miscellaneous Expense	49.00

Lisa Choy Associates
Bank Reconciliation
July 31, 19--

Bank statement balance, July 31							$2 7 6 4 40
Add deposits in transit		$ 2 5 0 00					
			9 8 00			3 4 8 00	
						$3 1 1 2 40	
Deduct outstanding checks:							
No. 387		$ 3 5 3 50					
No. 393		1 7 80					
No. 398		3 3 20				4 0 4 50	
Adjusted bank balance						$2 7 0 7 90	
Book balance, July 31						$3 1 3 0 90	
Deduct: Error on check no. 394*		$ 2 3 00					
NSF check		3 9 0 00					
Bank service charge		1 0 00				4 2 3 00	
Adjusted book balance						$2 7 0 7 90	
*Accounts Payable was debited in original entry.							

4 **EXERCISE 8A7 CASH SHORT AND OVER ENTRIES**   Based on the following information, prepare the weekly entries for cash receipts from service fees and cash short and over.

Date	Cash Register Receipt Amount	Actual Cash Counted
April 2	$268.50	$266.50
9	237.75	233.50
16	309.25	311.00
23	226.50	224.00
30	318.00	322.00

SERIES A PROBLEMS

2 **PROBLEM 8A1 BANK RECONCILIATION AND RELATED JOURNAL ENTRIES**   The balance in the checking account of Violette Enterprises as of October 31 is $4,765.00. The bank statement shows an ending balance of $4,235.00. The following information is discovered by comparing checks deposited and written and noting service charges and other debit and credit memos shown on the bank statement.

Deposits in transit:	10/26	$175.00
	10/28	334.00

Outstanding checks:	No. 1764	$ 47.00
	No. 1767	146.00
	No. 1781	369.00

Unrecorded ATM withdrawal*:	180.00
Bank service charge:	43.00
NSF check:	370.00

| Error on check no. 1754 | Checkbook shows it was for $72, but was actually written for $62. Accounts Payable was debited. |

*Funds were withdrawn by Guy Violette for personal use.

REQUIRED
1. Prepare a bank reconciliation as of October 31, 19--.
2. Prepare the required journal entries.

3   PROBLEM 8A2 PETTY CASH RECORD AND JOURNAL ENTRIES
On May 1 a petty cash fund was established for $150. The following vouchers were issued during May:

Date	Voucher No.	Purpose	Amount
May 1	1	postage due	$ 3.50
3	2	office supplies	11.00
5	3	auto repair (miscellaneous)	22.00
7	4	drawing (Joy Adams)	25.00
11	5	donation (Red Cross)	10.00
15	6	travel expenses	28.00
22	7	postage stamps	3.50
26	8	telephone call	5.00
30	9	donation (Boy Scouts)	30.00

REQUIRED
1. Prepare the journal entry to establish the petty cash fund.
2. Record the vouchers in the petty cash record. Total and rule the petty cash record.
3. Prepare the journal entry to replenish the petty cash fund. Make the appropriate entry in the petty cash record.

4   PROBLEM 8A3 CASH SHORT AND OVER ENTRIES   Listed below are the weekly cash register tape amounts for service fees and the related cash counts during the month of July.

Date	Cash Register Receipt Amount	Actual Cash Counted
July 2	$289.50	$287.00
9	311.50	311.50
16	306.00	308.50
23	317.50	315.00
30	296.00	299.50

REQUIRED

1. Prepare the journal entries to record the cash service fees and cash short and over for each of the five weeks.
2. Post to the cash short and over account (use account no. 573).
3. Determine the ending balance of the cash short and over account. Does it represent an expense or revenue?

SERIES B   EXERCISES

1 **EXERCISE 8B1 CHECKING ACCOUNT TERMS**   Match the following words with their definitions.

1. Banking number used to identify checks for deposit tickets
2. A card filled out to open a checking account
3. A machine from which withdrawals can be taken or deposits made to accounts
4. A place where relevant information is recorded about a check
5. A set of procedures designed to ensure proper accounting for transactions
6. A statement of account issued to each depositor once a month
7. A detailed listing of items being deposited to an account

a. bank statement
b. deposit ticket
c. signature card
d. internal control
e. check stub
f. ATM
g. ABA number

1 **EXERCISE 8B2 PREPARE DEPOSIT TICKET**   Based on the following information, prepare a deposit ticket.

Date:		November 15, 19--
Currency:		$283.00
Coin:		19.00
Checks:	No. 3-22	201.00
	No. 19-366	114.00
	No. 3-2	28.00

1 **EXERCISE 8B3 PREPARE CHECK AND STUB**   Based on the following information, prepare a check and stub.

Date: November 15,19--
Balance brought forward: $3,181.00
Deposit: (from Exercise 8B2)
Check to: R.J. Smith Co.
Amount: $120.00
For: Payment on account
Signature: Sign your name

2 **EXERCISE 8B4 BANK RECONCILIATION TERMINOLOGY** In a format similar to the following, indicate whether the action at the left will result in an addition to (+) or subtraction from (–) the ending bank balance or the ending checkbook balance.

	Ending Bank Balance	Ending Checkbook Balance
1. Service fee of $12 charged by bank		
2. Outstanding checks		
3. Error in checkbook: check recorded as $36 was actually for $28		
4. NSF check deposited earlier		
5. Bank credit memo advising they collected a note for us		
6. Deposits in transit to the bank		
7. Error in checkbook: check recorded as $182 was actually for $218		

2 **EXERCISE 8B5 PREPARE JOURNAL ENTRIES FOR BANK RECONCILIATION** Based on the following bank reconciliation information, prepare the journal entries.

Regina D'Alfonso Associates
Bank Reconciliation
July 31, 19--

Bank statement balance, July 31			$1 7 8 4 00
Add deposits in transit	$ 4 1 8 50		
	1 0 0 50		5 1 9 00
			$2 3 0 3 00
Deduct outstanding checks:			
No. 185	$ 2 0 6 50		
No. 203	3 1 7 40		
No. 210	5 6 10		5 8 0 00
Adjusted bank balance			$1 7 2 3 00
Book balance, July 31			$1 7 9 4 00
Add error on check no. 191*			1 0 00
			$1 8 0 4 00
Deduct: NSF check	$ 6 6 00		
Bank service charge	1 5 00		8 1 00
Adjusted book balance			$1 7 2 3 00
*Accounts Payable was debited in original entry.			

3 EXERCISE 8B6 PETTY CASH JOURNAL ENTRIES   Based on the following petty cash information, prepare (a) the journal entry to establish a petty cash fund, and (b) the journal entry to replenish the petty cash fund.

On October 1, 19--, a check was written in the amount of $200 to establish a petty cash fund. During October, the following vouchers were written for cash taken from the petty cash drawer:

Voucher No.	Account Debited	Amount
1	Postage Expense	$13.00
2	Miscellaneous Expense	17.00
3	John Flanagan, Drawing	45.00
4	Telephone Expense	36.00
5	Charitable Contributions Expense	50.00
6	Automobile Expense	29.00

4 EXERCISE 8B7 CASH SHORT AND OVER ENTRIES   Based on the following information, prepare the weekly entries for cash receipts from service fees and cash short and over.

Date	Cash Register Receipt Amount	Actual Cash Counted
June 1	$330.00	$333.00
8	297.00	300.00
15	233.00	231.00
22	302.00	296.50
29	316.00	312.00

SERIES B   PROBLEMS

2 PROBLEM 8B1 BANK RECONCILIATION AND RELATED JOURNAL ENTRIES   The balance in the checking account of Kyros Enterprises as of November 30, is $3,004.00. The bank statement shows an ending balance of $2,525.00. The following information is discovered by comparing checks deposited and written and noting service charges and other debit and credit memos shown on the bank statement.

Deposits in transit:	11/21	$125.00
	11/26	200.00
Outstanding checks: —	No. 322	17.00
	No. 324	105.00
	No. 327	54.00
Unrecorded ATM withdrawal*:		100.00
Bank service charge:		25.00
NSF check:		185.00

Error on check no. 321   Checkbook shows is was for $44, but was actually written for $64. Accounts Payable was debited.   _20.00

*Funds were withdrawn by Steve Kyros for personal use.

26 74

REQUIRED
1. Prepare a bank reconciliation as of November 30, 19--.
2. Prepare the required journal entries.

Bank Reconciliation on EXAM.

3   **PROBLEM 8B2 PETTY CASH RECORD AND JOURNAL ENTRIES**
On July 1, a petty cash fund was established for $100. The following vouchers were issued during July:

Date	Voucher No.	Purpose	Amount
July 1	1	office supplies	$ 3.00
3	2	donation (Goodwill)	15.00
5	3	travel expenses	5.00
7	4	postage due	2.00
8	5	office supplies	4.00
11	6	postage due	3.50
15	7	telephone call	5.00
21	8	travel expenses	11.00
25	9	withdrawal by owner (L. Bean)	20.00
26	10	copier repair (miscellaneous)	18.50

REQUIRED
1. Prepare the journal entry to establish the petty cash fund.
2. Record the vouchers in the petty cash record. Total and rule the petty cash record.
3. Prepare the journal entry to replenish the petty cash fund. Make the appropriate entry in the petty cash record.

4   **PROBLEM 8B3 CASH SHORT AND OVER ENTRIES**   Listed below are the weekly cash register tape amounts for service fees and the related cash counts during the month of July.

Date	Cash Register Receipt Amount	Actual Cash Counted
Aug. 1	$292.50	$295.00
8	305.00	301.50
15	286.00	286.00
22	330.25	332.75
29	298.50	295.00

REQUIRED
1. Prepare the journal entries to record the cash service fees and cash short and over for each of the five weeks.
2. Post to the cash short and over account. (Use account no. 573.)
3. Determine the ending balance of the cash short and over account. Does it represent an expense or revenue?

MASTERY PROBLEM

Turner Excavation maintains a checking account and has decided to open a petty cash fund. The following petty cash fund transactions occurred during July.

July   2 Established a petty cash fund by issuing check no. 301 for $100.00.
   5 Paid $25.00 from the petty cash fund for postage. Voucher no. 1.
   7 Paid $30.00 from the petty cash fund for delivery of flowers for the secretaries (miscellaneous expense). Voucher no. 2.
   8 Paid $20.00 from the petty cash fund to repair a tire on the company truck. Voucher no. 3.
   12 Paid $22.00 from the petty cash fund for a newspaper advertisement. Voucher no. 4.
   13 Issued check no. 303 to replenish the petty cash fund. (Total and rule the petty cash payments record. Record the balance and the amount needed to replenish the fund in the Description column of the petty cash payments record.)
   20 Paid $26.00 from the petty cash fund to reimburse an employee for expenses incurred to repair the company truck. Voucher no. 5.
   24 Paid $12.50 from the petty cash fund for telephone calls made from a phone booth. Voucher no. 6.
   28 Paid $25.00 from the petty cash fund as a contribution to the YMCA. Voucher no. 7.
   31 Issued check no. 308 to replenish the petty cash fund. (Total and rule the petty cash payments record. Record the balance and the amount needed to replenish the fund in the Description column of the petty cash payments record.)

The following additional transactions occurred during July.

July   5 Issued check no. 302 to pay office rent, $650.00.
   15 Issued check no. 304 for the purchase of office equipment, $525.00.
   17 Issued check no. 305 for the purchase of supplies, $133.00.
   18 Issued check no. 306 to pay attorney fees, $1,000.
   30 Issued check no. 307 to pay newspaper for an advertisement, $200.20.

REQUIRED

1. Record the petty cash transactions in a petty cash payments record. Use the following Distribution of Payments column headings: Truck Expense, Postage Expense, Charitable Contributions Expense, Telephone Expense, Advertising Expense, and Miscellaneous Expense. Total and rule the petty cash record.
2. Make all required general journal entries for cash transactions. (Note: The petty cash fund was established and replenished twice during July.)
3. The bank statement shown in Figure 8-13 was received in the mail. Deposits were made on July 6 for $3,500.00 and on July 29 for $2,350.00.

FIGURE 8-13   Bank Statement

Statement					Merchant's National Bank	

Turner Excavation
220 Main Street
Oakhurst, NJ 07755-1461

Reference Number 16 3247 5   Page Number
Statement Date July 31, 19--
Statement Instructions

Beginning Balance	No. of Deposits and Credits	We have added these deposits and credits totaling	No. of withdrawals and charges	We have subtracted these withdrawals and charges totaling	Resulting in a statement balance of
$1,250.25	1	$3,500.00	6	$1,512.50	$3,237.75

Document Count	Average Daily balance this statement period		Minimum balance this statement period	Date	Amount

If your account does not balance, please see reverse side and report any discrepancy to our Customer Service Department.

Date	Description	Amount	Balance
7/1	Beginning Balance		1,250.25
7/5	Check No. 301	-100.00	1,150.25
7/8	Check No. 302	-655.00	495.25
7/9	Deposit	3,500.00	3,995.25
7/15	Check No. 303	-97.00	3,898.25
7/20	Check No. 304	-525.00	3,373.25
7/28	Check No. 305	-133.00	3,240.25
7/31	Sevice Charge	-2.50	3,237.75

EC-Error Correction	OD-Overdrawn	RC-Return Check Charge
ATM-Automated Teller Machine	TR-Wire Transfer	D/N-Day/Night

Depositor agrees and Bank accepts business upon the terms and conditions of Bank's rules and regulations now in effect or as may be hereafter adopted.

The checkbook balance on July 31 is $4,331.55. Notice the discrepancy in check no. 302 that cleared the bank for $655.00. This check was written on July 5 for rent expense, but was incorrectly entered on the check stub and in the journal as $650.00. Prepare a bank reconciliation and make any necessary journal entries as of July 31.

9

Payroll Accounting: Employee Earnings and Deductions

Careful study of this chapter should enable you to:

LO1 Distinguish between employees and independent contractors.

LO2 Calculate employee earnings and deductions.

LO3 Prepare payroll records.

LO4 Account for employee earnings and deductions.

LO5 Describe various payroll record-keeping methods.

You work 40 hours at $6 an hour to earn $240. So why is your paycheck so much less than $240? What does your employer do with all that money deducted from your paycheck? Are the right amounts being deducted? To answer these questions, you need to know about employee payroll accounting.

The only contact most of us have with payroll is receiving a paycheck. Few of us have seen the large amount of record keeping needed to produce that paycheck.

Employers maintain complete payroll accounting records for two reasons. First, payroll costs are major expenditures for most companies. Payroll accounting records provide data useful in analyzing and controlling these expenditures. Second, federal, state, and local laws require employers to keep payroll records. Companies must accumulate payroll data both for the business as a whole and for each employee.

EMPLOYEES AND INDEPENDENT CONTRACTORS

LO1   Distinguish between employees and independent contractors.

Not every person who performs services for a business is considered an employee. An **employee** works under the control and direction of an employer. Examples include secretaries, maintenance workers, salesclerks, and plant supervisors. In contrast, an **independent contractor** performs a service for a fee and does not work under the control and direction of the company paying for the service. Examples of independent contractors include public accountants, real estate agents, and lawyers.

The distinction between an employee and an independent contractor is very important for payroll purposes. Government laws and regulations regarding payroll are much more complex for employees than for independent contractors. Employers must deduct certain taxes, maintain payroll records, and file numerous reports for all employees. Only one form must be filed for independent contractors. The payroll accounting procedures described in this chapter apply only to employer/employee relationships.

EMPLOYEE EARNINGS AND DEDUCTIONS

LO2   Calculate employee earnings and deductions.

Three steps are required to determine how much to pay an employee for a pay period.

1. Calculate total earnings.
2. Determine the amounts of deductions.
3. Subtract deductions from total earnings to compute net pay.

Salaries and Wages

Compensation for managerial or administrative services usually is called **salary.** A salary normally is expressed in biweekly (every two weeks), monthly, or annual terms. Compensation for skilled or unskilled labor usually is referred to as **wages.** Wages ordinarily are expressed in terms of hours, weeks, or units produced. The terms "salaries" and "wages" often are used interchangeably in practice.

The **Fair Labor Standards Act (FLSA)** requires employers to pay overtime at $1\frac{1}{2}$ times the regular rate to any hourly employee who works over 40 hours in a week. Some companies pay a higher rate for hours worked on Saturday or Sunday, but this is not required by the FLSA. Some salaried employees are exempt from the FLSA rules and are not paid overtime.

Computing Total Earnings

Compensation usually is based on the time worked during the payroll period. Sometimes earnings are based on sales or units of output during the period. When compensation is based on time, a record must be kept of the time worked by each employee. Time cards (Figure 9-1) are helpful for this purpose. In large businesses with computer-based timekeeping systems, plastic cards or badges with special barcodes (Figure 9-2) can be used.

To illustrate the computation of total earnings, look at Helen Kuzmik's time card in Figure 9-1. The card shows that Kuzmik worked 55 hours for the week.

FIGURE 9-1 Time Card

Westly, Inc.
Time Card - Hourly Payroll

Period Ending	Mo. Dec.	Day 19	Yr. 19--

Name of Dept. Sales

NAME (Print) Last: Kuzmik First: Helen

Payroll No. 25-1 Section A

1st. wk.	M	T	W	Th	F	Sa	Su	Totals
Reg. Sched.	8	8	8	8	8			40
Over-time	1	1	1	1	1	6		11
Dbl. Time							4	4
1st. wk.	**M**	**T**	**W**	**Th**	**F**	**Sa**	**Su**	**Totals**
Reg. Sched.								
Over-time								

Remarks

I certify that to the best of my knowledge the above is a true report of the attendence of the employee named.

T.M.
Department Head

FIGURE 9-2   Barcode Time Card

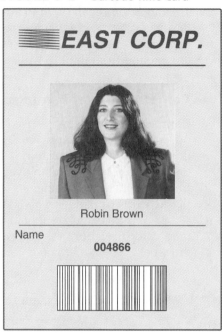

Kuzmik's regular rate of pay is $12 per hour. She is paid $1\frac{1}{2}$ times the regular rate for hours worked in excess of 40 per week, and twice the regular rate for hours worked on Sunday. Kuzmik's total earnings for the week ended December 19 are computed as follows:

Regular hours	40 hours
Overtime	11
Double time	4
Total hours worked	55 hours

40 hours × $12	$480
11 hours × $18 ($1\frac{1}{2}$ × $12 = $18)	198
4 hours (on Sunday) × $24 (2 × $12 = $24)	96
Total earnings for the week	$774

An employee who is paid a salary may also be entitled to premium pay for overtime. If this is the case, it is necessary to compute the regular hourly rate of pay before computing the overtime rate. To illustrate, assume that Linda Swaney has a salary of $2,288 a month plus $1\frac{1}{2}$ times the regular hourly rate for hours worked in excess of 40 per week. Swaney's overtime rate of pay is computed as follows:

$2,288 × 12 months	$27,456 annual pay
$27,456 ÷ 52 weeks	$528.00 pay per week
$528.00 ÷ 40 hours	$13.20 pay per regular hour
$13.20 × $1\frac{1}{2}$	$19.80 overtime pay per hour

If Swaney worked 50 hours during the week ended December 19, her total earnings for the week would be computed as follows:

40 hours × $13.20	$528.00
10 hours × $19.80	198.00
Total earnings for the week	$726.00

Deductions from Total Earnings

An employee's total earnings are called **gross pay.** Various deductions are made from gross pay to yield take-home or **net pay.** Deductions from gross pay fall into three major categories:

1. Federal (and possibly state and city) income tax withholding
2. Employees **FICA tax** withholding
3. Voluntary deductions

Employees Income Tax Withholding.   Federal law requires employers to withhold certain amounts from the total earnings of each employee. These withholdings are applied toward the payment of the employee's federal income tax. Four factors determine the amount to be withheld from an employee's gross pay each pay period.

1. Total earnings
2. Marital status
3. Number of withholding allowances claimed
4. Length of the pay period

Withholding Allowances.   Each employee is required to furnish the employer with an Employee's Withholding Allowance Certificate, Form W-4 (Figure 9-3). The marital status of the employee and the number of allowances claimed on Form W-4 determine the dollar amount of earnings subject to withholding. A **withholding allowance** exempts a specific dollar amount of an employee's gross pay from federal income tax withholding. In general, each employee is permitted one personal withholding allowance, one for a spouse who does not also claim an allowance, and one for each dependent.

An allowance certificate completed by Ken Istone is shown on page 276. Istone is married, has a spouse who does not claim an allowance, and has four dependent children. On line 5 of the W-4 form, Istone claims 6 allowances, calculated as follows:

Personal allowance	1
Spouse allowance	1
Allowances for dependents	4
Total withholding allowances	6

Wage-Bracket Method.   Employers may use the **wage-bracket method** to determine the amount of tax to be withheld from an employee's pay. The employee's gross pay for a specific time period is traced into the

Handwritten notes in margin:
1 ½
SST-.062   SSXGROSS
MEDICARE   .0145×gross
FIT   TABLE
STATE TAX   .275×Fed.
TDI   .013×GROSS

941 QUARTLY Fed. ANUALLY
940   FUT A TAX

FIGURE 9-3   Employee's Withholding Allowance Certificate (Form W-4)

.... Cut here and give the certificate to your employer. Keep the top portion for your records. ....

Form **W-4**	**Employee's Withholding Allowance Certificate**	OMB No. 1545-0010
Department of the Treasury Internal Revenue Service	▶ For Privacy Act and Paperwork Reduction Act Notice, see reverse.	19**95**

1 Type or print your first name and middle initial *Ken M.*	Last name *Istone*	2 Your social security number *393 58 8194*

| Home address (number and street or rural route)   *1546 Swallow Drive* | 3   ☐ Single ☒ Married ☐ Married, but withhold at higher Single rate. Note: *If married, but legally separated, or spouse is a nonresident alien, check the Single box.* |

| City or town, state, and ZIP code   *St. Louis, MO 63144-4752* | 4   If your last name differs from that on your social security card, check here and call 1-800-772-1213 for a new card . . . . . . ▶ ☐ |

5   Total number of allowances you are claiming (from line G above or from the worksheets on page 2 if they apply) . | 5 | *6* |
6   Additional amount, if any, you want withheld from each paycheck . . . . | 6 | $ |
7   I claim exemption from withholding for 1995 and I certify that I meet **BOTH** of the following conditions for exemption:
 ● Last year I had a right to a refund of **ALL** Federal income tax withheld because I had **NO** tax liability; **AND**
 ● This year I expect a refund of **ALL** Federal income tax withheld because I expect to have **NO** tax liability.
 If you meet both conditions, enter "EXEMPT" here . . . . ▶ | 7 |

Under penalties of perjury, I certify that I am entitled to the number of withholding allowances claimed on this certificate or entitled to claim exempt status.

Employee's signature ▶ *Ken M. Istone*   Date ▶ *January 3* , 19--

8   Employer's name and address (Employer: Complete 8 and 10 only if sending to the IRS) | 9 Office code (optional) | 10 Employer identification number |

Cat. No. 10220Q

appropriate wage-bracket table provided by the Internal Revenue Service (IRS). These tables cover various time periods, and there are separate tables for single and married taxpayers. Copies are provided in *Circular E—Employer's Tax Guide*, which may be obtained from any local IRS office.

Portions of weekly income tax wage-bracket withholding tables for single (not married) and married persons are illustrated in Figure 9-4. Assume that Ken Istone (who claims 6 allowances) had gross earnings of $545 for the week ended December 19, 19--. The table for married persons is used as follows:

> 1. Find the row for wages.
> 2. Find the column for withholding allowances.
> 3. Find the amount where they cross.

1. Find the row for wages of "at least $540, but less than $550."
2. Find the column headed "6 withholding allowances."
3. Where the row and column cross, $20 is given as the amount to be withheld.

For state or city income taxes, withholding generally is handled in one of two ways: (1) forms and tables similar to those provided by the IRS are used, or (2) an amount equal to a percentage of the federal withholding amount is withheld.

Employees FICA Tax Withholding. The Federal Insurance Contributions Act requires employers to withhold FICA taxes from employees' earnings. FICA taxes include amounts for both Social Security and Medicare programs. **Social Security taxes** provide pensions and disability benefits. **Medicare taxes** provide health insurance.

FIGURE 9-4 Federal Withholding Tax Table: Unmarried Persons

SINGLE Persons—**WEEKLY** Payroll Period

(For Wages Paid in 1995)

| If the wages are— | | And the number of withholding allowances claimed is— | | | | | | | | | | |
At least	But less than	0	1	2	3	4	5	6	7	8	9	10
		The amount of income tax to be withheld is—										
$300	$310	38	31	24	17	9	2	0	0	0	0	0
310	320	40	33	25	18	11	4	0	0	0	0	0
320	330	41	34	27	20	12	5	0	0	0	0	0
330	340	43	36	28	21	14	7	0	0	0	0	0
340	350	44	37	30	23	15	8	1	0	0	0	0
350	360	46	39	31	24	17	10	2	0	0	0	0
360	370	47	40	33	26	18	11	4	0	0	0	0
370	380	49	42	34	27	20	13	5	0	0	0	0
380	390	50	43	36	29	21	14	7	0	0	0	0
390	400	52	45	37	30	23	16	8	1	0	0	0
400	410	53	46	39	32	24	17	10	3	0	0	0
410	420	55	48	40	33	26	19	11	4	0	0	0
420	430	56	49	42	35	27	20	13	6	0	0	0
430	440	58	51	43	36	29	22	14	7	0	0	0
440	450	59	52	45	38	30	23	16	9	2	0	0
450	460	61	54	46	39	32	25	17	10	3	0	0
460	470	62	55	48	41	33	26	19	12	5	0	0
470	480	64	57	49	42	35	28	20	13	6	0	0
480	490	66	58	51	44	36	29	22	15	8	0	0
490	500	69	60	52	45	38	31	23	16	9	2	0
500	510	72	61	54	47	39	32	25	18	11	3	0
510	520	75	63	55	48	41	34	26	19	12	5	0
520	530	78	64	57	50	42	35	28	21	14	6	0
530	540	80	67	58	51	44	37	29	22	15	8	1
540	550	83	70	60	53	45	38	31	24	17	9	2
550	560	86	73	61	54	47	40	32	25	18	11	4
560	570	89	75	63	56	48	41	34	27	20	12	5
570	580	92	78	65	57	50	43	35	28	21	14	7
580	590	94	81	68	59	51	44	37	30	23	15	8
590	600	97	84	70	60	53	46	38	31	24	17	10
600	610	100	87	73	62	54	47	40	33	26	18	11
610	620	103	89	76	63	56	49	41	34	27	20	13
620	630	106	92	79	65	57	50	43	36	29	21	14
630	640	108	95	82	68	59	52	44	37	30	23	16
640	650	111	98	84	71	60	53	46	39	32	24	17
650	660	114	101	87	74	62	55	47	40	33	26	19
660	670	117	103	90	76	63	56	49	42	35	27	20
670	680	120	106	93	79	66	58	50	43	36	29	22
680	690	122	109	96	82	69	59	52	45	38	30	23
690	700	125	112	98	85	71	61	53	46	39	32	25
700	710	128	115	101	88	74	62	55	48	41	33	26
710	720	131	117	104	90	77	64	56	49	42	35	28
720	730	134	120	107	93	80	66	58	51	44	36	29
730	740	136	123	110	96	83	69	59	52	45	38	31
740	750	139	126	112	99	85	72	61	54	47	39	32
750	760	142	129	115	102	88	75	62	55	48	41	34
760	770	145	131	118	104	91	78	64	57	50	42	35
770	780	148	134	121	107	94	80	67	58	51	44	37
780	790	150	137	124	110	97	83	70	60	53	45	38
790	800	153	140	126	113	99	86	72	61	54	47	40
800	810	156	143	129	116	102	89	75	63	56	48	41
810	820	159	145	132	118	105	92	78	65	57	50	43
820	830	162	148	135	121	108	94	81	67	59	51	44
830	840	164	151	138	124	111	97	84	70	60	53	46
840	850	167	154	140	127	113	100	86	73	62	54	47
850	860	170	157	143	130	116	103	89	76	63	56	49
860	870	173	159	146	132	119	106	92	79	65	57	50
870	880	176	162	149	135	122	108	95	81	68	59	52
880	890	178	165	152	138	125	111	98	84	71	60	53
890	900	181	168	154	141	127	114	100	87	74	62	55
900	910	184	171	157	144	130	117	103	90	76	63	56
910	920	187	173	160	146	133	120	106	93	79	66	58
920	930	190	176	163	149	136	122	109	95	82	68	59
930	940	192	179	166	152	139	125	112	98	85	71	61
940	950	195	182	168	155	141	128	114	101	88	74	62
950	960	198	185	171	158	144	131	117	104	90	77	64
960	970	201	187	174	160	147	134	120	107	93	80	66
970	980	204	190	177	163	150	136	123	109	96	82	69
980	990	206	193	180	166	153	139	126	112	99	85	72
990	1,000	209	196	182	169	155	142	128	115	102	88	75
1,000	1,010	212	199	185	172	158	145	131	118	104	91	77
1,010	1,020	215	201	188	174	161	148	134	121	107	94	80
1,020	1,030	218	204	191	177	164	150	137	123	110	96	83
1,030	1,040	222	207	194	180	167	153	140	126	113	99	86
1,040	1,050	225	210	196	183	169	156	142	129	116	102	89
1,050	1,060	228	213	199	186	172	159	145	132	118	105	91
1,060	1,070	231	216	202	188	175	162	148	135	121	108	94
1,070	1,080	234	219	205	191	178	164	151	137	124	110	97
1,080	1,090	237	222	208	194	181	167	154	140	127	113	100
1,090	1,100	240	225	210	197	183	170	156	143	130	116	103
1,100	1,110	243	228	213	200	186	173	159	146	132	119	105
1,110	1,120	246	231	216	202	189	176	162	149	135	122	108
1,120	1,130	249	235	220	205	192	178	165	151	138	124	111
1,130	1,140	253	238	223	208	195	181	168	154	141	127	114
1,140	1,150	256	241	226	211	197	184	170	157	144	130	117
1,150	1,160	259	244	229	214	200	187	173	160	146	133	119
1,160	1,170	262	247	232	217	203	190	176	163	149	136	122
1,170	1,180	265	250	235	220	206	192	179	165	152	138	125
1,180	1,190	268	253	238	223	209	195	182	168	155	141	128
1,190	1,200	271	256	241	226	211	198	184	171	158	144	131
1,200	1,210	274	259	244	229	215	201	187	174	160	147	133
1,210	1,220	277	262	247	233	218	204	190	177	163	150	136
1,220	1,230	280	266	251	236	221	206	193	179	166	152	139
1,230	1,240	284	269	254	239	224	209	196	182	169	155	142
1,240	1,250	287	272	257	242	227	212	198	185	172	158	145

$1,250 and over Use Table 1(a) for a **SINGLE person** on page 32. Also see the instructions on page 30.

FIGURE 9-4   Federal Withholding Tax Table (continued): Married Persons

MARRIED Persons—**WEEKLY** Payroll Period

(For Wages Paid in 1995)

If the wages are—		And the number of withholding allowances claimed is—										
At least	But less than	0	1	2	3	4	5	6	7	8	9	10
		The amount of income tax to be withheld is—										
$290	$300	26	19	11	4	0	0	0	0	0	0	0
300	310	27	20	13	6	0	0	0	0	0	0	0
310	320	29	22	14	7	0	0	0	0	0	0	0
320	330	30	23	16	9	1	0	0	0	0	0	0
330	340	32	25	17	10	3	0	0	0	0	0	0
340	350	33	26	19	12	4	0	0	0	0	0	0
350	360	35	28	20	13	6	0	0	0	0	0	0
360	370	36	29	22	15	7	0	0	0	0	0	0
370	380	38	31	23	16	9	2	0	0	0	0	0
380	390	39	32	25	18	10	3	0	0	0	0	0
390	400	41	34	26	19	12	5	0	0	0	0	0
400	410	42	35	28	21	13	6	0	0	0	0	0
410	420	44	37	29	22	15	8	1	0	0	0	0
420	430	45	38	31	24	16	9	2	0	0	0	0
430	440	47	40	32	25	18	11	4	0	0	0	0
440	450	48	41	34	27	19	12	5	0	0	0	0
450	460	50	43	35	28	21	14	7	0	0	0	0
460	470	51	44	37	30	22	15	8	1	0	0	0
470	480	53	46	38	31	24	17	10	2	0	0	0
480	490	54	47	40	33	25	18	11	4	0	0	0
490	500	56	49	41	34	27	20	13	5	0	0	0
500	510	S7	50	43	36	28	21	14	7	0	0	0
510	520	59	52	44	37	30	23	16	8	1	0	0
520	530	60	53	46	39	31	24	17	10	3	0	0
530	540	62	55	47	40	33	26	19	11	4	0	0
540	550	63	56	49	42	34	27	20	13	6	0	0
550	560	65	58	50	43	36	29	22	14	7	0	0
560	570	66	59	52	45	37	30	23	16	9	1	0
570	580	68	61	53	46	39	32	25	17	10	3	0
580	590	69	62	55	48	40	33	26	19	12	4	0
590	600	71	64	56	49	42	35	28	20	13	6	0
600	610	72	65	58	51	43	36	29	22	15	7	0
610	620	74	67	59	52	45	38	31	23	16	9	2
620	630	75	68	61	54	46	39	32	25	18	10	3
630	640	77	70	62	55	48	41	34	26	19	12	5
640	650	78	71	64	57	49	42	35	28	21	13	6
650	660	80	73	65	58	51	44	37	29	22	15	8
660	670	81	74	67	60	52	45	38	31	24	16	9
670	680	83	76	68	61	54	47	40	32	25	18	11
680	690	84	77	70	63	55	48	41	34	27	19	12
690	700	86	79	71	64	57	50	43	35	28	21	14
700	710	87	80	73	66	58	51	44	37	30	22	15
710	720	89	82	74	67	60	53	46	38	31	24	17
720	730	90	83	76	69	61	54	47	40	33	25	18
730	740	92	85	77	70	63	56	49	41	34	27	20
740	750	93	86	79	72	64	57	50	43	36	28	21
750	760	95	88	80	73	66	59	52	44	37	30	23
760	770	96	89	82	75	67	60	53	46	39	31	24
770	780	98	91	83	76	69	62	55	47	40	33	26
780	790	99	92	85	78	70	63	56	49	42	34	27
790	800	101	94	86	79	72	65	58	50	43	36	29
800	810	102	95	88	81	73	66	59	52	45	37	30
810	820	104	97	89	82	75	68	61	53	46	39	32
820	830	105	98	91	84	76	69	62	55	48	40	33
830	840	108	100	92	85	78	71	64	56	49	42	35
840	850	111	101	94	87	79	72	65	58	51	43	36
850	860	113	103	95	88	81	74	67	59	52	45	38
860	870	116	104	97	90	82	75	68	61	54	46	39
870	880	119	106	98	91	84	77	70	62	55	48	41
880	890	122	108	100	93	85	78	71	64	57	49	42
890	900	125	111	101	94	87	80	73	65	58	51	44
900	910	127	114	103	96	88	81	74	67	60	52	45
910	920	130	117	104	97	90	83	76	68	61	54	47
920	930	133	119	106	99	91	84	77	70	63	55	48
930	940	136	122	109	100	93	86	79	71	64	57	50
940	950	139	125	112	102	94	87	80	73	66	58	51
950	960	141	128	114	103	96	89	82	74	67	60	53
960	970	144	131	117	105	97	90	83	76	69	61	54
970	980	147	133	120	107	99	92	85	77	70	63	56
980	990	150	136	123	109	100	93	86	79	72	64	57
990	1,000	153	139	126	112	102	95	88	80	73	66	59
1,000	1,010	155	142	128	115	103	96	89	82	75	67	60
1,010	1,020	158	145	131	118	105	98	91	83	76	69	62
1,020	1,030	161	147	134	121	107	99	92	85	78	70	63
1,030	1,040	164	150	137	123	110	101	94	86	79	72	65
1,040	1,050	167	153	140	126	113	102	95	88	81	73	66
1,050	1,060	169	156	142	129	115	104	97	89	82	75	68
1,060	1,070	172	159	145	132	118	105	98	91	84	76	69
1,070	1,080	175	161	148	135	121	108	100	92	85	78	71
1,080	1,090	178	164	151	137	124	110	101	94	87	79	72
1,090	1,100	181	167	154	140	127	113	103	95	88	81	74
1,100	1,110	183	170	156	143	129	116	104	97	90	82	75
1,110	1,120	186	173	159	146	132	119	106	98	91	84	77
1,120	1,130	189	175	162	149	135	122	108	100	93	85	78
1,130	1,140	192	178	165	151	138	124	111	101	94	87	80
1,140	1,150	195	181	168	154	141	127	114	103	96	88	81
1,150	1,160	197	184	170	157	143	130	117	104	97	90	83
1,160	1,170	200	187	173	160	146	133	119	106	99	91	84
1,170	1,180	203	189	176	163	149	136	122	109	100	93	86
1,180	1,190	206	192	179	165	152	138	125	111	102	94	87
1,190	1,200	209	195	182	168	155	141	128	114	103	96	89
1,200	1,210	211	198	184	171	157	144	131	117	105	97	90
1,210	1,220	214	201	187	174	160	147	133	120	106	99	92
1,220	1,230	217	203	190	177	163	150	136	123	109	100	93
1,230	1,240	220	206	193	179	166	152	139	125	112	102	95
1,240	1,250	223	209	196	182	169	155	142	128	115	103	96
1,250	1,260	225	212	198	185	171	158	145	131	118	105	98
1,260	1,270	228	215	201	188	174	161	147	134	120	107	99
1,270	1,280	231	217	204	191	177	164	150	137	123	110	101
1,280	1,290	234	220	207	193	180	166	153	139	126	113	102

Congress has frequently changed the tax rates and the maximum amounts of earnings subject to FICA taxes. For 1995, the Social Security rate is 6.2% on maximum earnings of $61,200. The Medicare rate is 1.45% on all earnings; there is no maximum.

To illustrate the calculation of FICA taxes, assume the following earnings for Sarah Cadrain:

	Earnings	
Pay Period	Week	Year-to-Date
Dec. 6–12	$1,200	$60,540
Dec. 13–19	$1,260	$61,800

For the week of December 6–12, FICA taxes on Cadrain's earnings would be:

Gross Pay	x	Tax Rate	=	Tax
$1,200		Social Security 6.2%		$74.40
		Medicare 1.45%		17.40
				$91.80

During the week of December 13–19, Cadrain's earnings for the calendar year went over the $61,200 Social Security maximum by $600 ($61,800 − $61,200). Therefore, $600 of her $1,260 earnings for the week would not be subject to the Social Security tax.

Year-to-date earnings	$61,800
Social Security maximum.	61,200
Amount not subject to Social Security tax	$ 600

The Social Security tax on Cadrain's December 13–19 earnings would be:

Gross pay	$1,260.00
Amount not subject to Social Security tax	600.00
Amount subject to Social Security tax	660.00
Tax rate	6.2%
Social Security tax	$ 40.92

Since there is no Medicare maximum, all of Cadrain's December 13–19 earnings would be subject to the Medicare tax.

Gross pay	$1,260.00
Tax rate	1.45%
Medicare tax	$ 18.27

The total FICA tax would be:

Social Security tax	$40.92
Medicare tax	18.27
Total FICA tax	$59.19

For the remainder of the calendar year, Cadrain's earnings would be subject only to Medicare taxes.

Voluntary Deductions.   In addition to the mandatory deductions from employee earnings for income and FICA taxes, many other deductions are possible. These deductions are usually voluntary and depend on specific agreements between the employee and employer. Examples of voluntary deductions are:

1. United States savings bond purchases
2. Health insurance premiums
3. Credit union deposits
4. Pension plan payments
5. Charitable contributions

Computing Net Pay

To compute an employee's net pay for the period, subtract all tax withholdings and voluntary deductions from the gross pay. Ken Istone's net pay for the week ended December 19 would be calculated as follows.

Gross pay		$545.00
Deductions:		
Federal income tax withholding	$20.00	
Social Security tax withholding	33.79	
Medicare tax withholding	7.90	
Health insurance premiums	10.00	
Total deductions		71.69
Net pay		$473.31

PAYROLL RECORDS

LO3   Prepare payroll records.

Payroll records should provide the following information for each employee:

1. Name, address, occupation, Social Security number, marital status, and number of withholding allowances.
2. Gross amount of earnings, date of payment, and period covered by each payroll.
3. Gross amount of earnings accumulated for the year.
4. Amounts of taxes and other items withheld.

Three types of payroll records are used to accumulate this information.

1. The payroll register
2. The payroll check with earnings statement attached
3. The employee's earnings record

These records can be prepared by either manual or automated methods. The illustrations in this chapter are based on a manual system. The forms and procedures illustrated are equally applicable to both manual and automated systems.

Payroll Register

A **payroll register** is a form used to assemble the data required at the end of each payroll period. Figure 9-5 illustrates Westly, Inc.'s, payroll register for the payroll period ended December 19, 19--. Detailed information on earnings, taxable earnings, deductions, and net pay is provided for each employee. Column headings for deductions may vary, depending on which deductions are commonly used by a particular business. The sources of key information in the register are indicated in Figure 9-5.

Westly, Inc., has eight employees. The first $61,200 of each employee's earnings is subject to Social Security tax. The Cumulative Total column, under the Earnings category, shows that Sarah Cadrain has exceeded this limit during the period. Thus, only $660 of her earnings for this pay period is subject to Social Security tax, as shown in the Taxable Earnings columns. The Taxable Earnings columns are needed for determining the Social Security tax and the employer's payroll taxes. Employers must pay unemployment tax on the first $7,000 of employee earnings and Social Security tax on the first $61,200. Employer payroll taxes are discussed in Chapter 10.

Regular deductions are made from employee earnings for federal income tax and Social Security and Medicare taxes. In addition, voluntary deductions are made for health insurance and United Way contributions, based on agreements with individual employees.

After the data for each employee have been entered, the amount columns in the payroll register should be totaled and the totals verified as follows:

Regular earnings		$4,743.00
Overtime earnings		692.00
Gross earnings		$5,435.00
Deductions:		
Federal income tax	$633.00	
Social Security tax	299.77	
Medicare tax	78.81	
Health insurance premiums	46.00	
United Way	40.00	1,097.58
Net amount of payroll		$4,337.42

In a computerized accounting system, the payroll software performs this proof. An error in the payroll register could cause the payment of an incorrect amount to an employee. It also could result in sending an incorrect amount to the government or other agencies for whom funds are withheld.

Payroll Check

Employees may be paid in cash or by check. In some cases, the employee does not even handle the paycheck. Rather, payment is made by **direct**

FIGURE 9-5 Payroll Register (Left Half)

PAYROLL

	NAME	ALLOW-ANCES	MARITAL STATUS	EARNINGS				TAXABLE EARNINGS		
				REGULAR	OVERTIME	TOTAL	CUMULATIVE TOTAL	UNEMPLOY. COMPENSATION	SOCIAL SECURITY	
1	Cadrain, Sarah	4	M	1 1 0 0 00	1 6 0 00	1 2 6 0 00	61 8 0 0 00		6 6 0 00	1
2	Guder, James	1	S	8 6 0 00	4 0 00	9 0 0 00	43 4 0 0 00		9 0 0 00	2
3	Istone, Ken	6	M	5 4 5 00		5 4 5 00	27 0 2 5 00		5 4 5 00	3
4	Kuzmik, Helen	2	M	4 8 0 00	2 9 4 00	7 7 4 00	31 0 0 0 00		7 7 4 00	4
5	Lee, Hoseoup	3	M	4 4 0 00		4 4 0 00	22 3 4 0 00		4 4 0 00	5
6	Swaney, Linda	2	S	5 2 8 00	1 9 8 00	7 2 6 00	27 5 0 0 00		7 2 6 00	6
7	Tucci, Paul	5	M	4 9 0 00		4 9 0 00	25 0 5 0 00		4 9 0 00	7
8	Wiles, Harry	1	S	3 0 0 00		3 0 0 00	6 3 0 0 00	3 0 0 00	3 0 0 00	8
9				4 7 4 3 00	6 9 2 00	5 4 3 5 00	244 4 1 5 00	3 0 0 00	4 8 3 5 00	9

Time cards, pay rates

Prior period total + current period earnings

Current below $7,000 cumul. total

Current below $61,200 cumul. total

FIGURE 9-5 Payroll Register (Right Half)

REGISTER—WEEK ENDED 12/19/--

	DEDUCTIONS							NET PAY	CHECK NO.	
	FEDERAL INCOME TAX	SOCIAL SEC. TAX	MEDICARE TAX	HEALTH INSURANCE	UNITED WAY	OTHER	TOTAL			
1	1 7 4 00	4 0 92	1 8 27				2 3 3 19	1 0 2 6 81	409	1
2	1 7 1 00	5 5 80	1 3 05		2 0 00		2 5 9 85	6 4 0 15	410	2
3	2 0 00	3 3 79	7 90	1 0 00			7 1 69	4 7 3 31	411	3
4	8 3 00	4 7 99	1 1 22	1 3 00	2 0 00		1 7 5 21	5 9 8 79	412	4
5	2 7 00	2 7 28	6 38	1 3 00			7 3 66	3 6 6 34	413	5
6	1 0 7 00	4 5 01	1 0 53				1 6 2 54	5 6 3 46	414	6
7	2 0 00	3 0 38	7 11	1 0 00			6 7 49	4 2 2 51	415	7
8	3 1 00	1 8 60	4 35				5 3 95	2 4 6 05	416	8
9	6 3 3 00	2 9 9 77	7 8 81	4 6 00	4 0 00		1 0 9 7 58	4 3 3 7 42		9

With-holding Tax Table

6.2% x Social Security taxable earnings

1.45% x total earnings

Specific employer– employee agreements

Total earnings – Total deductions

deposit or electronic funds transfer (EFT) by the employer to the employee's bank. The employee receives the earnings statement from the check and a nonnegotiable copy of the check indicating that the deposit has been made. Payment by check or direct deposit provides better internal accounting control than payment by cash.

Data needed to prepare a paycheck for each employee are contained in the payroll register. In a computer-based system, the paychecks and payroll register normally are prepared at the same time. The employer furnishes a statement of payroll deductions to each employee along with each paycheck. Paychecks with detachable earnings statements, like the one for Ken Istone illustrated in Figure 9-6, are widely used for this purpose. Before the check is deposited or cashed, the employee should detach the stub and keep it.

Employees Earnings Record

A separate record of each employee's earnings is called an **employees earnings record.** An employees earnings record for Ken M. Istone for a portion of the last quarter of the calendar year is illustrated in Figure 9-7.

FIGURE 9-6   Paycheck and Earnings Statement

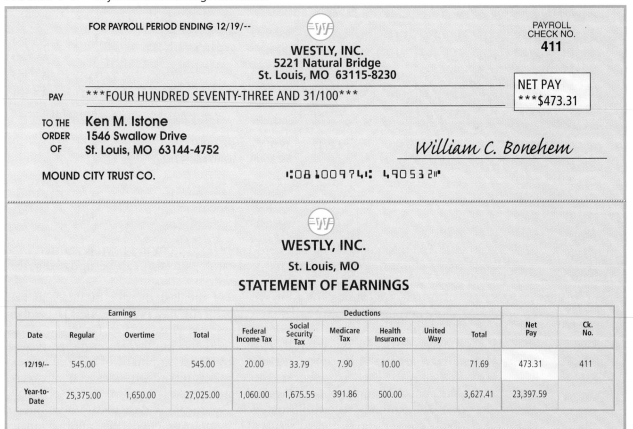

	Earnings			Deductions								
Date	Regular	Overtime	Total	Federal Income Tax	Social Security Tax	Medicare Tax	Health Insurance	United Way	Total	Net Pay	Ck. No.
12/19/--	545.00		545.00	20.00	33.79	7.90	10.00		71.69	473.31	411
Year-to-Date	25,375.00	1,650.00	27,025.00	1,060.00	1,675.55	391.86	500.00		3,627.41	23,397.59	

FIGURE 9-7   Employees Earnings Record (Left Half)

EMPLOYEES EARNINGS RECORD

19-- PERIOD ENDED	EARNINGS				TAXABLE EARNINGS	
	REGULAR	OVERTIME	TOTAL	CUMULATIVE TOTAL	UNEMPLOY. COMP.	SOCIAL SECURITY
11/28	5 4 5 00	7 5 00	6 2 0 00	25 2 4 0 00		6 2 0 00
12/5	5 4 5 00	7 5 00	6 2 0 00	25 8 6 0 00		6 2 0 00
12/12	5 4 5 00	7 5 00	6 2 0 00	26 4 8 0 00		6 2 0 00
12/19	5 4 5 00		5 4 5 00	27 0 2 5 00		5 4 5 00

GENDER		DEPARTMENT	OCCUPATION	SOC. SEC. NO.	MARITAL STATUS	ALLOWANCES
M	F					
✓		Maint.	Service	393-58-8194	M	6

FIGURE 9-7   Employees Earnings Record (Right Half)

FOR PERIOD ENDED   19--

DEDUCTIONS							CHECK NO.	AMOUNT
FEDERAL INCOME TAX	SOCIAL SEC. TAX	MEDICARE TAX	HEALTH INSURANCE	UNITED WAY	OTHER	TOTAL		
3 2 00	3 8 44	8 99	1 0 00			8 9 43	387	5 3 0 57
3 2 00	3 8 44	8 99	1 0 00			8 9 43	395	5 3 0 57
3 2 00	3 8 44	8 99	1 0 00			8 9 43	403	5 3 0 57
2 0 00	3 3 79	7 90	1 0 00			7 1 69	411	4 7 3 31

PAY RATE	DATE OF BIRTH	DATE HIRED	NAME/ADDRESS	EMPLOYEE NUMBER
$545/wk	8/17/64	1/3/87	Ken M. Istone 1546 Swallow Drive St. Louis, MO 63144-4752	3

The information in this record is obtained from the payroll register. In a computerized system, the employees earnings record can be updated at the same time the payroll register is prepared.

Istone's earnings for four weeks of the last quarter of the year are shown on this form. Note that the entry for the pay period ended December 19 is the same as that in the payroll register illustrated in Figure 9-5. This linkage between the payroll register and the employees earnings record always exists. The payroll register provides a summary of all employees' earnings for each pay period. The earnings record provides a summary of the annual earnings of an individual employee.

The earnings record illustrated in Figure 9-7 is designed to accumulate both quarterly and annual totals. The employer needs this information to prepare several reports. These reports will be discussed in Chapter 10.

ACCOUNTING FOR EMPLOYEE EARNINGS AND DEDUCTIONS

LO4   Account for employee earnings and deductions.

The payroll register described in the previous section provides complete payroll data for each pay period. But, the payroll register is not a journal. We still need to make a journal entry for payroll.

Journalizing Payroll Transactions

The totals at the bottom of the columns of the payroll register in Figure 9-5 show the following information.

Regular earnings		$4,743.00
Overtime earnings		692.00
Gross earnings		$5,435.00
Deductions:		
Federal income tax	$633.00	
Social Security tax	299.77	
Medicare tax	78.81	
Health insurance premiums	46.00	
United Way contributions	40.00	1,097.58
Net amount of payroll		$4,337.42

The payroll register column totals thus provide the basis for the following journal entry:

5	Dec.¹⁹⁻	19	Wages and Salaries Expense	5 4 3 5 00			5
6			Employees Income Tax Payable		6 3 3 00		6
7			Social Security Tax Payable		2 9 9 77		7
8			Medicare Tax Payable		7 8 81		8
9			Health Ins. Premiums Payable		4 6 00		9
10			United Way Contrib. Payable		4 0 00		10
11			Cash		4 3 3 7 42		11
12			Payroll for week ended				12
13			Dec. 19				13

Employee paychecks can be written from the regular bank account or from a special payroll bank account. Large businesses with many employees commonly use a payroll bank account. If Westly uses a payroll bank account, a single check for $4,337.42 is written to "Payroll Cash." Individual checks are then drawn on that account for the amount due to each employee. Otherwise, individual checks totaling $4,337.42 are written to the employees from the regular bank account.

LEARNING KEY   Wages and Salaries Expense is debited for the gross pay. A separate account is kept for each earnings deduction. Cash is credited for the net pay.

Notice two important facts about the payroll entry. First, Wages and Salaries Expense is debited for the gross pay of the employees. The expense to the employer is the gross pay, not the employees' net pay after deductions. Second, a separate account is kept for each deduction.

The accounts needed in entering deductions depend on the deductions involved. To understand the accounting for these deductions, consider what the employer is doing. By deducting amounts from employees' earnings, the employer is simply serving as an agent for the government and other groups. Amounts that are deducted from an employee's gross earnings must be paid by the employer to these groups. Therefore, a separate account should be kept for the liability for each type of deduction.

To help you understand the journal entry for payroll, let's examine the accounts involved. The seven accounts affected by the payroll entry shown above are as follows.

ACCOUNT	CLASSIFICATION
Wages and Salaries Expense	Expense
Employees Income Tax Payable	Liability
Social Security Tax Payable	Liability
Medicare Tax Payable	Liability
Health Insurance Premiums Payable	Liability
United Way Contributions Payable	Liability
Cash (or Payroll Cash)	Asset

Wages and Salaries Expense

This account is debited for the gross pay of all employees for each pay period. Sometimes, separate expense accounts are kept for the employees of different departments. Thus, separate accounts may be kept for Office Salaries Expense, Sales Salaries Expense, and Factory Wages Expense.

Wages and Salaries Expense	
Debit	Credit
gross pay of employees for each pay period	

Employees Income Tax Payable

This account is credited for the total federal income tax withheld from employees' earnings. The account is debited for amounts paid to the IRS. When all of the income taxes withheld have been paid, the account will have a zero balance. A state or city income tax payable account is used in a similar manner.

Employees Income Tax Payable

Debit	Credit
payment of income tax previously withheld	federal income tax withheld from employees' earnings

Social Security and Medicare Taxes Payable

These accounts are credited for (1) the Social Security and Medicare tax withheld from employees' earnings and (2) the Social Security and Medicare taxes imposed on the employer. Social Security and Medicare taxes imposed on the employer are discussed in Chapter 10. The accounts are debited for amounts paid to the IRS. When all of the Social Security and Medicare taxes have been paid, the accounts will have zero balances.

Social Security Tax Payable

Debit	Credit
payment of Social Security tax previously withheld or imposed	Social Security taxes (1) withheld from employees' earnings and (2) imposed on the employer

Medicare Tax Payable

Debit	Credit
payment of Medicare tax previously withheld or imposed	Medicare taxes (1) withheld from employees' earnings and (2) imposed on the employer

Other Deductions

Health Insurance Premiums Payable is credited for health insurance contributions deducted from an employee's pay. The account is debited for the subsequent payment of these amounts to the health insurer. United Way Contributions Payable is handled in a similar manner.

PAYROLL RECORD-KEEPING METHODS

LO5   Describe various payroll record-keeping methods.

You probably noticed that the same information appears in several places in the payroll records—in the payroll register, paycheck and stub, and employees earnings records. If all records are prepared by hand (a **manual system**), the same information would be recorded several times. Unless an employer has only a few employees, this can be very inefficient. Various approaches are available to make payroll accounting more efficient and accurate.

Both medium- and large-size businesses commonly use two approaches for payroll record keeping: payroll processing centers and electronic systems. A **payroll processing center** is a business that sells payroll record-keeping services. The employer provides the center with all basic employee data and each period's report of hours worked. The processing center maintains all payroll records and prepares each period's payroll checks. Payroll processing center fees tend to be much less than it would cost an employer to handle payroll internally.

An **electronic system** is a computer system based on a software package that performs all payroll record keeping and prepares payroll checks. In this system, only the employee number and hours worked need to be entered into a computer each pay period, as shown in Figure 9-8. All other payroll data needed to prepare the payroll records can be stored in the computer. The computer uses the employee number and hours worked to determine the gross pay, deductions, and net pay. The payroll register, checks, and employees earnings records are provided as outputs.

FIGURE 9-8 Electronic Payroll System

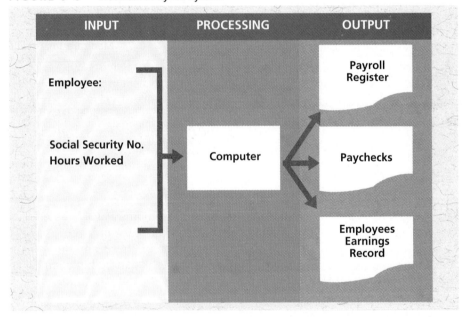

The same inputs and outputs are required in all payroll systems. Even with a computer, the data required for payroll processing have to be entered into the system at some point. The outputs—the payroll register, paychecks, and employees earnings records—are basically the same under each system.

KEY POINTS

1 Payroll accounting procedures apply only to employees, not to independent contractors.

2 Three steps are required to determine how much to pay an employee for a pay period:

1. Calculate total earnings.
2. Determine the amounts of deductions.
3. Subtract deductions from total earnings to compute net pay.

Deductions from gross pay fall into three categories:

1. Employees income tax withholding
2. Employees Social Security and Medicare taxes withholding
3. Voluntary deductions

Four factors determine the amount to be withheld from an employee's gross pay each pay period for federal income tax:

1. Total earnings
2. Marital status
3. Number of withholding allowances claimed
4. Length of the pay period

3 The payroll register and the employees earnings record are linked. The payroll register provides a summary of earnings of all employees for each pay period. The earnings record provides a summary of the annual earnings of an individual employee.

4 The totals at the bottom of the columns of the payroll register provide the basis for the journal entry for payroll.

Amounts withheld or deducted by the employer from employee earnings are credited to liability accounts. The employer must pay these amounts to the proper government groups and other appropriate groups.

5 In a manual payroll system, the same information may need to be recorded several times. An electronic payroll system is much more efficient.

KEY TERMS

direct deposit 281   The employee does not handle the paycheck; payment is made by the employer directly to the employee's bank.

electronic system 288   A computer system based on a software package that performs all payroll record keeping and prepares payroll checks.

employee 272   Person who works under the control and direction of an employer.

employees earnings record 283   A separate record of each employee's earnings.

Fair Labor Standards Act (FLSA) 273 Requires employers to pay overtime at 1½ times the regular rate to any hourly employee who works over 40 hours in a week.

FICA taxes 275 Payroll taxes withheld to provide Social Security and Medicare benefits.

gross pay 275 An employee's total earnings.

independent contractor 272 Person who performs a service for a fee and does not work under the control and direction of the company paying for the service.

manual system 287 Payroll system in which all records are prepared by hand.

Medicare taxes 276 Payroll taxes that are intended to provide health insurance benefits.

net pay 275 Gross pay less mandatory and voluntary deductions.

payroll processing center 288 A business that sells payroll record-keeping services.

payroll register 280 A form used to assemble the data required at the end of each payroll period.

salary 272 Compensation for managerial or administrative services.

Social Security taxes 276 Payroll taxes that are intended to provide pensions and disability benefits.

wage-bracket method 275 Employers determine the amount to withhold from an employee's gross pay for a specific time period from the appropriate wage-bracket table provided by the IRS.

wages 272 Compensation for skilled or unskilled labor.

withholding allowance 275 Exempts a specific dollar amount of an employee's gross pay from federal income tax withholding.

REVIEW QUESTIONS

1. Why is it important for payroll accounting purposes to distinguish between an employee and an independent contractor?
2. Name three major categories of deductions from an employee's gross pay.
3. Identify the four factors that determine the amount of federal income tax that is withheld from an employee's pay each pay period.
4. In general, an employee is entitled to withholding allowances for what purposes?
5. Identify the three payroll records usually needed by an employer.
6. Describe the information contained in the payroll register.
7. Why is it important to total and verify the totals of the payroll register after the data for each employee have been entered?
8. Distinguish between the payroll register and the employee earnings record.
9. Explain what an employer does with the amounts withheld from an employee's pay.
10. Explain why payroll processing centers and electronic systems are commonly used in payroll accounting.

MANAGING YOUR WRITING

The minimum wage originally was only $.25 an hour. Today it is $4.25 an hour. Assume that Congress is considering raising the minimum wage again and your United States representative is asking for public opinion on this issue. Write two letters to your representative, one with arguments for and the other with arguments against a higher minimum wage.

DEMONSTRATION PROBLEM

Carole Vohsen operates a pet grooming salon called Canine Coiffures. She has five employees, all of whom are paid on a weekly basis. Canine Coiffures uses a payroll register, individual employees earnings records, a journal, and a general ledger.

The payroll data for each employee for the week ended January 21, 19--, are given below. Employees are paid 1½ times the regular rate for work over 40 hours a week and double time for work on Sunday.

Name	Employee No.	No. of Allowances	Marital Status	Total Hours Worked Jan. 15–21	Rate	Total Earnings Jan. 1–14
DeNourie, Katie	1	2	S	44	$11.50	$1,058.00
Garriott, Pete	2	1	M	40	12.00	1,032.00
Martinez, Sheila	3	3	M	39	12.50	987.50
Parker, Nancy	4	4	M	42	11.00	957.00
Shapiro, John	5	2	S	40	11.50	931.50

Sheila Martinez is the manager of the Shampooing Department. Her Social Security number is 500-88-4189, and she was born April 12, 1969. She lives at 46 Darling Crossing; Norwich, CT 06360. Martinez was hired September 1 of last year.

Canine Coiffures uses a federal income tax withholding table. A portion of this weekly table is provided in Figure 9-4 on pages 277 and 278. Social Security tax is withheld at the rate of 6.2% of the first $61,200 earned, Medicare tax is withheld at the rate of 1.45%, and city earnings tax at the rate of 1%, both applied to gross pay. Garriott and Parker each have $14.00 and DeNourie and Martinez each have $4.00 withheld for health insurance. DeNourie, Martinez, and Shapiro each have $15.00 withheld to be invested in the groomers' credit union. Garriott and Shapiro each have $18.75 withheld under a savings bond purchase plan.

Canine Coiffures' payroll is met by drawing checks on its regular bank account. This week, the checks were issued in sequence, beginning with no. 811.

REQUIRED

1. Prepare a payroll register for Canine Coiffures for the week ended January 21, 19--. (In the Taxable Earnings/Unemployment Compensation column, enter the same amounts as in the Social Security column.) Total the amount columns, verify the totals, and rule with single and double lines.
2. Prepare an employees earnings record for Sheila Martinez for the week ended January 21, 19--.
3. Assuming that the wages for the week ended January 21 were paid on January 23, prepare the journal entry for the payment of this payroll.
4. Post the entry in requirement 3 to the affected accounts in the ledger of Canine Coiffures. Do not enter any amounts in the Balance columns. Use account numbers as follows: Cash—111; Employees Income Tax Payable—211; Social Security Tax Payable—212; Medicare Tax Payable—213; City Earnings Tax Payable—215; Health Insurance Premiums Payable—227; Credit Union Payable—228; Savings Bond Deductions Payable—261; Wages and Salaries Expense—542.

SOLUTION

1.

PAYROLL

	NAME	EMPLOYEE NO.	ALLOW-ANCES	MARITAL STATUS	EARNINGS				TAXABLE EARNINGS		
					REGULAR	OVERTIME	TOTAL	CUMULATIVE TOTAL	UNEMPLOY. COMPENSATION	SOCIAL SECURITY	
1	DeNourie, Katie	1	2	S	460 00	69 00	529 00	1587 00	529 00	529 00	1
2	Garriott, Pete	2	1	M	480 00		480 00	1512 00	480 00	480 00	2
3	Martinez, Sheila	3	3	M	487 50		487 50	1475 00	487 50	487 50	3
4	Parker, Nancy	4	4	M	440 00	33 00	473 00	1430 00	473 00	473 00	4
5	Shapiro, John	5	2	S	460 00		460 00	1391 50	460 00	460 00	5
6					2327 50	102 00	2429 50	7395 50	2429 50	2429 50	6
7											7

REGISTER—WEEK ENDED January 21, 19--

	DEDUCTIONS										NET PAY	CHECK NO.	
	FEDERAL INCOME TAX	SOCIAL SEC. TAX	MEDICARE TAX	CITY TAX	HEALTH INSURANCE	CREDIT UNION	OTHER		TOTAL				
1	57 00	32 80	7 67	5 29	4 00	15 00			121 76	407 24	811	1
2	47 00	29 76	6 96	4 80	14 00		US Sav. Bond	18 75	121 27	358 73	812	2
3	33 00	30 23	7 07	4 88	4 00	15 00			94 18	393 32	813	3
4	24 00	29 33	6 86	4 73	14 00				78 92	394 08	814	4
5	48 00	28 52	6 67	4 60		15 00	US Sav. Bond	18 75	121 54	338 46	815	5
6	209 00	150 64	35 23	24 30	36 00	45 00		37 50	537 67	1891 83		6
7												7

2.

EMPLOYEES EARNINGS RECORD

19-- PERIOD ENDED	EARNINGS				TAXABLE EARNINGS	
	REGULAR	OVERTIME	TOTAL	CUMULATIVE TOTAL	UNEMPLOY. COMP.	SOCIAL SECURITY
1/7						
1/14						
1/21	4 8 7 50		4 8 7 50	1 4 7 5 00	4 8 7 50	4 8 7 50
1/28						

GENDER		DEPARTMENT	OCCUPATION	SOC. SEC. NO.	MARITAL STATUS	EXEMPTIONS
M	F					
	✓	Shampooing	Manager	500-88-4189	M	3

FOR PERIOD ENDED   **19--**

DEDUCTIONS								CHECK NO.	AMOUNT
FEDERAL INCOME TAX	SOCIAL SEC. TAX	MEDICARE TAX	CITY TAX	HEALTH INSURANCE	CREDIT UNION	OTHER	TOTAL		
3 3 00	3 0 23	7 07	4 88	4 00	1 5 00		9 4 18	813	3 9 3 32

PAY RATE	DATE OF BIRTH	DATE HIRED	NAME/ADDRESS	EMPLOYEE NUMBER
$12.50	4/12/69	9/1/--	Sheila Martinez 46 Darling Crossing Norwich, CT 06360	3

3.

GENERAL JOURNAL   PAGE **1**

	DATE		DESCRIPTION	POST. REF.	DEBIT	CREDIT	
1	19- Jan.	23	Wages and Salaries Expense	542	2 4 2 9 50		1
2			Employees Income Tax Payable	211		2 0 9 00	2
3			Social Security Tax Payable	212		1 5 0 64	3
4			Medicare Tax Payable	213		3 5 23	4
5			City Earnings Tax Payable	215		2 4 30	5
6			Health Insurance Prem. Payable	227		3 6 00	6
7			Credit Union Payable	228		4 5 00	7
8			Savings Bond Deductions Payable	261		3 7 50	8
9			Cash	111		1 8 9 1 83	9
10			Payroll for week ended Jan. 21.				10

GENERAL LEDGER

ACCOUNT: Cash   **ACCOUNT NO.** 111

DATE	ITEM	POST. REF.	DEBIT	CREDIT	BALANCE DEBIT	BALANCE CREDIT
19-- Jan. 23		J1		1 8 9 1 83		

ACCOUNT: Employees Income Tax Payable   **ACCOUNT NO.** 211

DATE	ITEM	POST. REF.	DEBIT	CREDIT	BALANCE DEBIT	BALANCE CREDIT
19-- Jan. 23		J1		2 0 9 00		

ACCOUNT: Social Security Tax Payable   **ACCOUNT NO.** 212

DATE	ITEM	POST. REF.	DEBIT	CREDIT	BALANCE DEBIT	BALANCE CREDIT
19-- Jan. 23		J1		1 5 0 64		

ACCOUNT: Medicare Tax Payable   **ACCOUNT NO.** 213

DATE	ITEM	POST. REF.	DEBIT	CREDIT	BALANCE DEBIT	BALANCE CREDIT
19-- Jan. 23		J1		3 5 23		

ACCOUNT: City Earnings Tax Payable   **ACCOUNT NO.** 215

DATE	ITEM	POST. REF.	DEBIT	CREDIT	BALANCE DEBIT	BALANCE CREDIT
19-- Jan. 23		J1		2 4 30		

ACCOUNT: Health Insurance Premiums Payable   **ACCOUNT NO.** 227

DATE	ITEM	POST. REF.	DEBIT	CREDIT	BALANCE DEBIT	BALANCE CREDIT
19-- Jan. 23		J1		3 6 00		

ACCOUNT: Credit Union Payable   **ACCOUNT NO.** 228

DATE	ITEM	POST. REF.	DEBIT	CREDIT	BALANCE DEBIT	BALANCE CREDIT
19-- Jan. 23		J1		4 5 00		

ACCOUNT: Savings Bond Deductions Payable   **ACCOUNT NO.** 261

DATE	ITEM	POST. REF.	DEBIT	CREDIT	BALANCE DEBIT	BALANCE CREDIT
19-- Jan. 23		J1		3 7 50		

ACCOUNT: Wages and Salaries Expense   **ACCOUNT NO.** 542

DATE	ITEM	POST. REF.	DEBIT	CREDIT	BALANCE DEBIT	BALANCE CREDIT
19-- Jan. 23		J1	2 4 2 9 50			

SERIES A EXERCISES

2 **EXERCISE 9A1 COMPUTING NET PAY**   Mary Sue Guild works for a company that pays its employees 1¹/₂ times the regular rate for all hours worked in excess of 40 per week. Guild's pay rate is $10.00 per hour. Her wages are subject to deductions for federal income tax, Social Security tax, and Medicare tax. She is married and claims 4 withholding allowances. Guild has a ¹/₂-hour lunch break during an 8¹/₂-hour day. Her time card is shown below.

Name	Mary Sue Guild					
Week Ending	March 30, 19--					

Day	In	Out	In	Out	Hours Worked	
					Regular	Overtime
M	7:57	12:05	12:35	4:33	8	
T	7:52	12:09	12:39	5:05	8	1/2
W	7:59	12:15	12:45	5:30	8	1
T	8:00	12:01	12:30	6:31	8	2
F	7:56	12:05	12:34	4:30	8	
S	8:00	10:31				2 1/2

Complete the following:
(a) _____ regular hours × $10.00 per hour $_____
(b) _____ overtime hours × $15.00 per hour $_____
(c) Total gross wages $_____
(d) Federal income tax withholding (from tax tables in
     Figure 9-4, pages 277 and 278) $_____
(e) Social Security withholding at 6.2% $_____
(f) Medicare withholding at 1.45% $_____
(g) Total withholding $_____
(h) Net pay $_____

2 **EXERCISE 9A2 COMPUTING WEEKLY GROSS PAY**   Ryan Lawrence's regular hourly rate is $15.00. He receives 1¹/₂ times the regular rate for any hours worked over 40 a week and double the rate for work on Sunday. During the past week, Lawrence worked 8 hours each day Monday through Thursday, 10 hours on Friday, and 5 hours on Sunday. Compute Lawrence's gross pay for the past week.

2 **EXERCISE 9A3 COMPUTING OVERTIME RATE OF PAY AND GROSS WEEKLY PAY**   Artis Wilson receives a regular salary of $2,600 a month and is paid 1¹/₂ times the regular hourly rate for hours worked in excess of 40 per week.
(a) Calculate Wilson's overtime rate of pay.
(b) Calculate Wilson's total gross weekly pay if he works 45 hours during the week.

2 **EXERCISE 9A4 COMPUTING FEDERAL INCOME TAX**   Using the table in Figure 9-4 on pages 277 and 278, determine the amount of federal income tax an employer should withhold weekly for employees with the following marital status, earnings, and withholding allowances.

	Marital Status	Total Weekly Earnings	Number of Allowances	Amount of Withholding
(a)	S	$327.90	2	_____
(b)	S	$410.00	1	_____
(c)	M	$438.16	5	_____
(d)	S	$518.25	0	_____
(e)	M	$603.98	6	_____

2 **EXERCISE 9A5 CALCULATING SOCIAL SECURITY AND MEDICARE TAXES**   Assume a Social Security tax rate of 6.2% is applied to maximum earnings of $61,200 and a Medicare tax rate of 1.45% is applied to all earnings. Calculate the Social Security and Medicare tax for the following situations.

Cumul. Pay Before Current Weekly Payroll	Current Gross Pay	Year-to-Date Earnings	Soc. Sec. Maximum	Amount Over Max. Soc. Sec.	Amount Subject to Soc. Sec.	Soc. Sec. Tax Withheld	Medicare Tax Withheld
$22,000	$1,200	_____	$61,200	_____	_____	_____	_____
$54,000	$4,200	_____	$61,200	_____	_____	_____	_____
$58,600	$3,925	_____	$61,200	_____	_____	_____	_____
$60,600	$4,600	_____	$61,200	_____	_____	_____	_____

4 **EXERCISE 9A6 PAYROLL TRANSACTIONS**   On December 31, the payroll register of Hamstreet Associates indicated the following information:

Wages and Salaries Expense	$8,700.00
Employees Income Tax Payable	920.00
United Way Contributions Payable	200.00
Earnings subject to Social Security tax	8,000.00

Determine the amount of Social Security and Medicare taxes to be withheld and record the journal entry for the payroll, crediting Cash for the net pay.

4 **EXERCISE 9A7 PAYROLL JOURNAL ENTRY**   Journalize the following data taken from the payroll register of University Printing as of April 15, 19--.

Regular earnings	$5,418.00
Overtime earnings	824.00
Deductions:	
Federal income tax	593.00
Social Security tax	387.00
Medicare tax	90.51
Pension plan	90.00
Health insurance premiums	225.00
United Way contributions	100.00

SERIES A   PROBLEMS

2/4   **PROBLEM 9A1 GROSS PAY, DEDUCTIONS, AND NET PAY**
Donald Chin works for Northwest Supplies. His rate of pay is $8.50 per
hour and he is paid 1¹/₂ times the regular rate for all hours worked in
excess of 40 per week. During the last week of January of the current year
he worked 48 hours. Chin is married and claims 4 withholding allowances
on his W-4 form. His weekly wages are subject to the following deductions.

(a) Employees income tax (use Figure 9-4 on pages 277 and 278)
(b) Social Security tax at 6.2%
(c) Medicare tax at 1.45%
(d) Health insurance premium, $85.00
(e) Credit union, $125.00
(f) United Way contribution, $10.00

REQUIRED
1. Compute Chin's regular pay, overtime pay, gross pay, and net pay.
2. Journalize the payment of his wages for the week ended January 31,
       crediting Cash for the net amount.

2/3/4   **PROBLEM 9A2 PAYROLL REGISTER AND PAYROLL JOURNAL
ENTRY**   Don McCullum operates a travel agency called Don's Luxury
Travel. He has five employees, all of whom are paid on a weekly basis. The

travel agency uses a payroll register, individual employees earnings records,
and a general journal.

Don's Luxury Travel uses a weekly federal income tax withholding
table. The payroll data for each employee for the week ended March 22,
19--, are given below. Employees are paid 1¹/₂ times the regular rate for
working over 40 hours a week.

Name	No. of Allowances	Marital Status	Total Hours Worked Mar. 16–22	Rate	Total Earnings Jan. 1–Mar. 15
Ali, Loren	4	M	45	$11.00	$5,280.00
Carson, Judy	1	S	40	12.00	5,760.00
Ellis, Susan	3	M	43	9.50	4,560.00
Knox, Wayne	1	S	39	11.00	5,125.50
Paglione, Jim	2	M	40	10.50	4,720.50

Social Security tax is withheld from the first $61,200 of earnings at the
rate of 6.2%. Medicare tax is withheld at the rate of 1.45%, and city earnings
tax at the rate of 1%, both applied to gross pay. Ali and Knox have $15
withheld and Carson and Ellis have $5 withheld for health insurance. Ali
and Knox have $20 withheld to be invested in the travel agencies' credit
union. Carson has $38.75 withheld and Ellis $18.75 withheld under a savings bond purchase plan.

Don's Luxury Travel's payroll is met by drawing checks on its regular
bank account. The checks were issued in sequence, beginning with check
no. 423.

continued

REQUIRED

1. Prepare a payroll register for Don's Luxury Travel for the week ended March 22, 19--. (In the Taxable Earnings/Unemployment compensation column, enter the same amounts as in the Social Security column.) Total the amount columns, verify the totals, and rule with single and double lines.
2. Assuming that the wages for the week ended March 22 were paid on March 24, prepare the journal entry for the payment of the payroll.

3 **PROBLEM 9A3 EMPLOYEES EARNINGS RECORD**   Don's Luxury Travel in Problem 9A2 keeps employee earnings records. Judy Carson, employee number 62, is employed as a manager in the ticket sales department. She was born on May 8, 1959, and was hired on June 1 of last year. Her Social Security number is 544-67-1283. She lives at 28 Quarry Drive, Vernon, CT 06066.

REQUIRED

For the week ended March 22, complete an employees earnings record for Judy Carson. (Insert earnings data only for the week of March 22.)

SERIES B EXERCISES

2 **EXERCISE 9B1 COMPUTING NET PAY**   Tom Hallinan works for a company that pays its employees $1\frac{1}{2}$ times the regular rate for all hours worked in excess of 40 per week. Hallinan's pay rate is $12.00 per hour. His wages are subject to deductions for federal income tax, Social Security tax, and Medicare tax. He is married and claims 5 withholding allowances. Hallinan has a $\frac{1}{2}$-hour lunch break during an $8\frac{1}{2}$-hour day. His time card is shown below.

Name	Tom Hallinan					
Week Ending	March 30, 19--					

Day	In	Out	In	Out	Hours Worked	
					Regular	Overtime
M	7:55	12:02	12:32	5:33	8	1
T	7:59	12:04	12:34	6:05	8	1 1/2
W	7:59	12:05	12:35	4:30	8	
T	8:00	12:01	12:30	5:01	8	1/2
F	7:58	12:02	12:31	5:33	8	1
S	7:59	9:33				1 1/2

Complete the following:

(a) _____ regular hours × $12.00 per hour $_____
(b) _____ overtime hours × $18.00 per hour $_____
(c) Total gross wages $_____

continued

   (d) Federal income tax withholding (from tax tables in
Figure 9-4, pages 277 and 278)   \$_____

   (e) Social Security withholding at 6.2%   \$_____

   (f) Medicare withholding at 1.45%   \$_____

   (g) Total withholding   \$_____

   (h) Net pay   \$_____

2 **EXERCISE 9B2 COMPUTING WEEKLY GROSS PAY** William Brown's regular hourly rate is \$12.00. He receives 1½ times the regular rate for hours worked in excess of 40 a week and double the rate for work on Sunday. During the past week, Brown worked 8 hours each day Monday through Thursday, 11 hours on Friday, and 6 hours on Sunday. Compute Brown's gross pay for the past week.

2 **EXERCISE 9B3 COMPUTING OVERTIME RATE OF PAY AND GROSS WEEKLY PAY** Mike Fritz receives a regular salary of \$3,250 a month and is paid 1½ times the regular hourly rate for hours worked in excess of 40 per week.

(a) Calculate Fritz's overtime rate of pay. (Compute to the nearest half cent.)

(b) Calculate Fritz's total gross weekly pay if he works 46 hours during the week.

2 **EXERCISE 9B4 COMPUTING FEDERAL INCOME TAX** Using the table in Figure 9-4 on pages 277 and 278, determine the amount of federal income tax an employer should withhold weekly for employees with the following marital status, earnings, and withholding allowances.

	Marital Status	**Total Weekly Earnings**	**Number of Allowances**	**Amount of Withholding**
(a)	M	\$346.32	4	_____
(b)	M	\$390.00	3	_____
(c)	S	\$461.39	2	_____
(d)	M	\$522.88	6	_____
(e)	S	\$612.00	0	_____

2 **EXERCISE 9B5 CALCULATING SOCIAL SECURITY AND MEDICARE TAXES** Assume a Social Security tax rate of 6.2% is applied to maximum earnings of \$61,200 and a Medicare tax rate of 1.45% is applied to all earnings. Calculate the Social Security and Medicare tax for the following situations.

Cumul. Pay Before Current Weekly Payroll	**Current Gross Pay**	**Year-to-Date Earnings**	**Soc. Sec. Maximum**	**Amount Over Max. Soc. Sec.**	**Amount Subject to Soc. Sec.**	**Soc. Sec. Tax Withheld**	**Medicare Tax Withheld**
\$31,000	\$1,500	_____	\$61,200	_____	_____	_____	_____
\$53,000	\$2,860	_____	\$61,200	_____	_____	_____	_____
\$58,300	\$3,140	_____	\$61,200	_____	_____	_____	_____
\$60,600	\$2,920	_____	\$61,200	_____	_____	_____	_____

4 **EXERCISE 9B6 JOURNALIZING PAYROLL TRANSACTIONS** On November 30, the payroll register of Webster & Smith indicated the following information:

Wages and Salaries Expense	$9,400.00
Employees Income Tax Payable	985.00
United Way Contributions Payable	200.00
Earnings subject to Social Security tax	9,400.00

Determine the amount of Social Security and Medicare taxes to be withheld and record the journal entry for the payroll, crediting Cash for the net pay.

4 **EXERCISE 9B7 PAYROLL JOURNAL ENTRY** Journalize the following data taken from the payroll register of Himes Bakery as of June 12, 19--.

Regular earnings	$6,520.00
Overtime earnings	950.00
Deductions:	
Federal income tax	782.00
Social Security tax	463.14
Medicare tax	108.32
Pension plan	80.00
Health insurance premiums	190.00
United Way contributions	150.00

SERIES B   PROBLEMS

2/4 **PROBLEM 9B1 GROSS PAY, DEDUCTIONS, AND NET PAY**

Elyse Lin works for Columbia Industries. Her rate of pay is $9.00 per hour and she is paid 1½ times the regular rate for all hours worked in excess of 40 per week. During the last week of January of the current year she worked 46 hours. Lin is married and claims 5 withholding allowances on her W-4 form. Her weekly wages are subject to the following deductions.

(a) Employees income tax (use Figure 9-4 on pages 277 and 278)
(b) Social Security tax at 6.2%
(c) Medicare tax at 1.45%
(d) Health insurance premium, $92.00
(e) Credit union, $110.00
(f) United Way contribution, $5.00

REQUIRED
1. Compute Lin's regular pay, overtime pay, gross pay, and net pay.
2. Journalize the payment of her wages for the week ended January 31, crediting Cash for the net amount.

2/3/4 **PROBLEM 9B2 PAYROLL REGISTER AND PAYROLL JOURNAL ENTRY** Karen Jolly operates a bakery called Karen's Cupcakes. She has five employees, all of whom are paid on a weekly basis. Karen's Cupcakes uses a payroll register, individual employees earnings records, and a general journal.

continued

Karen's Cupcakes uses a weekly federal income tax withholding table. The payroll data for each employee for the week ended February 15, 19--, are given below. Employees are paid 1¹/₂ times the regular rate for working over 40 hours a week.

Name	No. of Allowances	Marital Status	Total Hours Worked Feb. 9–15	Rate	Total Earnings Jan. 1–Feb. 15
Barone, William	1	S	40	$10.00	$2,400.00
Hastings, Gene	4	M	45	12.00	3,360.00
Ridgeway, Ruth	3	M	46	8.75	2,935.00
Smith, Judy	4	M	42	11.00	2,745.00
Tarshis, Dolores	1	S	39	10.50	2,650.75

Social Security tax is withheld from the first $61,200 of earnings at the rate of 6.2%, Medicare tax is withheld at the rate of 1.45%, and city earnings tax at the rate of 1%, both applied to gross pay. Hastings and Smith have $35 withheld and Ridgeway and Tarshis have $15 withheld for health insurance. Ridgeway and Tarshis have $25 withheld to be invested in the bakers' credit union. Hastings has $18.75 withheld and Smith $43.75 withheld under a savings bond purchase plan.

Karen's Cupcakes payroll is met by drawing checks on its regular bank account. The checks were issued in sequence, beginning with no. 365.

REQUIRED

1. Prepare a payroll register for Karen's Cupcakes for the week ended February 15, 19--. (In the Taxable Earnings/Unemployment Compensation column, enter the same amounts as in the Social Security column.) Total the amount columns, verify the totals, and rule with single and double lines.
2. Assuming that the wages for the week ended February 15 were paid on February 17, prepare the journal entry for the payment of this payroll.

3 **PROBLEM 9B3 EMPLOYEES EARNINGS RECORD**   Karen's Cupcakes in Problem 9B2 keeps employees earnings records. William Barone, employee number 19, is employed as a baker in the desserts department. He was born on August 26, 1969, and was hired on October 1 of last year. His Social Security number is 342-73-4681. He lives at 30 Timber Lane, Willington, CT 06279.

REQUIRED

For the week ended February 15, complete an employees earnings record for William Barone. (Insert earnings data only for the week of February 15.)

MASTERY PROBLEM

Abigail Trenkamp owns and operates the Trenkamp Collection Agency. Listed below are the name, number of allowances claimed, marital status, information from time cards on hours worked each day, and the hourly rate of each employee. All hours worked in excess of 8 hours on weekdays are paid at 1¹/₂ times the regular rate. All weekend hours are paid at double the regular rate.

Trenkamp uses a weekly federal income tax withholding table (see Figure 9-4 on pages 277 and 278). Social Security tax is withheld at the rate of 6.2% for the first $61,200 earned. Medicare tax is withheld at 1.45% and state income tax at 3.5%. Each employee has $5.00 withheld for health insurance. All employees use payroll deduction to the credit union for varying amounts as listed below.

Trenkamp Collection Agency
Payroll Information for the Week Ended November 18,19--

Name	Employee No.	No. of Allowances	Marital Status	Regular Hours Worked							Hourly Rate	Credit Union Deposit	Total Earnings 1/1–11/18
				S	S	M	T	W	T	F			
Berling, James	1	3	M	2	2	9	8	8	9	10	$12.00	$149.60	$24,525.00
Merz, Linda	2	4	M	4	3	8	8	8	8	11	10.00	117.00	20,480.00
Goetz, Ken	3	5	M	0	0	6	7	8	9	10	11.00	91.30	21,500.00
Menick, Judd	4	2	M	8	8	0	0	8	8	9	11.00	126.50	22,625.00
Morris, Ruth	5	3	M	0	0	8	8	8	6	8	13.00	117.05	24,730.00
Heimbrock, Jacob	6	2	S	0	0	8	8	8	8	8	30.00	154.25	60,400.00
Townsley, Sarah	7	2	M	4	0	6	6	6	6	4	9.00	83.05	21,425.00
Salzman, Ben	8	4	M	6	2	8	8	6	6	6	11.00	130.00	6,635.00
Layton, Esther	9	4	M	0	0	8	8	8	8	8	11.00	88.00	5,635.00
Thompson, David	10	5	M	0	2	10	9	7	7	10	11.00	128.90	21,635.00
Wissman, Celia	11	2	S	8	0	4	8	8	8	9	13.00	139.11	24,115.00

The Trenkamp Collection Agency follows the practice of drawing a single check for the net amount of the payroll and depositing the check in a special payroll account at the bank. Individual checks issued were numbered consecutively, beginning with no. 331.

REQUIRED

1. Prepare a payroll register for Trenkamp Collection Agency for the week ended November 18, 19--. (In the Taxable Earnings/ Unemployment Compensation column, enter $365 for Salzman and $440 for Layton. Leave this column blank for all other employees.) Total the amount columns, verify the totals, and rule with single and double lines.

2. Assuming that the wages for the week ended November 18 were paid on November 21, prepare the journal entry for the payment of this payroll.

3. The current employees earnings record for Ben Salzman is provided in the working papers. Update Salzman's earnings record to reflect the November 18 payroll. Although this information should have been entered earlier, complete the required information on the earnings record. The necessary information is provided below.

Name	Ben F. Salzman
Address	12 Windmill Lane
	Trumbull, CT 06611

continued

Employee No.	8
Gender	Male
Department	Administration
Occupation	Office Manager
Social Security No.	446-46-6321
Marital Status	Married
Allowances	4
Pay Rate	$11.00 per hour
Date of Birth	4/5/64
Date Hired	7/22/--

10

Payroll Accounting: Employer Taxes and Reports

Careful study of this chapter should enable you to:

LO1 Describe and calculate employer payroll taxes.

LO2 Account for employer payroll taxes expense.

LO3 Describe employer reporting and payment responsibilities.

LO4 Describe and account for workers' compensation insurance.

You have worked the same job for nine months at $6 an hour and think you deserve a raise. When you approach your boss, you are told the business can't afford it. Besides, the boss says you already cost the business *more than* $6 an hour. How can this be? You know that in your paychecks you always take home *less than* $6 an hour. Is your boss being honest with you? To answer these questions, you need to know about employer payroll accounting.

The taxes we discussed in Chapter 9 had one thing in common—they all were levied on the employee. The employer withheld them from employees' earnings and paid them to the government. They did not add anything to the employer's payroll expenses.

In this chapter, we will examine several taxes that are imposed directly on the employer. All of these taxes represent additional payroll expenses.

EMPLOYER PAYROLL TAXES

LO1   Describe and calculate employer payroll taxes.

Most employers must pay FICA taxes, FUTA (Federal Unemployment Tax Act) taxes, and SUTA (State Unemployment Tax taxes).

Employer FICA Taxes

Employer FICA taxes are levied on employers at the same rates and on the same earnings bases as the employee FICA taxes. As explained in Chapter 9, for 1995 the Social Security component is 6.2% on maximum earnings of $61,200 for each employee. The Medicare component is 1.45% on all earnings.

 Use the information contained in the payroll register to compute employer payroll taxes.

The payroll register we saw in Chapter 9 is a key source of information for computing employer payroll taxes. That payroll register is reproduced in Figure 10-1. The Taxable Earnings Social Security column shows that $4,835 of employee earnings were subject to Social Security tax for the pay period. The employer's Social Security tax on these earnings is computed as follows:

Social Security Taxable Earnings x Tax Rate =   Tax
$4,835   6.2% $299.77

The Medicare tax applies to the total earnings of $5,435. The employer's Medicare tax on these earnings is computed as follows:

Total Earnings x Tax Rate =   Tax
$5,435   1.45% $78.81

These amounts plus the employees' Social Security and Medicare taxes withheld must be paid by the employer to the Internal Revenue Service (IRS).

Self-Employment Tax

Individuals who own and run their own business are considered self-employed. These individuals can be viewed as both employer and employee. They do not receive salary or wages from the business, but they do have earnings in the form of the business net income. **Self-employment income** is the net income of a trade or business run by an individual.

FIGURE 10-1 Payroll Register (Left Half)

PAYROLL

	NAME	ALLOW-ANCES	MARITAL STATUS	EARNINGS						TAXABLE EARNINGS				
				REGULAR	OVERTIME	TOTAL	CUMULATIVE TOTAL			UNEMPLOY. COMPENSATION	SOCIAL SECURITY		
1	Cadrain, Sarah	4	M	1 1 0 0 00	1 6 0 00	1 2 6 0 00	61 8 0 0 00				6 6 0 00	1
2	Guder, James	1	S	8 6 0 00	4 0 00	9 0 0 00	43 4 0 0 00				9 0 0 00	2
3	Istone, Ken	6	M	5 4 5 00		5 4 5 00	27 0 2 5 00				5 4 5 00	3
4	Kuzmik, Helen	2	M	4 8 0 00	2 9 4 00	7 7 4 00	31 0 0 0 00				7 7 4 00	4
5	Lee, Hoseoup	3	M	4 4 0 00		4 4 0 00	22 3 4 0 00				4 4 0 00	5
6	Swaney, Linda	2	S	5 2 8 00	1 9 8 00	7 2 6 00	27 5 0 0 00				7 2 6 00	6
7	Tucci, Paul	5	M	4 9 0 00		4 9 0 00	25 0 5 0 00				4 9 0 00	7
8	Wiles, Harry	1	S	3 0 0 00		3 0 0 00	6 3 0 0 00			3 0 0 00	3 0 0 00	8
9				4 7 4 3 00	6 9 2 00	5 4 3 5 00	244 4 1 5 00			3 0 0 00	4 8 3 5 00	9

Time cards, pay rates	Prior period total + current period earnings	Current below $7,000 cumul. total	Current below $61,200 cumul. total

Currently, persons earning self-employment income of $400 or more must pay a **self-employment tax**. Self-employment tax is a contribution to the FICA program. The tax rates are about double the Social Security and Medicare rates. They are applied to the same income bases as are used for the Social Security and Medicare taxes.

One half of the self-employment tax is a personal expense of the owner of the business. The other half is similar to the employer Social Security and Medicare taxes paid for each employee. This portion of the tax is considered a business expense and is debited to Self-Employment Tax.

Employer's FUTA Tax

The **FUTA (Federal Unemployment Tax Act) tax** is levied only on employers. It is not deducted from employees' earnings. The purpose of this tax is to raise funds to administer the combined federal/state unemployment compensation program. The maximum amount of earnings subject to the FUTA tax and the tax rate can be changed by Congress. The current rate is 6.2% applied to maximum earnings of $7,000 for each employee. But, employers are allowed a credit of up to 5.4% for participation in state unemployment programs. Thus, the effective federal rate is commonly 0.8%.

Gross FUTA rate	6.2%
Credit for SUTA (state unemployment taxes)	5.4%
Net FUTA rate	0.8%

FIGURE 10-1   Payroll Register (Right Half)

REGISTER—WEEK ENDED 12/19/--

	FEDERAL INCOME TAX	SOCIAL SEC. TAX	MEDICARE TAX	HEALTH INSURANCE	UNITED WAY	OTHER	TOTAL	NET PAY	CHECK NO.	
				DEDUCTIONS						
1	174 00	40 92	18 27				233 19	1026 81	409	1
2	171 00	55 80	13 05		20 00		259 85	640 15	410	2
3	20 00	33 79	7 90	10 00			71 69	473 31	411	3
4	83 00	47 99	11 22	13 00	20 00		175 21	598 79	412	4
5	27 00	27 28	6 38	13 00			73 66	366 34	413	5
6	107 00	45 01	10 53				162 54	563 46	414	6
7	20 00	30 38	7 11	10 00			67 49	422 51	415	7
8	31 00	18 60	4 35				53 95	246 05	416	8
9	633 00	299 77	78 81	46 00	40 00		1097 58	4337 42		9

With-holding Tax Table	6.2% x Social Security taxable earnings	1.45% x total earnings	Specific employer–employee agreements

To illustrate the computation of the FUTA tax, refer to Figure 10-1. The Taxable Earnings Unemployment Compensation column shows that only $300 of employee earnings were subject to the FUTA tax. This amount is so low because the payroll period is late in the calendar year (December 19, 19--). It is common for most employees to exceed the $7,000 earnings limit by this time. The FUTA tax is computed as shown in Figure 10-2.

FIGURE 10-2   Computation of FUTA Tax

	UNEMPLOY. COMPENSATION
5	
6	
7	
8	300 00
9	300 00
10	

FUTA Taxable Earnings x Tax Rate = Tax
$300   0.8% $2.40

Employer's State Unemployment Tax

The **state unemployment tax (SUTA)** is also levied only on employers in most states. The purpose of this tax is to raise funds to pay unemployment benefits. Tax rates and unemployment benefits vary among the states. The most common rate is 5.4% applied to maximum earnings of $7,000 for each

Tax Cheats Worldwide

Each year the U.S. Government collects billions of dollars from tax-payers—individuals and corporations. For tax year 1994 the Internal Revenue Service collected an estimated $555 billion dollars. It is also estimated that $150 billion will not be collected because of cheating.

There is no profile of the typical tax cheat, but one thing that most cheats have in common is the opportunity to cheat. Full-time salaried employees with only one employer have much less opportunity to cheat than individuals who are self-employed. It is relatively easy for independent contractors, sole proprietors, and others who are self-employed to fail to report a portion of their income.

Many cheaters are not caught, but those who are face back taxes, interest on back taxes, fines and penalties, legal fees, and prison. In an effort to catch cheaters and collect additional taxes the budget for audits in 1995 allows the IRS to target an additional half million returns.

The United States is not the only country where individuals and companies cheat on their taxes. In Argentina the government recently got tough with corporate tax cheats. Tax officials publicly named 150 large- and medium-sized companies suspected of underpaying taxes. The companies were given one week to pay their tax debt or face prosecution. It is estimated that these 150 companies underpaid their taxes by approximately $1 billion.

Source: Jonathan Friedland, "Argentina's Tax Collector Names Names," *The Wall Street Journal*, April 13, 1995.
Teresa Tritch, "The $150 Billion Tax Cheats," *Money*, April 1995.

employee. Most states have a **merit-rating system** to encourage employers to provide regular employment to workers. If an employer has very few former employees receiving unemployment compensation, the employer qualifies for a lower state unemployment tax rate. If an employer qualifies for a lower state rate, the full credit of 5.4% would still be allowed in computing the federal unemployment tax due.

Refer again to the payroll register in Figure 10-1. As we saw with the FUTA tax, only $300 of employee earnings for this pay period are subject to the state unemployment tax. The tax is computed as shown in Figure 10-3.

FIGURE 10-3   Computation of SUTA Tax

	UNEMPLOY. COMPENSATION
5	
6	
7	
8	3 0 0 00
9	3 0 0 00
10	

State Unemployment Taxable Earnings x Tax Rate = Tax

$300   5.4% $16.20

ACCOUNTING FOR EMPLOYER PAYROLL TAXES

LO2   Account for employer payroll taxes expense.

Now that we have computed the employer payroll taxes, we need to journalize them. It is common to debit all employer payroll taxes to a single account—Payroll Taxes Expense. However, we usually credit separate liability accounts for Social Security, Medicare, FUTA, and SUTA taxes payable.

Journalizing Employer Payroll Taxes

The employer payroll taxes computed in the previous section can be summarized as follows:

Employer's Social Security tax	$299.77
Employer's Medicare tax	78.81
FUTA tax	2.40
SUTA tax	16.20
Total employer payroll taxes	$397.18

These amounts provide the basis for the following journal entry:

5	Dec. 19-- 19	Payroll Taxes Expense		3 9 7 18		5
6		Social Security Tax Payable			2 9 9 77	6
7		Medicare Tax Payable			7 8 81	7
8		FUTA Tax Payable			2 40	8
9		SUTA Tax Payable			1 6 20	9
10		Employer payroll taxes for				10
11		week ended December 19				11

The steps needed to prepare this journal entry for employer payroll taxes are as follows.

STEP 1   Obtain the taxable earnings amounts from the Taxable Earnings columns of the payroll register. In this case, Social Security taxable earnings were $4,835; unemployment compensation taxable earnings were $300.

STEP 2   Compute the amount of employer Social Security tax by multiplying the total Social Security taxable earnings by 6.2%.

STEP 3   Compute the amount of Medicare tax by multiplying total earnings by 1.45%.

STEP 4   Compute the amount of FUTA tax by multiplying the total unemployment taxable earnings by 0.8%.

STEP 5   Compute the amount of SUTA tax by multiplying the total unemployment taxable earnings by 5.4%.

STEP 6   Prepare the appropriate journal entry using the amounts computed in steps 2 through 5.

To understand the journal entry for employer payroll taxes, let's examine the accounts involved.

Payroll Taxes Expense

The Social Security, Medicare, FUTA, and SUTA taxes imposed on the employer are expenses of doing business. Each of the employer taxes is debited to Payroll Taxes Expense.

Payroll Taxes Expense

Debit	Credit
Social Security, Medicare, FUTA, and SUTA taxes imposed on the employer	

Social Security and Medicare Taxes Payable

These are the same liability accounts used in Chapter 9 to record the Social Security and Medicare taxes withheld from employees' earnings. The accounts are credited to enter the Social Security and Medicare taxes imposed on the employer. They are debited when the taxes are paid to the IRS. When all of the Social Security and Medicare taxes have been paid, the accounts will have zero balances.

> **LEARNING KEY**   Social Security Tax Payable and Medicare Tax Payable for employer FICA taxes are the same liability accounts used to record the FICA taxes withheld from employees' earnings.

Social Security Tax Payable

Debit	Credit
payment of Social Security tax	Social Security taxes (1) withheld from employees' earnings and (2) imposed on the employer

Medicare Tax Payable

Debit	Credit
payment of Medicare tax	Medicare taxes (1) withheld from employees' earnings and (2) imposed on the employer

FUTA Tax Payable

A separate liability account entitled FUTA Tax Payable is kept for the employer's FUTA tax. This account is credited for the tax imposed on employers under the Federal Unemployment Tax Act. The account is debited when this tax is paid. When all of the FUTA taxes have been paid, the account will have a zero balance.

FUTA Tax Payable

Debit	Credit
payment of FUTA tax	FUTA tax imposed on the employer

SUTA Tax Payable

A separate liability account entitled SUTA Tax Payable is kept for the state unemployment tax. This account is credited for the tax imposed on employers under the state unemployment compensation laws. The account is debited when these taxes are paid. When all of the state unemployment taxes have been paid, the account will have a zero balance.

SUTA Tax Payable

Debit	Credit
state unemployment tax paid	state unemployment tax imposed on the employer

Total Payroll Cost of an Employee

It is interesting to note what it really costs to employ a person. The employer must, of course, pay the gross wages of an employee. In addition, the employer must pay payroll taxes on employee earnings up to certain dollar limits.

To illustrate, assume that an employee earns $26,000 a year. The total cost of this employee to the employer is calculated as follows.

Gross wages	$26,000
Employer Social Security tax (6.2% of $26,000)	1,612
Employer Medicare tax (1.45% of $26,000)	377
SUTA tax (5.4% of $7,000)	378
FUTA tax (0.8% of $7,000)	56
	$28,423

Thus, the total payroll cost of employing a person whose stated compensation is $26,000 is $28,423. Employer payroll taxes clearly are a significant cost of doing business.

REPORTING AND PAYMENT RESPONSIBILITIES

LO3   Describe employer reporting and payment responsibilities.

Employer payroll reporting and payment responsibilities fall into five areas:

1. Federal income tax withholding and Social Security and Medicare taxes
2. FUTA taxes
3. SUTA taxes
4. Employee Wage and Tax Statement (Form W-2)
5. Summary of employee wages and taxes

Federal Income Tax Withholding and Social Security and Medicare Taxes

Three important aspects of employer reporting and payment responsibilities for federal income tax withholding and Social Security and Medicare taxes are:

1. Determining when payments are due
2. Use of Form 8109, Federal Tax Deposit Coupon
3. Use of Form 941, Employer's Quarterly Federal Tax Return

When Payments Are Due.   The date by which federal income tax withholding and Social Security and Medicare taxes must be paid depends on the amount of these taxes. Figure 10-4 summarizes the deposit rules stated in *Circular E—Employer's Tax Guide.* In general, the larger the amount that needs to be deposited, the more frequently payments must be made. For simplicity, we will assume that deposits must be made 15 days after the end of each month.

FIGURE 10-4   Summary of Deposit Rules

DEPOSIT AMOUNT	DEPOSIT DUE
1. Less than $500 at the end of the current quarter	1. Pay with Form 941 at end of the month following end of the quarter
2. $500 or more at the end of the current quarter and $50,000 or less in total during the lookback period*	2. Deposit 15 days after end of the month
3. $500 or more at the end of the current quarter and more than $50,000 in total during the lookback period*	3. Deposit every other Wednesday or Friday, depending on the day of the week payroll payments are made
4. $100,000 or more on any day during current quarter	4. Deposit by the end of the next banking day

*The lookback period is the four quarters beginning July 1, two years ago, and ending June 30, one year ago.

Form 8109.   Deposits are made at a Federal Reserve Bank or other authorized commercial bank using Form 8109, Federal Tax Deposit Coupon (Figure 10-5). The **Employer Identification Number (EIN)** shown on this

FIGURE 10-5   Federal Tax Deposit Coupon (Form 8109)

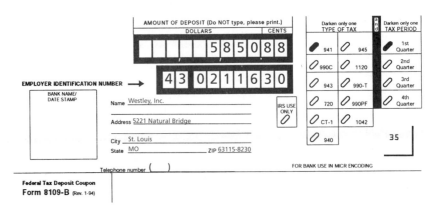

form is obtained by the employer from the IRS. This number identifies the employer and must be shown on all payroll forms and reports filed with the IRS.

The $5,850.88 deposit shown in Figure 10-5 for Westly was for the following taxes:

Employees' income tax withheld from wages		$2,526.80
Social Security tax:		
Withheld from employees' wages	$1,346.24	
Imposed on employer	1,346.24	2,692.48
Medicare tax:		
Withheld from employees' wages	$ 315.80	
Imposed on employer	315.80	631.60
Amount of check		$5,850.88

The journal entry for this deposit would be:

5		Employees Income Tax Payable	2 5 2 6 80		5
6		Social Security Tax Payable	2 6 9 2 48		6
7		Medicare Tax Payable	6 3 1 60		7
8		Cash		5 8 5 0 88	8
9		Deposit of employee federal			9
10		income tax and Social Security			10
11		and Medicare taxes			11

Paying a Worldwide Work Force

As companies enter the global marketplace they face new opportunities and challenges. Employee compensation is one of these challenges.

Just getting payroll checks to employees requires developing and implementing new procedures. One of the first things to consider is what currency will be used for payment. Employees who live and work in Japan during times when the U.S. dollar is falling against the Japanese yen will lose buying power if they are being paid in dollars. On the other hand, employees living and working in Mexico when the value of the peso is weak gain buying power if they are paid in dollars.

It is also important to decide exactly how wages are going to get from the company's bank to the employee. Waiting for international mail is not usually a good option. Electronic funds transfer is often a better choice.

Health insurance is often part of a compensation package. A health maintenance organization (HMO) that provides health care for local employees through a network of local physicians and hospitals is not appropriate for employees living halfway around the world.

These are not the only challenges to compensating employees in a global economy. Most companies seek advice from accounting and legal professionals who specialize in employee compensation.

Form 941.   Form 941, Employer's Quarterly Federal Tax Return, must be filed with the IRS at the end of the month following each calendar quarter. This form is a report of employee federal income tax and Social Security and Medicare tax withholding and employer Social Security and Medicare taxes for the quarter. A completed form for Westly for the first quarter of the calendar year is shown in Figure 10-6. Instructions for completing the form are provided with the form and in *Circular E.*

FUTA Taxes

Federal unemployment taxes must be calculated on a quarterly basis. If the accumulated liability exceeds $100, the total must be paid to a Federal Reserve Bank or other authorized commercial bank. The total is due by the end of the month following the close of the quarter. If the liability is $100 or less, no deposit is necessary. The amount is simply added to the amount to be deposited for the next quarter. FUTA taxes are deposited using Form 8109 (Figure 10-5).

Assume that Westly's accumulated FUTA tax liability for the first quarter of the calendar year is $408. Westly would use Form 8109 to deposit this amount on April 30. The journal entry for this transaction would be as follows:

15	19-- Apr.	30	FUTA Tax Payable			4 0 8 00				15
16			Cash				4 0 8 00	16
17			Paid federal unemployment					17
18			tax					18

Form 940.   In addition to making quarterly deposits, employers are required to file an annual report of federal unemployment tax on Form 940. This form must be filed with the IRS by January 31 following the end of the calendar year. Figure 10-7 shows a completed Form 940 for Westly. Instructions for completing the form are provided with the form and in *Circular E.*

SUTA Taxes

Deposit rules and forms for state unemployment taxes vary among the states. Deposits usually are required on a quarterly basis. Assume that Westly's accumulated state unemployment liability for the first quarter of the calendar year is $2,754. The journal entry for the deposit of this amount with the state on April 30 would be:

15	19-- Apr.	30	SUTA Tax Payable			2 7 5 4 00				15
16			Cash				2 7 5 4 00	16
17			Paid state unemployment tax					17

FIGURE 10-6   Employer's Quarterly Federal Tax Return (Form 941)

Form **941** (Rev. April 1994) Department of the Treasury Internal Revenue Service	4141	**Employer's Quarterly Federal Tax Return** ► **See separate instructions for information on completing this return.** Please type or print.

Enter state code for state in which deposits made . ► M:O (see page 2 of instructions).

Name (as distinguished from trade name)	Date quarter ended March 30,19--	OMB No. 1545-0029
Trade name, if any Westley, Inc.	Employer identification number 43-0211630	T
Address (number and street) 5221 Natural Bridge	City, state, and ZIP code St. Louis, Mo 63115-8230	FF
		FD
		FP
		I
		T

If address is different from prior return, check here ►

IRS Use

1 1 1 1 1 1 1 1 1 1   2   3 3 3 3 3 3   4 4 4

5 5 5   6   7   8 8 8 8 8   9 9 9   10 10 10 10 10 10 10 10 10 10

If you do not have to file returns in the future, check here ► ☐   and enter date final wages paid ►
If you are a seasonal employer, see **Seasonal employers** on page 2 and check here (see instructions) ►

1	Number of employees (except household) employed in the pay period that includes March 12th ►		8
2	Total wages and tips subject to withholding, plus other compensation	**2**	65,160 00
3	Total income tax withheld from wages, tips, and sick pay	**3**	7,595 80
4	Adjustment of withheld income tax for preceding quarters of calendar year	**4**	0
5	Adjusted total of income tax withheld (line 3 as adjusted by line 4—see instructions)	**5**	7,595 80
6a	Taxable social security wages . . . . $ 65,160 00 × 12.4% (.124) =	**6a**	8,079 84
b	Taxable social security tips . . . . . $ 0 × 12.4% (.124) =	**6b**	0
7	Taxable Medicare wages and tips . . . . . $ 65,160 00 × 2.9% (.029) =	**7**	1,889 64
8	Total social security and Medicare taxes (add lines 6a, 6b, and 7). Check here if wages are not subject to social security and/or Medicare tax . . . . ► ☐	**8**	9,969 48
9	Adjustment of social security and Medicare taxes (see instructions for required explanation) Sick Pay $ _____ ± Fractions of Cents $ _____ ± Other $ _____ =	**9**	0
10	Adjusted total of social security and Medicare taxes (line 8 as adjusted by line 9—see instructions)	**10**	9,969 48
11	**Total taxes** (add lines 5 and 10)	**11**	17,565 28
12	Advance earned income credit (EIC) payments made to employees, if any	**12**	
13	Net taxes (subtract line 12 from line 11). **This should equal line 17, column (d) below** (or line D of Schedule B (Form 941))	**13**	17,565 28
14	Total deposits for quarter, including overpayment applied from a prior quarter	**14**	17,565 28
15	**Balance due** (subtract line 14 from line 13). Pay to Internal Revenue Service	**15**	
16	**Overpayment,** if line 14 is more than line 13, enter excess here ► $ _____ and check if to be: ☐ Applied to next return **OR** ☐ Refunded.		

• **All filers:** If line 13 is less than $500, you need not complete line 17 or Schedule B.
• **Semiweekly depositors:** Complete Schedule B and check here . . . . ► ☐
• **Monthly depositors:** Complete line 17, columns (a) through (d) and check here . . . . ► ☒

17	**Monthly Summary of Federal Tax Liability.**		
(a) First month liability	**(b)** Second month liability	**(c)** Third month liability	**(d)** Total liability for quarter
5,850.88	5,690.77	6,023.63	17,565.28

Sign Here Under penalties of perjury, I declare that I have examined this return, including accompanying schedules and statements, and to the best of my knowledge and belief, it is true, correct, and complete.

Signature ► *William P. Jones*   Print Your Name and Title ► *Treasurer*   Date ► *4/30/--*

For Paperwork Reduction Act Notice, see page 0 of separate instructions.   Cat. No. 17001Z   Form **941** (Rev. 4-94)

♲ *Printed on recycled paper*

FIGURE 10-7   Employer's Annual Federal Unemployment (FUTA) Tax Return (Form 940)

Form **940**	**Employer's Annual Federal Unemployment (FUTA) Tax Return**	OMB No. 1545-0028
Department of the Treasury Internal Revenue Service	▶ **For Paperwork Reduction Act Notice, see separate instructions.**	19**94**

			T	
⌐ Name (as distinguished from trade name)	Calendar year ⌐		FF	
			FD	
Trade name, if any			FP	
Westley, Inc.			I	
Address and ZIP code	Employer identification number		T	
⌐ 5221 Natural Bridge St. Louis, MO 63115-8230	43 ⋮ 0211630 ⌐			

A Are you required to pay unemployment contributions to only one state? (If no, skip questions B and C.) . . ☒ **Yes** ☐ **No**

B Did you pay all state unemployment contributions by January 31, 1995? (If a 0% experience rate is granted, check "Yes.") (If no, skip question C.) . . . . ☒ **Yes** ☐ **No**

C Were all wages that were taxable for FUTA tax also taxable for your state's unemployment tax? . . . . . ☒ **Yes** ☐ **No**

If you answered "No" to any of these questions, you must file Form 940. If you answered "Yes" to all the questions, you may file Form 940-EZ, which is a simplified version of Form 940. You can get Form 940-EZ by calling 1-800-TAX-FORM (1-800-829-3676).

If you will not have to file returns in the future, check here, complete, and sign the return . . . . ▶ ☐

If this is an Amended Return, check here . . . . ▶ ☐

▮ **Computation of Taxable Wages**				
1	Total payments (including exempt payments) during the calendar year for services of employees .	**1**		258,954 00
2	Exempt payments. (Explain each exemption shown, attach additional sheets if necessary.) ▶	**2**	Amount paid	
3	Payments of more than $7,000 for services. Enter only amounts over the first $7,000 paid to each employee. Do not include payments from line 2. The $7,000 amount is the Federal wage base. Your state wage base may be different. **Do not use the state wage limitation**	**3**	203,254 00	
4	Total exempt payments (add lines 2 and 3)	**4**		203,254 00
5	**Total taxable wages** (subtract line 4 from line 1) . . . . ▶	**5**		55,700 00

Be sure to complete both sides of this return and sign in the space provided on the back.   Cat. No. 11234O   Form **940** (1994)

Employee Wage and Tax Statement

By January 31 of each year, employers must furnish each employee with a Wage and Tax Statement, Form W-2 (Figure 10-8). This form shows the total amount of wages paid to the employee and the amounts of taxes withheld during the preceding tax year. The employee's earnings record contains the information needed to complete this form.

Multiple copies of Form W-2 are needed for the following purposes:

- Copy A—Employer sends to Social Security Administration.
- Copy B—Employee attaches to federal income tax return.
- Copy C—Employee retains for personal records.

FIGURE 10-7 (continued)   Employer's Annual Federal Unemployment (FUTA) Tax Return (Form 940)

Form 940 (1994)   Page **2**

Tax Due or Refund

1	Gross FUTA tax. Multiply the wages in Part I, line 5, by .062						**1**		3,453|40
2	Maximum credit. Multiply the wages in Part I, line 5, by .054 . . .	**2**		3,007	80				

3   **Computation of tentative credit (Note:** *All taxpayers must complete the applicable columns.***)**

(a) Name of state	(b) State reporting number(s) as shown on employer's state contribution returns	(c) Taxable payroll (as defined in state act)	(d) State experience rate period		(e) State experience rate	(f) Contributions if rate had been 5.4% (col. (c) x .054)	(g) Contributions payable at experience rate (col. (c) x col. (e))	(h) Additional credit (col. (f) minus col.(g)). If 0 or less, enter -0-.	(i) Contributions actually paid to state
			From	To					
MO	36112	55,700.00	1/1/--	12/31/--	.054	3,007.80	3,007.80	-0-	3,007.80

3a	Totals . . . ▶	55,700.00							

3b	**Total tentative credit** (add line 3a, columns (h) and (i) only—see instructions for limitations on late payments) ▶			3,007|80
4				
5				
6	**Credit:** Enter the smaller of the amount in Part II, line 2, or line 3b.	**6**		3,007|80
7	**Total FUTA tax** (subtract line 6 from line 1)	**7**		445|60
8	Total FUTA tax deposited for the year, including any overpayment applied from a prior year . .	**8**		427|60
9	**Balance due** (subtract line 8 from line 7). This should be $100 or less. Pay to the Internal Revenue Service. See page 3 of the Instructions for Form 940 for details . . . . ▶	**9**		18|00
10	**Overpayment** (subtract line 7 from line 8). Check if it is to be: ☐ **Applied to next return,** or ☐ **Refunded** . . . . ▶	**10**		

Record of Quarterly Federal Unemployment Tax Liability *(Do not include state liability)*

Quarter	First	Second	Third	Fourth	Total for year
Liability for quarter	408.00	26.00	5.60	6.00	445.60

Under penalties of perjury, I declare that I have examined this return, including accompanying schedules and statements, and to the best of my knowledge and belief, it is true, correct, and complete, and that no part of any payment made to a state unemployment fund claimed as a credit was or is to be deducted from the payments to employees.

Signature ▶ *William P. Jones* Title (Owner, etc.) ▶ *Treasurer* Date ▶ *1/31/--*

- Copy D—Employer retains for business records.
- Copy 1—Employer sends to state or local tax department.
- Copy 2—Employee attaches to state or local income tax return.

Summary of Employee Wages and Taxes

Employers send Form W-3, Transmittal of Wage and Tax Statements (Figure 10-9), with Copy A of Forms W-2 to the Social Security Administration. Form W-3 must be filed by the last day of February following the end of each tax year. This form summarizes the employee earnings and tax information presented on Forms W-2 for the year. Information needed to complete Form W-3 is contained in the employees earnings records.

Summary of Reports and Payments

Keeping track of the many payroll reports, deposits, and due dates can be a challenge for an employer. Figure 10-10 shows a calendar that highlights the

FIGURE 10-8 Wage and Tax Statement (Form W-2)

a Control number		OMB No. 1545-0008		
b Employer's identification number 43-0211630			1 Wages, tips, other compensation 27,645.00	2 Federal income tax withheld 1,088.00
c Employer's name, address, and ZIP code Westley, Inc. 5221 Natural Bridge St. Louis, MO 63115-8230			3 Social security wages 27,645.00	4 Social security tax withheld 1,713.99
			5 Medicare wages and tips 27,645.00	6 Medicare tax withheld 400.85
			7 Social security tips	8 Allocated tips
d Employee's social security number 393-58-8194			9 Advance EIC payment	10 Dependent care benefits
e Employee's name, address, and ZIP code Ken M. Istone 1546 Swallow Dr. St. Louis, MO 63144-4752			11 Nonqualified plans	12 Benefits included in box 1
			13 See Instrs. for Form W-2	14 Other
			15 Statutory employee ☐ Deceased ☐ Pension plan ☐ Legal rep. ☐ 942 emp. ☐ Subtotal ☐ Deferred compensation ☐	
16 State Employer's state I.D. No.	17 State wages, tips, etc.	18 State income tax	19 Locality name 20 Local wages, tips, etc.	21 Local income tax

Department of the Treasury—Internal Revenue Service

Form **W-2** Wage and Tax Statement **1994**

For Paperwork Reduction Act Notice, see separate instructions.

Copy D For Employer

FIGURE 10-9 Transmittal of Wage and Tax Statements (Form W-3)

a Control number		OMB No. 1545-0008		
b **Kind of Payer**	941 ☒ Military ☐ 943 ☐ CT-1 ☐ 942 ☐ Medicare govt. emp. ☐		1 Wages, tips, other compensation 249,815.00	2 Federal income tax withheld 29,100.00
			3 Social security wages 247,955.00	4 Social security tax withheld 15,373.21
c Total number of statements 8	d Establishment number		5 Medicare wages and tips 249,815.00	6 Medicare tax withheld 3,622.32
e Employer's identification number 43-0211630			7 Social security tips	8 Allocated tips
f Employer's name Westley, Inc. 5221 Natural Bridge St. Louis, MO 63115-8230		YOUR COPY	9 Advance EIC payments	10 Dependent care benefits
			11 Nonqualified plans	12 Deferred compensation
			13 Adjusted total social security wages and tips 247,955.00	
			14 Adjusted total Medicare wages and tips 249,815.00	
g Employer's address and ZIP code				
h Other EIN used this year			15 Income tax withheld by third-party payer	
i Employer's state I.D. No. 21686001				

Form **W-3 Transmittal of Wage and Tax Statements 1994**

Department of the Treasury Internal Revenue Service

due dates for the various reports and deposits. The calendar assumes the following for an employer:

1. Undeposited FIT (federal income tax) and Social Security and Medicare taxes of $500 at the end of each quarter and less than $50,000 during the lookback period.

FIGURE 10-10 Payroll Calendar

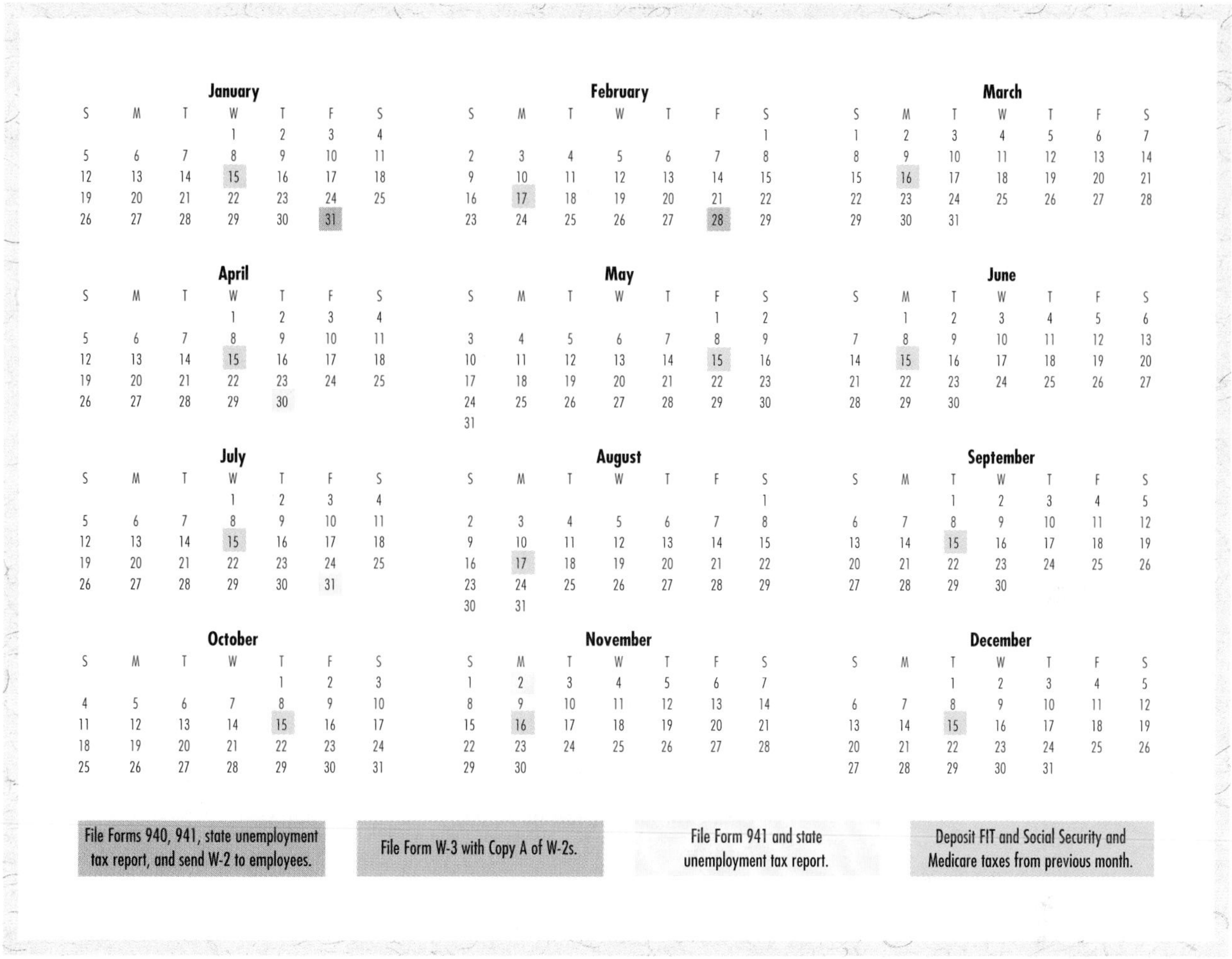

2. Undeposited FUTA taxes of more than $100 at the end of each quarter.
3. SUTA taxes deposited quarterly.

WORKERS' COMPENSATION INSURANCE

LO4 Describe and account for workers' compensation insurance.

Most states require employers to carry workers' compensation insurance. **Workers' compensation insurance** provides insurance for employees who suffer a job-related illness or injury.

The employer usually pays the entire cost of workers' compensation insurance. The cost of the insurance depends on the number of employees, riskiness of the job, and the company's accident history. For example, the insurance premium for workers in a chemical plant could be higher than that for office workers. Employers generally can obtain the insurance either from the state in which they operate or from a private insurance company.

The employer usually pays the premium at the beginning of the year, based on the estimated payroll for the year. At the end of the year, after the actual amount of payroll is known, an adjustment is made. If the employer has overpaid, a credit is received from the state or insurance company. If the employer has underpaid, an additional premium is paid.

To illustrate the accounting for workers' compensation insurance, assume that Lockwood Co. expects its payroll for the year to be $210,000. If Lockwood's insurance premium rate is 0.2%, its payment for workers' compensation insurance at the beginning of the year would be $420:

Estimated Payroll x Rate = Estimated Insurance Premium

$210,000   0.2% $420

The journal entry for the payment of this $420 premium would be:

7		Workers' Compensation Insur. Exp.		4 2 0 00			7
8		Cash			4 2 0 00		8
9		Paid insurance premium					9

If Lockwood's actual payroll for the year is $220,000, Lockwood would owe an additional premium of $20 at year end:

Actual Payroll	x	Rate	=	Insurance Premium
$220,000		0.2%		$440.00
Less estimated premium paid				420.00
Additional premium due				$ 20.00

The adjusting entry at year end for this additional expense would be:

11		Workers' Compensation Insur. Exp.		2 0 00			11
12		Workers' Compensation Insur. Pay.			2 0 00		12
13		Adjustment for insurance					13
14		premium					14

In T account form, the total Workers' Compensation Insurance Expense of $440.00 would look like this.

Workers' Compensation Insurance Expense

Debit	Credit
420.00	
20.00	
440.00	

If Lockwood's actual payroll for the year is only $205,000, Lockwood would be due a refund of $10:

Actual Payroll	x	Rate	= Insurance Premium
$205,000		0.2%	$410.00
Less estimated premium paid			420.00
Additional premium due			$(10.00)

The adjusting entry at year end for this refund due would be:

16		Insurance Refund Receivable	1 0 00		16
17		Workers' Compensation Insur. Exp.		1 0 00	17
18		Adjustment for insurance			18
19		premium			19

In T account form, the total Workers' Compensation Insurance Expense of $410 would look like this.

Workers' Compensation Insurance Expense

Debit	Credit
420.00	10.00
410.00	

KEY POINTS

1/2 Employer payroll taxes represent additional payroll expenses of the employer. The journal entry for payroll taxes is:

8		Payroll Taxes Expense	x x x xx		8
9		Social Security Tax Payable		x x x xx	9
10		Medicare Tax Payable		x x x xx	10
11		FUTA Tax Payable		x x x xx	11
12		SUTA Tax Payable		x x x xx	12

The steps to be followed in preparing this journal entry are as follows.

STEP 1 Obtain the taxable earnings amounts from the Taxable Earnings columns of the payroll register.

STEP 2 Compute the amount of employer Social Security tax by multiplying the Social Security taxable earnings by 6.2%.

STEP 3 Compute the amount of Medicare tax by multiplying total earnings by 1.45%.

STEP 4 Compute the amount of FUTA tax by multiplying the unemployment taxable earnings by 0.8%.

STEP 5 Compute the amount of SUTA tax by multiplying the unemployment taxable earnings by 5.4%.

STEP 6 Prepare the appropriate journal entry using the amounts computed in Steps 2 through 5.

3 Employer payroll reporting and payment responsibilities fall into five areas:

1. Federal income tax withholding and Social Security and Medicare taxes
2. FUTA taxes
3. SUTA taxes
4. Employee Wage and Tax Statement (Form W-2)
5. Summary of employee wages and taxes

Key forms needed in reporting and paying employer payroll taxes are:

1. Form 8109, Federal Tax Deposit Coupon
2. Form 941, Employer's Quarterly Federal Tax Return
3. Form 940, Employer's Annual Federal Unemployment Tax Return

By January 31 of each year, employers must provide each employee with a Wage and Tax Statement, Form W-2.

By February 28 of each year, employers must file Form W-3 and Copy A of Forms W-2 with the Social Security Administration.

4 Employers generally are required to carry and pay the entire cost of workers' compensation insurance.

KEY TERMS

employer FICA taxes 305 Taxes levied on employers at the same rates and on the same earnings bases as the employee FICA taxes.

Employer Identification Number (EIN) 312 A number that identifies the employer on all payroll forms and reports filed with the IRS.

FUTA (Federal Unemployment Tax Act) tax 306 A tax levied on employers to raise funds to administer the federal/state unemployment compensation program.

merit-rating system 308 A system to encourage employers to provide regular employment to workers.

self-employment income 305 The net income of a trade or business run by an individual.

self-employment tax 306 A contribution to the FICA program.

state unemployment tax (SUTA) 307 A tax levied on employers to raise funds to pay unemployment benefits.

workers' compensation insurance 319 Provides insurance for employees who suffer a job-related illness or injury.

REVIEW QUESTIONS

1. Why do employer payroll taxes represent an additional expense to the employer, whereas the various employee payroll taxes do not?
2. At what rate and on what earnings base is the employer's Social Security tax levied?
3. What is the purpose of the FUTA tax and who must pay it?
4. What is the purpose of the state unemployment tax and who must pay it?

5. What accounts are affected when employer payroll tax expenses are properly recorded?

6. Identify all items that are debited or credited to the (1) Social Security tax payable account and (2) Medicare tax payable account.

7. Explain why an employee whose gross salary is $20,000 costs an employer more than $20,000 to employ.

8. What is the purpose of Form 8109, Federal Tax Deposit Coupon?

9. What is the purpose of Form 941, Employer's Quarterly Federal Tax Return?

10. What is the purpose of Form 940, Employer's Annual Federal Unemployment Tax Return?

11. What information appears on Form W-2, the employee's Wage and Tax Statement?

12. What is the purpose of workers' compensation insurance and who must pay for it?

MANAGING YOUR WRITING

The Director of the Art Department, Wilson Watson, wants to hire new office staff. His boss tells him that to do so he must find in his budget not only the base salary for this position but an additional 30% for "fringe benefits." Watson explodes: "How in the world can fringe benefits cost 30% extra?" Write a memo to Watson explaining the costs that probably make up these fringe benefits.

DEMONSTRATION PROBLEM

The totals line from Hart Company's payroll register for the week ended December 31, 19--, is as follows:

(Left half)   **PAYROLL**

| | NAME | EMPLOYEE NO. | ALLOW-ANCES | MARITAL STATUS | EARNINGS | | | | TAXABLE EARNINGS | |
					REGULAR	OVERTIME	TOTAL	CUMULATIVE TOTAL	UNEMPLOY. COMPENSATION	SOCIAL SECURITY
1	Totals				3 5 0 0 00	3 0 0 00	3 8 0 0 00	197 6 0 0 00	4 0 0 00	3 8 0 0 00	1

REGISTER—PERIOD ENDED December 31, 19--   **(Right half)**

| | | | | | DEDUCTIONS | | | | NET PAY | CHECK NO. |
	FEDERAL INCOME TAX	SOCIAL SEC. TAX	MEDICARE TAX	HEALTH INSURANCE	UNITED WAY	OTHER	TOTAL		
1	3 8 0 00	2 3 5 60	5 5 10	5 0 00	1 0 0 00		8 2 0 70	2 9 7 9 30	1

Payroll taxes are imposed as follows: Social Security, 6.2%; Medicare, 1.45%; FUTA, 0.8%; and SUTA, 5.4%.

REQUIRED

1. a. Prepare the journal entry for payment of this payroll on December 31, 19--.

b. Prepare the journal entry for the employer's payroll taxes for the period ended December 31, 19--.

2. Hart Company had the following balances in its general ledger *after* the entries for requirement (1) were made:

Employees Income Tax Payable	$1,520.00
Social Security Tax Payable	1,847.00
Medicare Tax Payable	433.00
FUTA Tax Payable	27.20
SUTA Tax Payable	183.60

a. Prepare the journal entry for payment of the liabilities for employees federal income taxes and Social Security and Medicare taxes on January 15, 19--.

b. Prepare the journal entry for payment of the liability for FUTA tax on January 31, 19--.

c. Prepare the journal entry for payment of the liability for SUTA tax on January 31, 19--.

3. Hart Company paid a premium of $280 for workers' compensation insurance based on estimated payroll as of the beginning of the year. Based on actual payroll as of the end of the year, the premium is $298. Prepare the adjusting entry to reflect the underpayment of the insurance premium.

SOLUTION

1, 2, 3.

GENERAL JOURNAL   PAGE 1

	DATE		DESCRIPTION	POST. REF.	DEBIT	CREDIT	
1	Dec.	31	Wages and Salaries Expense		3 8 0 0 00		1
2			Employees Income Tax Payable			3 8 0 00	2
3			Social Security Tax Payable			2 3 5 60	3
4			Medicare Tax Payable			5 5 10	4
5			Health Insurance Premiums Pay.			5 0 00	5
6			United Way Contributions Pay.			1 0 0 00	6
7			Cash			2 9 7 9 30	7
8			To record Dec. 31 payroll				8
9							9
10	Dec.	31	Payroll Taxes Expense		3 1 5 50		10
11			Social Security Tax Payable			2 3 5 60	11
12			Medicare Tax Payable			5 5 10	12
13			FUTA Tax Payable			3 20	13
14			SUTA Tax Payable			2 1 60	14
15			Employer payroll taxes for				15
16			week ended Dec. 31				16

18	Jan.	15	Employees Income Tax Payable		1 5 2 0 00				18
19			Social Security Tax Payable		1 8 4 7 00				19
20			Medicare Tax Payable		4 3 3 00				20
21			Cash			3 8 0 0 00		21
22			Paid employees federal income,				22
23			Social Security, and Medicare				23
24			taxes				24
25							25
26	Jan.	31	FUTA Tax Payable		2 7 20				26
27			Cash			2 7 20		27
28			Paid FUTA tax				28
29							29
30	Jan.	31	SUTA Tax Payable		1 8 3 60				30
31			Cash			1 8 3 60		31
32			Paid SUTA tax				32
33							33
34	Jan.	31	Workers' Compensation Insur. Exp.		1 8 00				34
35			Workers' Compensation Insur. Pay.			1 8 00		35
36			Adjustment for insurance				36
37			premium				37

SERIES A EXERCISES

1/2 **EXERCISE 10A1 JOURNAL ENTRY FOR EMPLOYER PAYROLL TAXES**   Portions of the payroll register for Barney's Bagels for the week ended July 15 are shown below. The SUTA tax rate is 5.4% and the FUTA tax rate is 0.8%, both of which are levied on the first $7,000 of earnings. The Social Security tax rate is 6.2% on the first $61,200 of earnings. The Medicare rate is 1.45% on gross earnings.

Barney's Bagels
Payroll Register

Total Earnings	Total Taxable Earnings of All Employees	
	Unemployment Compensation	Social Security
$12,200	$10,500	$12,200

Calculate the employer's payroll taxes expense and prepare the journal entry to record the employer's payroll taxes expense for the week ended July 15, of the current year.

1/2 **EXERCISE 10A2 EMPLOYER PAYROLL TAXES**   Earnings for several employees for the week ended March 12, 19--, are as follows:

		Taxable Earnings	
Employee Name	**Total Earnings**	**Unemployment Compensation**	**Social Security**
Aus, Glenn E.	$ 700	$200	$ 700
Diaz, Charles K.	350	350	350
Knapp, Carol S.	1,200	—	1,200
Mueller, Deborah F.	830	125	830
Yeager, Jackie R.	920	35	920

Calculate the employer's payroll taxes expense and prepare the journal entry as of March 12, 19--, assuming that FUTA tax is 0.8%, SUTA tax is 5.4%, Social Security tax is 6.2%, and Medicare tax is 1.45%.

1/2 **EXERCISE 10A3 TAXABLE EARNINGS AND EMPLOYER'S PAYROLL TAXES JOURNAL ENTRY**   Selected information from the payroll register of Raynette's Boutique for the week ended September 14, 19--, is as follows. Social Security tax is 6.2% on the first $61,200 of earnings for each employee. Medicare tax is 1.45% of gross earnings. FUTA tax is 0.8% and SUTA tax is 5.4% on the first $7,000 of earnings.

	Cumulative Pay Before Current Earnings	**Current Gross Pay**	Taxable Earnings	
Employee Name			**Unemployment Compensation**	**Social Security**
Adams, John R.	$ 6,800	$1,250		
Ellis, Judy A.	6,300	1,100		
Lewis, Arlene S.	54,200	2,320		
Mason, Jason W.	53,900	2,270		
Yates, Ruby L.	27,650	1,900		
Zielke, Ronald M.	59,330	2,680		

Calculate the amount of taxable earnings for unemployment, Social Security, and Medicare taxes, and prepare the journal entry to record the employer's payroll taxes as of September 14, 19--.

3 **EXERCISE 10A4 JOURNAL ENTRY FOR PAYMENT OF EMPLOYER'S PAYROLL TAXES**   Bruce Brown owns a business called Brown Construction Co. He does his banking at Citizens National Bank in Portland, Oregon. The amounts in his general ledger for payroll taxes and the employees' withholding of Social Security, Medicare, and Federal income tax payable as of April 15 of the current year are as follows:

Social Security tax payable (includes both employer and employee)	$3,750
Medicare tax payable (includes both employer and employee)	875
FUTA tax payable	200
SUTA tax payable	1,350
Employees income tax payable	2,275

continued

Journalize the payment of the Form 941 deposit (i.e. Social Security, Medicare, and federal income tax) to Citizens National Bank and the payment of the SUTA tax to the state of Oregon as of April 15, 19--.

1 **EXERCISE 10A5 TOTAL COST OF EMPLOYEE** J.B. Kenton employs Sharla Knox at a salary of $32,000 a year. Kenton is subject to employer Social Security taxes at a rate of 6.2% and Medicare taxes at a rate of 1.45% on Sharla's salary. In addition, Kenton must pay SUTA tax at a rate of 5.4% and FUTA tax at a rate of 0.8% on the first $7,000 of Knox's salary.
Compute the total cost to Kenton of employing Knox for the year.

4 **EXERCISE 10A6 WORKERS' COMPENSATION INSURANCE AND ADJUSTMENT** General Manufacturing estimated that its total payroll for the coming year would be $425,000. The workers' compensation insurance premium rate is 0.2%.

REQUIRED

1. Calculate the estimated workers' compensation insurance premium and prepare the journal entry for the payment as of January 2, 19--.
2. Assume that General Manufacturing's actual payroll for the year is $432,000. Calculate the total insurance premium owed and prepare a journal entry as of December 31, 19--, to record the adjustment for the underpayment. The actual payment of the additional premium will take place in January of the next year.

SERIES A PROBLEMS

1/2 **PROBLEM 10A1 CALCULATING PAYROLL TAXES EXPENSE AND PREPARING JOURNAL ENTRY** Selected information from the

payroll register of Anderson's Dairy for the week ended May 7, 19--, is shown below. SUTA tax is withheld at the rate of 5.4% and the FUTA tax at the rate of 0.8%, both on the first $7,000 of earnings. Social Security tax on the employer is 6.2% on the first $61,200 of earnings and Medicare tax is 1.45% on gross earnings.

	Cumulative Pay Before Current Earnings	Current Weekly Earnings	Taxable Earnings	
Employee Name			**Unemployment Compensation**	**Social Security**
Barnum, Alex	$ 6,750	$ 820		
Duel, Richard	6,340	725		
Hunt, J.B.	23,460	1,235		
Larson, Susan	6,950	910		
Mercado, Denise	59,850	2,520		
Swan, Judy	15,470	1,125		
Yates, Keith	28,675	1,300		

continued

REQUIRED

1. Calculate the total employer payroll taxes for these employees.
2. Prepare the journal entry to record the employer payroll taxes as of May 7, 19--.

2 **PROBLEM 10A2 JOURNALIZING AND POSTING PAYROLL ENTRIES** The Cascade Company has four employees. All are paid on a monthly basis. The fiscal year of the business is July 1 to June 30. Payroll taxes are imposed as follows.

1. Social Security tax of 6.2% withheld from employees' wages on the first $61,200 of earnings and Medicare tax withheld at 1.45% of gross earnings.
2. Social Security tax of 6.2% imposed on the employer on the first $61,200 of earnings and Medicare tax of 1.45% on gross earnings.
3. SUTA tax of 5.4% imposed on the employer on the first $7,000 of earnings.
4. FUTA tax of 0.8% imposed on the employer on the first $7,000 of earnings.

The accounts kept by Cascade include the following:

Account Number	Title	Balance on July 1
111	Cash	$50,200
211	Employees Income Tax Payable	1,015
212	Social Security Tax Payable	1,458
213	Medicare Tax Payable	342
221	FUTA Tax Payable	164
222	SUTA Tax Payable	810
261	Savings Bond Deductions Payable	350
542	Wages and Salaries Expense	0
552	Payroll Taxes Expense	0

The following transactions relating to payrolls and payroll taxes occurred during July and August.

July 15 Paid $2,815 covering the following June taxes:

Social Security tax	$ 1,458
Medicare tax	342
Employees income tax withheld	1,015
Total	$ 2,815

31 July payroll:

Total wages and salaries expense		$12,000
Less amounts withheld:		
Social Security tax	$ 744	
Medicare tax	174	
Employees income tax	1,020	
Savings bond deductions	350	2,288
Net amount paid		$ 9,712

continued

July   31 Purchased savings bonds for employees,
              $700
        31 Data for completing employer's payroll
              taxes expense for July:
                Social Security taxable wages $12,000
                Unemployment taxable wages   3,000

Aug.   15 Paid $2,856 covering the following July
              taxes:
                Social Security tax $ 1,488
                Medicare tax   348
                Employees income tax withheld   1,020
                Total $ 2,856

        15 Paid SUTA tax for the quarter, $972
        15 Paid FUTA tax, $188

REQUIRED
1. Journalize the preceding transactions using a general journal.
2. Open T accounts for the payroll expenses and liabilities. Enter the beginning balances and post the transactions recorded in the journal.

4   **PROBLEM 10A3 WORKERS' COMPENSATION INSURANCE AND ADJUSTMENT**   Willamette Manufacturing estimated that its total payroll for the coming year would be $650,000. The workers' compensation insurance premium rate is 0.3%.

REQUIRED
1. Calculate the estimated workers' compensation insurance premium and prepare the journal entry for the payment as of January 2, 19--.
2. Assume that Willamette Manufacturing's actual payroll for the year was $672,000. Calculate the total insurance premium owed and prepare a journal entry as of December 31, 19--, to record the adjustment for the underpayment. The actual payment of the additional premium will take place in January of the next year.
3. Assume instead that Willamette Manufacturing's actual payroll for the year was $634,000. Prepare a journal entry as of December 31, 19--, for the total amount that should be refunded. The refund will not be received until the next year.

SERIES B   EXERCISES

1/2   **EXERCISE 10B1 JOURNAL ENTRY FOR EMPLOYER PAYROLL TAXES**   Portions of the payroll register for Kathy's Cupcakes for the week ended June 21 are on the next page. The SUTA tax rate is 5.4% and the FUTA tax rate is 0.8%, both on the first $7,000 of earnings. The Social Security tax rate is 6.2% on the first $61,200 of earnings. The Medicare rate is 1.45% on gross earnings.   *continued*

Kathy's Cupcakes
Payroll Register

Total Taxable Earnings of All Employees

Total Earnings	Unemployment Compensation	Social Security
$15,680	$12,310	$15,680

Calculate the employer's payroll taxes expense and prepare the journal entry to record the employer's payroll taxes expense for the week ended June 21 of the current year.

1/2 **EXERCISE 10B2 EMPLOYER PAYROLL TAXES** Earnings for several employees for the week ended April 7, 19--, are as follows:

		Taxable Earnings	
Employee Name	Total Earnings	Unemployment Compensation	Social Security
Boyd, Glenda, L.	$ 850	$300	$ 850
Evans, Sheryl N.	970	225	970
Fox, Howard J.	830	830	830
Jacobs, Phyllis J.	1,825	—	1,825
Roh, William R.	990	25	990

Calculate the employer's payroll taxes expense and prepare the journal entry as of April 7, 19--, assuming that FUTA tax is 0.8%, SUTA tax is 5.4%, Social Security tax is 6.2%, and Medicare tax is 1.45%.

1/2 **EXERCISE 10B3 TAXABLE EARNINGS AND EMPLOYER'S PAYROLL TAXES JOURNAL ENTRY** Selected information from the payroll register of Howard's Cutlery for the week ended October 7, 19--, is presented below. Social Security tax is 6.2% on the first $61,200 of earnings for each employee. Medicare tax is 1.45% on gross earnings. FUTA tax is 0.8% and SUTA tax is 5.4% on the first $7,000 of earnings.

	Cumulative Pay Before Current Earnings	Current Gross Pay	Taxable Earnings	
Employee Name			Unemployment Compensation	Social Security
Carlson, David J.	$ 6,635	$ 950		
Davis, Patricia S.	6,150	1,215		
Lewis, Arlene S.	54,375	2,415		
Nixon, Robert R.	53,870	1,750		
Shippe, Lance W.	24,830	1,450		
Watts, Brandon Q.	59,800	2,120		

Calculate the amount of taxable earnings for unemployment, Social Security, and Medicare taxes, and prepare the journal entry to record the employer's payroll taxes as of October 7, 19--.

3   **EXERCISE 10B4 JOURNAL ENTRY FOR PAYMENT OF EMPLOYER'S PAYROLL TAXES**   Francis Baker owns a business called Baker Construction Co. She does her banking at the American National Bank in Seattle, Washington. The amounts in her general ledger for payroll taxes and employees' withholding of Social Security, Medicare, and federal income tax payable as of July 15 of the current year are as follows:

Social Security tax payable (includes both employer and employee)	$6,375
Medicare tax payable (includes both employer and employee)	1,500
FUTA tax payable	336
SUTA tax payable	2,268
Employees federal income tax payable	4,830

Journalize the payment of the Form 941 deposit (i.e., Social Security, Medicare, and federal income tax) to the American National Bank and the payment of the state unemployment tax to the state of Washington as of July 15, 19--.

1   **EXERCISE 10B5 TOTAL COST OF EMPLOYEE**   B.F. Goodson employs Eduardo Gonzales at a salary of $46,000 a year. Goodson is subject to employer Social Security taxes at a rate of 6.2% and Medicare taxes at a rate of 1.45% on Eduardo's salary. In addition, Goodson must pay SUTA tax at a rate of 5.4% and FUTA tax at a rate of 0.8% on the first $7,000 of Gonzales' salary.

Compute the total cost to Goodson of employing Gonzales for the year.

4   **EXERCISE 10B6 WORKERS' COMPENSATION INSURANCE AND ADJUSTMENT**   Columbia Industries estimated that its total payroll for the coming year would be $385,000. The workers' compensation insurance premium rate is 0.2%.

REQUIRED
1. Calculate the estimated workers' compensation insurance premium and prepare the journal entry for the payment as of January 2, 19--.
2. Assume that Columbia Industries' actual payroll for the year is $396,000. Calculate the total insurance premium owed and prepare a journal entry as of December 31, 19--, to record the adjustment for the underpayment. The actual payment of the additional premium will take place in January of the next year.

SERIES B   PROBLEMS

1/2   **PROBLEM 10B1 CALCULATING PAYROLL TAXES EXPENSE AND PREPARING JOURNAL ENTRY**   Selected information from the payroll register of Wray's Drug Store for the week ended July 7, 19--, is shown on the next page. SUTA tax is withheld at the rate of 5.4% and FUTA tax at the rate of 0.8%, both on the first $7,000 of earnings. Social Security tax on the employer is 6.2% on the first $61,200 of earnings and Medicare tax is 1.45% on gross earnings.

Employee Name	Cumulative Pay Before Current Earnings	Current Weekly Earnings	Taxable Earnings Unemployment Compensation	Social Security
Ackers, Alice	$ 6,460	$ 645		
Conley, Dorothy	27,560	1,025		
Davis, James	6,850	565		
Lawrence, Kevin	52,850	2,875		
Rawlings, Judy	16,350	985		
Tester, Leonard	22,320	835		
Vadillo, Raynette	59,360	2,540		

REQUIRED

1. Calculate the total employer payroll taxes for these employees.
2. Prepare the journal entry to record the employer payroll taxes as of July 7, 19--.

2   **PROBLEM 10B2 JOURNALIZING AND POSTING PAYROLL ENTRIES**   The Oxford Company has five employees. All are paid on a monthly basis. The fiscal year of the business is June 1 to May 31. Payroll taxes are imposed as follows:

1. Social Security tax of 6.2% to be withheld from employees' wages on the first $61,200 of earnings and Medicare tax of 1.45% on gross earnings.
2. Social Security tax of 6.2% imposed on the employer on the first $61,200 of earnings and Medicare tax of 1.45% on gross earnings.
3. SUTA tax of 5.4% imposed on the employer on the first $7,000 of earnings.
4. FUTA tax of 0.8% imposed on the employer on the first $7,000 of earnings.

The accounts kept by the Oxford Company include the following:

Account Number	Title	Balance on June 1
111	Cash	$48,650
211	Employees Income Tax Payable	1,345
212	Social Security Tax Payable	1,823
213	Medicare Tax Payable	427
221	FUTA Tax Payable	360
222	SUTA Tax Payable	920
261	Savings Bond Deductions Payable	525
542	Wages and Salaries Expense	0
552	Payroll Taxes Expense	0

The following transactions relating to payrolls and payroll taxes occurred during June and July.

June 15 Paid $3,595.00 covering the
following May taxes:

Social Security tax	$ 1,823.00
Medicare tax	427.00
Employees income tax withheld	1,345.00
Total	$ 3,595.00

30 June payroll:

Total wages and salaries expense		$14,700.00
Less amounts withheld:		
Social Security tax	$ 911.40	
Medicare tax	213.15	
Employees income tax	1,280.00	
Savings bond deductions	525.00	2,929.55
Net amount paid		$11,770.45

30 Purchased savings bonds for
employees, $1,050.00

30 Data for completing employer's
payroll taxes expense for June:

Social Security taxable wages	$14,700.00
Unemployment taxable wages	4,500.00

July 15 Paid $3,529.10 covering the
following June taxes:

Social Security tax	$ 1,822.80
Medicare tax	426.30
Employees income tax withheld	1,280.00
Total	$ 3,529.10

15 Paid SUTA tax, $1,163.00
15 Paid FUTA tax, $396.00

REQUIRED

1. Journalize the preceding transactions using a general journal.
2. Open T accounts for the payroll expenses and liabilities. Enter the beginning balances and post the transactions recorded in the journal.

4 **PROBLEM 10B3 WORKERS' COMPENSATION INSURANCE AND ADJUSTMENT**   Multnomah Manufacturing estimated that its total payroll for the coming year would be $540,000. The workers' compensation insurance premium rate is 0.2%.

REQUIRED

1. Calculate the estimated workers' compensation insurance premium and prepare the journal entry for the payment as of January 2, 19--.
2. Assume that Multnomah Manufacturing's actual payroll for the year was $562,000. Calculate the total insurance premium owed and prepare a journal entry as of December 31, 19--, to record the adjustment for the underpayment. The actual payment of the additional premium will take place in January of the next year.   *continued*

3. Assume instead that Multnomah Manufacturing's actual payroll for the year was $532,000. Prepare a journal entry as of December 31, 19--, for the total amount that should be refunded. The refund will not be received until the next year.

MASTERY PROBLEM

The totals line from Nix Company's payroll register for the week ended March 31, 19--, is as follows:

(Left half)   **PAYROLL REGISTER**

| | NAME | EMPLOYEE NO. | ALLOW-ANCES | MARITAL STATUS | EARNINGS | | | CUMULATIVE TOTAL | TAXABLE EARNINGS | | |
					REGULAR	OVERTIME	TOTAL		UNEMPLOY. COMPENSATION	SOCIAL SECURITY	
1	Totals				5 4 0 0 00	1 0 0 00	5 5 0 0 00	71 5 0 0 00	5 0 0 0 00	5 5 0 0 00	1

FOR PERIOD ENDED   March 31, 19--   **(Right half)**

| | DEDUCTIONS | | | | | | | NET PAY | CHECK NO. |
	FEDERAL INCOME TAX	SOCIAL SEC. TAX	MEDICARE TAX	HEALTH INSURANCE	LIFE INSURANCE	OTHER	TOTAL		
1	5 0 0 00	3 4 1 00	7 9 75	1 6 5 00	2 0 0 00		1 2 8 5 75	4 2 1 4 25	1

Payroll taxes are imposed as follows: Social Security tax, 6.2%; Medicare tax, 1.45%; FUTA tax, 0.8%, and SUTA tax, 5.4%.

REQUIRED

1. **a.** Prepare the journal entry for payment of this payroll on March 31, 19--.
   b. Prepare the journal entry for the employer's payroll taxes for the period ended March 31, 19--.
2. Nix Company had the following balances in its general ledger *before* the entries for requirement (1) were made:

Employees income tax payable	$2,500
Social Security tax payable	2,008
Medicare tax payable	470
FUTA tax payable	520
SUTA tax payable	3,510

   a. Prepare the journal entry for payment of the liabilities for federal income taxes and Social Security and Medicare taxes on April 15, 19--.
   b. Prepare the journal entry for payment of the liability for FUTA tax on April 30, 19--.
   c. Prepare the journal entry for payment of the liability for SUTA tax on April 30, 19--.
3. Nix Company paid a premium of $420 for workers' compensation insurance based on the estimated payroll as of the beginning of the year. Based on actual payroll as of the end of the year, the premium is only $400. Prepare the adjusting entry to reflect the overpayment of the insurance premium at the end of the year (December 31, 19--).

INDEX

Page references in bold indicate defined terms.

A